Library of America, a nonprofit organization,
champions our nation's cultural heritage
by publishing America's greatest writing in
authoritative new editions and providing resources
for readers to explore this rich, living legacy.

THE ESSENTIAL DEBATE
ON THE CONSTITUTION

THE ESSENTIAL
DEBATE ON THE
CONSTITUTION

FEDERALIST AND ANTIFEDERALIST
SPEECHES AND WRITINGS

*The brilliant battle of ideas
that still shapes the nation*

Robert J. Allison and Bernard Bailyn, *editors*

THE LIBRARY OF AMERICA

Contents

Preface

BY BERNARD BAILYN

I WRITE THESE WORDS at a time when the Founders' Constitution is being tested as never before in the two centuries and more of the nation's existence. Their intricate constitutional design, worked out in the Convention of 1787 and debated for months in 1788, was for a national state strong enough to provide for citizens' needs and to compete in the world's great affairs without intruding on the citizens' freedoms. But they knew how delicate free states are and how difficult it would be for their descendants to preserve the constitutional republic they were creating. The dominant theme in everything they said and wrote in the great ratification debate of 1787–88 was to prevent the free republican state they were creating from descending into a tyrannical or what they called an "arbitrary" state—what we call an authoritarian or fascist state—in which a charismatic demagogue would cut through or ignore or distort the structure of law, install his corrupt minions in high office, protect them by use of the pardoning power, and block citizens' freedom to speak and to challenge those who ruled. They knew only too well, from history and from their contemporary world, how such a debasement of free states could happen. They had seen it again and again. And they knew, and assumed, that beyond all the crucial constitutional details that the states were debating lay basic assumptions on which the entire edifice of freedom rested.

They assumed that while party zealots and men of selfish ambition would always be present, there must also, always, be informed men of independent judgment who would serve the public interest without seeking benefits to themselves and who were not intimidated by ruthless magistrates. But they were not blind optimists. They believed that man in his deepest nature was selfish and corrupt—that the lust for wealth and power was so overwhelming that no one should ever be entrusted with unqualified authority. The Constitution's intricate system of checks and balances would help, but they feared that there

might not be virtue enough for success. Could not some ignorant but clever and ruthless leader manipulate and then sweep
aside the delicate structure of constitutional government to
satisfy his passion for power and establish a corrupt regime?
Madison, in the Federalist papers and in the Virginia ratifying
convention, put it directly. "As there is a degree of depravity
in mankind which requires a certain degree of circumspection
and distrust; So there are other qualities in human nature,
which justify a certain portion of esteem and confidence."

> I go on this great republican principle, that the people
> will have virtue and intelligence to select men of virtue
> and wisdom. Is there no virtue among us? If there be not
> we are in a wretched situation. No theoretical checks—
> no form of government can render us secure.

The same anxious but optimistic thought came with embel-
lishments from Hamilton. He knew that in proportion that
riches and luxury prevail, virtue will tend to become a mere
"graceful appendage of wealth, and the tendency of things will
be to depart from the republican standard." But he still believed
that "the supposition of universal venality in human nature is
little less an error in political reasoning than the supposition of
universal rectitude. The institution of delegated power implies
that there is a portion of virtue and honor among mankind,
which may be a reasonable foundation of confidence."

The Founders assumed also that they would succeed in preserving the free state they were creating only if the people retained the right to challenge the government in open, public
expression. If that failed, if the public press was in some way
muzzled or undermined and the corrupt regime monopolized
the public discourse immune from public challenges, the free
state would be in mortal danger. Jefferson put it dramatically.
If, he wrote, I had to choose between "a government without
newspapers, or newspapers without a government, I should
not hesitate a moment to prefer the latter." The only way to
safeguard public liberty, he added, is to give the people "full
information of their affairs thro' the channel of public papers
[that should] penetrate the whole mass of the people." For, he
said, the basis of our governments is the opinion of the people.

And they assumed, even without saying so, that beyond

everything else that a free state required for its survival lay respect for the law and for the courts that enforced and defined it. Many of the Founders were lawyers: Jefferson, Hamilton, Adams, Wilson, Dickinson, Jay, Iredell, Ellsworth, Patrick Henry, and others. And those who were not lawyers by profession learned something of the law in the public debates, and shared the respect for the law and the courts as foundations of free states. A magistrate at any level who disparaged the courts and defied or twisted the course of justice could only be a despot who would rule for his own sake and was a danger to the people's freedoms. But they knew how difficult impartial adherence to the law could be. The entire struggle with Britain in the 1760s and '70s had been a struggle over law—Parliament's law—which they knew they were defying, and so it was only gradually and in desperation that they came to accept their defiance as legitimate. And nothing is more revealing of their respect for law and the courts than the speed with which states moved to reinstitute in republican terms the legal systems they had known. For they knew that regimes dominated by men and not by law would lead to anarchy, which would inevitably become the "arbitrary" state they so deeply feared.

It was fear—of the encroachment of authoritarian rule—that drove the fierce debate of 1787–88 on to its conclusion, and it was passion—for the highest ideals of statecraft—that kept the debates aloft from the squalor of angry disagreements. Both are revealed in the pages that follow, which contain the essential documentation of what the Founders achieved.

It was Madison, speaking in Congress a decade after the struggle had subsided and the nation had been established, who saw what had happened most clearly. The Constitution, he said, that had come from the Convention of 1787

> was nothing more than the draft of a plan, nothing but a dead letter, until life and validity were breathed into it by the voice of the people, speaking through the several State Conventions. If we were to look, therefore, for the meaning of the [Constitution] beyond the face of the instrument, we must look for it, not in the General Convention, which proposed, but in the State Conventions, which accepted and ratified the Constitution.

Introduction

BY ROBERT J. ALLISON

THE QUESTION OF POWER obsessed the Constitution's framers, and most Americans of the day. Power, a malevolent force, would crush liberty. They had learned from history and experience how free states had become dictatorships.

Power they had seen in its concrete form in the 1760s and 1770s, in the persons of British governors, ministers, and troops exerting control over them. They had resisted, having read in history that free states could be corrupted or usurped into autocracies. And they knew that autocratic power would be the end of liberty.

In the Revolution's early years it was easy to denounce power and those who abused it. But now they had to wield power, and create a system of power, but also ensure that power would not crush liberty. The ratifying conventions debated a system that its creators thought would divide and control power, making it safe for a free people. But would it work? Did this experiment, as Patrick Henry declaimed, deny all the experience of mankind?

For eleven months, in an extraordinary philosophical discussion and important political debate, they argued about this. How can you create a power center that will not destroy liberty? No one had done it before.

Prominent political actors and thinkers—Benjamin Franklin, George Washington, James Madison, Alexander Hamilton, all politicians and intelligentsia of the age were engaged in this debate, but so were many more obscure men and women whose lives and liberties were equally bound up in the decision. The debate took place in newspapers, pamphlets, town meetings, legislative halls, and in the conventions each state called to decide on ratification. The convention that had framed the Constitution had met in secret; not a word of its debates was leaked to the public during the weeks and months of its deliberations. But the state ratifying conventions were public and their debates were published in detail in the newspapers. Madison later wrote that to understand the Constitution's meaning, we should look not to the convention that proposed it, but the state conventions that debated it. The Constitution as proposed was "nothing but a dead letter, until life and validity were breathed into it" in the state ratifying conventions "by the voice of the people."[1]

Along with their conventions, advocates on all sides wrote in newspapers and pamphlets, under pseudonyms such as A Federal Farmer (against), Civis (for), Americanus (for), Giles Hickory (for), Cato (against), A Landholder (for), Brutus (against), and Publius (for). All agreed that the future of the American union was at stake, as was the future of liberty. They had just fought a war to preserve liberty, not only for the people of the American states, but for the entire world.

The framers believed the system's very structure would preserve liberty by dividing power among branches of government, and between the states and the federal government. Ambition would check ambition, and would prevent the kind of tyrannical usurpation of which the world gave too many examples.

The opponents of ratification recognized the current system's flaws but saw worse in the new plan. The President could be re-elected perpetually; the House of Representatives was too small, and each representative's district too big, to make it an adequate voice for the people; the President and a handful of Senators could collude to frame treaties surrendering sovereignty; Congress would arm and discipline militias, depriving people in the states of the power to defend themselves against tyranny; the federal government's taxation would destroy any revenue sources within the states; and above all, the omission of a bill of rights left the people's liberties at risk.

Supporters argued that a bill of rights would be unnecessary, if not dangerous. The Constitution granted the government specific powers in Article I, section 8. Powers not granted were reserved to the states or the people. The Constitution divided and separated powers, having ambition check ambition

---

[1]James Madison in Congress, April 6, 1796, quoted in Pauline Maier, *Ratification: The People Debate the Constitution 1787–1788* (New York: Simon & Schuster, 2010), xvii.

and power counter power. The Constitution created a balance between branches of government—legislative, executive, and judicial—and between levels of government—state and federal.

But for the opponents this was not enough. They wanted a different system that would prevent centralization of power and more effectively protect the people against an expanding government.

Only a near defeat in the Massachusetts ratifying convention convinced the Constitution's supporters to compromise—adopt the proposed Constitution first, and once it was in operation, add a bill of rights to limit the government's power to trample on liberty. The result of the ratification debate is a balance of power and liberty, a Constitution that is a bill of powers granted to the government, with built-in attempts to restrain that power, and a Bill of Rights, an explicit limit on that government's power.

Under this complicated structure Americans have governed themselves ever since. Some of the divisive issues of 1787 remain familiar: taxation and the national debt; the role of the President; the role of Congress, the role of the federal courts; the power of the states, the rights of individuals and of minorities in a system in which the majority governs. Other questions that divided them have been resolved. New questions and challenges have emerged since, and will continue to do so.

During the Convention's secret proceedings, Elizabeth Powell, a Philadelphia neighbor, asked Franklin: "Well Doctor, what have we got a republic or a monarchy." "A republic," he replied, "if you can keep it."[2]

That we continue to argue under the system devised in 1787, amended in response to their opponents' arguments, is the greatest proof of the framers' skill. Creating the republic was their greatest accomplishment. Keeping it is our biggest challenge.

---

[2]"Papers of Dr. James McHenry on the Federal Convention of 1787." *American Historical Review* 11, no. 3 (April 1906): 618.

PART 1:
THE DEBATE OPENS

As THE Philadelphia Convention finished its work on September 17, 1787, **Benjamin Franklin** called on the delegates to support the Constitution unanimously. He knew it would encounter strong opposition, and warned that if each delegate went home and reported his own objections, the entire project would fail. Three delegates —Edmund Randolph and George Mason from Virginia and Elbridge Gerry from Massachusetts—still refused to sign, but on Franklin's motion the Convention reported that the Constitution had "the unanimous consent of the states present." Newspapers reprinted Franklin's speech three dozen times, making his closing words to the Convention the opening of the ratification debate. Ratification was far from certain. **Alexander Hamilton** knew it would be difficult— powerful interests in the states would oppose it. If ratification failed, Hamilton thought a civil war likely. **James Wilson** launched the public campaign with a speech in Philadelphia. His explanation of why the Constitution lacked a Bill of Rights—"every power not given is reserved"—failed to convince his audience, and Wilson became a target for the opposition to attack.

Brutus and *Cato*, two anonymous New Yorkers, wrote effective opposition essays. *Cato* may have been Abraham Yates, Jr., a prominent New York political leader, and his brother Robert Yates, an Albany judge and a delegate to the Convention (he had left in July), may have been *Brutus*. Whoever they were, *Brutus* and *Cato* recognized the need for a stronger federal system, but thought the Constitution as written would threaten individual liberty and the power of the states. In **A Political Dialogue**, "Mr. Grumble" was vexed that all his neighbors in Massachusetts supported the Constitution because a stronger government would revive trade. Although Mr. Grumble had no specific arguments against the new plan, their unanimity troubled him.

From New York City, where the Confederation Congress was meeting, **James Madison** wrote to **Thomas Jefferson**, the American minister to France, outlining the emerging political alliances, and arguing that the very structure of the new political system would prevent the formation of majority factions. In reply, Jefferson found much to admire in the Constitution, but also much he did not like: the lack of a Bill of Rights, and the President's eligibility for re-election. In New York Hamilton launched *The Federalist*, a series of newspaper essays in support of ratification, warning that failure to adopt the new Constitution would result in the "dismemberment of the Union" and "the general misfortune of mankind." Using the shared pseudonym *Publius*, Hamilton would write fifty-one *Federalist* essays, Madison, twenty-nine, and John Jay, five.

Benjamin Franklin: Speech at the Conclusion of the Constitutional Convention

Philadelphia, September 17, 1787

I confess that I do not entirely approve of this Constitution at present, but Sir, I am not sure I shall never approve it: For having lived long, I have experienced many Instances of being oblig'd, by better Information or fuller Consideration, to change Opinions even on important Subjects, which I once thought right, but found to be otherwise. It is therefore that the older I grow the more apt I am to doubt my own Judgment and to pay more Respect to the Judgment of others. Most Men indeed as well as most Sects in Religion, think themselves in Possession of all Truth, and that wherever others differ from them it is so far Error. Steele, a Protestant, in a Dedication tells the Pope, that the only Difference between our two Churches in their Opinions of the Certainty of their Doctrine, is, the Romish Church is infallible, and the Church of England is never in the Wrong. But tho' many private Persons think almost as highly of their own Infallibility, as that of their Sect, few express it so naturally as a certain French lady, who in a little Dispute with her Sister, said, I don't know how it happens, Sister, but I meet with no body but myself that's *always* in the right. *Il n'y a que moi qui a toujours raison.*

In these Sentiments, Sir, I agree to this Constitution, with all its Faults, if they are such: because I think a General Government necessary for us, and there is no *Form* of Government but what may be a Blessing to the People if well administred; and I believe farther that this is likely to be well administred for a Course of Years, and can only end in Despotism as other Forms have done before it, when the People shall become so corrupted as to need Despotic Government, being incapable of any other. I doubt too whether any other Convention we can obtain, may be able to make a better Constitution: For when you assemble a Number of Men to have the Advantage of their joint Wisdom, you inevitably assemble with those Men all their Prejudices, their Passions, their Errors of Opinion, their local

Interests, and their selfish Views. From such an Assembly can a perfect Production be expected? It therefore astonishes me, Sir, to find this System approaching so near to Perfection as it does; and I think it will astonish our Enemies, who are waiting with Confidence to hear that our Councils are confounded, like those of the Builders of Babel, and that our States are on the Point of Separation, only to meet hereafter for the Purpose of cutting one another's Throats. Thus I consent, Sir, to this Constitution because I expect no better, and because I am not sure that it is not the best. The Opinions I have had of its Errors, I sacrifice to the Public Good. I have never whisper'd a Syllable of them abroad. Within these Walls they were born, & here they shall die. If every one of us in returning to our Constituents were to report the Objections he has had to it, and endeavour to gain Partizans in support of them, we might prevent its being generally received, and thereby lose all the salutary Effects & great Advantages resulting naturally in our favour among foreign Nations, as well as among ourselves, from our real or apparent Unanimity. Much of the Strength and Efficiency of any Government, in procuring & securing Happiness to the People depends on Opinion, on the general Opinion of the Goodness of that Government as well as of the Wisdom & Integrity of its Governors. I hope therefore that for our own Sakes, as a Part of the People, and for the Sake of our Posterity, we shall act heartily & unanimously in recommending this Constitution, wherever our Influence may extend, and turn our future Thoughts and Endeavours to the Means of having it well administred.—

On the whole, Sir, I cannot help expressing a Wish, that every Member of the Convention, who may still have Objections to it, would with me on this Occasion doubt a little of his own Infallibility, and to make *manifest* our *Unanimity*, put his Name to this Instrument.—

Then the Motion was made for adding the last Formula, viz Done in Convention by the unanimous Consent &c—which was agreed to and added—accordingly.

Alexander Hamilton: Conjectures About the New Constitution

late September 1787

The new constitution has in favour of its success these circumstances—a very great weight of influence of the persons who framed it, particularly in the universal popularity of General Washington—the good will of the commercial interest throughout the states which will give all its efforts to the establishment of a government capable of regulating protecting and extending the commerce of the Union—the good will of most men of property in the several states who wish a government of the union able to protect them against domestic violence and the depredations which the democratic spirit is apt to make on property; and who are besides anxious for the respectability of the nation—the hopes of the Creditors of the United States that a general government possessing the means of doing it will pay the debt of the Union—a strong belief in the people at large of the insufficiency of the present confederation to preserve the existence of the Union and of the necessity of the union to their safety and prosperity; of course a strong desire of a change and a predisposition to receive well the propositions of the Convention.

Against its success is to be put the dissent of two or three important men in the Convention; who will think their characters pleged to defeat the plan—the influence of many *inconsiderable* men in possession of considerable offices under the state governments who will fear a diminution of their consequence, power and emolument by the establishment of the general government and who can hope for nothing there—the influence of some *considerable* men in office possessed of talents and popularity who partly from the same motives and partly from a desire of *playing a part* in a convulsion for their own aggrandisement will oppose the quiet adoption of the new government—(some considerable men out of office, from motives of ambition may be disposed to act the same part)—add to these causes the disinclination of the people to

5

taxes, and of course to a strong government—the opposition of all men much in debt who will not wish to see a government established one object of which is to restrain the means of cheating Creditors—the democratical jealousy of the people which may be alarmed at the appearance of institutions that may seem calculated to place the power of the community in few hands and to raise a few individuals to stations of great preeminence—and the influence of some foreign powers who from different motives will not wish to see an energetic government established throughout the states.

In this view of the subject it is difficult to form any judgment whether the plan will be adopted or rejected. It must be essentially a matter of conjecture. The present appearances and all other circumstances considered the probability seems to be on the side of its adoption.

But the causes operating against its adoption are powerful and there will be nothing astonishing in the Contrary.

If it do not finally obtain, it is probable the discussion of the question will beget such struggles animosities and heats in the community that this circumstance conspiring with the *real necessity* of an essential change in our present situation will produce civil war. Should this happen, whatever parties prevail it is probable governments very different from the present in their principles will be established. A dismemberment of the Union and monarchies in different portions of it may be expected. It may however happen that no civil war will take place; but several republican confederacies be established between different combinations of the particular states.

A reunion with Great Britain, from universal disgust at a state of commotion, is not impossible, though not much to be feared. The most plausible shape of such a business would be the establishment of a son of the present monarch in the supreme government of this country with a family compact.

If the government be adopted, it is probable general Washington will be the President of the United States. This will insure a wise choice of men to administer the government and a good administration. A good administration will conciliate the confidence and affection of the people and perhaps enable the government to acquire more consistency than the proposed constitution seems to promise for so great a Country. It may

then triumph altogether over the state governments and reduce them to an intire subord nation, dividing the larger states
into smaller districts. The *organs* of the general government
may also acquire additional strength.

If this should not be the case, in the course of a few years,
it is probable that the contests about the boundaries of power
between the particular government's and the general government and the *momentum* of the larger states in such contests
will produce a dissolution of the Union. This after all seems to
be the most likely result.

But it is almost arrogance in so complicated a subject, depending so intirely on the incalculable fluctuations of the human passions, to attempt even a conjecture about the event.

It will be Eight or Nine months before any certain judgment
can be formed respecting the adoption of the Plan.

James Wilson: Speech at a Public Meeting

Philadelphia, October 6, 1787

Mr. Wilson then rose, and delivered a long and eloquent speech upon the principles of the Fœderal Constitution proposed by the late convention. The outlines of this speech we shall endeavour to lay before the public, as tending to reflect great light upon the interesting subject now in general discussion.

Mr. Chairman and Fellow Citizens, Having received the honor of an appointment to represent you in the late convention, it is perhaps, my duty to comply with the request of many gentlemen whose characters and judgments I sincerely respect, and who have urged, that this would be a proper occasion to lay before you any information which will serve to explain and elucidate the principles and arrangements of the constitution, that has been submitted to the consideration of the United States. I confess that I am unprepared for so extensive and so important a disquisition; but the insidious attempts which are clandestinely and industriously made to pervert and destroy the new plan, induce me the more readily to engage in its defence; and the impressions of four months constant attention to the subject, have not been so easily effaced as to leave me without an answer to the objections which have been raised.

It will be proper however, before I enter into the refutation of the charges that are alledged, to mark the leading descrimination between the state constitutions, and the constitution of the United States. When the people established the powers of legislation under their separate governments, they invested their representatives with every right and authority which they did not in explicit terms reserve; and therefore upon every question, respecting the jurisdiction of the house of assembly, if the frame of government is silent, the jurisdiction is efficient and complete. But in delegating fœderal powers, another criterion was necessarily introduced, and the congressional authority is to be collected, not from tacit implication, but from the positive grant expressed in the instrument of union. Hence it is evident, that in the former case every thing which is not reserved is given, but in the latter the reverse of the proposition prevails, and every thing which is not given, is reserved. This distinction being recognized, will furnish an answer to those who think the omission of a bill of rights, a defect in the proposed constitution: for it would have been superfluous and absurd to have stipulated with a fœderal body of our own creation, that we should enjoy those privileges, of which we are not divested either by the intention or the act, that has brought that body into existence. For instance, the liberty of the press, which has been a copious source of declamation and opposition, what controul can proceed from the fœderal government to shackle or destroy that sacred palladium of national freedom? If indeed, a power similar to that which has been granted for the regulation of commerce, had been granted to regulate literary publications, it would have been as necessary to stipulate that the liberty of the press should be preserved inviolate, as that the impost should be general in its operation. With respect likewise to the particular district of ten miles, which is to be made the seat of fœderal government, it will undoubtedly be proper to observe this salutary precaution, as there the legislative power will be exclusively lodged in the president, senate, and house of representatives of the United States. But this could not be an object with the convention, for it must naturally depend upon a future compact, to which the citizens immediately interested will, and ought to be parties; and there is no reason to suspect that so popular a privilege will in that case be neglected. In truth then, the proposed system possesses no influence whatever upon the press, and it would have been merely nugatory to have introduced a formal declaration upon the subject—nay, that very declaration might have been construed to imply that some degree of power was given, since we undertook to define its extent.

Another objection that has been fabricated against the new constitution, is expressed in this disingenuous form—"the trial by jury is abolished in civil cases." I must be excused, my fellow citizens, if upon this point, I take advantage of my professional experience to detect the futility of the assertion. Let it be remembered then, that the business of the Fœderal Convention was not local, but general; not limited to the views and establishments of a single state, but co-extensive with the continent, and comprehending the views and establishments of thirteen independent sovereignties. When therefore, this subject was in discussion, we were involved in difficulties which pressed on all sides, and no precedent could be discovered to direct our course. The cases open to a trial by jury differed in the different states, it was therefore impracticable on that ground to have made a general rule. The want of uniformity would have rendered any reference to the practice of the states idle and useless; and it could not, with any propriety, be said that "the trial by jury shall be as heretofore," since there has never existed any fœderal system of jurisprudence to which the declaration could relate. Besides, it is not in all cases that the trial by jury is adopted in civil questions, for causes depending in courts of admiralty, such as relate to maritime captures, and such as are agitated in courts of equity, do not require the intervention of that tribunal. How then, was the line of discrimination to be drawn? The convention found the task too difficult for them, and they left the business as it stands, in the fullest confidence that no danger could possibly ensue, since the proceedings of the supreme court, are to be regulated by the congress, which is a faithful representation of the people; and the oppression of government is effectually barred, by declaring that in all criminal cases the trial by jury shall be preserved.

This constitution, it has been further urged, is of a pernicious tendency, because it tolerates a standing army in the time of peace.—This has always been a topic of popular declamation; and yet, I do not know a nation in the world, which has not found it necessary and useful to maintain the appearance of strength in a season of the most profound tranquility. Nor is it a novelty with us; for under the present articles of confederation, congress certainly possesses this reprobated power, and the exercise of that power is proved at this moment by her cantonments along the banks of the Ohio. But what would be our national situation were it otherwise? Every principle of policy must be subverted, and the government must declare war, before they are prepared to carry it on. Whatever may be the provocation, however important the object in view, and however necessary dispatch and secrecy may be, still the declaration must precede the preparation, and the enemy will be informed of your intention, not only before you are equipped for an attack, but even before you are fortified for a defence. The consequence is too obvious to require any further delineation, and no man, who regards the dignity and safety of his country, can deny the necessity of a military force, under the controul and with the restrictions which the new constitution provides.

Perhaps there never was a charge made with less reasons than that which predicts the institution of a baneful aristocracy in the fœderal senate. This body branches into two characters, the one legislative, and the other executive. In its legislative character it can effect no purpose, without the co-operation of the house of representatives, and in its executive character, it can accomplish no object, without the concurrence of the president. Thus fettered, I do not know any act which the senate can of itself perform, and such dependance necessarily precludes every idea of influence and superiority. But I will confess that in the organization of this body, a compromise between contending interests is descernible; and when we reflect how various are the laws, commerce, habits, population, and extent of the confederated states, this evidence of mutual concession and accommodation ought rather to command a generous applause, than to excite jealousy and reproach. For my part, my admiration can only be equalled by my astonishment, in beholding so perfect a system, formed from such heterogeneous materials.

The next accusation I shall consider, is that which represents the fœderal constitution as not only calculated, but designedly framed, to reduce the state governments to mere corporations, and eventually to annihilate them. Those who have employed the term corporation upon this occasion, are not perhaps aware of its extent. In common parlance, indeed, it is generally applied to petty associations for the ease and conveniency of a few individuals; but in its enlarged sense, it will comprehend the government of Pennsylvania, the existing union of the states, and even this projected system is nothing more than a formal act of incorporation. But upon what pretence can it be alledged that it was designed to annihilate the state governments? For, I will undertake to prove that upon their existence, depends the existence of the fœderal plan. For this purpose, permit me to call your attention to the manner in which the president, senate, and house of representatives, are proposed to be appointed. The president is to be chosen by electors, nominated in such manner as the legislature of each state may direct; so that if there is no legislature, there can be no electors, and consequently the office of president cannot be supplied. The senate is to be composed of two senators from each state, chosen by the legislature; and therefore if there is no legislature, there can be no senate. The house of representatives, is to be composed of members chosen every second year by the people of the several states, and the electors in each state shall have the qualifications requisite for electors of the most numerous branch of the state legislature,—unless therefore, there is a state legislature, that qualification cannot be ascertained, and the popular branch of the fœderal constitution must likewise be extinct. From this view, then it is evidently absurd to suppose, that the annihilation of the separate governments will result from their union; or, that having that intention, the authors of the new system would have bound their connection with such indissoluble ties. Let me here advert to an arrangement highly advantageous, for you will perceive, without prejudice to the powers of the legislature in the election of senators, the people at large will acquire an additional privilege in returning members to the house of representatives—whereas, by the present confederation, it is the legislature alone that appoints the delegates to Congress.

The power of direct taxation has likewise been treated as an improper delegation to the fœderal government; but when we consider it as the duty of that body to provide for the national safety, to support the dignity of the union, and to discharge the debts contracted upon the collective faith of the states for their common benefit, it must be acknowledged, that those upon whom such important obligations are imposed, ought in justice and in policy to possess every means requisite for a faithful performance of their trust. But why should we be alarmed with visionary evils? I will venture to predict, that the great revenue of the United States must, and always will be raised by impost, for, being at once less obnoxious, and more productive, the interest of the government will be best promoted by the accommodation of the people. Still however, the objects of direct taxation should be within reach in all cases of emergency; and there is no more reason to apprehend oppression in the mode of collecting a revenue from this resource, than in the form of an impost, which, by universal assent, is left to the authority of the fœderal government. In either case, the force of civil institutions will be adequate to the purpose; and the dread of military violence, which has been assiduously disseminated, must eventually prove the mere effusion of a wild imagination, or a factious spirit. But the salutary consequences that must flow from thus enabling the government to receive and support the credit of the union, will afford another answer to the objections upon this ground. The State of Pennsylvania particularly, which has encumbered itself with the assumption of a great proportion of the public debt, will derive considerable relief and advantage; for, as it was the imbecility of the present confederation, which gave rise to the funding law, that law must naturally expire, when a competent and energetic fœderal system shall be substituted—the state will then be discharged from an extraordinary burthen, and the national creditor will find it to be his interest to return to his original security.

After all, my fellow citizens, it is neither extraordinary or unexpected, that the constitution offered to your consideration, should meet with opposition. It is the nature of man to pursue his own interest, in preference to the public good; and I do not mean to make any personal reflection, when I add, that it is the interest of a very numerous, powerful, and respectable body to counteract and destroy the excellent work produced by the late convention. All the offices of government, and all the appointments for the administration of justice and the collection of the public revenue, which are transferred from the individual to the aggregate sovereignty of the states, will necessarily turn the stream of influence and emolument into a new channel. Every person therefore, who either enjoys, or expects to enjoy, a place of profit under the present establishment, will object to the proposed innovation; not, in truth, because it is injurious to the liberties of his country, but because it affects his schemes of wealth and consequence. I will confess indeed, that I am not a blind admirer of this plan of government, and that there are some parts of it, which if my wish had prevailed, would certainly have been altered. But, when I reflect how widely men differ in their opinions, and that every man (and the observation applies likewise to every state) has an equal pretension to assert his own, I am satisfied that any thing nearer to perfection could not have been accomplished. If there are errors, it should be remembered, that the seeds of reformation are sown in the work itself, and the concurrence of two thirds of the congress may at any time introduce alterations and amendments. Regarding it then, in every point of view, with a candid and disinterested mind, I am bold to assert, that it is the best form of government which has ever been offered to the world.

> Mr. Wilson's speech was frequently interrupted with loud and unanimous testimonies of approbation, and the applause which was reiterated at the conclusion, evinced the general sense of its excellence, and the conviction which it had impressed upon every mind.

Brutus I

New York Journal, October 18, 1787

To the CITIZENS *of the* STATE *of* NEW-YORK.

When the public is called to investigate and decide upon a question in which not only the present members of the community are deeply interested, but upon which the happiness and misery of generations yet unborn is in great measure suspended, the benevolent mind cannot help feeling itself peculiarly interested in the result.

In this situation, I trust the feeble efforts of an individual, to lead the minds of the people to a wise and prudent determination, cannot fail of being acceptable to the candid and dispassionate part of the community. Encouraged by this consideration, I have been induced to offer my thoughts upon the present important crisis of our public affairs.

Perhaps this country never saw so critical a period in their political concerns. We have felt the feebleness of the ties by which these United-States are held together, and the want of sufficient energy in our present confederation, to manage, in some instances, our general concerns. Various expedients have been proposed to remedy these evils, but none have succeeded. At length a Convention of the states has been assembled, they have formed a constitution which will now, probably, be submitted to the people to ratify or reject, who are the fountain of all power, to whom alone it of right belongs to make or unmake constitutions, or forms of government, at their pleasure. The most important question that was ever proposed to your decision, or to the decision of any people under heaven, is before you, and you are to decide upon it by men of your own election, chosen specially for this purpose. If the constitution, offered to your acceptance, be a wise one, calculated to preserve the invaluable blessings of liberty, to secure the inestimable rights of mankind, and promote human happiness, then, if you accept it, you will lay a lasting foundation of happiness for millions yet unborn; generations to come will rise up and call you blessed. You may rejoice in the prospects of this

vast extended continent becoming filled with freemen, who
will assert the dignity of human nature. You may solace yourselves with the idea, that society, in this favoured land, will fast
advance to the highest point of perfection; the human mind
will expand in knowledge and virtue, and the golden age be,
in some measure, realised. But if, on the other hand, this form
of government contains principles that will lead to the subversion of liberty—if it tends to establish a despotism, or, what
is worse, a tyrannic aristocracy; then, if you adopt it, this only
remaining assylum for liberty will be shut up, and posterity will
execrate your memory.

Momentous then is the question you have to determine, and
you are called upon by every motive which should influence a
noble and virtuous mind, to examine it well, and to make up
a wise judgment. It is insisted, indeed, that this constitution
must be received, be it ever so imperfect. If it has its defects, it
is said, they can be best amended when they are experienced.
But remember, when the people once part with power, they
can seldom or never resume it again but by force. Many instances can be produced in which the people have voluntarily
increased the powers of their rulers; but few, if any, in which
rulers have willingly abridged their authority. This is a sufficient reason to induce you to be careful, in the first instance,
how you deposit the powers of government.

With these few introductory remarks, I shall proceed to a
consideration of this constitution.

The first question that presents itself on the subject is,
whether a confederated government be the best for the United
States or not? Or in other words, whether the thirteen United
States should be reduced to one great republic, governed by
one legislature, and under the direction of one executive and
judicial; or whether they should continue thirteen confederated republics, under the direction and controul of a supreme
federal head for certain defined national purposes only?

This enquiry is important, because, although the government reported by the convention does not go to a perfect and
entire consolidation, yet it approaches so near to it, that it
must, if executed, certainly and infallibly terminate in it.

This government is to possess absolute and uncontroulable
power, legislative, executive and judicial, with respect to every

object to which it extends, for by the last clause of section 8th, article 1st, it is declared "that the Congress shall have power to make all laws which shall be necessary and proper for carrying into execution the foregoing powers, and all other powers vested by this constitution, in the government of the United States; or in any department or office thereof." And by the 6th article, it is declared "that this constitution, and the laws of the United States, which shall be made in pursuance thereof, and the treaties made, or which shall be made, under the authority of the United States, shall be the supreme law of the land; and the judges in every state shall be bound thereby, any thing in the constitution, or law of any state to the contrary notwithstanding." It appears from these articles that there is no need of any intervention of the state governments, between the Congress and the people, to execute any one power vested in the general government, and that the constitution and laws of every state are nullified and declared void, so far as they are or shall be inconsistent with this constitution, or the laws made in pursuance of it, or with treaties made under the authority of the United States.—The government then, so far as it extends, is a complete one, and not a confederation. It is as much one complete government as that of New-York or Massachusetts, has as absolute and perfect powers to make and execute all laws, to appoint officers, institute courts, declare offences, and annex penalties, with respect to every object to which it extends, as any other in the world. So far therefore as its powers reach, all ideas of confederation are given up and lost. It is true this government is limited to certain objects, or to speak more properly, some small degree of power is still left to the states, but a little attention to the powers vested in the general government, will convince every candid man, that if it is capable of being executed, all that is reserved for the individual states must very soon be annihilated, except so far as they are barely necessary to the organization of the general government. The powers of the general legislature extend to every case that is of the least importance—there is nothing valuable to human nature, nothing dear to freemen, but what is within its power. It has authority to make laws which will affect the lives, the liberty, and property of every man in the United States; nor can the constitution or laws of any state, in any way prevent or impede the full and complete execution of every power given. The legislative power is competent to lay taxes, duties, imposts, and excises;—there is no limitation to this power, unless it be said that the clause which directs the use to which those taxes, and duties shall be applied, may be said to be a limitation: but this is no restriction of the power at all, for by this clause they are to be applied to pay the debts and provide for the common defence and general welfare of the United States; but the legislature have authority to contract debts at their discretion; they are the sole judges of what is necessary to provide for the common defence, and they only are to determine what is for the general welfare; this power therefore is neither more nor less, than a power to lay and collect taxes, imposts, and excises, at their pleasure; not only the power to lay taxes unlimited, as to the amount they may require, but it is perfect and absolute to raise them in any mode they please. No state legislature, or any power in the state governments, have any more to do in carrying this into effect, than the authority of one state has to do with that of another. In the business therefore of laying and collecting taxes, the idea of confederation is totally lost, and that of one entire republic is embraced. It is proper here to remark, that the authority to lay and collect taxes is the most important of any power that can be granted; it connects with it almost all other powers, or at least will in process of time draw all other after it; it is the great mean of protection, security, and defence, in a good government, and the great engine of oppression and tyranny in a bad one. This cannot fail of being the case, if we consider the contracted limits which are set by this constitution, to the late governments, on this article of raising money. No state can emit paper money—lay any duties, or imposts, on imports, or exports, but by consent of the Congress; and then the net produce shall be for the benefit of the United States: the only mean therefore left, for any state to support its government and discharge its debts, is by direct taxation; and the United States have also power to lay and collect taxes, in any way they please. Every one who has thought on the subject, must be convinced that but small sums of money can be collected in any country, by direct taxes, when the fœderal government begins to exercise the right of taxation in all its parts, the legislatures of the several states will find it impossible to raise monies to support their governments. Without money they cannot be supported, and they must dwindle away, and, as before observed, their powers absorbed in that of the general government.

It might be here shewn, that the power in the federal legislative, to raise and support armies at pleasure, as well in peace as in war, and their controul over the militia, tend, not only to a consolidation of the government, but the destruction of liberty.—I shall not, however, dwell upon these, as a few observations upon the judicial power of this government, in addition to the preceding, will fully evince the truth of the position.

The judicial power of the United States is to be vested in a supreme court, and in such inferior courts as Congress may from time to time ordain and establish. The powers of these courts are very extensive; their jurisdiction comprehends all civil causes, except such as arise between citizens of the same state; and it extends to all cases in law and equity arising under the constitution. One inferior court must be established, I presume, in each state, at least, with the necessary executive officers appendant thereto. It is easy to see, that in the common course of things, these courts will eclipse the dignity, and take away from the respectability, of the state courts. These courts will be, in themselves, totally independent of the states, deriving their authority from the United States, and receiving from them fixed salaries; and in the course of human events it is to be expected, that they will swallow up all the powers of the courts in the respective states.

How far the clause in the 8th section of the 1st article may operate to do away all idea of confederated states, and to effect an entire consolidation of the whole into one general government, it is impossible to say. The powers given by this article are very general and comprehensive, and it may receive a construction to justify the passing almost any law. A power to make all laws, which shall be *necessary and proper*, for carrying into execution, all powers vested by the constitution in the government of the United States, or any department or officer thereof, is a power very comprehensive and definite, and may, for ought I know, be exercised in such manner as entirely to abolish the state legislatures. Suppose the legislature of a state should pass a law to raise money to support their government and pay the state debt, may the Congress repeal this law, because it may prevent the collection of a tax which they may think proper and necessary to lay, to provide for the general welfare of the United States? For all laws made, in pursuance of this constitution, are the supreme law of the land, and the judges in every state shall be bound thereby, any thing in the constitution or laws of the different states to the contrary notwithstanding.—By such a law, the government of a particular state might be overturned at one stroke, and thereby be deprived of every means of its support.

It is not meant, by stating this case, to insinuate that the constitution would warrant a law of this kind; or unnecessarily to alarm the fears of the people, by suggesting, that the federal legislature would be more likely to pass the limits assigned them by the constitution, than that of an individual state, further than they are less responsible to the people. But what is meant is, that the legislature of the United States are vested with the great and uncontroulable powers, of laying and collecting taxes, duties, imposts, and excises; of regulating trade, raising and supporting armies, organizing, arming, and disciplining the militia, instituting courts, and other general powers. And are by this clause invested with the power of making all laws, *proper and necessary*, for carrying all these into execution; and they may so exercise this power as entirely to annihilate all the state governments, and reduce this country to one single government. And if they may do it, it is pretty certain they will; for it will be found that the power retained by individual states, small as it is, will be a clog upon the wheels of the government of the United States; the latter therefore will be naturally inclined to remove it out of the way. Besides, it is a truth confirmed by the unerring experience of ages, that every man, and every body of men, invested with power, are ever disposed to increase it, and to acquire a superiority over every thing that stands in their way. This disposition, which is implanted in human nature, will operate in the federal legislature to lessen and ultimately to subvert the state authority, and having such advantages, will most certainly succeed, if the federal government succeeds at all. It must be very evident then, that what this constitution wants of being a complete consolidation of the several parts of the union into one complete government, possessed of perfect legislative, judicial, and executive powers, to all intents and purposes, it will necessarily acquire in its exercise and operation.

Let us now proceed to enquire, as I at first proposed, whether it be best the thirteen United States should be reduced to one great republic, or not? It is here taken for granted, that all agree in this, that whatever government we adopt, it ought to be a free one; that it should be so framed as to secure the liberty of the citizens of America, and such an one as to admit of a full, fair, and equal representation of the people. The question then will be, whether a government thus constituted, and founded on such principles, is practicable, and can be exercised over the whole United States, reduced into one state?

If respect is to be paid to the opinion of the greatest and wisest men who have ever thought or wrote on the science of government, we shall be constrained to conclude, that a free republic cannot succeed over a country of such immense extent, containing such a number of inhabitants, and these encreasing in such rapid progression as that of the whole United States. Among the many illustrious authorities which might be produced to this point, I shall content myself with quoting only two. The one is the baron de Montesquieu, spirit of laws, chap. xvi. vol. I. "It is natural to a republic to have only a small territory, otherwise it cannot long subsist. In a large republic there are men of large fortunes, and consequently of less moderation; there are trusts too great to be placed in any single subject; he has interest of his own; he soon begins to think that he may be happy, great and glorious, by oppressing his fellow citizens; and that he may raise himself to grandeur on the ruins of his country. In a large republic, the public good is sacrificed to a thousand views; it is subordinate to exceptions, and depends on accidents. In a small one, the interest of the public is easier perceived, better understood, and more within the reach of every citizen; abuses are of less extent, and of course are less protected." Of the same opinion is the marquis Beccarari.

History furnishes no example of a free republic, any thing like the extent of the United States. The Grecian republics were of small extent; so also was that of the Romans. Both of these, it is true, in process of time, extended their conquests over large territories of country; and the consequence was, that their governments were changed from that of free governments to those of the most tyrannical that ever existed in the world.

Not only the opinion of the greatest men, and the experience of mankind, are against the idea of an extensive republic, but a variety of reasons may be drawn from the reason and nature of things, against it. In every government, the will of the sovereign is the law. In despotic governments, the supreme authority being lodged in one, his will is law, and can be as easily expressed to a large extensive territory as to a small one. In a pure democracy the people are the sovereign, and their will is declared by themselves; for this purpose they must all come together to deliberate, and decide. This kind of government cannot be exercised, therefore, over a country of any considerable extent; it must be confined to a single city, or at least limited to such bounds as that the people can conveniently assemble, be able to debate, understand the subject submitted to them, and declare their opinion concerning it.

In a free republic, although all laws are derived from the consent of the people, yet the people do not declare their consent by themselves in person, but by representatives, chosen by them, who are supposed to know the minds of their constituents, and to be possessed of integrity to declare this mind.

In every free government, the people must give their assent to the laws by which they are governed. This is the true criterion between a free government and an arbitrary one. The former are ruled by the will of the whole, expressed in any manner they may agree upon; the latter by the will of one, or a few. If the people are to give their assent to the laws, by persons chosen and appointed by them, the manner of the choice and the number chosen, must be such, as to possess, be disposed, and consequently qualified to declare the sentiments of the people; for if they do not know, or are not disposed to speak the sentiments of the people, the people do not govern, but the sovereignty is in a few. Now, in a large extended country, it is impossible to have a representation, possessing the sentiments, and of integrity, to declare the minds of the people, without having it so numerous and unwieldly, as to be subject in great measure to the inconveniency of a democratic government.

The territory of the United States is of vast extent; it now contains near three millions of souls, and is capable of containing much more than ten times that number. Is it practicable for a country, so large and so numerous as they will soon become, to elect a representation, that will speak their sentiments, without their becoming so numerous as to be incapable of transacting public business? It certainly is not.

In a republic, the manners, sentiments, and interests of the people should be similar. If this be not the case, there will be a constant clashing of opinions; and the representatives of one part will be continually striving against those of the other. This will retard the operations of government, and prevent such conclusions as will promote the public good. If we apply this remark to the condition of the United States, we shall be convinced that it forbids that we should be one government. The United States includes a variety of climates. The productions of the different parts of the union are very variant, and their interests, of consequence, diverse. Their manners and habits differ as much as their climates and productions; and their sentiments are by no means coincident. The laws and customs of the several states are, in many respects, very diverse, and in some opposite; each would be in favor of its own interests and customs, and, of consequence, a legislature, formed of representatives from the respective parts, would not only be too numerous to act with any care or decision, but would be composed of such heterogenous and discordant principles, as would constantly be contending with each other.

The laws cannot be executed in a republic, of an extent equal to that of the United States, with promptitude.

The magistrates in every government must be supported in the execution of the laws, either by an armed force, maintained at the public expence for that purpose; or by the people turning out to aid the magistrate upon his command, in case of resistance.

In despotic governments, as well as in all the monarchies of Europe, standing armies are kept up to execute the commands of the prince or the magistrate, and are employed for this purpose when occasion requires: But they have always proved the destruction of liberty, and is abhorrent to the spirit of a free republic. In England, where they depend upon the parliament for their annual support, they have always been complained of as oppressive and unconstitutional, and are seldom employed in executing of the laws; never except on extraordinary occasions, and then under the direction of a civil magistrate.

A free republic will never keep a standing army to execute its laws. It must depend upon the support of its citizens. But when a government is to receive its support from the aid of the citizens, it must be so constructed as to have the confidence, respect, and affection of the people. Men who, upon the call of the magistrate, offer themselves to execute the laws, are influenced to do it either by affection to the government, or from fear; where a standing army is at hand to punish offenders, every man is actuated by the latter principle, and therefore, when the magistrate calls, will obey: but, where this is not the case, the government must rest for its support upon the confidence and respect which the people have for their government and laws. The body of the people being attached, the government will always be sufficient to support and execute its laws, and to operate upon the fears of any faction which may be opposed to it, not only to prevent an opposition to the execution of the laws themselves, but also to compel the most of them to aid the magistrate; but the people will not be likely to have such confidence in their rulers, in a republic so extensive as the United States, as necessary for these purposes. The confidence which the people have in their rulers, in a free republic, arises from their knowing them, from their being responsible to them for their conduct, and from the power they have of displacing them when they misbehave: but in a republic of the extent of this continent, the people in general would be acquainted with very few of their rulers: the people at large would know little of their proceedings, and it would be extremely difficult to change them. The people in Georgia and New-Hampshire would not know one another's mind, and therefore could not act in concert to enable them to effect a general change of representatives. The different parts of so extensive a country could not possibly be made acquainted with the conduct of their representatives, nor be informed of the reasons upon which measures were founded. The consequence will be, they will have no confidence in their legislature, suspect them of ambitious views, be jealous of every measure they adopt, and will not support the laws they pass. Hence the government will be nerveless and inefficient, and no way will be left to render it otherwise, but by establishing an armed force to execute the laws at the point of the bayonet—a government of all others the most to be dreaded.

In a republic of such vast extent as the United-States, the legislature cannot attend to the various concerns and wants of its different parts. It cannot be sufficiently numerous to be acquainted with the local condition and wants of the different districts, and if it could, it is impossible it should have sufficient time to attend to and provide for all the variety of cases of this nature, that would be continually arising.

In so extensive a republic, the great officers of government would soon become above the controul of the people, and abuse their power to the purpose of aggrandizing themselves, and oppressing them. The trust committed to the executive offices, in a country of the extent of the United-States, must be various and of magnitude. The command of all the troops and navy of the republic, the appointment of officers, the power of pardoning offences, the collecting of all the public revenues, and the power of expending them, with a number of other powers, must be lodged and exercised in every state, in the hands of a few. When these are attended with great honor and emolument, as they always will be in large states, so as greatly to interest men to pursue them, and to be proper objects for ambitious and designing men, such men will be ever restless in their pursuit after them. They will use the power, when they have acquired it, to the purposes of gratifying their own interest and ambition, and it is scarcely possible, in a very large republic, to call them to account for their misconduct, or to prevent their abuse of power.

These are some of the reasons by which it appears, that a free republic cannot long subsist over a country of the great extent of these states. If then this new constitution is calculated to consolidate the thirteen states into one, as it evidently is, it ought not to be adopted.

Though I am of opinion, that it is a sufficient objection to this government, to reject it, that it creates the whole union into one government, under the form of a republic, yet if this objection was obviated, there are exceptions to it, which are so material and fundamental, that they ought to determine every man, who is a friend to the liberty and happiness of mankind, not to adopt it. I beg the candid and dispassionate attention of my countrymen while I state these objections—they are such as have obtruded themselves upon my mind upon a careful attention to the matter, and such as I sincerely believe are well founded. There are many objections, of small moment, of which I shall take no notice—perfection is not to be expected in any thing that is the production of man—and if I did not in my conscience believe that this scheme was defective in the fundamental principles—in the foundation upon which a free and equal government must rest—I would hold my peace.

A Political Dialogue

Massachusetts Centinel (Boston), October 24, 1787

Mr. GRUMBLE. Sad times! neighbour *Union*, sad times!

Mr. UNION. Why, what is the matter, neighbour *Grumble*?

Mr. GRUMBLE. Why, all our liberties are going to be swallowed up; *the whole country* is in a confederacy to ruin us—I remember the glorious times when every man had a right to speak what he thought.

Mr. UNION. Why, who hinders you now?

Mr. GRUMBLE. Who?—Why every body:—When this report of the Convention came to hand, I thought I would go and talk about it to my neighbours; so I went to the Barber's shop, and taking up the paper, so says I, "it seems this monster which is to devour the liberties of the people is come forth."—Immediately the whole shop was in alarm—Mr. *Razor*'s hand trembled so with indignation, that I thought he would have cut my throat—and the whole shop looked as if they did not care if he had. What's that you say, said a surly *Ship-Carpenter*, do you mean that I and my family should starve? Let us come at him, said a *Blacksmith, Painter, Rope-Maker, Sail-Maker, Corker*, and *Joiner*—the Federal Constitution is the only thing which can save us, and our children, from starving.—Out of the shop with the rascal, said half a dozen different tradesmen. It was in vain I applied to a *Merchant* for protection, he assured me that for want of a Federal Government he had sunk a fortune by importing cargoes under the State imposts, and was undersold by goods from Connecticut—and even my friend *Simon Meek*, the Quaker, who delights in healing quarrels, would not interfere, but cooly told me—"*Friend Grumble, whilst we are in the flesh, we should be obedient to the powers which may be ordained over us.*" In fine, I was driven from the shop in the plight of the Israelitish ambassadours.—I ran with my complaint to our reverend *Pastor*, who told me that to be bound by this law of equity, was perfect freedom, and bid me beware of the leaven of the Pharisees.—The *Doctor* who tends my sick child, was in the same story—and the honest man from the country, who brings me my winter's cyder, *vowed* it would have been *right cute* if they had kicked me out of the shop, for *his town* thought the new Constitution was altogether up to the *notch*. In a word, every man I have conversed with, has been ready to knock my brains out, if I said a word against it—Do you call these liberty times?

Mr. UNION. Well, but neighbour, what are your objections to the new Constitution?

Mr. GRUMBLE. Why, as to the matter, I can't say I have any, but then what vexes me is, that they won't let me say a word against it—it shews, neighbour, there is some trick in it.

Mr. UNION. But neighbour this is indeed a country of liberty, and every man may speak his mind, especially on a subject which is presented to you, for your consideration—but if all orders and degrees of people oppose your speaking against this proposed constitution, the conclusion is, that the whole people, both see the necessity, and give their warmest approbation of it. And indeed, neighbour, it is no wonder, when we consider the horrours of our present situation—the decay of our trade and manufactures—the scarcity of money—the failure of publick credit—the distraction of our publick affairs, and the distress of individuals, which have all arisen from a want of this very Federal Government—it is no wonder, I say, if men who are so deeply interested, should not be able to sit patiently, and hear revilings against the only remedy which can be applied with success, to our present grievances.

No man is intended to be deprived of a freedom of speech, but the few individuals who oppose the Federal Government, must not be surprised to find, that the *Merchant* and *Trader*, who have been ruined for the want of an efficient Federal Government to regulate trade—will resent it—that the *Landholder* who has been taxed so high that the produce of his farm would scarcely pay its rates—will resent it:—And out of the abundance of the heart, the long train of industrious *Tradesmen*, who are now spending their past earnings, or selling their tools for a subsistence—will resent it—nay, the whole body of an almost ruined people, will despise and execrate the wretch who dares blaspheme the POLITICAL SAVIOUR OF OUR COUNTRY.

James Madison to Thomas Jefferson

New York Octr. 24. 1787.

DEAR SIR

My two last, though written for the two last Packets, have unluckily been delayed till this conveyance. The first of them was sent from Philada. to Commodore Jones in consequence of information that he was certainly to go by the Packet then about to sail. Being detained here by his business with Congress, and being unwilling to put the letter into the mail without my approbation which could not be obtained in time, he detained the letter also. The second was sent from Philada. to Col. Carrington, with a view that it might go by the last packet at all events in case Commodore Jones should meet with further detention here. By ill luck he was out of Town, and did not return till it was too late to make use of the opportunity. Neither of the letters were indeed of much consequence at the time, and are still less so now. I let them go forward nevertheless as they may mention some circumstances not at present in my recollection, and as they will prevent a chasm in my part of [   ] correspondence which I have so many motives to cherish by an exact punctuality.

Your favor of June 20. has been already acknowledged. The last Packet from France brought me that of August 2d. I have recd. also by the Mary Capt. Howland the three Boxes for W.H. B.F. and myself. The two first have been duly forwarded. The contents of the last are a valuable addition to former literary remittances and lay me under additional obligations, which I shall always feel more strongly than I express. The articles included for Congress have been delivered & those for the two Universities and for General Washington have been forwarded, as have been the various letters for your friends in Virginia and elsewhere. The parcel of rice referred to in your letter to the Delegates of S. Carolina has met with some accident. No account whatever can be gathered concerning it. It probably was not shipped from France. Ubbo's book I find was not omitted as you seem to have apprehended. The charge for it however is, which I must beg you to supply. The duplicate vol. of the Encyclopedie, I left in Virginia, and it is uncertain when I shall have an opportunity of returning it. Your Spanish duplicates will I fear be hardly vendible. I shall make a trial wherever a chance presents itself. A few days ago I recd. your favor of the 15 of Augst. via L'Orient & Boston. The letters inclosed along with it were immediately sent on to Virga.

You will herewith receive the result of the Convention, which continued its Session till the 17th. of September. I take the liberty of making some observations on the subject which will help to make up a letter, if they should answer no other purpose.

It appeared to be the sincere and unanimous wish of the Convention to cherish and preserve the Union of the States. No proposition was made, no suggestion was thrown out, in favor of a partition of the Empire into two or more Confederacies.

It was generally agreed that the objects of the Union could not be secured by any system founded on the principle of a confederation of sovereign States. A *voluntary* observance of the federal law by all the members, could never be hoped for. A *compulsive* one could evidently never be reduced to practice, and if it could, involved equal calamities to the innocent & the guilty, the necessity of a military force both obnoxious & dangerous, and in general, a scene resembling much more a civil war, than the administration of a regular Government.

Hence was embraced the alternative of a Government which instead of operating, on the States, should operate without their intervention on the individuals composing them: and hence the change in the principle and proportion of representation.

This ground-work being laid, the great objects which presented themselves were 1. to unite a proper energy in the Executive and a proper stability in the Legislative departments, with the essential characters of Republican Government. 2. to draw a line of demarkation which would give to the General Government every power requisite for general purposes, and leave to the States every power which might be most beneficially administered by them. 3. to provide for the different interests of different parts of the Union. 4. to adjust the clashing pretensions of the large and small States. Each of these objects was pregnant with difficulties. The whole of them together formed a task more difficult than can be well concieved by those who were not concerned in the execution of it. Adding to these considerations the natural diversity of human opinions on all new and complicated subjects, it is impossible to consider the degree of concord which ultimately prevailed as less than a miracle.

The first of these objects as it respects the Executive, was peculiarly embarrassing. On the question whether it should consist of a single person, or a plurality of co-ordinate members, on the mode of appointment, on the duration in office, on the degree of power, on the re-eligibility, tedious and reiterated discussions took place. The plurality of co-ordinate members had finally but few advocates. Governour Randolph was at the head of them. The modes of appointment proposed were various, as by the people at large—by electors chosen by the people—by the Executives of the States—by the Congress, some preferring a joint ballot of the two Houses—some a separate concurrent ballot allowing to each a negative on the other house—some a nomination of several candidates by one House, out of whom a choice should be made by the other. Several other modifications were started. The expedient at length adopted seemed to give pretty general satisfaction to the members. As to the duration in office, a few would have preferred a tenure during good behaviour—a considerable number would have done so, in case an easy & effectual removal by impeachment could be settled. It was much agitated whether a long term, seven years for example, with a subsequent & perpetual ineligibility, or a short term with a capacity to be re-elected, should be fixed. In favor of the first opinion were urged the danger of a gradual degeneracy of re-elections from time to time, into first a life and then a heriditary tenure, and the favorable effect of an incapacity to be reappointed, on the independent exercise of the Executive authority. On the other side it was contended that the prospect of necessary degradation, would discourage the most dignified characters from aspiring to the office, would take away the principal motive to the faithful discharge of its duties—the hope of being rewarded with a reappointment, would stimulate ambition to violent efforts for holding over the constitutional term—and instead of producing an independent administration, and a firmer defence of the constitutional rights of the department, would render the officer

more indifferent to the importance of a place which he would
soon be obliged to quit for ever, and more ready to yield to
the incroachmts. of the Legislature of which he might again
be a member. The questions concerning the degree of power
turned chiefly on the appointment to offices, and the controul
on the Legislature. An *absolute* appointment to all offices—to
some offices—to no offices, formed the scale of opinions on
the first point. On the second, some contended for an absolute
negative, as the only possible mean of reducing to practice, the
theory of a free Government which forbids a mixture of the
Legislative & Executive powers. Others would be content with
a revisionary power to be overruled by three fourths of both
Houses. It was warmly urged that the judiciary department
should be associated in the revision. The idea of some was that
a separate revision should be given to the two departments—
that if either objected two thirds; if both three fourths, should
be necessary to overrule.

In forming the Senate, the great anchor of the Government,
the questions as they came within the first object turned mostly
on the mode of appointment, and the duration of it. The different modes proposed were, 1. by the House of Representatives 2. by the Executive, 3. by electors chosen by the people
for the purpose. 4. by the State Legislatures. On the point of
duration, the propositions descended from good-behavior to
four years, through the intermediate terms of nine, seven, six,
& five years. The election of the other branch was first determined to be triennial, and afterwards reduced to biennial.

The second object, the due partition of power, between the
General & local Governments, was perhaps of all, the most
nice and difficult. A few contended for an entire abolition of
the States; some for indefinite power of Legislation in the Congress, with a negative on the laws of the States: some for such
a power without a negative: some for a limited power of legislation, with such a negative: the majority finally for a limited
power without the negative. The question with regard to the
Negative underwent repeated discussions, and was finally rejected by a bare majority. As I formerly intimated to you my
opinion in favor of this ingredient, I will take this occasion of
explaining myself on the subject. Such a check on the States
appears to me necessary 1. to prevent encroachments on the

General authority. 2. to prevent instability and injustice in the legislation of the States.

1. Without such a check in the whole over the parts, our system involves the evil of imperia in imperio. If a compleat supremacy some where is not necessary in every Society, a controuling power at least is so, by which the general authority may be defended against encroachments of the subordinate authorities, and by which the latter may be restrained from encroachments on each other. If the supremacy of the British Parliament is not necessary as has been contended, for the harmony of that Empire; it is evident I think that without the royal negative or some equivalent controul, the unity of the system would be destroyed. The want of some such provision seems to have been mortal to the antient Confederacies, and to be the disease of the modern. Of the Lycian Confederacy little is known. That of the Amphyctions is well known to have been rendered of little use whilst it lasted, and in the end to have been destroyed by the predominance of the local over the federal authority. The same observation may be made, on the authority of Polybius, with regard to the Achæan League. The Helvetic System scarcely amounts to a Confederacy, and is distinguished by too many peculiarities, to be a ground of comparison. The case of the United Netherlands is in point. The authority of a Statholder, the influence of a Standing army, the common interest in the conquered possessions, the pressure of surrounding danger, the guarantee of foreign powers, are not sufficient to secure the authority and interests of the generality, agst. the antifederal tendency of the provincial sovereignties. The German Empire is another example. A Hereditary chief with vast independent resources of wealth and power, a federal Diet, with ample parchment authority, a regular Judiciary establishment, the influence of the neighbourhood of great & formidable Nations, have been found unable either to maintain the subordination of the members, or to prevent their mutual contests & encroachments. Still more to the purpose is our own experience both during the war and since the peace. Encroachments of the States on the general authority, sacrifices of national to local interests, interferences of the measures of different States, form a great part of the history of our political system. It may be said that the new Constitution is founded on

different principles, and will have a different operation. I admit the difference to be material. It presents the aspect rather of a feudal system of republics, if such a phrase may be used, than of a Confederacy of independent States. And what has been the progress and event of the feudal Constitutions? In all of them a continual struggle between the head and the inferior members, until a final victory has been gained in some instances by one, in others, by the other of them. In one respect indeed there is a remarkable variance between the two cases. In the feudal system the sovereign, though limited, was independent; and having no particular sympathy of interests with the great Barons, his ambition had as full play as theirs in the mutual projects of usurpation. In the American Constitution The general authority will be derived entirely from the subordinate authorities. The Senate will represent the States in their political capacity; the other House will represent the people of the States in their individual capacity. The former will be accountable to their constituents at moderate, the latter at short periods. The President also derives his appointment from the States, and is periodically accountable to them. This dependence of the General, on the local authorities, seems effectually to guard the latter against any dangerous encroachments of the former: Whilst the latter, within their respective limits, will be continually sensible of the abridgment of their power, and be stimulated by ambition to resume the surrendered portion of it. We find the representatives of Counties and corporations in the Legislatures of the States, much more disposed to sacrifice the aggregate interest, and even authority, to the local views of their Constituents: than the latter to the former. I mean not by these remarks to insinuate that an esprit de corps will not exist in the national Government or that opportunities may not occur, of extending its jurisdiction in some points. I mean only that the danger of encroachments is much greater from the other side, and that the impossibility of dividing powers of legislation, in such a manner, as to be free from different constructions by different interests, or even from ambiguity in the judgment of the impartial, requires some such expedient as I contend for. Many illustrations might be given of this impossibility. How long has it taken to fix, and how imperfectly is yet fixed the legislative power of corporations, though that power is subordinate in the most compleat manner? The line of distinction between the power of regulating trade and that of drawing revenue from it, which was once considered as the barrier of our liberties, was found on fair discussion, to be absolutely undefinable. No distinction seems to be more obvious than that between spiritual and temporal matters. Yet wherever they have been made objects of Legislation, they have clashed and contended with each other, till one or the other has gained the supremacy. Even the boundaries between the Executive, Legislative & Judiciary powers, though in general so strongly marked in themselves, consist in many instances of mere shades of difference. It may be said that the Judicial authority under our new system will keep the States within their proper limits, and supply the place of a negative on their laws. The answer is, that it is more convenient to prevent the passage of a law, than to declare it void after it is passed; that this will be particularly the case, where the law aggrieves individuals, who may be unable to support an appeal agst. a State to the supreme Judiciary; that a State which would violate the Legislative rights of the Union, would not be very ready to obey a Judicial decree in support of them, and that a recurrence to force, which in the event of disobedience would be necessary, is an evil which the new Constitution meant to exclude as far as possible.

2. A constitutional negative on the laws of the States seems equally necessary to secure individuals agst. encroachments on their rights. The mutability of the laws of the States is found to be a serious evil. The injustice of them has been so frequent and so flagrant as to alarm the most stedfast friends of Republicanism. I am persuaded I do not err in saying that the evils issuing from these sources contributed more to that uneasiness which produced the Convention. and prepared the public mind for a general reform, than those which accrued to our national character and interest from the inadequacy of the Confederation to its immediate objects. A reform therefore which does not make provision for private rights, must be materially defective. The restraints agst. paper emissions, and violations of contracts are not sufficient. Supposing them to be effectual as far as they go, they are short of the mark. Injustice may be effected by such an infinitude of legislative expedients, that where the disposition exists it can only be controuled by

some provision which reaches all cases whatsoever. The partial provision made, supposes the disposition which will evade it. It may be asked how private rights will be more secure under the Guardianship of the General Government than under the State Governments, since they are both founded on the republican principle which refers the ultimate decision to the will of the majority, and are distinguished rather by the extent within which they will operate, than by any material difference in their structure. A full discussion of this question would, if I mistake not, unfold the true principles of Republican Government, and prove in contradiction to the concurrent opinions of theoretical writers, that this form of Government, in order to effect its purposes, must operate not within a small but an extensive sphere. I will state some of the ideas which have occurred to me on this subject. Those who contend for a simple Democracy, or a pure republic, actuated by the sense of the majority, and operating within narrow limits, assume or suppose a case which is altogether fictitious. They found their reasoning on the idea, that the people composing the Society, enjoy not only an equality of political rights; but that they have all precisely the same interests, and the same feelings in every respect. Were this in reality the case, their reasoning would be conclusive. The interest of the majority would be that of the minority also; the decisions could only turn on mere opinion concerning the good of the whole, of which the major voice would be the safest criterion; and within a small sphere, this voice could be most easily collected, and the public affairs most accurately managed. We know however that no Society ever did or can consist of so homogeneous a mass of Citizens. In the savage State indeed, an approach is made towards it; but in that State little or no Government is necessary. In all civilized Societies, distinctions are various and unavoidable. A distinction of property results from that very protection which a free Government gives to unequal faculties of acquiring it. There will be rich and poor; creditors and debtors; a landed interest, a monied interest, a mercantile interest, a manufacturing interest. These classes may again be subdivided according to the different productions of different situations & soils, & according to different branches of commerce, and of manufactures. In addition to these natural distinctions, artificial ones will be founded, on accidental differences in political, religious or other opinions, or an attachment to the persons of leading individuals. However erroneous or ridiculous these grounds of dissention and faction, may appear to the enlightened Statesman, or the benevolent philosopher, the bulk of mankind who are neither Statesmen nor Philosophers, will continue to view them in a different light. It remains then to be enquired whether a majority having any common interest, or feeling any common passion, will find sufficient motives to restrain them from oppressing the minority. An individual is never allowed to be a judge or even a witness in his own cause. If two individuals are under the biass of interest or enmity agst. a third, the rights of the latter could never be safely referred to the majority of the three. Will two thousand individuals be less apt to oppress one thousand, or two hundred thousand, one hundred thousand? Three motives only can restrain in such cases. 1. a prudent regard to private or partial good, as essentially involved in the general and permanent good of the whole. This ought no doubt to be sufficient of itself. Experience however shews that it has little effect on individuals, and perhaps still less on a collection of individuals, and least of all on a majority with the public authority in their hands. If the former are ready to forget that honesty is the best policy; the last do more. They often proceed on the converse of the maxim: that whatever is politic is honest. 2. respect for character. This motive is not found sufficient to restrain individuals from injustice, and loses its efficacy in proportion to the number which is to divide the praise or the blame. Besides as it has reference to public opinion, which is that of the majority, the Standard is fixed by those whose conduct is to be measured by it. 3. Religion. The inefficacy of this restraint on individuals is well known. The conduct of every popular Assembly, acting on oath, the strongest of religious ties, shews that individuals join without remorse in acts agst. which their consciences would revolt, if proposed to them separately in their closets. When Indeed Religion is kindled into enthusiasm, its force like that of other passions is increased by the sympathy of a multitude. But enthusiasm is only a temporary state of Religion, and whilst it lasts will hardly be seen with pleasure at the helm. Even in its coolest state, it has been much oftener a motive to oppression than a restraint from it. If then there must be different interests and parties in Society; and a majority when united by a common interest or passion can not be restrained from oppressing the minority, what remedy can be found in a republican Government, where the majority must ultimately decide, but that of giving such an extent to its sphere, that no common interest or passion will be likely to unite a majority of the whole number in an unjust pursuit. In a large Society, the people are broken into so many interests and parties, that a common sentiment is less likely to be felt, and the requisite concert less likely to be formed, by a majority of the whole. The same security seems requisite for the civil as for the religious rights of individuals. If the same sect form a majority and have the power, other sects will be sure to be depressed. Divide et impera, the reprobated axiom of tyranny, is under certain qualifications, the only policy, by which a republic can be administered on just principles. It must be observed however that this doctrine can only hold within a sphere of a mean extent. As in too small a sphere oppressive combinations may be too easily formed agst. the weaker party; so in too extensive a one, a defensive concert may be rendered too difficult against the oppression of those entrusted with the administration. The great desideratum in Government is, so to modify the sovereignty as that it may be sufficiently neutral between different parts of the Society to controul one part from invading the rights of another, and at the same time sufficiently controuled itself, from setting up an interest adverse to that of the entire Society. In absolute monarchies, the Prince may be tolerably neutral towards different classes of his subjects, but may sacrifice the happiness of all to his personal ambition or avarice. In small republics, the sovereign will is controuled from such a sacrifice of the entire Society, but is not sufficiently neutral towards the parts composing it. In the extended Republic of the United States, The General Government would hold a pretty even balance between the parties of particular States, and be at the same time sufficiently restrained by its dependence on the community, from betraying its general interests.

Begging pardon for this immoderate digression I return to the third object abovementioned, the adjustment of the different interests of different parts of the Continent. Some contended for an unlimited power over trade including exports as well as imports, and over slaves as well as other imports; some for such a power, provided the concurrence of two thirds of both House were required; Some for such a qualification of the power, with an exemption of exports and slaves, others for an exemption of exports only. The result is seen in the Constitution. S. Carolina & Georgia were inflexible on the point of the slaves.

The remaining object created more embarrassment, and a greater alarm for the issue of the Convention than all the rest put together. The little States insisted on retaining their equality in both branches, unless a compleat abolition of the State Governments should take place; and made an equality in the Senate a sine qua non. The large States on the other hand urged that as the new Government was to be drawn principally from the people immediately and was to operate directly on them, not on the States; and consequently as the States wd. lose that importance which is now proportioned to the importance of their voluntary compliances with the requisitions of Congress, it was necessary that the representation in both Houses should be in proportion to their size. It ended in the compromise which you will see, but very much to the dissatisfaction of several members from the large States.

It will not escape you that three names only from Virginia are subscribed to the Act. Mr. Wythe did not return after the death of his lady. Docr. MClurg left the Convention some time before the adjournment. The Governour and Col. Mason refused to be parties to it. Mr. Gerry was the only other member who refused. The objections of the Govr. turn principally on the latitude of the general powers, and on the connection established between the President and the Senate. He wished that the plan should be proposed to the States with liberty to them to suggest alterations which should all be referred to another general Convention, to be incorporated into the plan as far as might be judged expedient. He was not inveterate in his opposition, and grounded his refusal to subscribe pretty much on his unwillingness to commit himself, so as not to be at liberty to be governed by further lights on the subject. Col. Mason left Philada. in an exceeding ill humour indeed. A number of little circumstances arising in part from the impatience which prevailed towards the close of the business, conspired to whet his acrimony. He returned to Virginia with a fixed disposition to prevent the adoption of the plan if possible. He considers the want of a Bill of Rights as a fatal objection. His other objections are to the substitution of the Senate in place of an Executive Council & to the powers vested in that body— to the powers of the Judiciary—to the vice President being made President of the Senate—to the smallness of the number of Representatives—to the restriction on the States with regard to ex post facto laws—and most of all probably to the power of regulating trade, by a majority only of each House. He has some other lesser objections. Being now under the necessity of justifying his refusal to sign, he will of course muster every possible one. His conduct has given great umbrage to the County of Fairfax, and particularly to the Town of Alexandria. He is already instructed to promote in the Assembly the calling a Convention, and will probably be either not deputed to the Convention, or be tied up by express instructions. He did not object in general to the powers vested in the National Government, so much as to the modification. In some respects he admitted that some further powers would have improved the system. He acknowledged in particular that a negative on the State laws, and the appointment of the State Executives ought to be ingredients; but supposed that the public mind would not now bear them, and that experience would hereafter produce these amendments.

The final reception which will be given by the people at large to the proposed System can not yet be decided. The Legislature of N. Hampshire was sitting when it reached that State and was well pleased with it. As far as the sense of the people there has been expressed, it is equally favorable. Boston is warm and almost unanimous in embracing it. The impression on the Country is not yet known. No symptoms of disapprobation have appeared. The Legislature of that State is now sitting, through which the sense of the people at large will soon be promulged with tolerable certainty. The paper money faction in Rh. Island is hostile. The other party zealously attached to it. Its passage through Connecticut is likely to be very smooth and easy. There seems to be less agitation in this State than any where. The discussion of the subject seems confined to the newspapers. The principal characters are known to be friendly. The Governour's party which has hitherto been the popular & most numerous one, is supposed to be on the opposite side; but considerable reserve is practised, of which he sets the example. N. Jersey takes the affirmative side of course. Meetings of the people are declaring their approbation, and instructing their representatives. Penna. will be divided. The City of Philada., the Republican party, the Quakers, and most of the Germans espouse the Constitution. Some of the Constitutional leaders, backed by the western Country will oppose. An unlucky ferment on the subject in their Assembly just before its late adjournment has irritated both sides, particularly the opposition, and by redoubling the exertions of that party may render the event doubtful. The voice of Maryland I understand from pretty good authority, is, as far as it has been declared, strongly in favor of the Constitution. Mr. Chase is an enemy, but the Town of Baltimore which he now represents, is warmly attached to it, and will shackle him as far as they can. Mr. Paca will probably be, as usual, in the politics of Chase. My information from Virginia is as yet extremely imperfect. I have a letter from Genl. Washington which speaks favorably of the impression within a circle of some extent; and another from Chancellor Pendleton which expresses his full acceptance of the plan, and the popularity of it in his district. I am told also that Innis and Marshall are patrons of it. In the opposite scale are Mr. James Mercer, Mr. R. H. Lee, Docr. Lee and their connections of course, Mr. M. Page according to Report, and most of the Judges & Bar of the general Court. The part which Mr. Henry will take is unknown here. Much will depend on it. I had taken it for granted from a variety of circumstances that he wd. be in the opposition, and still think that will be the case. There are reports however which favor a contrary supposition. From the States South of Virginia nothing has been heard. As the deputation from S. Carolina consisted of some of its weightiest characters, who have returned unanimously zealous in favor of the Constitution, it is probable that State will readily embrace it. It is not less probable, that N. Carolina will follow the example unless that of Virginia should counterbalance it. Upon the whole, although, the public mind will not be fully known, nor finally settled for a considerable time, appearances at present augur a more prompt, and general adoption of the Plan than could have been well expected.

When the plan came before Congs. for their sanction, a very serious effort was made by R. H. Lee & Mr. Dane from Masts. to embarrass it. It was first contended that Congress could not properly give any positive countenance to a measure which had for its object the subversion of the Constitution under which they acted. This ground of attack failing, the former gentleman urged the expediency of sending out the plan with amendments, & proposed a number of them corresponding with the objections of Col. Mason. This experiment had still less effect. In order however to obtain unanimity it was necessary to couch the resolution in very moderate terms.

Mr. Adams has recd. permission to return, with thanks for his Services. No provision is made for supplying his place, or keeping up any represention there. Your reappointment for three years will be notified from the Office of F. Affrs. It was *made without a negative eight states* being *present. Connecticut however put in a blank ticket* the *sense of* that *state having been declared against embassies. Massachusets betrayed some scruple* on *like ground.* Every *personal consideration* was *avowed & I beleive with sincerity* to have *militated against these scruples.* It seems to be understood that letters to & from the foreign Ministers of the U.S. are not free of Postage: but that the charge is to be allowed in their accounts.

The exchange of our French for Dutch Creditors has not been countenanced either by Congress or the Treasury Board. The paragraph in your last letter to Mr. Jay, on the subject of applying a loan in Holland to the discharge of the pay due to the foreign Officers has been referred to the Board since my arrival here. No report has yet been made. But I have little idea that the proposition will be adopted. Such is the state & prospect of our fiscal department that any new loan however small, that should now be made, would probably subject us to the reproach of premeditated deception. The balance of Mr. Adams' last loan will be wanted for the interest due in Holland, and with all the income here, will, it is feared, not save our credit in Europe from further wounds. It may well be doubted whether the present Govt. can be kept alive thro' the ensuing year, or untill the new one may take its place.

Upwards of 100,000 Acres of the surveyed lands of the U.S. have been disposed of in open market. Five million of unsurveyed have been sold by private contract to a N. England Company, at ⅔ of a dollar per acre, payment to be made in the principal of the public securities. A negociation is nearly closed with a N. Jersey Company for two million more on like terms, and another commenced with a Company of this City for four million. Col. Carrington writes more fully on this subject.

You will receive herewith the desired information from Alderman Broome in the case of Mr. Burke. Also the Virga. Bill on crimes & punishments. Sundry alterations having been made in conformity to the sense of the House in its latter stages, it is less accurate & methodical than it ought to have been. To these papers I add a Speech of Mr. C. P. on the Missippi. business. It is printed under precautions of secrecy, but surely could not have been properly exposed to so much risk of publication. You will find also among the Pamplets & papers I send by Commodore Jones, another printed speech of the same Gentleman. The Musæum, Magazine, & Philada. Gazettes, will give you a tolerable idea of the objects of present attention.

The summer crops in the Eastern & Middle States have been extremely plentiful. Southward of Virga. They differ in different places. On the whole I do not know that they are bad in that region. In Virginia the drought has been unprecedented, particularly between the falls of the Rivers & the Mountains. The Crops of Corn are in general alarmingly short. In Orange I find there will be scarcely subsistence for the inhabitants. I have not heard from Albemarle. The crops of Tobo. are every where said to be pretty good in point of quantity; & the quality unusually fine. The crops of wheat were also in general excellent in quality & tolerable in quantity.

Novr. 1. Commodore Jones having preferred another vessel to the packet, has remained here till this time. The interval has produced little necessary to be added to the above. The Legislature of Massts. has it seems taken up the Act of the Convention, and have appointed or probably will appoint an early day for its State Convention. There are letters also from Georgia which denote a favorable disposition. I am informed from Richmond that the New Election-law from the Revised Code produced a pretty full House of Delegates, as well as a Senate, on the first day. It had previously had equal effect in producing full meetings of the freeholders for the County elections. A very decided majority of the Assembly is said to be zealous in favor of the New Constitution. The same is said of the Country at large. It appears however that individuals of great weight both within & without the Legislature are opposed to it. A letter I just have from Mr. A. Stuart, names Mr. Henry, Genl. Nelson, W. Nelson, the family of Cabels, St. George Tucker, John Taylor and the Judges of the Genl. Court except P. Carrington. The other opponents he describes as of too little note to be mentioned, which gives a negative information of the Characters on the other side. All are agreed that the plan must be submitted to a Convention.

We hear from Georgia that that State is threatened with a dangerous war with the Creek Indians. The alarm is of so serious a nature, that law-martial has been proclaimed, and they are proceeding to fortify even the Town of Savannah. The idea there, is that the Indians derive their motives as well as their means from their Spanish neighbours. Individuals complain also that their fugitive slaves are encouraged by East Florida. The policy of this is explained by supposing that it is considered as a discouragement to the Georgians to form settlements near the Spanish boundaries.

There are but few States on the spot here which will survive the expiration of the federal year; and it is extremely uncertain when a Congress will again be formed. We have not yet heard who are to be in the appointment of Virginia for the next year. With the most affectionate attachment I remain Dear Sr. Your Obed friend & servant

JS. MADISON JR.

Thomas Jefferson to James Madison

Dear Sir

My last to you was of Oct. 8. by the Count de Moustier. Yours of July 18. Sep. 6. & Oct. 24. have been successively received, yesterday, the day before & three or four days before that. I have only had time to read the letters, the printed papers communicated with them, however interesting, being obliged to lie over till I finish my dispatches for the packet, which dispatches must go from hence the day after tomorrow. I have much to thank you for. First and most for the cyphered paragraph respecting myself. These little informations are very material towards forming my own decisions. I would be glad even to know when any individual member thinks I have gone wrong in any instance. If I know myself it would not excite ill blood in me, while it would assist to guide my conduct, perhaps to justify it, and to keep me to my duty, alert. I must thank you too for the information in Thos. Burke's case, tho' you will have found by a subsequent letter that I have asked of you a further investigation of that matter. It is to gratify the lady who is at the head of the Convent wherein my daughters are, & who, by her attachment & attention to them, lays me under great obligations. I shall hope therefore still to receive from you the result of the further enquiries my second letter had asked. The parcel of rice which you informed me had miscarried accompanied my letter to the Delegates of S. Carolina. Mr. Bourgoin was to be the bearer of both and both were delivered together into the hands of his relation here who introduced him to me, and who at a subsequent moment undertook to convey them to Mr. Bourgoin. This person was an engraver particularly recommended to Dr. Franklin & mr. Hopkinson. Perhaps he may have mislaid the little parcel of rice among his baggage. I am much pleased that the sale of Western lands is so succesful. I hope they will absorb all the Certificates of our Domestic debt speedily in the first place, and that then offered for cash they will do the same by our foreign one.

The season admitting only of operations in the Cabinet, and these being in a great measure secret, I have little to fill a letter. I will therefore make up the deficiency by adding a few words on the Constitution proposed by our Convention. I like much the general idea of framing a government which should go on of itself peaceably, without needing continual recurrence to the state legislatures. I like the organization of the government into Legislative, Judiciary & Executive. I like the power given the Legislature to levy taxes, and for that reason solely approve of the greater house being chosen by the people directly. For tho' I think a house chosen by them will be very illy qualified to legislate for the Union, for foreign nations &c. yet this evil does not weigh against the good of preserving inviolate the fundamental principle that the people are not to be taxed but by representatives chosen immediately by themselves. I am captivated by the compromise of the opposite claims of the great & little states, of the latter to equal, and the former to proportional influence. I am much pleased too with the substitution of the method of voting by persons, instead of that of voting by states: and I like the negative given to the Executive with a third of either house, though I should have liked it better had the Judiciary been associated for that purpose, or invested with a similar and separate power. There are other good things of less moment. I will now add what I do not like. First the omission of a bill of rights providing clearly & without the aid of sophisms for freedom of religion, freedom of the press, protection against standing armies, restriction against monopolies, the eternal & unremitting force of the habeas corpus laws, and trials by jury in all matters of fact triable by the laws of the land & not by the law of Nations. To say, as mr. Wilson does, that a bill of rights was not necessary because all is reserved in the case of the general government which is not given, while in the particular ones all is given which is not reserved, might do for the Audience to whom it was addressed, but is surely a gratis dictum, opposed by strong inferences from the body of the instrument, as well as from the omission of the clause of our present confederation which had declared that in express terms. It was a hard conclusion to say because there has been no uniformity among the states as to the cases triable by jury, because some have been so incautious as to abandon this mode of trial, therefore the more prudent states shall be reduced to the same level of calamity. It would have been much more just & wise to have concluded the other way that as most of the states had judiciously preserved this palladium, those who had wandered should be brought back to it, and to have established general right instead of general wrong. Let me add that a bill of rights is what the people are entitled to against every government on earth, general or particular, & what no just government should refuse or rest on inference. The second feature I dislike, and greatly dislike, is the abandonment in every instance of the necessity of rotation in office, and most particularly in the case of the President. Experience concurs with reason in concluding that the first magistrate will always be re-elected if the constitution permits it. He is then an officer for life. This once observed it becomes of so much consequence to certain nations to have a friend or a foe at the head of our affairs that they will interfere with money & with arms. A Galloman or an Angloman will be supported by the nation he befriends. If once elected, and at a second or third election outvoted by one or two votes, he will pretend false votes, foul play, hold possession of the reins of government, be supported by the states voting for him, especially if they are the central ones lying in a compact body themselves & separating their opponents: and they will be aided by one nation of Europe, while the majority are aided by another. The election of a President of America some years hence will be much more interesting to certain nations of Europe than ever the election of a king of Poland was. Reflect on all the instances in history antient & modern, of elective monarchies, and say if they do not give foundation for my fears. The Roman emperors, the popes, while they were of any importance, the German emperors till they became hereditary in practice, the kings of Poland, the Deys of the Ottoman dependancies. It may be said that if elections are to be attended with these disorders, the seldomer they are renewed the better. But experience shews that the only way to prevent disorder is to render them uninteresting by frequent changes. An incapacity to be elected a second time would have been the only effectual preventative. The power of removing him every fourth year by the vote of the people is a power which will not be exercised. The king of Poland is removeable every day by the Diet, yet he is never removed. Smaller objections are the Appeal in fact as well as law, and the binding all persons Legislative Executive & Judiciary by oath to maintain that constitution. I do not pretend to decide what would be the best method of procuring the establishment of the manifold good things in this constitution, and of getting rid of the bad. Whether by adopting it in hopes of future amendment, or, after it has been duly weighed & canvassed by the people, after seeing the parts they generally dislike, & those they generally approve, to say to them 'We see now what you wish. Send together your deputies again, let them frame a constitution for you omitting what you have condemned, & establishing the powers you approve. Even these will be a great addition to the energy of your government.' At all events I hope you will not be discouraged from other trials, if the present one should fail of it's full effect. I have thus told you freely what I like & dislike: merely as a matter of curiosity, for I know your own judgment has been formed on all these points after having heard every thing which could be urged on them. I own I am not a friend to a very energetic government. It is always oppressive. The late rebellion in Massachusets has given more alarm than I think it should have done. Calculate that one rebellion in 13 states in the course of 11 years, is but one for each state in a century & a half. No country should be so long without one. Nor will any degree of power in the hands of government prevent insurrections. France, with all it's despotism, and two or three hundred thousand men always in arms has had three insurrections in the three years I have been here in every one of which greater numbers were engaged than in Massachusets & a great deal more blood was spilt. In Turkey, which Montesquieu supposes more despotic, insurrections are the events of every day. In England, where the hand of power is lighter than here, but heavier than with us they happen every half dozen years. Compare again the ferocious depredations of their insurgents with the order, the moderation & the almost self extinguishment of ours. After all, it is my principle that the will of the Majority should always prevail. If they approve the proposed Convention in all it's parts, I shall concur in it chearfully, in hopes that they will amend it whenever they shall find it work wrong. I think our governments will remain virtuous for many centuries; as long as they are chiefly agricultural; and this will be as long as there shall be vacant lands in any part of America. When they get piled upon one another in large cities, as in Europe, they will become corrupt as in Europe. Above all things I hope the education of the common people will be attended to; convinced that on their good sense we may rely with the most security for the preservation of a due degree of liberty. I have tired you by this time with my disquisitions & will therefore only add assurances of the sincerity of those sentiments of esteem & attachment with which I am Dear Sir your affectionate friend & servant

Th: Jefferson

P.S. The instability of our laws is really an immense evil. I think it would be well to provide in our constitutions that there shall always be a twelve-month between the ingrossing a bill & passing it: that it should then be offered to it's passage without changing a word: and that if circumstances should be thought to require a speedier passage, it should take two thirds of both houses instead of a bare majority.

Cato III

New York Journal, October 25, 1787

To the CITIZENS *of the* STATE *of* NEW-YORK.

In the close of my last introductory address, I told you, that my object in future would be to take up this new form of national government, to compare it with the experience and opinions of the most sensible and approved political authors, and to show you that its principles, and the exercise of them will be dangerous to your liberty and happiness.

Although I am conscious that this is an arduous undertaking, yet I will perform it to the best of my ability.

The freedom, equality, and independence which you enjoyed by nature, induced you to consent to a political power. The same principles led you to examine the errors and vices of a British superintendence, to divest yourselves of it, and to reassume a new political shape. It is acknowledged that there are defects in this, and another is tendered to you for acceptance; the great question then, that arises on this new political principle, is, whether it will answer the ends for which it is said to be offered to you, and for which all men engage in political society, to wit, the mutual preservation of their lives, liberties, and estates.

The recital, or premises on which this new form of government is erected, declares a consolidation or union of all the thirteen parts, or states, into one great whole, under the firm of the United States, for all the various and important purposes therein set forth.—But whoever seriously considers the immense extent of territory comprehended within the limits of the United States, together with the variety of its climates, productions, and commerce, the difference of extent, and number of inhabitants in all; the dissimilitude of interest, morals, and policies, in almost every one, will receive it as an intuitive truth, that a consolidated republican form of government therein, can never *form a perfect union, establish justice, insure domestic tranquility, promote the general welfare, and secure the blessings of liberty to you and your posterity,* for to these objects it must be directed: this unkindred legislature therefore, composed of interests opposite and dissimilar in their nature, will in its exercise, emphatically be, like a house divided against itself.

The governments of Europe have taken their limits and form from adventitious circumstances, and nothing can be argued on the motive of agreement from them; but these adventitious political principles, have nevertheless produced effects that have attracted the attention of philosophy, which has established axioms in the science of politics therefrom, as irrefragable as any in Euclid. It is natural, says Montesquieu, *to a republic to have only a small territory, otherwise it cannot long subsist: in a large one, there are men of large fortunes, and consequently of less moderation; there are too great deposits to intrust in the hands of a single subject, an ambitious person soon becomes sensible that he may be happy, great, and glorious by oppressing his fellow citizens, and that he might raise himself to grandeur, on the ruins of his country. In large republics, the public good is sacrificed to a thousand views; in a small one the interest of the public is easily perceived, better understood, and more within the reach of every citizen; abuses have a less extent, and of course are less protected*—he also shews you, that the duration of the republic of Sparta, was owing to its having continued with the same extent of territory after all its wars, and that the ambition of Athens and Lacedemon to command and direct the union, lost them their liberties, and gave them a monarchy.

From this picture, what can you promise yourselves, on the score of consolidation of the United States, into one government—impracticability in the just exercise of it—your freedom insecure—even this form of government limited in its continuance—the employments of your country disposed of to the opulent, to whose contumely you will continually be an object—you must risque much, by indispensibly placing trusts of the greatest magnitude, into the hands of individuals, whose ambition for power, and agrandisement, will oppress and grind you—where, from the vast extent of your territory, and the complication of interests, the science of government will become intricate and perplexed, and too misterious for you to understand, and observe; and by which you are to be conducted into a monarchy, either limited or despotic; the latter, Mr. Locke remarks, *is a government derived from neither nature, nor compact.*

Political liberty, the great Montesquieu again observes, *consists in security, or at least in the opinion we have of security*; and this *security* therefore, or the *opinion*, is best obtained in moderate governments, where the mildness of the laws, and the equality of the manners, beget a confidence in the people, which produces this security, or the opinion. This moderation in governments, depends in a great measure on their limits, connected with their political distribution.

The extent of many of the states in the Union, is at this time, almost too great for the superintendence of a republican form of government, and must one day or other, revolve into more vigorous ones, or by separation be reduced into smaller, and more useful, as well as moderate ones. You have already observed the feeble efforts of Massachusetts against their insurgents; with what difficulty did they quell that insurrection; and is not the province of main at this moment, on the eve of separation from her. The reason of these things is, that for the security of the *property* of the community, in which expressive term Mr. Lock makes life, liberty, and estate, to consist—the wheels of a free republic are necessarily slow in their operation; hence in large free republics, the evil sometimes is not only begun, but almost completed, before they are in a situation to turn the current into a contrary progression: the extremes are also too remote from the usual seat of government, and the laws therefore too feeble to afford protection to all its parts, and insure *domestic tranquility* without the aid of another principle. If, therefore, this state, and that of N. Carolina, had an army under their controul, they never would have lost Vermont, and Frankland, nor the state of Massachusetts suffer an insurrection, or the dismemberment of her fairest district, but the exercise of a principle which would have prevented these things, if we may believe the experience of ages, would have ended in the destruction of their liberties.

Will this consolidated republic, if established, in its exercise beget such confidence and compliance, among the citizens of these states, as to do without the aid of a standing army—I deny that it will.—The malcontents in each state, who will

not be a few, nor the least important, will be exciting factions
against it—the fear of a dismemberment of some of its parts,
and the necessity to enforce the execution of revenue laws (a
fruitful source of oppression) on the extremes and in the other
districts of the government, will incidentally, and necessarily
require a permanent force, to be kept on foot—will not political security, and even the opinion of it, be extinguished?
can mildness and moderation exist in a government, where the
primary incident in its exercise must be force? will not violence
destroy confidence, and can equality subsist, where the extent,
policy, and practice of it, will naturally lead to make odious
distinctions among citizens?

The people, who may compose this national legislature from
the southern states, in which, from the mildness of the climate, the fertility of the soil, and the value of its productions,
wealth is rapidly acquired, and where the same causes naturally
lead to luxury, dissipation, and a passion for aristocratic distinctions; where slavery is encouraged, and liberty of course, less
respected, and protected; who know not what it is to acquire
property by their own toil, nor to œconomise with the sav-
ings of industry—will these men therefore be as tenacious of
the liberties and interests of the more northern states, where
freedom, independence, industry, equality, and frugality, are
natural to the climate and soil, as men who are your own citizens, legislating in your own state, under your inspection, and
whose manners, and fortunes, bear a more equal resemblance
to your own?

It may be suggested, in answer to this, that whoever is a citizen of one state, is a citizen of each, and that therefore he will
be as interested in the happiness and interest of all, as the one
he is delegated from; but the argument is fallacious, and, whoever has attended to the history of mankind, and the principles
which bind them together as parents, citizens, or men, will
readily perceive it. These principles are, in their exercise, like
a pebble cast on the calm surface of a river, the circles begin
in the center, and are small, active, and forcible, but as they
depart from that point, they lose their force, and vanish into
calmness.

The strongest principle of union resides within our domestic walls. The ties of the parent exceed that of any other; as

we depart from home, the next general principle of union is amongst citizens of the same state, where acquaintance, habits, and fortunes, nourish affection, and attachment; enlarge the circle still further, &, as citizens of different states, though we acknowledge the same national denomination, we lose the ties of acquaintance, habits, and fortunes, and thus, by degrees, we lessen in our attachments, till, at length, we no more than acknowledge a sameness of species. Is it therefore, from certainty like this, reasonable to believe, that inhabitants of Georgia, or New-Hampshire, will have the same obligations towards you as your own, and preside over your lives, liberties, and property, with the same care and attachment? Intuitive reason, answers in the negative.

In the course of my examination of the principals of consolidation of the states into one general government, many other reasons against it have occurred, but I flatter myself, from those herein offered to your consideration, I have convinced you that it is both presumptious and impracticable consistent with your safety. To detain you with further remarks, would be useless—I shall however, continue in my following numbers, to anilise this new government, pursuant to my promise.

Publius (Alexander Hamilton)
The Federalist No. 1

Independent Journal (New York), October 27, 1787

To the People of the State of New York.

AFTER an unequivocal experience of the inefficacy of the subsisting Fœderal Government, you are called upon to deliberate on a new Constitution for the United States of America. The subject speaks its own importance; comprehending in its consequences, nothing less than the existence of the UNION, the safety and welfare of the parts of which it is composed, the fate of an empire, in many respects, the most interesting the world. It has been frequently remarked, that it seems to have been reserved to the people of this country, by their conduct and example, to decide the important question, whether societies of men are really capable or not, of establishing good government from reflection and choice, or whether they are forever destined to depend, for their political constitutions, on accident and force. If there be any truth in the remark, the crisis, at which we are arrived, may with propriety be regarded as the æra in which that decision is to be made; and a wrong election of the part we shall act, may, in this view, deserve to be considered as the general misfortune of mankind.

This idea will add the inducements of philanthropy to those of patriotism to heighten the sollicitude, which all considerate and good men must feel for the event. Happy will it be if our choice should be directed by a judicous estimate of our true interests, unperplexed and unbiassed by considerations not connected with the public good. But this is a thing more ardently to be wished, than seriously to be expected. The plan offered to our deliberations, affects too many particular interests, innovates upon too many local institutions, not to involve in its discussion a variety of objects foreign to its merits, and of views, passions and prejudices little favourable to the discovery of truth.

Among the most formidable of the obstacles which the new Constitution will have to encounter, may readily be distinguished the obvious interest of a certain class of men in every State to resist all changes which may hazard a diminution of the power, emolument and consequence of the offices they hold under the State-establishments—and the perverted ambition of another class of men, who will either hope to aggrandise themselves by the confusions of their country, or will flatter themselves with fairer prospects of elevation from the subdivision of the empire into several partial confederacies, than from its union under one government.

It is not, however, my design to dwell upon observations of this nature. I am well aware that it would be disingenuous to resolve indiscriminately the opposition of any set of men (merely because their situations might subject them to suspicion) into interested or ambitious views: Candour will oblige us to admit, that even such men may be actuated by upright intentions; and it cannot be doubted, that much of the opposition which has made its appearance, or may hereafter make its appearance, will spring from sources, blameless at least, if not respectable, the honest errors of minds led astray by preconceived jealousies and fears. So numerous indeed and so powerful are the causes, which serve to give a false bias to the judgment, that we upon many occasions, see wise and good men on the wrong as well as on the right side of questions, of the first magnitude to society. This circumstance, if duly attended to, would furnish a lesson of moderation of those, who are ever so much persuaded of their being in the right, in any controversy. And a further reason for caution, in this respect, might be drawn from the reflection, that we are not always sure, that those who advocate the truth are influenced by purer principles than their antagonists. Ambition, avarice, personal animosity, party opposition, and many other motives, not more laudable than these, are apt to operate as well upon those who support as upon those who oppose the right side of a question. Were there not even these inducements to moderation, nothing could be more illjudged than that intolerant spirit, which has, at all times, characterised political parties. For, in politics as in religion, it is equally absurd to aim at making proselytes by fire and sword. Heresies in either can rarely be cured by persecution.

And yet however just these sentiments will be allowed to be, we have already sufficient indications, that it will happen in this as in all former cases of great national discussion. A torrent of angry and malignant passions will be let loose. To judge from the conduct of the opposite parties, we shall be led to conclude, that they will mutually hope to evince the justness of their opinions, and to increase the number of their converts by the loudness of their declamations, and by the bitterness of their invectives. An enlightened zeal for the energy and efficiency of government will be stigmatised, as the off-spring of a temper fond of despotic power and hostile to the principles of liberty. An overscrupulous jealousy of danger to the rights of the people, which is more commonly the fault of the head than of the heart, will be represented as mere pretence and artifice; the bait for popularity at the expence of public good. It will be forgotten, on the one hand, that jealousy is the usual concomitant of violent love, and that the noble enthusiasm of liberty is too apt to be infected with a spirit of narrow and illiberal distrust. On the other hand, it will be equally forgotten, that the vigour of government is essential to the security of liberty; that, in the contemplation of a sound and well informed judgment, their interest can never be separated; and that a dangerous ambition more often lurks behind the specious mask of zeal for the rights of the people, than under the forbidding appearance of zeal for the firmness and efficiency of government. History will teach us, that the former has been found a much more certain road to the introduction of despotism, than the latter, and that of those men who have overturned the liberties of republics the greatest number have begun their carreer, by paying an obsequious court to the people, commencing Demagogues and ending Tyrants.

In the course of the preceeding observations I have had an eye, my Fellow Citizens, to putting you upon your guard against all attempts, from whatever quarter, to influence your decision in a matter of the utmost moment to your welfare by any impressions other than those which may result from the evidence of truth. You will, no doubt, at the same time, have collected from the general scope of them that they proceed from a source not unfriendly to the new Constitution. Yes, my Countrymen, I own to you, that, after having given it an attentive consideration, I am clearly of opinion, it is your interest to adopt it. I am convinced, that this is the safest course for your liberty, your dignity, and your happiness. I effect not reserves, which I do not feel. I will not amuse you with an appearance of deliberation, when I have decided. I frankly acknowledge to you my convictions, and I will freely lay before you the reasons on which they are founded. The consciousness of good intentions disdains ambiguity. I shall not however multiply professions on this head. My motives must remain in the depository of my own breast: My arguments will be open to all, and may be judged of by all. They shall at least be offered in a spirit, which will not disgrace the cause of truth.

I propose in a series of papers to discuss the following interesting particulars—*The utility of the UNION to your political prosperity—The insufficiency of the present Confederation to preserve that Union—The necessity of a government at least equally energetic with the one proposed to the attainment of this object—The conformity of the proposed constitution to the true principles of republican government—Its analogy to your own state constitution*—and lastly, *The additional security, which its adoption will afford to the preservation of that species of government, to liberty and to property.*

In the progress of this discussion I shall endeavour to give a satisfactory answer to all the objections which shall have made their appearance that may seem to have any claim to your attention.

It may perhaps be thought superfluous to offer arguments to prove the utility of the UNION, a point, no doubt, deeply engraved on the hearts of the great body of the people in every state, and one, which it may be imagined has no adversaries. But the fact is, that we already hear it whispered in the private circles of those who oppose the new constitution, that the Thirteen States are of too great extent for any general system, and that we must of necessity resort to separate confederacies of distinct portions of the whole.* This doctrine will, in all probability, be gradually propagated, till it has votaries enough to countenance an open avowal of it. For nothing can be more evident, to those who are able to take an enlarged view of the

---

*The same idea, tracing the arguments to their consequences, is held out in several of the late publications against the New Constitution.

subject than the alternative of an adoption of the new Constitution, or a dismemberment of the Union. It will therefore be of use to begin by examining the advantages of that Union, the certain evils and the probable dangers, to which every State will be exposed from its dissolution. This shall accordingly constitute the subject of my next address.

PUBLIUS.

PART 2:
OPPOSITION ORGANIZES

ELBRIDGE GERRY had announced on the Convention's final day that he opposed the Constitution. It gave too much power to the national government, it lacked a Bill of Rights, and it would exacerbate, rather than relieve, tensions between proponents of democracy ("the worst he thought of all political evils") and their opponents ("as violent in the opposite extreme"). Still, in his subsequent letter to the Massachusetts General Court, he called on supporters and opponents to engage in a reasoned debate, which would produce much information and could lead to a happy issue. The Constitution's most sustained critique came in the **Letters from the Federal Farmer**, whose anonymous author saw many good features in the plan to correct the Confederation's fatal flaws. But the Federal Farmer faulted the Constitution for inadequate representation of the people. Though the Federal Farmer's identity remains a mystery, "the Republican" to whom he wrote was New York Governor George Clinton, a powerful force in his state and an opponent of a stronger national government. **Jefferson** wrote to William Stephens Smith, John Adams's son-in-law, discussing the new plan's positive and negative features. Jefferson disputed the claim that the United States was stumbling into anarchy and chaos. He did not see Shays' Rebellion, the tax revolt in Massachusetts in 1786–87, as a threat, but as a salutary demonstration of the American devotion to liberty. **George Mason**, who left Philadelphia "in a very ill humor indeed" according to Madison, had been one of the most active members of the Philadelphia Convention, and was the principal author of Virginia's constitution. He became one of the Constitution's leading critics, unhappy that it lacked a Bill of Rights, that simple majorities in Congress could pass tariff laws hurting Virginia's economy, and that the slave trade could continue for twenty years. Mason's "Objections" would be published throughout the states—though some newspapers in northern states, where tariffs would give an economic boost, omitted his objection to the power of Congress to regulate commerce. New York delegates **Robert Yates** and **John Lansing, Jr.**, explained their opposition to Governor Clinton.

Elbridge Gerry to the
Massachusetts General Court

Massachusetts Centinel (Boston), November 3, 1787

Hon. Mr. GERRY's objections to signing the National Constitution.

(The following Letter, on the subject of the American Constitution, from the Hon. ELBRIDGE GERRY, Esq. one of the Delegates representing this Commonwealth in the late Federal Convention, to the Legislature, was on Wednesday last read in the Senate and sent down to the House of Representatives, where it was yesterday read and sent up. As it contains opinions on a subject of the first importance to our country at this day, we have obtained a copy of it for insertion—and are happy to have it in our power thus early to communicate it to the publick.)

NEW-YORK, 18*th October*, 1787.

GENTLEMEN, I have the honour to inclose, pursuant to my commission, the constitution proposed by the federal Convention.

To this system I gave my dissent, and shall submit my objections to the honourable Legislature.

It was painful for me, on a subject of such national importance, to differ from the respectable members who signed the constitution: But conceiving as I did, that the liberties of America were not secured by the system, it was my duty to oppose it.—

My principal objections to the plan, are, that there is no adequate provision for a representation of the people—that they have no security for the right of election—that some of the powers of the Legislature are ambiguous, and others indefinite and dangerous—that the Executive is blended with and will have an undue influence over the Legislature—that the judicial department will be oppressive—that treaties of the highest importance may be formed by the President with the advice of two thirds of a *quorum* of the Senate—and that the system is without the security of a bill of rights. These are objections which are not local, but apply equally to all the States.

As the Convention was called for "the *sole* and *express* purpose of revising the Articles of Confederation, and reporting to Congress and the several Legislatures such alterations and provisions as shall render the Federal Constitution adequate to the exigencies of government and the preservation of the union," I did not conceive that these powers extended to the formation of the plan proposed, but the Convention being of a different *opinion*, I acquiesced in *it*, being fully convinced that to preserve the union, an efficient government was indispensibly necessary; and that it would be difficult to make proper amendments to the articles of Confederation.

The Constitution proposed has few, if any *federal* features, but is rather a system of *national* government: Nevertheless, in many respects I think it has great merit, and by proper amendments, may be adapted to the "exigencies of government," and preservation of liberty.

The question on this plan involves others of the highest importance—1st. Whether there shall be a dissolution of the *federal* government? 2dly. Whether the several State Governments shall be so altered, as in effect to be dissolved? and 3dly. Whether in lieu of the *federal* and *State* Governments, the *national* Constitution now proposed shall be substituted without amendment? Never perhaps were a people called on to decide a question of greater magnitude—Should the citizens of America adopt the plan as it now stands, their liberties may be lost: Or should they reject it altogether Anarchy may ensue. It is evident therefore, that they should not be precipitate in their decisions; that the subject should be well understood, lest they should refuse to *support* the government, after having *hastily* accepted it.

If those who are in favour of the Constitution, as well as those who are against it, should preserve moderation, their discussions may afford much information and finally direct to an happy issue.

It may be urged by some, that an *implicit* confidence should be placed in the Convention: But, however respectable the members may be who signed the Constitution, it must be admitted, that a free people are the proper guardians of their rights and liberties—that the greatest men may err—and that their errours are sometimes, of the greatest magnitude.

Others may suppose, that the Constitution may be safely adopted, because therein provision is made to *amend* it: But cannot *this object* be better attained before a ratification, than after it? And should a *free* people adopt a form of Government, under conviction that it wants amendment?

And some may conceive, that if the plan is not accepted by the people, they will not unite in another: But surely whilst they have the power to amend, they are not under the necessity of rejecting it.

I have been detained here longer than I expected, but shall leave this place in a day or two for Massachusetts, and on my arrival shall submit the reasons (if required by the Legislature) on which my objections are grounded.

I shall only add, that as the welfare of the union requires a better Constitution than the Confederation, I shall think it my duty as a citizen of Massachusetts, to support that which shall be finally adopted, sincerely hoping it will secure the liberty and happiness of America.

I have the honour to be, Gentlemen, with the highest respect for the honourable Legislature and yourselves, your most obedient, and very humble servant, E. GERRY.

Letters from the Federal Farmer
to The Republican

New York, November 8, 1787

LETTER I.

OCTOBER 8th, 1787.

DEAR SIR, My letters to you last winter, on the subject of a well balanced national government for the United States, were the result of free enquiry; when I passed from that subject to enquiries relative to our commerce, revenues, past administration, &c. I anticipated the anxieties I feel, on carefully examining the plan of government proposed by the convention. It appears to be a plan retaining some federal features; but to be the first important step, and to aim strongly to one consolidated government of the United States. It leaves the powers of government, and the representation of the people, so unnaturally divided between the general and state governments, that the operations of our system must be very uncertain. My uniform federal attachments, and the interest I have in the protection of property, and a steady execution of the laws, will convince you, that, if I am under any biass at all, it is in favor of any general system which shall promise those advantages. The instability of our laws increase my wishes for firm and steady government; but then, I can consent to no government, which, in my opinion, is not calculated equally to preserve the rights of all orders of men in the community. My object has been to join with those who have endeavoured to supply the defects in the forms of our governments by a steady and proper administration of them. Though I have long apprehended that fraudulent debtors, and embarrassed men, on the one hand, and men, on the other, unfriendly to republican equality, would produce an uneasiness among the people, and prepare the way, not for cool and deliberate reforms in the governments, but for changes calculated to promote the interests of particular orders of men. Acquit me, sir, of any agency in the formation of the new system; I shall be satisfied with seeing, if it shall be adopted, a prudent administration. Indeed I am so much convinced of the

66

truth of Pope's maxim, that "That which is best administered is best," that I am much inclined to subscribe to it from experience. I am not disposed to unreasonably contend about forms. I know our situation is critical, and it behoves us to make the best of it. A federal government of some sort is necessary. We have suffered the present to languish; and whether the confederation was capable or not originally of answering any valuable purposes, it is now but of little importance. I will pass by the men, and states, who have been particularly instrumental in preparing the way for a change, and, perhaps, for governments not very favourable to the people at large. A constitution is now presented, which we may reject, or which we may accept, with or without amendments; and to which point we ought to direct our exertions, is the question. To determine this question, with propriety, we must attentively examine the system itself, and the probable consequences of either step. This I shall endeavour to do, so far as I am able, with candour and fairness; and leave you to decide upon the propriety of my opinions, the weight of my reasons, and how far my conclusions are well drawn. Whatever may be the conduct of others, on the present occasion, I do not mean, hastily and positively to decide on the merits of the constitution proposed. I shall be open to conviction, and always disposed to adopt that which, all things considered, shall appear to me to be most for the happiness of the community. It must be granted, that if men hastily and blindly adopt a system of government, they will as hastily and as blindly be led to alter or abolish it; and changes must ensue, one after another, till the peaceable and better part of the community will grow weary with changes, tumults and disorders, and be disposed to accept any government, however despotic, that shall promise stability and firmness.

The first principal question that occurs, is, Whether, considering our situation, we ought to precipitate the adoption of the proposed constitution? If we remain cool and temperate, we are in no immediate danger of any commotions; we are in a state of perfect peace, and in no danger of invasions; the state governments are in the full exercise of their powers; and our governments answer all present exigencies, except the regulation of trade, securing credit, in some cases, and providing for the interest, in some instances, of the public debts; and whether we adopt a change, three or nine months hence, can make but little odds with the private circumstances of individuals; their happiness and prosperity, after all, depend principally upon their own exertions. We are hardly recovered from a long and distressing war: The farmers, fishmen, &c. have not yet fully repaired the waste made by it. Industry and frugality are again assuming their proper station. Private debts are lessened, and public debts incurred by the war, have been, by various ways, diminished; and the public lands have now become a productive source for diminishing them much more. I know uneasy men, who wish very much to precipitate, do not admit all these facts; but they are facts well known to all men who are thoroughly informed in the affairs of this country. It must, however, be admitted, that our federal system is defective, and that some of the state governments are not well administered; but, then, we impute to the defects in our governments, many evils and embarrassments which are most clearly the result of the late war. We must allow men to conduct on the present occasion, as on all similar one's. They will urge a thousand pretences to answer their purposes on both sides. When we want a man to change his condition, we describe it as miserable, wretched, and despised; and draw a pleasing picture of that which we would have him assume. And when we wish the contrary, we reverse our descriptions. Whenever a clamor is raised, and idle men get to work, it is highly necessary to examine facts carefully, and without unreasonably suspecting men of falshood, to examine, and enquire attentively, under what impressions they act. It is too often the case in political concerns, that men state facts not as they are, but as they wish them to be; and almost every man, by calling to mind past scenes, will find this to be true.

Nothing but the passions of ambitious, impatient, or disorderly men, I conceive, will plunge us into commotions, if time should be taken fully to examine and consider the system proposed. Men who feel easy in their circumstances, and such as are not sanguine in their expectations relative to the consequences of the proposed change, will remain quiet under the existing governments. Many commercial and monied men, who are uneasy, not without just cause, ought to be respected; and, by no means, unreasonably disappointed in their expectations and hopes; but as to those who expect employments under the new constitution; as to those weak and ardent men who always expect to be gainers by revolutions, and whose lot it generally is to get out of one difficulty into another, they are very little to be regarded: and as to those who designedly avail themselves of this weakness and ardor, they are to be despised. It is natural for men, who wish to hasten the adoption of a measure, to tell us, now is the crisis—now is the critical moment which must be seized, or all will be lost: and to shut the door against free enquiry, whenever conscious the thing presented has defects in it, which time and investigation will probably discover. This has been the custom of tyrants and their dependants in all ages. If it is true, what has been so often said, that the people of this country cannot change their condition for the worse, I presume it still behoves them to endeavour deliberately to change it for the better. The fickle and ardent, in any community, are the proper tools for establishing despotic government. But it is deliberate and thinking men, who must establish and secure governments on free principles. Before they decide on the plan proposed, they will enquire whether it will probably be a blessing or a curse to this people.

The present moment discovers a new face in our affairs. Our object has been all along, to reform our federal system, and to strengthen our governments—to establish peace, order and justice in the community—but a new object now presents. The plan of government now proposed, is evidently calculated totally to change, in time, our condition as a people. Instead of being thirteen republics, under a federal head, it is clearly designed to make us one consolidated government. Of this, I think, I shall fully convince you, in my following letters on this subject. This consolidation of the states has been the object of several men in this country for some time past. Whether such a change can ever be effected in any manner; whether it can be effected without convulsions and civil wars; whether such a change will not totally destroy the liberties of this country—time only can determine.

To have a just idea of the government before us, and to shew that a consolidated one is the object in view, it is necessary not only to examine the plan, but also its history, and the politics of its particular friends.

The confederation was formed when great confidence was placed in the voluntary exertions of individuals, and of the respective states; and the framers of it, to guard against usurpation, so limited and checked the powers, that, in many respects, they are inadequate to the exigencies of the union. We find, therefore, members of congress urging alterations in the federal system almost as soon as it was adopted. It was early proposed to vest congress with powers to levy an impost, to regulate trade, &c. but such was known to be the caution of the states in parting with power, that the vestment, even of these, was proposed to be under several checks and limitations. During the war, the general confusion, and the introduction of paper money, infused in the minds of people vague ideas respecting government and credit. We expected too much from the return of peace, and of course we have been disappointed. Our governments have been new and unsettled; and several legislatures, by making tender, suspension, and paper money laws, have given just cause of uneasiness to creditors. By these and other causes, several orders of men in the community have been prepared, by degrees, for a change of government; and this very abuse of power in the legislatures, which, in some cases, has been charged upon the democratic part of the community, has furnished aristocratical men with those very weapons, and those very means, with which, in great measure, they are rapidly effecting their favourite object. And should an oppressive government be the consequence of the proposed change, posterity may reproach not only a few overbearing, unprincipled men, but those parties in the states which have misused their powers.

The conduct of several legislatures, touching paper money, and tender laws, has prepared many honest men for changes in government, which otherwise they would not have thought of—when by the evils, on the one hand, and by the secret instigations of artful men, on the other, the minds of men were become sufficiently uneasy, a bold step was taken, which is usually followed by a revolution, or a civil war. A general convention for mere commercial purposes was moved for—the authors of this measure saw that the people's attention was turned solely to the amendment of the federal system; and that, had the idea of a total change been started, probably no state would have appointed members to the convention. The idea of destroying, ultimately, the state government, and forming one consolidated system, could not have been admitted—a convention, therefore, merely for vesting in congress power to regulate trade, was proposed. This was pleasing to the commercial towns; and the landed people had little or no concern about it. September, 1786, a few men from the middle states met at Annapolis, and hastily proposed a convention to be held in May, 1787, for the purpose, generally, of amending the confederation—this was done before the delegates of Massachusetts, and of the other states arrived—still not a word was said about destroying the old constitution, and making a new one—The states still unsuspecting, and not aware that they were passing the Rubicon, appointed members to the new convention, for the sole and express purpose of revising and amending the confederation—and, probably, not one man in ten thousand in the United States, till within these ten or twelve days, had an idea that the old ship was to be destroyed. and he put to the alternative of embarking in the new ship presented, or of being left in danger of sinking—The States, I believe, universally supposed the convention would report alterations in the confederation, which would pass an examination in congress, and after being agreed to there, would be confirmed by all the legislatures, or be rejected. Virginia made a very respectable appointment, and placed at the head of it the first man in America:—In this appointment there was a mixture of political characters; but Pennsylvania appointed principally those men who are esteemed aristocratical. Here the favourite moment for changing the government was evidently discerned by a few men, who seized it with address. Ten other states appointed, and tho' they chose men principally connected with commerce and the judicial department yet they appointed many good republican characters—had they all attended we should now see, I am persuaded, a better system presented. The non-attendance of eight or nine men, who were appointed members of the convention, I shall ever consider as a very unfortunate event to the United States.—Had they attended, I am pretty clear that the result of the convention would not have had that strong tendency to aristocracy now discernable in every part of the plan. There would not have been so great an accumulation of powers especially as to the internal police of the country, in a few hands as the constitution reported proposes to vest in them—the young visionary men, and the consolidating aristocracy, would have been more restrained than they have been. Eleven states met in the convention, and after four months close attention, presented the new constitution, to be adopted or rejected by the people. The uneasy and fickle part of the community may be prepared to receive any form of government; but, I presume, the enlightened and substantial part will give any constitution, presented for their adoption, a candid and thorough examination; and silence those designing or empty men, who weakly and rashly attempt to precipitate the adoption of a system of so much importance—We shall view the convention with proper respect—and, at the same time, that we reflect there were men of abilities and integrity in it, we must recollect how disproportionably the democratic and aristocratic parts of the community were represented.—Perhaps the judicious friends and opposers of the new constitution will agree, that it is best to let it rest solely on its own merits, or be condemned for its own defects.

In the first place, I shall premise, that the plan proposed, is a plan of accommodation—and that it is in this way only, and by giving up a part of our opinions, that we can ever expect to obtain a government founded in freedom and compact. This circumstance candid men will always keep in view, in the discussion of this subject.

The plan proposed appears to be partly federal, but principally however, calculated ultimately to make the states one consolidated government.

The first interesting question, therefore, suggested, is, how far the states can be consolidated into one entire government on free principles. In considering this question extensive objects are to be taken into view, and important changes in the forms of government to be carefully attended to in all their consequences. The happiness of the people at large must be the great object with every honest statesman, and he will direct every movement to this point. If we are so situated as a people, as not to be able to enjoy equal happiness and advantages under one government, the consolidation of the states cannot be admitted.

There are three different forms of free government under which the United States may exist as one nation; and now is, perhaps, the time to determine to which we will direct our views. 1. Distinct republics connected under a federal head. In this case the respective state governments must be the principal guardians of the peoples rights, and exclusively regulate their internal police; in them must rest the balance of government. The congress of the states, or federal head, must consist of delegates amenable to, and removeable by the respective states: This congress must have general directing powers; powers to require men and monies of the states; to make treaties; peace and war; to direct the operations of armies, &c. Under this federal modification of government, the powers of congress would be rather advisary or recommendatory than coercive. 2. We may do away the several state governments, and form or consolidate all the states into one entire government, with one executive, one judiciary, and one legislature, consisting of senators and representatives collected from all parts of the union: In this case there would be a compleat consolidation of the states. 3. We may consolidate the states as to certain national objects, and leave them severally distinct independent republics, as to internal police generally. Let the general government consist of an executive, a judiciary, and balanced legislature, and its powers extend exclusively to all foreign concerns, causes arising on the seas, to commerce, imports, armies, navies, Indian affairs, peace and war, and to a few internal concerns of the community; to the coin, post-offices, weights and measures, a general plan for the militia, to naturalization, *and, perhaps to bankruptcies,* leaving the internal police of the community, in other respects, exclusively to the state governments; as the administration of justice in all causes arising internally, the laying and collecting of internal taxes, and the forming of the militia according to a general plan prescribed. In this case there would be a compleat consolidation, *quoad* certain objects only.

Touching the first, or federal plan, I do not think much can be said in its favor: The sovereignity of the nation, without coercive and efficient powers to collect the strength of it, cannot always be depended on to answer the purposes of government; and in a congress of representatives of sovereign states, there must necessarily be an unreasonable mixture of powers in the same hands.

As to the second, or compleat consolidating plan, it deserves to be carefully considered at this time, by every American: If it be impracticable, it is a fatal error to model our governments, directing our views ultimately to it.

The third plan, or partial consolidation, is, in my opinion, the only one that can secure the freedom and happiness of this people. I once had some general ideas that the second plan was practicable, but from long attention, and the proceedings of the convention, I am fully satisfied, that this third plan is the only one we can with safety and propriety proceed upon. Making this the standard to point out, with candour and fairness, the parts of the new constitution which appear to be improper, is my object. The convention appears to have proposed the partial consolidation evidently with a view to collect all powers ultimately, in the United States into one entire government; and from its views in this respect, and from the tenacity, of the small states to have an equal vote in the senate, probably originated the greatest defects in the proposed plan.

Independant of the opinions of many great authors, that a free elective government cannot be extended over large territories, a few reflections must evince, that one government and general legislation alone never can extend equal benefits to all parts of the United States: Different laws, customs, and opinions exist in the different states, which by a uniform system of laws would be unreasonably invaded. The United States contain about a million of square miles, and in half a century will, probably, contain ten millions of people; and from the center to the extremes is about 800 miles.

Before we do away the state governments, or adopt measures that will tend to abolish them, and to consolidate the states into one entire government several principles should be considered and facts ascertained:—These, and my examination into the essential parts of the proposed plan, I shall pursue in my next.

LETTER II.

OCTOBER 9, 1787.

DEAR SIR, The essential parts of a free and good government are a full and equal representation of the people in the legislature, and the jury trial of the vicinage in the administration of justice—a full and equal representation, is that which possesses the same interests, feelings, opinions, and views the people themselves would were they all assembled—a fair representation, therefore, should be so regulated, that every order of men in the community, according to the common course of elections, can have a share in it—in order to allow professional men, merchants, traders, farmers, mechanics, &c. to bring a just proportion of their best informed men respectively into the legislature, the representation must be considerably numerous—We have about 200 state senators in the United States, and a less number than that of federal representatives cannot, clearly, be a full representation of this people, in the affairs of internal taxation and police, were there but one legislature for the whole union. The representation cannot be equal, or the situation of the people proper for one government only—if the extreme parts of the society cannot be represented as fully as the central—It is apparently impracticable that this should be the case in this extensive country—it would be impossible to collect a representation of the parts of the country five, six, and seven hundred miles from the seat of government.

Under one general government alone, there could be but one judiciary, one supreme and a proper number of inferior courts. I think it would be totally impracticable in this case to preserve a due administration of justice, and the real benefits of the jury trial of the vicinage—there are now supreme courts in each state in the union; and a great number of county and other courts subordinate to each supreme court—most of these supreme and inferior courts are itinerant, and hold their sessions in different parts every year of their respective states, counties and districts—with all these moving courts, our citizens, from the vast extent of the country must travel very considerable distances from home to find the place where justice is administered. I am not for bringing justice so near to individuals as to afford them any temptation to engage in law suits; though I think it one of the greatest benefits in a good government, that each citizen should find a court of justice within a reasonable distance, perhaps, within a day's travel of his home; so that, without great inconveniences and enormous expences, he may have the advantages of his witnesses and jury—it would be impracticable to derive these advantages from one judiciary—the

one supreme court at most could only set in the centre of the
union, and move once a year into the centre of the eastern and
southern extremes of it—and, in this case, each citizen, on an
average, would travel 150 or 200 miles to find this court—that,
however, inferior courts might be properly placed in the different counties, and districts of the union, the appellate jurisdiction would be intolerable and expensive.

If it were possible to consolidate the states, and preserve the
features of a free government, still it is evident that the middle
states, the parts of the union, about the seat of government,
would enjoy great advantages, while the remote states would
experience the many inconveniences of remote provinces.
Wealth, offices, and the benefits of government would collect
in the centre: and the extreme states; and their principal towns,
become much less important.

There are other considerations which tend to prove that
the idea of one consolidated whole, on free principles, is ill-
founded—the laws of a free government rest on the confidence
of the people, and operate gently—and never can extend their
influence very far—if they are executed on free principles,
about the centre, where the benefits of the government induce
the people to support it voluntarily; yet they must be executed
on the principles of fear and force in the extremes—This has
been the case with every extensive republic of which we have
any accurate account.

There are certain unalienable and fundamental rights, which
in forming the social compact, ought to be explicitly ascertained and fixed—a free and enlightened people, in forming
this compact, will not resign all their rights to those who govern, and they will fix limits to their legislators and rulers, which
will soon be plainly seen by those who are governed, as well
as by those who govern: and the latter will know they cannot be passed unperceived by the former, and without giving a general alarm—These rights should be made the basis
of every constitution; and if a people be so situated, or have
such different opinions that they cannot agree in ascertaining
and fixing them, it is a very strong argument against their at-
tempting to form one entire society, to live under one system
of laws only.—I confess, I never thought the people of these
states differed essentially in these respects; they having derived

all these rights from one common source, the British systems; and having in the formation of their state constitutions, discovered that their ideas relative to these rights are very similar. However, it is now said that the states differ so essentially in these respects, and even in the important article of the trial by jury, that when assembled in convention, they can agree to no words by which to establish that trial, or by which to ascertain and establish many other of these rights, as fundamental articles in the social compact. If so, we proceed to consolidate the states on no solid basis whatever.

But I do not pay much regard to the reasons given for not bottoming the new constitution on a better bill of rights. I still believe a complete federal bill of rights to be very practicable. Nevertheless I acknowledge the proceedings of the convention furnish my mind with many new and strong reasons, against a complete consolidation of the states. They tend to convince me, that it cannot be carried with propriety very far—that the convention have gone much farther in one respect than they found it practicable to go in another; that is, they propose to lodge in the general government very extensive powers—*powers* nearly, if not altogether, complete and unlimited, over the purse and the sword. But, in its organization, they furnish the strongest proof that the proper limbs, or parts of a government, to support and execute those powers on proper principles (or in which they can be safely lodged) cannot be formed. These powers must be lodged somewhere in every society; but then they should be lodged where the strength and guardians of the people are collected. They can be wielded, or safely used, in a free country only by an able executive and judiciary, a respectable senate, and a secure, full, and equal representation of the people. I think the principles I have premised or brought into view, are well founded—I think they will not be denied by any fair reasoner. It is in connection with these, and other solid principles, we are to examine the constitution. It is not a few democratic phrases, or a few well formed features, that will prove its merits; or a few small omissions that will produce its rejection among men of sense; they will enquire what are the essential powers in a community, and what are nominal ones; where and how the essential powers shall be lodged to secure government, and to secure true liberty.

In examining the proposed constitution carefully, we must clearly perceive an unnatural separation of these powers from the substantial representation of the people. The state governments will exist, with all their governors, senators, representatives, officers and expences; in these will be nineteen-twentieths of the representatives of the people; they will have a near connection, and their members an immediate intercourse with the people; and the probability is, that the state governments will possess the confidence of the people, and be considered generally as their immediate guardians.

The general government will consist of a new species of executive, a small senate, and a very small house of representatives. As many citizens will be more than three hundred miles from the seat of this government as will be nearer to it, its judges and officers cannot be very numerous, without making our government very expensive. Thus will stand the state and the general governments, should the constitution be adopted without any alterations in their organization; but as to powers, the general government will possess all essential ones, at least on paper, and those of the states a mere shadow of power. And therefore, unless the people shall make some great exertions to restore to the state governments their powers in matters of internal police; as the powers to lay and collect, exclusively, internal taxes, to govern the militia, and to hold the decisions of their own judicial courts upon their own laws final, the balance cannot possibly continue long; but the state governments must be annihilated, or continue to exist for no purpose.

It is however to be observed, that many of the essential powers given the national government are not exclusively given; and the general government may have prudence enough to forbear the exercise of those which may still be exercised by the respective states. But this cannot justify the impropriety of giving powers, the exercise of which prudent men will not attempt, and imprudent men will, or probably can, exercise only in a manner destructive of free government. The general government, organized as it is, may be adequate to many valuable objects, and be able to carry its laws into execution on proper principles in several cases; but I think its warmest friends will not contend, that it can carry all the powers proposed to be lodged in it into effect, without calling to its aid a military force, which must very soon destroy all elective governments in the country, produce anarchy, or establish despotism. Though we cannot have now a complete idea of what will be the operations of the proposed system, we may, allowing things to have their common course, have a very tolerable one. The powers lodged in the general government, if exercised by it, must intimately effect the internal police of the states, as well as external concerns; and there is no reason to expect the numerous state governments, and their connections, will be very friendly to the execution of federal laws in those internal affairs, which hitherto have been under their own immediate management. There is more reason to believe, that the general government, far removed from the people, and none of its members elected oftener than once in two years, will be forgot or neglected, and its laws in many cases disregarded, unless a multitude of officers and military force be continually kept in view, and employed to enforce the execution of the laws, and to make the government feared and respected. No position can be truer than this,—That in this country either neglected laws, or a military execution of them, must lead to a revolution, and to the destruction of freedom. Neglected laws must first lead to anarchy and confusion; and a military execution of laws is only a shorter way to the same point—despotic government.

LETTER II.

OCTOBER 10th, 1787.

DEAR SIR, The great object of a free people must be so to form their government and laws and so to administer them as to create a confidence in, and respect for the laws; and thereby induce the sensible and virtuous part of the community to declare in favor of the laws, and to support them without an expensive military force. I wish, though I confess I have not much hope, that this may be the case with the laws of Congress under the new Constitution. I am fully convinced that we must organize the national government on different principles, and make the parts of it more efficient, and secure in it more effectually the different interests in the community; or else leave in the state governments some powers propose to be lodged in it—at least till such an organization shall be found to be practicable. Not sanguine in my expectations of a good federal administration and satisfied, as I am, of the impracticability of consolidating the states, and at the same time of preserving the rights of the people at large, I believe we ought still to leave some of those powers in the state governments, in which the people, in fact, will still be represented—to define some other powers proposed to be vested in the general government, more carefully, and to establish a few principles to secure a proper exercise of the powers given it. It is not my object to multiply objections, or to contend about inconsiderable powers or amendments. I wish the system adopted with a few alterations; but those, in my mind, are essential ones; if adopted without, every good citizen will acquiesce, though I shall consider the duration of our governments, and the liberties of this people, very much dependant on the administration of the general government. A wise and honest administration, may make the people happy under any government; but necessity only can justify even our leaving open avenues to the abuse of power, by wicked, unthinking, or ambitious men. I will examine, first, the organization of the proposed government, in order to judge; 2d. with propriety, what powers are improperly, at least prematurely lodged in it. I shall examine, 3d, the undefined powers; and 4th, those powers, the exercise of which is not secured on safe and proper ground.

First. As to the organization—the house of representatives, the democrative branch, as it is called, is to consist of 65 members: that is, about one representative for fifty thousand inhabitants, to be chosen biennially—the federal legislature may increase this number to one for every thirty thousand inhabitants, abating fractional numbers in each state.—Thirty-three representatives will make a quorum for doing business, and a majority of those present determine the sense of the house.—I have no idea that the interests, feelings, and opinions of three or four millions of people, especially touching internal taxation, can be collected in such a house.—In the nature of things, nine times in ten, men of the elevated classes in the community only can be chosen—Connecticut, for instance, will have five representatives—not one man in a hundred of those who form the democrative branch in the state legislature, will on a fair computation, be one of the five—The people of this country, in one sense, may all be democratic;

but if we make the proper distinction between the few men of wealth and abilities, and consider them, as we ought, as the natural aristocracy of the country, and the great body of the people, the middle and lower classes, as the democracy, this federal representative branch will have but very little democracy in it, even this small representation is not secured on proper principles.—The branches of the legislature are essential parts of the fundamental compact, and ought to be so fixed by the people, that the legislature cannot alter itself by modifying the elections of its own members. This, by a part of Art. 1. Sect. 4. the general legislature may do, it may evidently so regulate elections as to secure the choice of any particular description of men.—It may make the whole state one district—make the capital, or any places in the state, the place or places of election—it may declare that the five men (or whatever the number may be the state may chuse) who shall have the most votes shall be considered as chosen—In this case it is easy to perceive how the people who live scattered in the inland towns will bestow their votes on different men— and how few men in a city, in any order or profession, may unite and place any five men they p ease highest among those that may be voted for—and all this may be done constitutionally, and by those silent operations, which are not immediately perceived by the people in general.—I know it is urged, that the general legislature will be disposed to regulate elections on fair and just principles:—This may be true—good men will generally govern well with almost any constitution: But why in laying the foundation of the social system, need we unnecessarily have a door open to improper regulations?—This is a very general and unguarded clause, and many evils may flow from that part which authorises the congress to regulate elections—Were it omitted, the regulations of elections would be solely in the respective states, where the people are substantially represented; and where the elections ought to be regulated, otherwise to secure a representation from all parts of the community, in making the constitution, we ought to provide for dividing each state into a proper number of districts, and for confining the electors in each district to the choice of some men, who shall have a permanent interest and residence in it; and also for this essential object, that the representative elected shall have a majority of the votes of those electors who shall attend and give their votes.

In considering the practicability of having a full and equal representation of the people from all parts of the union, not only distances and different opinions, customs, and views, common in extensive tracts of country, are to be taken into view, but many differences peculiar to Eastern, Middle, and Southern States. These differences are not so perceivable among the members of congress, and men of general information in the state, as among the men who would properly form the democratic branch. The Eastern states are very democratic, and composed chiefly of moderate freeholders: they have but few rich men and no slaves; the Southern states are composed chiefly of rich planters and slaves; they have but few moderate freeholders, and the prevailing influence, in them, is generally a dissipated aristocracy: The Middle states partake partly of the Eastern, and partly of the Southern character.

Perhaps, nothing could be more disjointed, unweildly and incompetent to doing business with harmony and dispatch, than a federal house of representatives properly numerous for the great objects of taxation, &c. collected from the several states; whether such men would ever act in concert; whether they would not worry along a few years, and then be the means of separating the parts of the union, is very problematical?— View this system in whatever form we can, propriety brings us still to this point, a federal government possessed of general and complete powers, as to those national objects which cannot well come under the cognizance of the internal laws of the respective states, and this federal government, accordingly, consisting of branches not very numerous.

The house of representatives is on the plan of consolidation, but the senate is entirely on the federal plan; and Delaware will have as much constitutional influence in the senate, as the largest state in the union; and in this senate are lodged legislative, executive and judicial powers: Ten states in this union urge that they are small states, nine of which were present in the convention.—They were interested in collecting large powers into the hands of the senate, in which each state still will have its equal share of power. I suppose it was impracticable for the three large states, as they were called, to get the senate formed on any other principles:—But this only proves, that we cannot form one general government on equal and just principles— and proves, that we ought not to lodge in it such extensive powers before we are convinced of the practicability of organizing it on just and equal principles. The senate will consist of two members from each state, chosen by the state legislatures, every sixth year. The clause referred to, respecting the elections of representatives, empowers the general legislature to regulate the elections of senators also, "except as to the places of chusing senators."—There is, therefore, but little more security in the elections than in those of representatives:—Fourteen senators make a quorum for business, and a majority of the senators present give the vote of the senate, except in giving judgment upon an impeachment, or in making treaties, or in expelling a member, when two thirds of the senators present must agree.—The members of the legislature are not excluded from being elected to any military offices, or any civil offices, except those created, or the emoluments of which shall be increased by themselves: two-thirds of the members present, of either house, may expel a member at pleasure.—The senate is an independent branch of the legislature, a court for trying impeachments, and also a part of the executive, having a negative in the making of all treaties, and in appointing almost all officers.

The vice-president is not a very important, if not an unnecessary part of the system—he may be a part of the senate at one period, and act as the supreme executive magistrate at another—The election of this officer, as well as of the president of the United States seems to be properly secured; but when we examine the powers of the president, and the forms of the executive, we shall perceive that the general government, in this part, will have a strong tendency to aristocracy, or the government of the few. The executive is, in fact, the president and senate in all transactions of any importance; the president is connected with, or tied to the senate; he may always act with the senate, but never can effectually counteract its views: The president can appoint no officer, civil or military, who shall not be agreeable to the senate; and the presumption is, that the will of so important a body will not be very easily controuled, and that it will exercise its powers with great address.

In the judicial department, powers ever kept distinct in well balanced governments, are no less improperly blended in the hands of the same men—in the judges of the supreme court is lodged, the law, the equity and the fact. It is not necessary to pursue the minute organical parts of the general government proposed.—There were various interests in the convention, to be reconciled, especially of large and small states; of carrying and non-carrying states; and of states more and states less democratic—vast labour and attention were by the convention bestowed on the organization of the parts of the constitution offered; still it is acknowledged, there are many things radically wrong in the essential parts of this constitution—but it is said, that these are the result of our situation:—On a full examination of the subject, I believe it; but what do the laborious inquiries and determinations of the convention prove? If they prove any thing, they prove that we cannot consolidate the states on proper principles: The organization of the government presented proves, that we cannot form a general government in which all power can be safely lodged; and a little attention to the parts of the one proposed will make it appear very evident, that all the powers proposed to be lodged in it, will not be then well deposited, either for the purposes of government, or the preservation of liberty. I will suppose no abuse of powers in those cases, in which the abuse of it is not well guarded against—I will suppose the words authorising the general government to regulate the elections of its own members struck out of the plan, or free district elections, in each state, amply secured.—That the small representation provided for shall be as fair and equal as it is capable of being made—I will suppose the judicial department regulated on pure principles, by future laws, as far as it can be by the constitution, and consist with the situation of the country—still there will be an unreasonable accumulation of powers in the general government, if all be granted, enumerated in the plan proposed. The plan does not present a well balanced government: The senatorial branch of the legislative and the executive are substantially united, and the president, or the first executive magistrate, may aid the senatorial interest when weakest, but never can effectually support the democratic, however it may be oppressed;—the excellency, in my mind, of a well balanced government is that it consists of distinct branches, each sufficiently strong and independant to keep its own station, and to aid either of the other branches which may occasionally want aid.

The convention found that any but a small house of representatives would be expensive, and that it would be impracticable to assemble a large number of representatives. Not only the determination of the convention in this case, but the situation of the states, proves the impracticability of collecting, in any one point, a proper representation.

The formation of the senate, and the smallness of the house, being, therefore, the result of our situation, and the actual state of things, the evils which may attend the exercise of many powers in this national government may be considered as without a remedy.

All officers are impeachable before the senate only—before the men by whom they are appointed, or who are consenting to the appointment of these officers. No judgment of conviction, on an impeachment, can be given unless two thirds of the senators agree. Under these circumstances the right of impeachment, in the house, can be of but little importance: the house cannot expect often to convict the offender; and, therefore, probably, will but seldom or never exercise the right. In addition to the insecurity and inconveniences attending this organization beforementioned, it may be observed, that it is extremely difficult to secure the people against the fatal effects of corruption and influence. The power of making any law will be in the president, eight senators, and seventeen representatives, relative to the important objects enumerated in the constitution. Where there is a small representation a sufficient number to carry any measure, may, with ease, be influenced by bribes, offices and civilities; they may easily form private juntoes, and out-door meetings, agree on measures, and carry them by silent votes.

Impressed, as I am, with a sense of the difficulties there are in the way of forming the parts of a federal government on proper principles, and seeing a government so unsubstantially organized, after so arduous an attempt has been made, I am led to believe, that powers ought to be given to it with great care and caution.

In the second place it is necessary, therefore, to examine the extent, and the probable operations of some of those extensive powers proposed to be vested in this government. These powers, legislative, executive, and judicial, respect internal as well as external objects. Those respecting external objects, as all foreign concerns, commerce, imposts, all causes arising on the seas, peace and war, and Indian affairs, can be lodged no where else, with any propriety, but in this government. Many powers that respect internal objects ought clearly to be lodged in it; as those to regulate trade between the states, weights and measures, the coin or current monies, post-offices, naturalization, &c. These powers may be exercised without essentially effecting the internal police of the respective states: But powers to lay and collect internal taxes, to form the militia, to make bankrupt laws, and to decide on appeals, questions arising on the internal laws of the respective states, are of a very serious nature, and carry with them almost all other powers. These taken in connection with the others, and powers to raise armies and build navies, proposed to be lodged in this government, appear to me to comprehend all the essential powers in the community, and those which will be left to the states will be of no great importance.

A power to lay and collect taxes at discretion, is, in itself, of very great importance. By means of taxes, the government may command the whole or any part of the subject's property. Taxes may be of various kinds; but there is a strong distinction between external and internal taxes. External taxes are impost duties, which are laid on imported goods; they may usually be collected in a few seaport towns, and of a few individuals, though ultimately paid by the consumer; a few officers can collect them, and they can be carried no higher than trade will bear, or smuggling permit—that in the very nature of commerce, bounds are set to them. But internal taxes, as poll and land taxes, excise, duties on all written instruments, &c. may fix themselves on every person and species of property in the community; they may be carried to any lengths, and in proportion as they are extended, numerous officers must be employed to assess them, and to enforce the collection of them. In the United Netherlands the general government has compleat powers, as to external taxation; but as to internal taxes, it makes requisitions on the provinces. Internal taxation in this country is more important, as the country is so very extensive. As many assessors and collectors of federal taxes will be above three hundred miles from the seat of the federal government as will be less. Besides, to lay and collect internal taxes, in this extensive country, must require a great number of congressional ordinances, immediately operating upon the body of the people; these must continually interfere with the state laws, and thereby produce disorder and general dissatisfaction, till the one system of laws or the other, operating upon the same subjects, shall be abolished. These ordinances alone, to say nothing of those respecting the militia, coin, commerce, federal judiciary, &c. &c. will probably soon defeat the operations of the state laws and governments.

Should the general government think it politic, as some administrations (if not all) probably will, to look for a support in a system of influence, the government will take every occasion to multiply laws, and officers to execute them, considering these as so many necessary props for its own support. Should this system of policy be adopted, taxes more productive than the impost duties will, probably, be wanted to support the government, and to discharge foreign demands, without leaving any thing for the domestic creditors. The internal sources of taxation then must be called into operation, and internal tax laws and federal assessors and collectors spread over this immense country. All these circumstances considered, is it wise, prudent, or safe, to vest the powers of laying and collecting internal taxes in the general government, while imperfectly organized and inadequate; and to trust to amending it hereafter, and making it adequate to this purpose? It is not only unsafe but absurd to lodge power in a government before it is fitted to receive it? It is confessed that this power and representation ought to go together. Why give the power first? Why give the power to the few, who, when possessed of it, may have address enough to prevent the increase of representation? Why not keep the power, and, when necessary, amend the constitution, and add to its other parts this power, and a proper increase of representation at the same time? Then men who may want the power will be under strong inducements to let in the people, by their representatives, into the government, to hold their due

proportion of this power. If a proper representation be impracticable, then we shall see this power resting in the states, where
it at present ought to be, and not inconsiderately given up.

When I recollect how lately congress, conventions, legislatures and people, contended in the cause of liberty, and carefully weighed the importance of taxation, I can scarcely believe
we are serious in proposing to vest the powers of laying and
collecting internal taxes in a government so imperfectly organized for such purposes. Should the United States be taxed
by a house of representatives of two hundred members, which
would be about fifteen members for Connecticut, twenty-five
for Massachusetts, &c. still the middle and lower classes of
people could have no great share, in fact, in taxation. I am
aware it is said, that the representation proposed by the new
constitution is sufficiently numerous; it may be for many purposes; but to suppose that this branch is sufficiently numerous
to guard the rights of the people in the administration of the
government, in which the purse and sword is placed, seems
to argue that we have forgot what the true meaning of representation is. I am sensible also, that it is said that congress
will not attempt to lay and collect internal taxes; that it is necessary for them to have the power, though it cannot probably
be exercised.—I admit that it is not probable that any prudent
congress will attempt to lay and collect internal taxes, especially
direct taxes: but this only proves, that the power would be
improperly lodged in congress, and that it might be abused by
imprudent and designing men.

I have heard several gentlemen, to get rid of objections to
this part of the constitution, attempt to construe the powers
relative to direct taxes, as those who object to it would have
them; as to these, it is said, that congress will only have power
to make requisitions, leaving it to the states to lay and collect
them. I see but very little colour for this construction, and
the attempt only proves that this part of the plan cannot be
defended. By this plan there can be no doubt, but that the
powers of congress will be complete as to all kinds of taxes
whatever—Further, as to internal taxes, the state governments
will have concurrent powers with the general government, and
both may tax the same objects in the same year; and the objection that the general government may suspend a state tax,

as a necessary measure for the promoting the collection of a federal tax, is not without foundation.—As the states owe large debts, and have large demands upon them individually, there clearly would be a propriety in leaving in their possession exclusively, some of the internal sources of taxation, at least until the federal representation shall be properly encreased: The power in the general government to lay and collect internal taxes, will render its powers respecting armies, navies and the militia, the more exceptionable. By the constitution it is proposed that congress shall have power "to raise and support armies, but no appropriation of money to that use shall be for a longer term than two years; to provide and maintain a navy; to provide for calling forth the militia to execute the laws of the union; suppress insurrections. and repel invasions: to provide for organizing, arming, and disciplining the militia: reserving to the states the right to appoint the officers, and to train the militia according to the discipline prescribed by congress;" congress will have unlimited power to raise armies, and to engage officers and men for any number of years; but a legislative act applying money for their support can have operation for no longer term than two years, and if a subsequent congress do not within the two years renew the appropriation, or further appropriate monies for the use of the army, the army, will be left to take care of itself. When an army shall once be raised for a number of years, it is not probable that it will find much difficulty in getting congress to pass laws for applying monies to its support. I see so many men in America fond of a standing army, and especially among those who probably will have a large share in administering the federal system; it is very evident to me, that we shall have a large standing army as soon as the monies to support them can be possibly found. An army is a very agreeable place of employment for the young gentlemen of many families. A power to raise armies must be lodged some where; still this will not justify the lodging this power in a bare majority of so few men without any checks; or in the government in which the great body of the people, in the nature of things, will be only nominally represented. In the state governments the great body of the people, the yeomanry, &c. of the country, are represented: It is true they will chuse the members of congress, and may now and then chuse a man of their own way of thinking; but it is impossible for forty, or thirty thousand people in this country, one time in ten to find a man who can possess similar feelings, views, and interests with themselves: Powers to lay and collect taxes and to raise armies are of the greatest moment; for carrying them into effect, laws need not be frequently made, and the yeomanry, &c. of the country ought substantially to have a check upon the passing of these laws; this check ought to be placed in the legislatures, or at least, in the few men the common people of the country, will, probably, have in congress, in the true sense of the word, "from among themselves." It is true, the yeomanry of the country possess the lands, the weight of property, possess arms, and are too strong a body of men to be openly offended—and, therefore, it is urged, they will take care of themselves, that men who shall govern will not dare pay any disrespect to their opinions. It is easily perceived, that if they have not their proper negative upon passing laws in congress, or on the passage of laws relative to taxes and armies, they may in twenty or thirty years be by means imperceptible to them, totally deprived of that boasted weight and strength: This may be done in a great measure by congress, if disposed to do it, by modelling the militia. Should one fifth, or one eighth part of the men capable of bearing arms, be made a select militia, as has been proposed, and those the young and ardent part of the community, possessed of but little or no property, and all the others put upon a plan that will render them of no importance, the former will answer all the purposes of an army, while the latter will be defenceless. The state must train the militia in such form and according to such systems and rules as Congress shall prescribe: and the only actual influence the respective states will have respecting the militia will be in appointing the officers. I see no provision made for calling out the *posse commitatus* for executing the laws of the union, but provision is made for Congress to call forth the militia for the execution of them—and the militia in general, or any select part of it, may be called out under military officers, instead of the sheriff to enforce an execution of federal laws, in the first instance and thereby introduce an entire military execution of the laws. I know that powers to raise taxes, to regulate the military strength of the community on some uniform plan, to provide for its defence and internal order, and for duly executing the laws, must be lodged somewhere; but still we ought not to lodge them, as evidently to give one another of them in the community, undue advantages over others; or commit the many to the mercy, prudence, and moderation of the few. And so far as it may be necessary to lodge any of the peculiar powers in the general government, a more safe exercise of them ought to be secured, by requiring the consent of two-thirds or three-fourths of congress thereto—until the federal representation can be increased, so that the democratic members in Congress may stand some tolerable chance of a reasonable negative, in behalf of the numerous, important, and democratic part of the community.

I am not sufficiently acquainted with the laws and internal police of all the states to discern fully, how general bankrupt laws, made by the union, would effect them, or promote the public good. I believe the property of debtors, in the several states, is held responsible for their debts in modes and forms very different. If uniform bankrupt laws can be made without producing real and substantial inconveniences, I wish them to be made by Congress.

There are some powers proposed to be lodged in the general government in the judicial department, I think very unnecessarily, I mean powers respecting questions arising upon the internal laws of the respective states. It is proper the federal judiciary should have powers co-extensive with the federal legislature—that is, the power of deciding finally on the laws of the union. By Art. 3. Sect. 2. the powers of the federal judiciary are extended (among other things) to all cases between a state and citizens of another state—between citizens of different states—between a state or the citizens thereof, and foreign states, citizens or subjects. Actions in all these cases, except against a state government. are now brought and finally determined in the law courts of the states respectively; and as there are no words to exclude these courts of their jurisdiction in these cases, they will have concurrent jurisdiction with the inferior federal courts in them; and, therefore, if the new constitution be adopted without any amendment in this respect, all those numerous actions. now brought in the state courts between our citizens and foreigners, between citizens of different states, by state governments against foreigners, and by state governments against citizens of other states, may also be brought in the federal courts; and an appeal will lay in them from the state courts, or federal inferior courts, to the supreme judicial court of the union. In almost all these cases, either party may have the trial by jury in the state courts; excepting paper money and tender laws, which are wisely guarded against in the proposed constitution; justice may be obtained in these courts on reasonable terms; they must be more competent to proper decisions on the laws of their respective states, than the federal courts can possibly be. I do not, in any point of view, see the need of opening a new jurisdiction to these causes— of opening a new scene of expensive law suits—of suffering foreigners, and citizens of different states, to drag each other many hundred miles into the federal courts. It is true, those courts may be so organized by a wise and prudent legislature, as to make the obtaining of justice in them tolerably easy; they may in general be organized on the common law principles of the country: But this benefit is by no means secured by the constitution. The trial by jury is secured only in those few criminal cases, to which the federal laws will extend—as crimes committed on the seas, against the laws of nations, treason, and counterfeiting the federal securities and coin: But even in these cases, the jury trial of the vicinage is not secured— particularly in the large states, a citizen may be tried for a crime committed in the state, and yet tried in some states 500 miles from the place where it was committed; but the jury trial is not secured at all in civil causes. Though the convention have not established this trial, it is to be hoped that congress, in putting the new system into execution, will do it by a legislative act, in all cases in which it can be done with propriety. Whether the jury trial is not excluded in the supreme judicial court, is an important question. By Art. 3. Sect. 2. all cases affecting ambassadors, other public ministers, and consuls, and in those cases in which a state shall be party, the supreme court shall have jurisdiction. In all the other cases before mentioned, the supreme court shall have appellate jurisdiction, both as to LAW and FACT, with such exception, and under such regulations, as the congress shall make. By court is understood a court con- sisting of judges; and the idea of a jury is excluded. This court, or the judges, are to have jurisdiction on appeals, in all the cases enumerated, as to law and fact; the judges are to decide the law and try the fact, and the trial of the fact being assigned to the judges by the constitution, a jury for trying the fact is excluded; however, under the exceptions and powers to make regulations, Congress may, perhaps, introduce the jury, to try the fact in most necessary cases.

There can be but one supreme court in which the final juris-diction will centre in all federal causes—except in cases where appeals by law shall not be allowed: The judicial powers of the federal courts extends in law and equity to certain cases: and, therefore, the powers to determine on the law, in equity, and as to the fact, all will concentre in the supreme court:—These powers, which by this constitution are blended in the same hands, the same judges, are in Great-Britain deposited in dif-ferent hands—to wit, the decision of the law in the law judges, the decision in equity in the chancellor, and the trial of the fact in the jury. It is a very dangerous thing to vest in the same judge power to decide on the law, and also general powers in equity; for if the law restrain him, he is only to step into his shoes of equity, and give what judgment his reason or opin-ion may dictate; we have no precedents in this country, as yet, to regulate the divisions as in equity in Great-Britain; equity, therefore, in the supreme court for many years, will be mere discretion. I confess in the constitution of this supreme court, as left by the constitution, I do not see a spark of freedom or a shadow of our own or the British common law.

This court is to have appellate jurisdiction in all the other cases before-mentioned: Many sensible men suppose that cases before mentioned respect, as well the criminal cases as the civil ones, mentioned antecedently in the constitution, if so an appeal is allowed in criminal cases—contrary to the usual sense of law. How far it may be proper to admit a foreigner or the citizen of another state to bring actions against state gov-ernments, which have failed in performing so many promises made during the war, is doubtful: How far it may be proper so to humble a state, as to bring it to answer to an individual in a court of law, is worthy of consideration; the states are now subject to no such actions; and this new jurisdiction will sub-ject the states, and many defendants to actions, and processes, which were not in the contemplation of the parties, when the contract was made; all engagements existing between citizens of different states, citizens and foreigners, states and foreigners; and states and citizens of other states were made the parties contemplating the remedies then existing on the laws of the states—and the new remedy proposed to be given in the federal courts, can be founded on no principle whatever.

LETTER IV.

OCTOBER 12th, 1787.

DEAR SIR, It will not be possible to establish in the federal courts the jury trial of the vicinage so well as in the state courts.

Third. There appears to me to be not only a premature deposit of some important powers in the general government—but many of those deposited there are undefined, and may be used to good or bad purposes as honest or designing men shall prevail. By Art. 1, Sect. 2, representatives and direct taxes shall be apportioned among the several states, &c.—same art. sect. 8, the Congress shall have powers to lay and collect taxes, duties, &c. for the common defence and general welfare, but all duties, imposts and excises, shall be uniform throughout the United States: By the first recited clause, direct taxes shall be apportioned on the states. This seems to favour the idea suggested by some sensible men and writers, that Congress, as to direct taxes, will only have power to make requisitions; but the latter clause, power to lay and collect taxes, &c. seems clearly to favour the contrary opinion, and, to my mind, the true one, that Congress shall have power to tax immediately individuals, without the intervention of the state legislatures; in fact the first clause appears to me only to provide that each state shall pay a certain portion of the tax, and the latter to provide that Congress shall have power to lay and collect taxes, that is to assess upon, and to collect of the individuals in the state, the states quota; but these still I consider as undefined powers, because judicious men understand them differently.

It is doubtful whether the vice president is to have any qualifications; none are mentioned; but he may serve as president, and it may be inferred, he ought to be qualified therefore as the president; but the qualifications of the president are required only of the person to be elected president. By art. the 2, sect. 2.

"But the Congress may by law vest the appointment of such inferior officers as they think proper in the president alone, in the courts of law, or in the heads of the departments:" Who are inferior officers? May not a Congress disposed to vest the appointment of all officers in the president, under this clause, vest the appointment of almost every officer in the president alone, and destroy the check mentioned in the first part of the clause, and lodged in the senate. It is true, this check is badly lodged, but then some check upon the first magistrate in appointing officers, ought, it appears by the opinion of the convention, and by the general opinion, to be established in the constitution. By art. 3, sect. 2, the supreme court shall have appellate jurisdiction as to law and facts with such exceptions, &c. to what extent is it intended the exceptions shall be carried—Congress may carry them so far as to annihilate substantially the appellate jurisdiction, and the clause be rendered of very little importance.

4th. There are certain rights which we have always held sacred in the United States, and recognized in all our constitutions, and which, by the adoption of the new constitution, its present form will be left unsecured. By article 6, the proposed constitution, and the laws of the United States, which shall be made in pursuance thereof; and all treaties made, or which shall be made under the authority of the United States, shall be the supreme law of the land; and the judges in every state shall be bound thereby; any thing in the constitution or laws of any state to the contrary notwithstanding.

It is to be observed that when the people shall adopt the proposed constitution it will be their last and supreme act; it will be adopted not by the people of New-Hampshire, Massachusetts, &c. but by the people of the United States; and whenever this constitution, or any part of it, shall be incompatible with the antient customs, rights, the laws or the constitutions heretofore established in the United States, it will entirely abolish them and do them away: And not only this, but the laws of the United States which shall be made in pursuance of the federal constitution will be also supreme laws, and whenever they shall be incompatible with those customs, rights, laws or constitutions heretofore established, they will also entirely abolish them and do them away.

By the article before recited, treaties also made under the authority of the United States, shall be the supreme law: It is not said that these treaties shall be made in pursuance of the constitution—nor are there any constitutional bounds set to those who shall make them: The president and two thirds of the senate will be empowered to make treaties indefinitely, and when these treaties shall be made, they will also abolish all laws and state constitutions incompatible with them. This power in the president and senate is absolute, and the judges will be bound to allow full force to whatever rule, article or thing the president and senate shall establish by treaty, whether it be practicable to set any bounds to those who make treaties, I am not able to say: if not, it proves that this power ought to be more safely lodged.

The federal constitution, the laws of congress made in pursuance of the constitution, and all treaties must have full force and effect in all parts of the United States; and all other laws, rights and constitutions which stand in their way must yield: It is proper the national laws should be supreme, and superior to state or district laws; but then the national laws ought to yield to unalienable or fundamental rights—and national laws, made by a few men, should extend only to a few national objects. This will not be the case with the laws of congress: To have any proper idea of their extent, we must carefully examine the legislative, executive and judicial powers proposed to be lodged in the general government, and consider them in connection with a general clause in art. 1. sect. 8. in these words (after enumerating a number of powers) "To make all laws which shall be necessary and proper for carrying into execution the foregoing powers, and all other powers vested by this constitution in the government of the United States, or in any department or officer thereof."—The powers of this government as has been observed, extend to internal as well as external objects, and to those objects to which all others are subordinate; it is almost impossible to have a just conception of these powers, or of the extent and number of the laws which may be deemed necessary and proper to carry them into effect, till we shall come to exercise those powers and make the laws. In making laws to carry those powers into effect, it will be expected, that a wise and prudent congress will pay respect to the opinions of a free people, and bottom their laws on those principles which have been considered as essential and fundamental in the British, and in our government: But a congress of a different character will not be bound by the constitution to pay respect to those principles.

It is said, that when the people make a constitution, and delegate powers, that all powers not delegated by them to those who govern, is reserved in the people; and that the people, in the present case, have reserved in themselves, and in their state governments, every right and power not expressly given by the federal constitution to those who shall administer the national government. It is said, on the other hand, that the people, when they make a constitution, yield all power not expressly reserved to themselves. The truth is, in either case, it is mere matter of opinion, and men usually take either side of the argument, as will best answer their purposes: But the general presumption being, that men who govern, will, in doubtful cases, construe laws and constitutions most favourably for encreasing their own powers; all wise and prudent people, in forming constitutions, have drawn the line, and carefully described the powers parted with and the powers reserved. By the state constitutions, certain rights have been reserved in the people; or rather, they have been recognized and established in such a manner, that state legislatures are bound to respect them, and to make no laws infringing upon them. The state legislatures are obliged to take notice of the bills of rights of their respective states. The bills of rights, and the state constitutions, are fundamental compacts only between those who govern, and the people of the same state.

In the year 1788 the people of the United States make a federal constitution, which is a fundamental compact between them and their federal rulers these rulers, in the nature of things, cannot be bound to take notice of any other compact. It would be absurd for them, in making laws, to look over thirteen, fifteen, or twenty state constitutions, to see what rights are established as fundamental, and must not be infringed upon, in making laws in the society. It is true, they would be bound to do it if the people, in their federal compact, should refer to the state constitutions, recognize all parts not inconsistent with the federal constitution, and direct their federal rulers to take notice of them accordingly; but this is not the case, as the plan stands proposed at present; and it is absurd, to suppose so unnatural an idea is intended or implied, I think my opinion is not only founded in reason, but I think it is supported by the report of the convention itself. If there are a number of rights established by the state constitutions, and which will remain sacred, and the general government is bound to take notice of them—it must take notice of one as well as another; and if unnecessary to recognize or establish one by the federal constitution, it would be unnecessary to recognize or establish another by it. If the federal constitution is to be construed so far in connection with the state constitutions, as to leave the trial by jury in civil causes, for instance, secured; on the same principles it would have left the trial by jury in criminal causes, the benefits of the writ of habeas corpus, &c. secured; they all stand on the same footing; they are the common rights of Americans, and have been recognized by the state constitutions: But the convention found it necessary to recognize or re-establish the benefits of that writ, and the jury trial in criminal cases. As to EXPOST FACTO laws, the convention has done the same in one case, and gone further in another. It is a part of the compact between the people of each state and their rulers, that no EXPOST FACTO laws shall be made. But the convention, by Art. I. Sect. 10. have put a sanction upon this part even of the state compacts. In fact, the 9th and 10th Sections in Art. I. in the proposed constitution, are no more nor less, than a partial bill of rights; they establish certain principles as part of the compact upon which the federal legislators and officers can never infringe. It is here wisely stipulated, that the federal legislature shall never pass a bill of attainder, or EXPOST FACTO law; that no tax shall be laid on articles exported, &c. The establishing of one right implies the necessity of establishing another and similar one.

On the whole, the position appears to me to be undeniable, that this bill of rights ought to be carried farther, and some other principles established, as a part of this fundamental compact between the people of the United States and their federal rulers.

It is true, we are not disposed to differ much, at present, about religion; but when we are making a constitution, it is to be hoped, for ages and millions yet unborn, why not establish the free exercise of religion, as a part of the national compact. There are other essential rights, which we have justly understood to be the rights of freemen; as freedom from hasty and unreasonable search warrants, warrants not founded on oath, and not issued with due caution, for searching and seizing men's papers, property, and persons. The trials by jury in civil causes, it is said, varies so much in the several states, that no words could be found for the uniform establishment of it. If so the federal legislation will not be able to establish it by any general laws. I confess I am of opinion it may be established, but not in that beneficial manner in which we may enjoy it, for the reasons beforementioned. When I speak of the jury trial of the vicinage, or the trial of the fact in the neighbourhood,—I do not lay so much stress upon the circumstance of our being tried by our neighbours: in this enlightened country men may be probably impartially tried by those who do not live very near them: but the trial of facts in the neighbourhood is of great importance in other respects. Nothing can be more essential than the cross examining witnesses, and generally before the triers of the facts in question. The common people can establish facts with much more ease with oral than written evidence; when trials of facts are removed to a distance from the homes of the parties and witnesses, oral evidence becomes intolerably expensive, and the parties must depend on written evidence, which to the common people is expensive and almost useless; it must be frequently taken ex-parte, and but very seldom leads to the proper discovery of truth.

The trial by jury is very important in another point of view. It is essential in every free country, that common people should have a part and share of influence, in the judicial as well as in the legislative department. To hold open to them the offices of senators, judges, and officers to fill which an expensive education is required, cannot answer any valuable purposes for them; they are not in a situation to be brought forward and to fill those offices; these, and most other offices of any considerable importance, will be occupied by the few. The few, the well born, &c. as Mr. Adams calls them, in judicial decisions as well as in legislation, are generally disposed, and very naturally too, to favour those of their own description.

The trial by jury in the judicial department, and the collection of the people by their representatives in the legislature, are those fortunate inventions which have procured for them, in this country, their true proportion of influence, and the wisest and most fit means of protecting themselves in the community. Their situation, as jurors and representatives, enables them to acquire information and knowledge in the affairs and government of the society; and to come forward, in turn, as the centinels and guardians of each other. I am very sorry that even a few of our countrymen should consider jurors and representatives in a different point of view, as ignorant troublesome bodies, which ought not to have any share in the concerns of government.

I confess I do not see in what cases the congress can, with any pretence of right, make a law to suppress the freedom of the press; though I am not clear, that congress is restrained from laying any duties whatever on printing, and from laying duties particularly heavy on certain pieces printed, and perhaps congress may require large bonds for the payment of these duties. Should the printer say, the freedom of the press was secured by the constitution of the state in which he lived, congress might, and perhaps, with great propriety, answer, that the federal constitution is the only compact existing between them and the people; in this compact the people have named no others, and therefore congress, in exercising the powers assigned them, and in making laws to carry them into execution, are restrained by nothing beside the federal constitution, any more than a state legislature is restrained by a compact between the magistrates and people of a county, city, or town of which the people, in forming the state constitution, have taken no notice.

It is not my object to enumerate rights of inconsiderable importance; but there are others, no doubt, which ought to be established as a fundamental part of the national system.

It is worthy observation, that all treaties are made by foreign nations with a confederacy of thirteen states—that the western country is attached to thirteen states—thirteen states have jointly and severally engaged to pay the public debts.—Should a new government be formed of nine, ten, eleven, or twelve states, those treaties could not be considered as binding on the foreign nations who made them. However, I believe the probability to be, that if nine states adopt the constitution, the others will.

It may also be worthy our examination, how far the provision for amending this plan, when it shall be adopted, is of any importance. No measures can be taken towards amendments, unless two-thirds of the Congress, or two-thirds of the legislatures of the several states shall agree.—While power is in the hands of the people, or democratic part of the community, more especially as at present, it is easy, according to the general course of human affairs, for the few influential men in the community, to obtain conventions, alterations in government, and to persuade the common people they may change for the better, and to get from them a part of the power: But when power is once transferred from the many to the few, all changes become extremely difficult; the government, in this case, being beneficial to the few, they will be exceedingly artful and adroit in preventing any measures which may lead to a change; and nothing will produce it, but great exertions and severe struggles on the part of the common people. Every man of reflection must see, that the change now proposed, is a transfer of power from the many to the few, and the probability is, the artful and ever active aristocracy, will prevent all peaceable measures for changes, unless when they shall discover some favourable moment to increase their own influence. I am sensible, thousands of men in the United States, are disposed to adopt the proposed constitution, though they perceive it to be essentially defective, under an idea that amendment of it, may be obtained when necessary. This is a pernicious idea, it argues a servility of character totally unfit for the support of free government; it is very repugnant to that perpetual jealousy respecting liberty, so absolutely necessary in all free states, spoken of by Mr. Dickinson.—However, if our countrymen are so soon changed, and the language of 1774, is become odious to them, it will be in vain to use the language of freedom, or to attempt to rouse them to free enquiries: But I shall never believe this is the case with them, whatever present appearances may be, till I shall have very strong evidence indeed of it.

LETTER V

OCTOBER 13th, 1787.

DEAR SIR, Thus I have examined the federal constitution as far as a few days leisure would permit. It opens to my mind a new scene; instead of seeing powers cautiously lodged in the hands of numerous legislators, and many magistrates, we see all important powers collecting in one centre, where a few men will possess them almost at discretion. And instead of checks in the formation of the government, to secure the rights of the people against the usurpations of those they appoint to govern, we are to understand the equal division of lands among our people, and the strong arm furnished them by nature and situation, are to secure them against those usurpations. If there are advantages in the equal division of our lands, and the strong and manly habits of our people, we ought to establish governments calculated to give duration to them, and not governments which never can work naturally, till that equality of property, and those free and manly habits shall be destroyed; these evidently are not the natural basis of the proposed constitution.—No man of reflection, and skilled in the science of government, can suppose these will move on harmoniously together for ages, or even for fifty years. As to the little circumstances commented upon, by some writers, with applause—as the age of a representative, of the president, &c.—they have, in my mind, no weight in the general tendency of the system.

There are, however, in my opinion, many good things in the proposed system. It is founded on elective principles, and the deposits of powers in different hands, is essentially right.— The guards against those evils we have experienced in some states in legislation are valuable indeed: but the value of every feature in this system is vastly lessened for the want of that one important feature in a free government, a representation of the people. Because we have sometimes abused democracy, I am not among those men who think a democratic branch a nuisance; which branch shall be sufficiently numerous, to admit some of the best informed men of each order in the community into the administration of government.

While the radical defects in the proposed system are not so soon discovered, some temptations to each state, and to many classes of men to adopt it, are very visible. It uses the democratic language of several of the state constitutions, particularly that of Massachusetts; the eastern states will receive advantages so far as the regulation of trade, by a bare majority, is committed to it: Connecticut and New-Jersey will receive their share of a general impost:—The middle states will receive the advantages surrounding the seat of government:—The southern states will receive protection, and have their negroes represented in the legislature, and large back countries will soon have a majority in it.—This system promises a large field of employment to military gentlemen, and gentlemen of the law; and in case the government shall be executed without convulsions, it will afford security to creditors, to the clergy, salary-men and others depending on money payments. So far as the system promises justice and reasonable advantages, in these respects, it ought to be supported by all honest men; but whenever it promises unequal and improper advantages to any particular states, or orders of men, it ought to be opposed.

I have, in the course of these letters observed, that there are many good things in the proposed constitution, and I have endeavoured to point out many important defects in it. I have admitted that we want a federal system—that we have a system presented, which, with several alterations, may be made a tolerable good one—I have admitted there is a well founded uneasiness among creditors and mercantile men. In this situation of things, you ask me what I think ought to be done? My opinion in this case is only the opinion of an individual, and so far only as it corresponds with the opinions of the honest and substantial part of the community, is it entitled to consideration. Though I am fully satisfied that the state conventions ought most seriously to direct their exertions to altering and amending the system proposed before they shall adopt it—yet I have not sufficiently examined the subject, or formed an opinion, how far it will be practicable for those conventions to carry their amendments. As to the idea, that it will be in vain for those conventions to attempt amendments, it cannot be admitted; it is impossible to say whether they can or not until the attempt shall be made: and when it shall be determined, by experience, that the conventions cannot agree in amendments, it will then be an important question before the people of the United States, whether they will adopt or not the system proposed in its present form. This subject of consolidating the states is new; and because forty or fifty men have agreed in a system, to suppose the good sense of this country, an enlightened nation, must adopt it without examination, and though in a state of profound peace, without endeavouring to amend those parts they perceive are defective, dangerous to freedom, and destructive of the valuable principles of republican government—is truly humiliating. It is true there may be danger in delay; but there is danger in adopting the system in its present form; and I see the danger in either case will arise principally from the conduct and views of two very unprincipled parties in the United States—two fires, between which the honest and substantial people have long found themselves situated. One party is composed of little insurgents, men in debt, who want no law, and who want a share of the property of others; these are called levellers, Shayites, &c. The other party is composed of a few, but more dangerous men, with their servile dependents; these avariciously grasp at all power and property; you may discover in all the actions of these men, an evident dislike to free and equal governments, and they will go systematically to work to change, essentially, the forms of government in this country; these are called aristocrates, morrisites, &c. &c. Between these two parties is the weight of the community; the men of middling property, men not in debt on the one hand, and men, on the other, content with republican governments, and not aiming at immense fortunes, offices, and power. In 1786, the little insurgents, the levellers, came forth, invaded the rights of others, and attempted to establish governments according to their wills. Their movements evidently gave encouragement to the other party, which, in 1787, has taken the political field, and with its fashionable dependents, and the tongue and the pen, is endeavouring to establish, in great haste, a politer kind of government. These two parties, which will probably be opposed or united as it may suit their interests and views, are really insignificant, compared with the solid, free, and independent part of the community. It is not my intention to suggest, that either of these parties, and the real friends of the proposed constitution, are the same men. The fact is, these aristocrats support and hasten the adoption of the proposed constitution, merely because they think it is a stepping stone to their favourite object. I think I am well founded in this idea; I think the general politics of these men support it, as well as the common observation among them, That the proffered plan is the best that can be got at present, it will do for a few years, and lead to something better. The sensible and judicious part of the community will carefully weigh all these circumstances; they will view the late convention as a respectable assembly of men—America probably never will see an assembly of men of a like number, more respectable. But the members of the convention met without knowing the sentiments of one man in ten thousand in these states respecting the new ground taken. Their doings are but the first attempts in the most important scene ever opened. Though each individual in the state conventions will not, probably, be so respectable as each individual in the federal convention, yet as the state conventions will probably consist of fifteen hundred or two thousand men of abilities, and versed in the science of government, collected from all parts of the community and from all orders of men, it must be acknowledged that the weight of respectability will be in them—In them will be collected the solid sense and the real political character of the country. Being revisers of the subject, they will possess peculiar advantages. To say that these conventions ought not to attempt, coolly and deliberately, the revision of the system, or that they cannot amend it, is very foolish or very assuming. If these conventions, after examining the system, adopt it, I shall be perfectly satisfied, and wish to see men make the administration of the government an equal blessing to all orders of men. I believe the great body of our people to be virtuous and friendly to good government, to the protection of liberty and property; and it is the duty of all good men, especially of those who are placed as centinels to guard their rights—it is their duty to examine into the prevailing politics of parties, and to disclose them—while they avoid exciting undue suspicions, to lay facts before the people, which will enable them to form a proper judgment. Men, who wish the people of this country to determine for themselves, and deliberately to fit the government to their situation, must feel some degree of indignation at those attempts to hurry the adoption of a system, and to shut the door against examination. The very attempts create suspicions, that those who make them have secret views, or see some defects in the system, which, in the hurry of affairs, they expect will escape the eye of a free people.

What can be the views of those gentlemen in Pennsylvania, who precipitated decisions on this subject? What can be the views of those gentlemen in Boston, who countenanced the Printers in shutting up the press against a fair and free investigation of this important system in the usual way. The members of the convention have done their duty—why should some of them fly to their states—almost forget a propriety of behaviour, and precipitate measures for the adoption of a system of their own making? I confess candidly, when I consider these circumstances in connection with the unguarded parts of the system I have mentioned, I feel disposed to proceed with very great caution, and to pay more attention than usual to the conduct of particular characters. If the constitution presented be a good one, it will stand the test with a well informed people: all are agreed there shall be state conventions to examine it; and we must believe it will be adopted, unless we suppose it is a bad one, or that those conventions will make false divisions respecting it. I admit improper measures are taken against the adoption of the system as well for it—all who object to the plan proposed ought to point out the defects objected to, and to propose those amendments with which they can accept it, or to propose some other system of government, that the public mind may be known, and that we may be brought to agree in some system of government, to strengthen and execute the present, or to provide a substitute. I consider the field of enquiry just opened, and that we are to look to the state conventions for ultimate decisions on the subject before us; it is not to be presumed, that they will differ about small amendments, and lose a system when they shall have made it substantially good; but touching the essential amendments, it is to be presumed the several conventions will pursue the most rational measures to agree in and obtain them; and such defects as they shall discover and not remove, they will probably notice, keep them in view as the ground work of future amendments, and in the firm and manly language which every free people ought to use, will suggest to those who may here-after administer the government, that it is their expectation, that the system will be so organized by legislative acts, and the government so administered, as to render those defects as little injurious as possible.—Our countrymen are entitled to an honest and faithful government; to a government of laws and not of men; and also to one of their chusing—as a citizen of the country, I wish to see these objects secured, and licentious, assuming, and overbearing men restrained; if the constitution or social compact be vague and unguarded, then we depend wholly upon the prudence, wisdom and moderation of those who manage the affairs of government; or on what, probably, is equally uncertain and precarious, the success of the people oppressed by the abuse of government, in receiving it from the hands of those who abuse it, and placing it in the hands of those who will use it well.

In every point of view, therefore, in which I have been able, as yet, to contemplate this subject, I can discern but one rational mode of proceeding relative to it; and that is to examine it with freedom and candour, to have state conventions some months hence, which shall examine coolly every article, clause, and word in the system proposed, and to adopt it with such amendments as they shall think fit. How far the state conventions ought to pursue the mode prescribed by the federal convention of adopting or rejecting the plan in toto, I leave it to them to determine. Our examination of the subject hitherto has been rather of a general nature. The republican characters in the several states, who wish to make this plan more adequate to security of liberty and property, and to the duration of the principles of a free government, will, no doubt, collect their opinions to certain points, and accurately define those alterations and amendments they wish; if it shall be found they essentially disagree in them, the conventions will then be able to determine whether to adopt the plan as it is, or what will be proper to be done.

Under these impressions, and keeping in view the improper and unadvisable lodgment of powers in the general government, organized as it at present is, touching internal taxes, armies and militia, the elections of its own members, causes between citizens of different states, &c. and the want of a more perfect bill of rights, &c.—I drop the subject for the present, and when I shall have leisure to revise and correct my ideas respecting it, and to collect into points the opinions of those who wish to make the system more secure and safe, perhaps I may proceed to point out particularly for your consideration, the amendments which ought to be ingrafted into this system, not only in conformity to my own, but the deliberate opinions of others—you will with me perceive, that the objections to the plan proposed may, by a more leisure examination be set in a stronger point of view, especially the important one, that there is no substantial representation in the people provided for in a government, in which the most essential powers, even as to the internal police of the country, is proposed to be lodged.

I think the honest and substantial part of the community, will wish to see this system altered, permanency and consistency given to the constitution we shall adopt; and therefore they will be anxious to apportion the powers to the features and organization of the government, and to see abuse in the exercise of power more effectually guarded against. It is suggested, that state officers, from interested motives will oppose the constitution itself—I see no reason for this, their places in general will not be effected, but new openings to offices and places of profit must evidently be made by the adoption of the constitution in its present form.

Thomas Jefferson to William Stephens Smith

Paris Nov. 13. 1787.

DEAR SIR

I am now to acknolege the receipt of your favors of October the 4th. 8th. and 26th. In the last you apologize for your letters of introduction to Americans coming here. It is so far from needing apology on your part, that it calls for thanks on mine. I endeavor to shew civilities to all the Americans who come here, and who will give me opportunities of doing it: and it is a matter of comfort to know from a good quarter what they are, and how far I may go in my attentions to them.—Can you send me Woodmason's bills for the two copying presses for the M. de la fayette, and the M. de Chastellux? The latter makes one article in a considerable account, of old standing, and which I cannot present for want of this article.—I do not know whether it is to yourself or Mr. Adams I am to give my thanks for the copy of the new constitution. I beg leave through you to place them where due. It will be yet three weeks before I shall receive them from America. There are very good articles in it: and very bad. I do not know which preponderate. What we have lately read in the history of Holland, in the chapter on the Stadtholder, would have sufficed to set me against a Chief magistrate eligible for a long duration, if I had ever been disposed towards one: and what we have always read of the elections of Polish kings should have forever excluded the idea of one continuable for life. Wonderful is the effect of impudent and persevering lying. The British ministry have so long hired their gazetteers to repeat and model into every form lies about our being in anarchy, that the world has at length believed them, the English nation has believed them, the ministers themselves have come to believe them, and what is more wonderful, we have believed them ourselves. Yet where does this anarchy exist? Where did it ever exist, except in the single instance of Massachusets? And can history produce an instance of a rebellion so honourably conducted? I say nothing of it's motives. They were founded in ignorance, not wickedness. God forbid we should ever be 20. years without such a rebellion. The people can not be all, and always, well informed. The part which is wrong will be discontented in proportion to the importance of the facts they misconceive. If they remain quiet under such misconceptions it is a lethargy, the forerunner of death to the public liberty. We have had 13. states independant 11. years. There has been one rebellion. That comes to one rebellion in a century and a half for each state. What country before ever existed a century and half without a rebellion? And what country can preserve it's liberties if their rulers are not warned from time to time that their people preserve the spirit of resistance? Let them take arms. The remedy is to set them right as to facts, pardon and pacify them. What signify a few lives lost in a century or two? The tree of liberty must be refreshed from time to time with the blood of patriots and tyrants. It is it's natural manure. Our Convention has been too much impressed by the insurrection of Massachusets: and in the spur of the moment they are setting up a kite to keep the hen yard in order. I hope in god this article will be rectified before the new constitution is accepted.—You ask me if any thing transpires here on the subject of S. America? Not a word. I know that there are combustible materials there, and that they wait the torch only. But this country probably will join the extinguishers.—The want of facts worth communicating to you has occasioned me to give a little loose to dissertation. We must be contented to amuse, when we cannot inform. Present my respects to Mrs. Smith, and be assured of the sincere esteem of Dear Sir Your friend & servant,

TH: JEFFERSON

George Mason: Objections to the Constitution

circulated early October 1787, published in full
in the *Virginia Journal* (Alexandria), November 22, 1787

To the PRINTERS of the VIRGINIA JOURNAL
and ALEXANDRIA ADVERTISER.

Gentlemen, At this important crisis when we are about to determine upon a government which is not to effect us for a month, for a year, or for our lives: but which, it is probable, will extend its consequences to the remotest posterity, it behoves every friend to the rights and privileges of man, and particularly those who are interested in the prosperity and happiness of this country, to step forward and offer their sentiments upon the subject in an open, candid and independent manner.—Let the constitution proposed by the late Convention be dispassionately considered and fully canvassed.—Let no citizen of the United States of America, who is capable of discussing the important subject, retire from the field.—And, above all, let no one disseminate his objections to, or his reasons for approving of the constitution in such a manner as to gain partizans to his opinion, without giving them an opportunity of seeing how effectually his sentiments may be controverted, or how far his arguments may be invalidated.—For when a man of acknowledged abilities and great influence (and particularly one who has paid attention to the subject) *hands forth* his opinion, upon a matter of general concern, among those upon whom he has reason to think it will make the most favorable impression, without submitting it to the test of a public investigation, he may be truly said to take an undue advantage of his influence, and appearances would justify a supposition that he wished to effect, in a clandestine manner, that which he could not accomplish by an open and candid application to the public.

I expected, Gentlemen, that Col. Mason's objections to the proposed constitution would have been conveyed to the public, before this time, through the channel of your, or some other paper, but as my expectations, in that respect, have not yet been gratified, I shall take the liberty to send you a copy of

them for publication, which I think must be highly acceptable
to a number of your customers who have not had an opportunity of seeing them in manuscript.

"*Objections to the Constitution of Government formed by the Convention.*

"There is no declaration of rights; and the laws of the general
government being paramount to the laws and constitutions
of the several States, the declarations of rights in the separate
States are no security. Nor are the people secured even in the
enjoyment of the benefits of the common law, which stands
here upon no other foundation than its having been adopted
by the respective acts forming the constitutions of the several
States.

"In the House of Representatives there is not the substance,
but the shadow only of representation; which can never produce proper information in the Legislature, or inspire confidence in the people; the laws will therefore be generally made
by men little concerned in, and unacquainted with their effects
and consequences.*

"The Senate have the power of altering all money-bills,
and of originating appropriations of money, and the salaries
of the officers of their own appointment in conjunction with
the President of the United States; although they are not the
representatives of the people, or amenable to them.

"These with their other great powers (viz. their power in
the appointment of ambassadors and other public officers, in
making treaties, and in trying all impeachments) their influence upon and connection with the supreme executive from
these causes, their duration of office, and their being a constant
existing body almost continually sitting, joined with their being one complete branch of the Legislature, will destroy any
balance in the government, and enable them to accomplish
what usurpations they please upon the rights and liberties of
the people.

"The judiciary of the United States is so constructed and
extended as to absorb and destroy the judiciaries of the several

---

*Col. Mason acknowledges that this objection was in some degree lessened
by inserting the word *thirty* instead of *forty*, as it was at first determined, in the
3d clause of the 2d section of the 1st article.

States; thereby rendering law as tedious, intricate and expensive, and justice as unattainable by a great part of the community, as in England, and enabling the rich to oppress and ruin the poor.

"The President of the United States has no constitutional council (a thing unknown in any safe and regular government) he will therefore be unsupported by proper information and advice; and will be generally directed by minions and favorites—or he will become a tool to the Senate—or a Council of State will grow out of the principal officers of the great departments; the worst and most dangerous of all ingredients for such a council in a free country; for they may be induced to join in any dangerous or oppressive measures, to shelter themselves, and prevent an inquiry into their own misconduct in office; whereas had a constitutional council been formed (as was proposed) of six members, viz. two from the eastern, two from the middle, and two from the southern States, to be appointed by vote of the States in the House of Representatives, with the same duration and rotation in office as the Senate, the Executive would always have had safe and proper information and advice, the President of such a council might have acted as Vice-President of the United States, pro tempore, upon any vacancy or disability of the chief Magistrate; and long continued sessions of the Senate would in a great measure have been prevented.

"From this fatal defect of a constitutional council has arisen the improper power of the Senate, in the appointment of public officers, and the alarming dependance and connection between that branch of the Legislature and the supreme Executive.

"Hence also sprung that unnecessary and dangerous officer the Vice-President; who for want of other employment is made President of the Senate; thereby dangerously blending the executive and legislative powers; besides always giving to some one of the States an unnecessary and unjust preeminence over the others.

"The President of the United States has the unrestrained power of granting pardons for treason; which may be sometimes exercised to screen from punishment those whom he had secretly instigated to commit the crime, and thereby prevent a discovery of his own guilt.

"By declaring all treaties supreme laws of the land, the Executive and the Senate have, in many cases, an exclusive power of legislation; which might have been avoided by proper distinctions with respect to treaties, and requiring the assent of the House of Representatives, where it could be done with safety.

"By requiring only a majority to make all commercial and navigation laws, the five southern States (whose produce and circumstances are totally different from that of the eight northern and eastern States) will be ruined; for such rigid and premature regulations may be made, as will enable the merchants of the northern and eastern States not only to demand an exorbitant freight, but to monopolize the purchase of the commodities at their own price, for many years: To the great injury of the landed interest, and impoverishment of the people: And the danger is the greater, as the gain on one side will be in proportion to the loss on the other. Whereas requiring two-thirds of the members present in both houses would have produced mutual moderation, promoted the general interest and removed an insuperable objection to the adoption of the government.

"Under their own construction of the general clause at the end of the enumerated powers, the Congress may grant monopolies in trade and commerce, constitute new crimes, inflict unusual and severe punishments, and extend their power as far as they shall think proper; so that the State Legislatures have no security for the powers now presumed to remain to them; or the people for their rights.

"There is no declaration of any kind for preserving the liberty of the press, the trial by jury in civil causes; nor against the danger of standing armies in time of peace.

"The State Legislatures are restrained from laying export duties on their own produce.

"The general Legislature is restrained from prohibiting the further importation of slaves for twenty odd years; though such importations render the United States weaker, and more vulnerable, and less capable of defence.

"Both the general Legislature and the State Legislatures are expressly prohibited making ex post facto laws; though there never was nor can be a Legislature but must and will make such laws, when necessity and the public safety require them, which will hereafter be a breach of all the constitutions in the Union, and afford precedents for other innovations.

"This government will commence in a moderate aristocracy; it is at present impossible to foresee whether it will, in its operation, produce a monarchy, or a corrupt oppressive aristocracy; it will most probably vibrate some years between the two, and then terminate between the one and the other."

Many of the foregoing objections and the reasonings upon them, appear to be calculated more to alarm the fears of the people, than to answer any good or valuable purpose.—Some of them are raised upon so slender a foundation as would render it doubtful whether they were the production of Col. *Mason*'s abilities, if an incontestible evidence of their being so could not be adduced.

November 19, 1787.

Robert Yates and John Lansing, Jr., to Governor George Clinton

Daily Advertiser (New York), January 14, 1788

Albany, Dec. 21, 1787.

SIR, We do ourselves the honor to advise your Excellency, that, in pursuance of concurrent resolutions of the Honorable Senate and Assembly, we have, together with Mr. Hamilton, attended the Convention appointed for revising the articles of Confederation, and reporting amendments to the same.

It is with the sincerest concern we observe, that in the prosecution of the important objects of our mission, we have been reduced to the disagreeable alternative of either exceeding the powers delegated to us, and giving our assent to measures which we conceived destructive of the political happiness of the citizens of the United States; or opposing our opinion to that of a body of respectable men, to whom those citizens had given the most unequivocal proofs of confidence. Thus circumstanced, under these impressions, to have hesitated would have been to be culpable. We therefore gave the principles of the Constitution, which has received the sanction of a majority of the Convention, our decided and unreserved dissent; but we must candidly confess, that we should have been equally opposed to any system, however modified, which had in object the consolidation of the United States into one Government.

We beg leave briefly to state some cogent reasons which, among others, influenced us to decide against a consolidation of the States. These are reducible into two heads.

First. The limited and well defined powers under which we acted, and which could not, on any possible construction, embrace an idea of such magnitude as to assent to a general Constitution in subversion of that of the State.

Secondly. A conviction of the impracticability of establishing a general Government, pervading every part of the United States, and extending essential benefits to all.

Our powers were explicit, and confined to the *sole and express purpose of revising the articles of Confederation*, and reporting such alterations and provisions therein, as should render the Federal Constitution adequate to the exigencies of Government, and the preservation of the Union.

From these expressions, we were led to believe that a system of consolidated Government, could not, in the remotest degree, have been in contemplation of the Legislature of this State, for that so important a trust, as the adopting measures which tended to deprive the State Government of its most essential rights of Sovereignty, and to place it in a dependent situation, could not have been confided, by implication, and the circumstance, that the acts of the Convention were to receive a State approbation, in the last resort, forcibly corroborated the opinion, that our powers could not involve the subversion of a Constitution, which being immediately derived from the people, could only be abolished by their express consent, and not by a Legislature, possessing authority vested in them for its preservation. Nor could we suppose, that if it had been the intention of the Legislature to abrogate the existing Confederation, they would, in such pointed terms, have directed the attention of their delegates to the revision and amendment of it, in total exclusion of every other idea.

Reasoning in this manner, we were of opinion, that the leading feature of every amendment ought to be the preservation of the individual States, in their uncontroled constitutional rights; and that, in reserving these, a mode might have been devised, of granting to the Confederacy, the monies arising from a general system of revenue, the power of regulating commerce, and enforcing the observance of Foreign treaties, and other necessary matters of less moment.

Exclusive of our objections, originating from the want of power, we entertained an opinion that a general Government, however guarded by declarations of rights or cautionary provisions, must unavoidably, in a short time, be productive of the destruction of the civil liberty of such citizens who could be effectually coerced by it; by reason of the extensive territory of the United States; the dispersed situation of its inhabitants, and the insuperable difficulty of controling or counteracting the views of a set of men (however unconstitutional and oppressive their acts might be) possessed of all the powers of Government, and who, from their remoteness from their constituents, and necessary permanency of office, could not be supposed to be uniformly actuated by an attention to their welfare and happiness; that however wise and energetic the principles of the general Government might be, the extremities of the United States could not be kept in due submission and obedience to its laws at the distance of many hundred miles from the seat of Government; that if the general Legislature was composed of so numerous a body of men as to represent the interest of all the inhabitants of the United States in the usual and true ideas of representation, the expence of supporting it would become intolerably burthensome, and that if a few only were invested with a power of legislation, the interests of a great majority of the inhabitants of the United States must necessarily be unknown, or if known even in the first stages of the operations of the new Government, unattended to.

These reasons were in our opinion conclusive against any system of consolidated Government: to that recommended by the Convention we suppose most of them forcibly apply.

It is not our intention to pursue this subject further than merely to explain our conduct in the discharge of the trust which the Honorable the Legislature reposed in us—interested however, as we are in common with our fellow citizens in the result, we cannot forbear to declare that we have the strongest apprehensions that a Government so organized as that recommended by the Convention, cannot afford that security to equal and permanent liberty, which we wished to make an invariable object of our pursuit.

We were not present at the completion of the New Constitution; but before we left the Convention, its principles were so well established as to convince us that no alteration was to be expected, to conform it to our ideas of expediency and safety. A persuasion that our further attendance would be fruitless and unavailing, rendered us less solicitious to return.

We have thus explained our motives for opposing the adoption of the National Constitution, which we conceived it our duty to communicate to your Excellency, to be submitted to the consideration of the Hon. Legislature.

We have the Honor to be, with the greatest Respect, your Excellency's most obedient and very humble Servants,

PART 3:
TOWARD A NEW UNDERSTANDING OF POLITICS

Two of the Revolution's elder statesmen, **Samuel Adams** of Massachusetts and **Richard Henry Lee** of Virginia, feared that the new Constitution would obliterate the state governments and leave no protection for civil liberty. **James Madison** in **Federalist 10** countered this fear, arguing that by extending the sphere of the republic to encompass more diverse interests the structure of the new system would make difficult the forming of a single tyrannical majority. **Roger Sherman** reminded Connecticut readers that their state Bill of Rights was only a "paper protection." **Oliver Ellsworth** addressed the concerns of pious Congregationalists and Anglicans in Connecticut who feared that the lack of religious tests for officeholders would open the way for nonbelievers to wield power. The new Constitution did not have the "cob-web barriers" of religious tests that promoted religious persecution and blatant hypocrisy, but instead trusted the people to elect "sincere friends of religion." **John Stevens, Jr.**, in New Jersey argued that the new system protected liberty by having the different parts of the government check usurpations of power by the other parts. *Brutus IV* warned that under the Constitution a small number of men would hold power in the House of Representatives—with only thirty-three members required for a quorum, seventeen members could form a majority. **Alexander Hamilton** in **Federalist 23** and *Brutus VII* debated Congress's power over the military—a debate that quickly turned to Congress's power over revenue, with Hamilton continuing that discussion in **Federalist 30**.

Publius (James Madison)
The Federalist No. 10

Daily Advertiser (New York), November 22, 1787

To the People of the State of New-York.

Among the numerous advantages promised by a well constructed Union, none deserves to be more accurately developed than its tendency to break and control the violence of
faction. The friend of popular governments, never finds himself so much alarmed for their character and fate, as when he
contemplates their propensity to this dangerous vice. He will
not fail therefore to set a due value on any plan which, without violating the principles to which he is attached, provides
a proper cure for it. The instability, injustice and confusion
introduced into the public councils, have in truth been the
mortal diseases under which popular governments have every where perished; as they continue to be the favorite and
fruitful topics from which the adversaries to liberty derive their
most specious declamations. The valuable improvements made
by the American Constitutions on the popular models, both
ancient and modern, cannot certainly be too much admired;
but it would be an unwarrantable partiality, to contend that
they have as effectually obviated the danger on this side as was
wished and expected. Complaints are every where heard from
our most considerate and virtuous citizens, equally the friends
of public and private faith, and of public and personal liberty;
that our governments are too unstable; that the public good is
disregarded in the conflicts of rival parties; and that measures
are too often decided, not according to the rules of justice, and
the rights of the minor party; but by the superior force of an
interested and over-bearing majority. However anxiously we
may wish that these complaints had no foundation, the evidence of known facts will not permit us to deny that they are
in some degree true. It will be found indeed, on a candid review of our situation, that some of the distresses under which
we labor, have been erroneously charged on the operation of
our governments; but it will be found, at the same time, that

other causes will not alone account for many of our heaviest misfortunes; and particularly, for that prevailing and increasing distrust of public engagements, and alarm for private rights, which are echoed from one end of the continent to the other. These must be chiefly, if not wholly, effects of the unsteadiness and injustice, with which a factious spirit has tainted our public administration.

By a faction I understand a number of citizens, whether amounting to a majority or minority of the whole, who are united and actuated by some common impulse of passion, or of interest, adverse to the rights of other citizens, or to the permanent and aggregate interests of the community.

There are two methods of curing the mischiefs of faction: the one, by removing its causes; the other, by controling its effects.

There are again two methods of removing the causes of faction: the one by destroying the liberty which is essential to its existence; the other, by giving to every citizen the same opinions, the same passions, and the same interests.

It could never be more truly said than of the first remedy, that it is worse than the disease. Liberty is to faction, what air is to fire, an aliment without which it instantly expires. But it could not be a less folly to abolish liberty, which is essential to political life, because it nourishes faction, than it would be to wish the annihilation of air, which is essential to animal life, because it imparts to fire its destructive agency.

The second expedient is as impracticable, as the first would be unwise. As long as the reason of man continues fallible, and he is at liberty to exercise it, different opinions will be formed. As long as the connection subsists between his reason and his self-love, his opinions and his passions will have a reciprocal influence on each other; and the former will be objects to which the latter will attach themselves. The diversity in the faculties of men from which the rights of property originate, is not less an insuperable obstacle to a uniformity of interests. The protection of these faculties is the first object of Government. From the protection of different and unequal faculties of acquiring property, the possession of different degrees and kinds of property immediately results: and from the influence of these on the sentiments and views of the respective proprietors, ensues a division of the society into different interests and parties.

The latent causes of faction are thus sown in the nature of man; and we see them every where brought into different degrees of activity, according to the different circumstances of civil society. A zeal for different opinions concerning religion, concerning Government, and many other points, as well of speculation as of practice; an attachment to different leaders ambitiously contending for pre-eminence and power; or to persons of other descriptions whose fortunes have been interesting to the human passions, have in turn divided mankind into parties, inflamed them with mutual animosity, and rendered them much more disposed to vex and oppress each other, than to co-operate for their common good. So strong is this propensity of mankind to fall into mutual animosities, that where no substantial occasion presents itself, the most frivolous and fanciful distinctions have been sufficient to kindle their unfriendly passions, and excite their most violent conflicts. But the most common and durable source of factions, has been the various and unequal distribution of property. Those who hold, and those who are without property, have ever formed distinct interests in society. Those who are creditors, and those who are debtors, fall under a like discrimination. A landed interest, a manufacturing interest, a mercantile interest, a monied interest, with many lesser interests, grow up of necessity in civilized nations, and divide them into different classes, actuated by different sentiments and views. The regulation of these various and interfering interests forms the principal task of modern Legislation, and involves the spirit of party and faction in the necessary and ordinary operations of Government.

No man is allowed to be a judge in his own cause; because his interest would certainly bias his judgment, and, not improbably, corrupt his integrity. With equal, nay with greater reason, a body of men, are unfit to be both judges and parties, at the same time; yet, what are many of the most important acts of legislation, but so many judicial determinations, not indeed concerning the rights of single persons, but concerning the rights of large bodies of citizens; and what are the different classes of legislators, but advocates and parties to the causes which they determine? Is a law proposed concerning private debts? It is a question to which the creditors are parties on one side, and the debtors on the other. Justice ought to hold the balance between them. Yet the parties are and must be themselves the judges; and the most numerous party, or, in other words, the most powerful faction must be expected to prevail. Shall domestic manufactures be encouraged, and in what degree, by restrictions on foreign manufactures? are questions which would be differently decided by the landed and the manufacturing classes; and probably by neither, with a sole regard to justice and the public good. The apportionment of taxes on the various descriptions of property, is an act which seems to require the most exact impartiality; yet there is perhaps no legislative act in which greater opportunity and temptation are given to a predominant party, to trample on the rules of justice. Every shilling with which they over-burden the inferior number, is a shilling saved to their own pockets.

It is in vain to say, that enlightened statesmen will be able to adjust these clashing interests, and render them all subservient to the public good. Enlightened statesmen will not always be at the helm: Nor, in many cases, can such an adjustment be made at all, without taking into view indirect and remote considerations, which will rarely prevail over the immediate interest which one party may find in disregarding the rights of another, or the good of the whole.

The inference to which we are brought, is, that the *causes* of faction cannot be removed; and that relief is only to be sought in the means of controling its *effects*.

If a faction consists of less than a majority, relief is supplied by the republican principle, which enables the majority to defeat its sinister views by regular vote: It may clog the administration, it may convulse the society; but it will be unable to execute and mask its violence under the forms of the Constitution. When a majority is included in a faction, the form of popular government on the other hand enables it to sacrifice to its ruling passion or interest, both the public good and the rights of other citizens. To secure the public good, and private rights, against the danger of such a faction, and at the same time to preserve the spirit and the form of popular government, is then the great object to which our enquiries are directed: Let me add that it is the great desideratum, by which alone this form of government can be rescued from the opprobrium under which it has so long labored, and be recommended to the esteem and adoption of mankind.

By what means is this object attainable? Evidently by one of two only. Either the existence of the same passion or interest in a majority at the same time, must be prevented; or the majority, having such co-existent passion or interest, must be rendered, by their number and local situation, unable to concert and carry into effect schemes of oppression. If the impulse and the opportunity be suffered to coincide, we well know that neither moral nor religious motives can be relied on as an adequate control. They are not found to be such on the injustice and violence of individuals, and lose their efficacy in proportion to the number combined together; that is, in proportion as their efficacy becomes needful.

From this view of the subject, it may be concluded, that a pure Democracy, by which I mean, a Society, consisting of a small number of citizens, who assemble and administer the Government in person, can admit of no cure for the mischiefs of faction. A common passion or interest will, in almost every case, be felt by a majority of the whole; a communication and concert results from the form of Government itself; and there is nothing to check the inducements to sacrifice the weaker party, or an obnoxious individual. Hence it is, that such Democracies have ever been spectacles of turbulence and contention; have ever been found incompatible with personal security, or the rights of property; and have in general been as short in their lives, as they have been violent in their deaths. Theoretic politicians, who have patronized this species of Government, have erroneously supposed, that by reducing mankind to a perfect equality in their political rights, they would, at the same time, be perfectly equalized and assimilated in their possessions, their opinions, and their passions.

A Republic, by which I mean a Government in which the scheme of representation takes place, opens a different prospect, and promises the cure for which we are seeking. Let us examine the points in which it varies from pure Democracy, and we shall comprehend both the nature of the cure, and the efficacy which it must derive from the Union.

The two great points of difference between a Democracy and a Republic are, first, the delegation of the Government, in the latter, to a small number of citizens elected by the rest: secondly, the greater number of citizens, and greater sphere of country, over which the latter may be extended.

The effect of the first difference is, on the one hand to refine and enlarge the public views, by passing them through the medium of a chosen body of citizens, whose wisdom may best discern the true interest of their country, and whose patriotism and love of justice, will be least likely to sacrifice it to temporary or partial considerations. Under such a regulation, it may well happen that the public voice pronounced by the representatives of the people, will be more consonant to the public good, than if pronounced by the people themselves convened for the purpose. On the other hand, the effect may be inverted. Men of factious tempers, of local prejudices, or of sinister designs, may by intrigue, by corruption or by other means, first obtain the suffrages, and then betray the interests of the people. The question resulting is, whether small or extensive Republics are most favorable to the election of proper guardians of the public weal; and it is clearly decided in favor of the latter by two obvious considerations.

In the first place it is to be remarked that however small the Republic may be, the Representatives must be raised to a certain number, in order to guard against the cabals of a few; and that however large it may be, they must be limited to a certain number, in order to guard against the confusion of a multitude. Hence the number of Representatives in the two cases, not being in proportion to that of the Constituents, and being proportionally greatest in the small Republic, it follows, that if the proportion of fit characters, be not less, in the large than in the small Republic, the former will present a greater option, and consequently a greater probability of a fit choice.

In the next place, as each Representative will be chosen by a greater number of citizens in the large than in the small Republic, it will be more difficult for unworthy candidates to practise with success the vicious arts, by which elections are too often carried; and the suffrages of the people being more free, will be more likely to centre on men who possess the most attractive merit, and the most diffusive and established characters.

It must be confessed, that in this, as in most other cases, there is a mean, on both sides of which inconveniencies will be found to lie. By enlarging too much the number of electors, you render the representative too little acquainted with all their local circumstances and lesser interests; as by reducing it too much, you render him unduly attached to these, and too little fit to comprehend and pursue great and national objects. The Federal Constitution forms a happy combination in this respect; the great and aggregate interests being referred to the national, the local and particular, to the state legislatures.

The other point of difference is, the greater number of citizens and extent of territory which may be brought within the compass of Republican, than of Democratic Government; and it is this circumstance principally which renders factious combinations less to be dreaded in the former, than in the latter. The smaller the society, the fewer probably will be the distinct parties and interests composing it; the fewer the distinct parties and interests, the more frequently will a majority be found of the same party; and the smaller the number of individuals composing a majority, and the smaller the compass within which they are placed, the more easily will they concert and execute their plans of oppression. Extend the sphere, and you take in a greater variety of parties and interests; you make it less probable that a majority of the whole will have a common motive to invade the rights of other citizens; or if such a common motive exists, it will be more difficult for all who feel it to discover their own strength, and to act in unison with each other. Besides other impediments, it may be remarked, that where there is a consciousness of unjust or dishonorable purposes, communication is always checked by distrust, in proportion to the number whose concurrence is necessary.

Hence it clearly appears, that the same advantage, which a Republic has over a Democracy, in controling the effects of faction, is enjoyed by a large over a small Republic—is enjoyed by the Union over the States composing it. Does this advantage consist in the substitution of Representatives, whose enlightened views and virtuous sentiments render them superior to local prejudices, and to schemes of injustice? It will not be denied, that the Representation of the Union will be most likely to possess these requisite endowments. Does it consist in the greater security afforded by a greater variety of parties, against the event of any one party being able to outnumber and oppress the rest? In an equal degree does the encreased variety of parties, comprised within the Union, encrease this security. Does it, in fine, consist in the greater obstacles opposed to the concert and accomplishment of the secret wishes of an unjust and interested majority? Here, again, the extent of the Union gives it the most palpable advantage.

The influence of factious leaders may kindle a flame within their particular States, but will be unable to spread a general conflagration through the other States: a religious sect, may degenerate into a political faction in a part of the Confederacy; but the variety of sects dispersed over the entire face of it, must secure the national Councils against any danger from that source: a rage for paper money, for an abolition of debts, for an equal division of property, or for any other improper or wicked project, will be less apt to pervade the whole body of the Union, than a particular member of it; in the same proportion as such a malady is more likely to taint a particular county or district, than an entire State.

In the extent and proper structure of the Union, therefore, we behold a Republican remedy for the diseases most incident to Republican Government. And according to the degree of pleasure and pride, we feel in being Republicans, ought to be our zeal in cherishing the spirit, and supporting the character of Federalists.

A Countryman (Roger Sherman) II

New Haven Gazette (Connecticut), November 22, 1787

To the PEOPLE *of* Connecticut.

It is fortunate that you have been but little distressed with that torrent of impertinence and folly, with which the newspaper politicians have overwhelmed many parts of our country.

It is enough that you should have heard, that one party has seriously urged, that we should adopt the *New Constitution* because it has been approved by *Washington* and *Franklin*: and the other, with all the solemnity of apostolic address to *Men, Brethren, Fathers, Friends and Countrymen*, have urged that we should reject, as dangerous, every clause thereof, because that *Washington* is more used to command as a soldier, than to reason as a politician—*Franklin* is *old*—others are *young*—and *Wilson* is *haughty*. You are too well informed to decide by the opinion of others, and too independent to need a caution against undue influence.

Of a very different nature, tho' only one degree better than the other reasoning, is all that sublimity of *nonsense* and *alarm*, that has been thundered against it in every shape of *metaphoric terror*, on the subject of a *bill of rights*, the *liberty of the press, rights of conscience, rights of taxation and election, trials in the vicinity, freedom of speech, trial by jury*, and a *standing army*. These last are undoubtedly important points, much too important to depend on mere paper protection. For, guard such privileges by the strongest expressions, still if you leave the legislative and executive power in the hands of those who are or may be disposed to deprive you of them—you are but slaves. Make an absolute monarch—give him the supreme authority, and guard as much as you will by bills of right, your liberty of the press, and trial by jury;—he will find means either to take them from you, or to render them useless.

The only real security that you can have for all your important rights must be in the nature of your government. If you suffer any man to govern you who is not strongly interested in supporting your privileges, you will certainly lose them. If you

are about to trust your liberties with people whom it is necessary to bind by stipulation, that they shall not keep a standing
army, your stipulation is not worth even the trouble of writing.
No bill of rights ever yet bound the supreme power longer
than the *honey moon* of a new married couple, unless the *rulers
were interested* in preserving the rights; and in that case they
have always been ready enough to declare the rights, and to
preserve them when they were declared.—The famous English
Magna Charta is but an act of parliament, which every subsequent parliament has had just as much constitutional power
to repeal and annul, as the parliament which made it had to
pass it at first. But the security of the nation has always been,
that their government was so formed, that at least *one branch*
of their legislature must be strongly interested to preserve the
rights of the nation.

You have a bill of rights in Connecticut (i.e.) your legislature many years since enacted that the subjects of this state
should enjoy certain privileges. Every assembly since that time,
could, by the same authority, enact that the subjects should
enjoy none of those privileges; and the only reason that it has
not long since been so enacted, is that your legislature were
as strongly interested in preserving those rights as any of the
subjects; and this is your only security that it shall not be so enacted at the next session of assembly: and it is security enough.

Your General Assembly under your present constitution are
supreme. They may keep troops on foot in the most profound
peace, if they think proper. They have heretofore abridged the
trial by jury in some causes, and they can again in all. They can
restrain the press, and may lay the most burdensome taxes if
they please, and who can forbid? But still the people are perfectly safe that not one of these events shall take place so long
as the members of the General assembly are as much interested, and interested in the same manner as the other subjects.

On examining the new proposed constitution, there can not
be a question, but that there is authority enough lodged in the
proposed federal Congress, if abused, to do the greatest injury.
And it is perfectly idle to object to it, that there is no bill of
rights, or to propose to add to it a provision that a trial by
jury shall in no case be omitted, or to patch it up by adding a
stipulation in favor of the press, or to guard it by removing the

paltry objection to the right of Congress to regulate the time and manner of elections.

If you can not prove by the best of all evidence, viz. by the *interest of the rulers*, that this authority will not be abused, or at least that those powers are not more likely to be abused by the Congress, than by those who now have the same powers, you must by no means adopt the constitution:—No, not with all the bills of rights and all the stipulations in favour of the people that can be made.

But if the members of Congress are to be interested just as you and I are, and just as the members of our present legislatures are interested, we shall be just as safe, with even supreme power, (if that were granted) in Congress, as in the General Assembly. If the members of Congress can take no improper step which will not affect them as much as it does us, we need not apprehend that they will usurp authorities not given them to injure that society of which they are a part.

The sole question, (so far as any apprehension of tyranny and oppression is concerned) ought to be, how are Congress formed? how far are the members interested to preserve your rights? how far have you a controul over them?—Decide this, and then all the questions about their power may be dismissed for the amusement of those politicians whose business it is to catch flies, or may occasionally furnish subjects for *George Bryan's* POMPOSITY, or the declamations of *Cato—An Old Whig—Son of Liberty—Brutus—Brutus junior—An Officer of the Continental Army,*—the more contemptible *Timoleon—* and the residue of that rabble of writers.

Brutus IV

New York Journal, November 29, 1787

To the PEOPLE *of the State of* NEW-YORK.

There can be no free government where the people are not possessed of the power of making the laws by which they are governed, either in their own persons, or by others substituted in their stead.

Experience has taught mankind, that legislation by representatives is the most eligible, and the only practicable mode in which the people of any country can exercise this right, either prudently or beneficially. But then, it is a matter of the highest importance, in forming this representation, that it be so constituted as to be capable of understanding the true interests of the society for which it acts, and so disposed as to pursue the good and happiness of the people as its ultimate end. The object of every free government is the public good, and all lesser interests yield to it. That of every tyrannical government, is the happiness and aggrandisement of one, or a few, and to this the public felicity, and every other interest must submit.—The reason of this difference in these governments is obvious. The first is so constituted as to collect the views and wishes of the whole people in that of their rulers, while the latter is so framed as to separate the interests of the governors from that of the governed. The principle of self love, therefore, that will influence the one to promote the good of the whole, will prompt the other to follow its own private advantage. The great art, therefore, in forming a good constitution, appears to be this, so to frame it, as that those to whom the power is committed shall be subject to the same feelings, and aim at the same objects as the people do, who transfer to them their authority. There is no possible way to effect this but by an equal, full and fair representation; this, therefore, is the great desideratum in politics. However fair an appearance any government may make, though it may possess a thousand plausible articles and be decorated with ever so many ornaments, yet if it is deficient in this essential principle of a full and just representation of the people, it will be only like a painted sepulcher—For, without this it cannot be a free government; let the administration of it be good or ill, it still will be a government, not according to the will of the people, but according to the will of a few.

To test this new constitution then, by this principle, is of the last importance—It is to bring it to the touch-stone of national liberty, and I hope I shall be excused, if, in this paper, I pursue the subject commenced in my last number, to wit, the necessity of an equal and full representation in the legislature.—In that, I showed that it was not equal, because the smallest states are to send the same number of members to the senate as the largest, and, because the slaves, who afford neither aid or defence to the government, are to encrease the proportion of members. To prove that it was not a just or adequate representation, it was urged, that so small a number could not resemble the people, or possess their sentiments and dispositions. That the choice of members would commonly fall upon the rich and great, while the middling class of the community would be excluded. That in so small a representation there was no security against bribery and corruption.

The small number which is to compose this legislature, will not only expose it to the danger of that kind of corruption, and undue influence, which will arise from the gift of places of honor and emolument, or the more direct one of bribery, but it will also subject it to another kind of influence no less fatal to the liberties of the people, though it be not so flagrantly repugnant to the principles of rectitude. It is not to be expected that a legislature will be found in any country that will not have some of its members, who will pursue their private ends, and for which they will sacrifice the public good. Men of this character are, generally, artful and designing, and frequently possess brilliant talents and abilities; they commonly act in concert, and agree to share the spoils of their country among them; they will keep their object ever in view, and follow it with constancy. To effect their purpose, they will assume any shape, and, Proteus like, mould themselves into any form—where they find members proof against direct bribery or gifts of offices, they will endeavor to mislead their minds by specious and false reasoning, to impose upon their unsuspecting honesty by an affectation of zeal for the public good; they will form juntos, and hold out-door meetings; they will operate upon the good nature of their opponents, by a thousand little attentions, and seize them into compliance by the earnestness of solicitation. Those who are acquainted with the manner of conducting business in public assemblies, know how prevalent art and address are in carrying a measure, even over men of the best intentions, and of good understanding. The firmest security against this kind of improper and dangerous influence, as well as all other, is a strong and numerous representation: in such a house of assembly, so great a number must be gained over, before the private views of individuals could be gratified that there could be scarce a hope of success. But in the fœderal assembly, seventeen men are all that is necessary to pass a law. It is probable, it will seldom happen that more than twenty-five will be requisite to form a majority, when it is considered what a number of places of honor and emolument will be in the gift of the executive, the powerful influence that great and designing men have over the honest and unsuspecting, by their art and address, their soothing manners and civilities, and their cringing flattery, joined with their affected patriotism; when these different species of influence are combined, it is scarcely to be hoped that a legislature, composed of so small a number, as the one proposed by the new constitution, will long resist their force. A farther objection against the feebleness of the representation is, that it will not possess the confidence of the people. The execution of the laws in a free government must rest on this confidence, and this must be founded on the good opinion they entertain of the framers of the laws. Every government must be supported, either by the people having such an attachment to it, as to be ready, when called upon, to support it, or by a force at the command of the government, to compel obedience. The latter mode destroys every idea of a free government; for the same force that may be employed to compel obedience to good laws, might, and probably would be used to wrest from the people their constitutional liberties.—Whether it is practicable to have a representation for the whole union sufficiently numerous to obtain that confidence which is necessary for the purpose of internal taxation, and other powers to which this proposed government extends, is an important question. I am clearly of opinion, it is not, and therefore I have stated this in my first number, as one of the reasons against going into so an entire consolidation of the states—one of the most capital errors in the system, is that of extending the powers of the fœderal government to objects to which it is not adequate, which it cannot exercise without endangering public liberty, and which it is not necessary they should possess, in order to preserve the union and manage our national concerns; of this, however, I shall treat more fully in some future paper—But, however this may be, certain it is, that the representation in the legislature is not so formed as to give reasonable ground for public trust.

In order for the people safely to repose themselves on their rulers, they should not only be of their own choice. But it is requisite they should be acquainted with their abilities to manage the public concerns with wisdom. They should be satisfied that those who represent them are men of integrity, who will pursue the good of the community with fidelity; and will not be turned aside from their duty by private interest, or corrupted by undue influence; and that they will have such a zeal for the good of those whom they represent, as to excite them to be deligent in their service; but it is impossible the people of the United States should have sufficient knowledge of their representatives, when the numbers are so few, to acquire any rational satisfaction on either of these points. The people of this state will have very little acquaintance with those who may be chosen to represent them; a great part of them will, probably, not know the characters of their own members, much less that of a majority of those who will compose the fœderal assembly; they will consist of men, whose names they have never heard, and of whose talents and regard for the public good, they are total strangers to; and they will have no persons so immediately of their choice so near them, of their neighbours and of their own rank in life, that they can feel themselves secure in trusting their interests in their hands. The representatives of the people cannot, as they now do, after they have passed laws, mix with the people, and explain to them the motives which induced the adoption of any measure, point out its utility, and remove objections or silence unreasonable clamours against it.—The number will be so small that but a very few of the most sensible and respectable yeomanry of the country can ever have any knowledge of them: being so far removed from the people, their station will be elevated and important, and they will be considered as ambitious and designing. They will not be viewed by the people as part of themselves, but as a body distinct from them, and having separate interests to pursue; the consequence will be, that a perpetual jealousy will exist in the minds of the people against them; their conduct will be narrowly watched; their measures scrutinized; and their laws opposed, evaded, or reluctantly obeyed. This is natural, and exactly corresponds with the conduct of individuals towards those in whose hands they intrust important concerns. If the person confided in, be a neighbour with whom his employer is intimately acquainted, whose talents, he knows, are sufficient to manage the business with which he is charged, his honesty and fidelity unsuspected, and his friendship and zeal for the service of his principal unquestionable, he will commit his affairs into his hands with unreserved confidence, and feel himself secure; all the transactions of the agent will meet with the most favorable construction, and the measures he takes will give satisfaction. But, if the person employed be a stranger, whom he has never seen, and whose character for ability or fidelity he cannot fully learn—If he is constrained to choose him, because it was not in his power to procure one more agreeable to his wishes, he will trust him with caution, and be suspicious of all his conduct.

If then this government should not derive support from the good will of the people, it must be executed by force, or not executed at all; either case would lead to the total destruction of liberty.—The convention seemed aware of this, and have therefore provided for calling out the militia to execute the laws of the union. If this system was so framed as to command that respect from the people, which every good free government will obtain, this provision was unnecessary—the people would support the civil magistrate. This power is a novel one, in free governments—these have depended for the execution of the laws on the Posse Comitatus, and never raised an idea, that the people would refuse to aid the civil magistrate in executing those laws they themselves had made. I shall now dismiss the subject of the incompetency of the representation, and proceed, as I promised, to shew, that, impotent as it is, the people have no security that they will enjoy the exercise of the right of electing this assembly, which, at best, can be considered but as the shadow of representation.

By section 4, article 1, the Congress are authorized, at any time, by law, to make, or alter, regulations respecting the time, place, and manner of holding elections for senators and representatives, except as to the places of choosing senators. By this clause the right of election itself, is, in a great measure, transferred from the people to their rulers.—One would think, that if any thing was necessary to be made a fundamental article of the original compact, it would be, that of fixing the branches of the legislature, so as to put it out of its power to alter itself by modifying the election of its own members at will and pleasure. When a people once resign the privilege of a fair election, they clearly have none left worth contending for.

It is clear that, under this article, the fœderal legislature may institute such rules respecting elections as to lead to the choice of one description of men. The weakness of the representation, tends but too certainly to confer on the rich and *well-born*, all honours; but the power granted in this article, may be so exercised, as to secure it almost beyond a possibility of controul. The proposed Congress may make the whole state one district, and direct, that the capital (the city of New-York, for instance) shall be the place for holding the election; the consequence would be, that none but men of the most elevated rank in society would attend, and they would as certainly choose men of their own class; as it is true what the *Apostle Paul* saith, that "no man ever yet hated his own flesh, but nourisheth and cherisheth it."—They may declare that those members who have the greatest number of votes, shall be considered as duly elected; the consequence would be that the people, who are dispersed in the interior parts of the state, would give their votes for a variety of candidates, while any order, or profession, residing in populous places, by uniting their interests, might procure whom they pleased to be chosen—and by this means the representatives of the state may be elected by one tenth part of the people who actually vote. This may be effected constitutionally, and by one of those silent operations which frequently takes place without being noticed, but which often produces such changes as entirely to alter a government, subvert a free constitution, and rivet the chains on a free people before they perceive they are forged. Had the power of regulating elections been left under the direction of the state legislatures, where the people are not only nominally but substantially represented, it would have been secure; but if it was taken out of their hands, it surely ought to have been fixed on such a basis as to have put it out of the power of the fœderal legislature to deprive the people of it by law. Provision should have been made for marking out the states into districts, and for choosing, by a majority of votes, a person out of each of them of permanent property and residence in the district which he was to represent.

If the people of America will submit to a constitution that will vest in the hands of any body of men a right to deprive them by law of the privilege of a fair election, they will submit to almost any thing. Reasoning with them will be in vain, they must be left until they are brought to reflection by feeling oppression—they will then have to wrest from their oppressors, by a strong hand, that which they now possess, and which they may retain if they will exercise but a moderate share of prudence and firmness.

I know it is said that the dangers apprehended from this clause are merely imaginary, that the proposed general legislature will be disposed to regulate elections upon proper principles, and to use their power with discretion, and to promote the public good. On this, I would observe, that constitutions are not so necessary to regulate the conduct of good rulers as to restrain that of bad ones.—Wise and good men will exercise power so as to promote the public happiness under any form of government. If we are to take it for granted, that those who administer the government under this system, will always pay proper attention to the rights and interests of the people, nothing more was necessary than to say who should be invested with the powers of government, and leave them to exercise it at will and pleasure. Men are apt to be deceived both with respect to their own dispositions and those of others. Though this truth is proved by almost every page of the history of nations, to wit, that power, lodged in the hands of rulers to be used at discretion, is almost always exercised to the oppression of the people, and the aggrandizement of themselves; yet most men think if it was lodged in their hands they would not employ it in this manner.—Thus when the prophet *Elisha* told *Hazael*, "I know the evil that thou wilt do unto the children of Israel; their strong holds wilt thou set on fire, and their young men, wilt thou slay with the sword, and wilt dash their children, and rip up their women with child." Hazael had no idea that he ever should be guilty of such horrid cruelty, and said to the prophet, "Is thy servant a dog that he should do this great thing." Elisha, answered, "The Lord hath shewed me that thou shalt be king of Syria." The event proved, that Hazael only wanted an opportunity to perpetrate these enormities without restraint, and he had a disposition to do them, though he himself knew it not.

Americanus (John Stevens, Jr.) III

Daily Advertiser (New York), November 30, 1787

"It is natural for a Republic to have only a small territory." It may be thought by some an unpardonable piece of temerity in me to deny the truth of this maxim of the celebrated Civilian, in so decisive a tone as I have ventured to do in a former paper. To satisfy those therefore, whose delicacy may be hurt on this occasion, I hope I shall be able before I finish this paper to bring about a perfect reconciliation between the Baron and myself; and thus deprive Cato of the assistance of this powerful auxiliary, on this occasion at least. It is manifest from a variety of passages, that Montesquieu's idea of a Republic, was a Government in which the collective body of the people, as in Democracy, or of the nobles, as in Aristocracy, possessed a share in the management of public affairs: Thus he tells us "the people in whom the supreme power resides ought to have the management of every thing within their reach." "It is likewise a fundamental law in Democracies, that the people should have the sole power to enact laws." It is obvious that to collect the suffrages of a numerous people, scattered over a wide extent of country on every law, on every public measure, would be utterly impracticable. According therefore to his idea of a Republican Government, this maxim of his, that a Republic should be confined to a small territory, is certainly a very just one. Should I be able to prove that the Governments of these States are founded on principles totally different from those which Montesquieu here had in view, it will then be manifest that Cato has lugged him into a controversy in which he is no ways concerned.

The Republics of antiquity were chiefly Democratic, those of modern date are chiefly Aristocratic. As to Aristocracies we have nothing to do with them. But let us enquire a little into the nature and genius of the ancient Republics of Greece and Rome. Cato's maxim, "that the safety of the people in a Republic depends on the share or proportion they have in the Government," seem to have been deemed by them indispensibly necessary; indeed, as they had no idea of appointing representatives to legislate for them, they had no other alternative; either the people collectively must retain to themselves a voice in the management of public affairs, or all pretensions to liberty must be resigned. To obviate the natural tendency of this radical defect in the frame of their Governments, they were under an absolute necessity of recurring to violent methods. To support these wretched institutions, the laws of nature herself were subverted. The life of a citizen was one continued effort of self-denial and restraint. Every social passion—all the finer feelings of the heart—the tender ties of parent and child—every enjoyment, whether of sentiment or of sense—every thing in short which renders life desirable, was relinquished. The Romans did not carry this system of self-denial to that extreme as was done by some of the Grecian States. They found however that a rigid attention to manners was indispensibly necessary. Magistrates were appointed for the express purpose of inspecting into the lives and conduct of every citizen—the public good superceded every consideration of a private nature—fathers condemned their own sons to the axe. Let it not be thought however that this exalted degree of patriotism—this rigid system of mortification and self-denial was the effect of choice; no! far from it. it was necessity that imposed it on them.—This magnanimous people saw plainly that their safety depended upon keeping up this austerity of manners. As from the very nature of this sort of Government there can be no regular checks established for preventing the abuse of power, the people are in a great measure constrained to rely on the patriotism and personal virtue of those citizens who compose the Government.

The Grecians and Romans have however infinite merit in subjecting themselves to so severe a discipline, in foregoing so many of the blessings and enjoyments of this life, for the sake of liberty.

The history of these States affords us very striking instances of the astonishing force of this passion of the human heart, when man is placed in a situation proper for displaying it.

Without a due attention to these distinctive properties of the Republics of antiquity, we cannot form an adequate idea of the immense advantages of a representative legislature. The people of Rome, of Sparta, &c. were obliged to keep a constant eye on the conduct of their rulers for this reason, and that they might be enabled to exercise their right of a personal vote on public affairs, it was absolutely necessary that the citizens be confined within a small compass.

But if matters can be so ordered, that by appointing Representatives, the people can have the business of the State transacted in a better manner than they can possibly do it themselves, there is then no determining what may be the extent of the state. Thus it will be found that the Government of the most extensive State of the Union, though greater perhaps than all the States of Greece put together, may be administered with infinitely more care and safety than was any one of them, though comprehended within the limits of a few square miles.

The major part of mankind are slaves to sound—the writings of a great man, who has distinguished himself in any of the walks of science, in a short time become "irrefragable axioms." Thus, thro' the indolence and inattention of some, and the knavery of others, error becomes at length so firmly established as to baffle, for a long time, the assaults of philosophy and truth.

And thus it is, that with those who suffer themselves to be carried away by a name, and attend not to things, the application Cato makes of Montesquieu's maxim to the Government of these States, would pass currently and without opposition. But this would be to sacrifice sense to sound with a vengeance.

The political institutions we have contrived and adopted in this new world differ as widely from the republics of the old, whether antient or modern, as does a well constructed edifice, where elegance and utility unite and harmonize, differ from a huge mishapen pile reared by Gothic ignorance and barbarity.

I have already remarked, that a Republic confined to a small territory, must, from its own nature, be incident to great inconvenience. Faction, instability, and frequent revolutions, are inherent properties. Besides, that its weakness exposes it to continual danger from the enterprizes of ambitious neighbours. What a capital improvement then is representation to a Republican Government. By this simple expedient can the sense of the people of an extensive Empire be collected with ease and certainty. By this admirable contrivance, the care and attention of Government is extended equally to every part—the wants and wishes of the most remote corners are known and attended to. But what is of infinite importance, a Government on this plan can be so constructed, as that the different parts of it shall form mutual checks on each other. This is not all, a number of lesser communities may be united under one head; and thus form an extensive Empire. But this new combination will give still greater security to liberty, because more checks will be added. The Government of the Union, and those of the States individually, will be watchful centinels on the conduct of each other. By this means the usurpations of power are guarded against, and liberty secured without the interference of the collective body of the people. Until this important discovery in the art of Government was made, the people themselves formed almost the only check on the Government. For, from the necessity of the case, the right of proposing new laws to the consideration of the people, necessarily devolved upon those who were entrusted with the execution of those laws. Now it may easily be conceived, that to counteract the sinister views of their rulers, it required the utmost circumspection in the people—indeed it was impossible, by the most active and vigilant attention to public officers, for the people to avoid being dupes to the artifices of designing men. This indeed is a business the people are by no means calculated for. Conscious of this inability, the Romans procured the establishment of tribunes, who were to be the guardians of the people's rights, and to defend their privileges against the power of the Senate and the Consuls. How well this expedient answered the end, history will inform us. All that train of unavoidable mischiefs, which necessarily attends the interference of the people in the management of public affairs, instantly vanish when we have recourse to a representative Legislature. Nothing more is then necessary to place liberty on the firmest basis, than the frequent recurrence of elections—that representation be adequate and proportionate—and that the Representatives be tied down from interfering in any shape, in the Executive parts of Government, but confined absolutely to the business of their mission, which should be Legislation solely. If these things are attended to, the people need be under no apprehensions about the management of affairs. From the very nature of things, these Representatives cannot fail of proving the faithful and effectual guardians of the people. Here then we have that grand desideratum, that has hitherto been wanting in all the popular Governments we are acquainted with, that the people may repose confidence in Government, without danger of its being abused. As these Representatives are chosen only for a short period, at the expiration of which, they are again reduced to the level of their fellow-citizens; and as, during their continuance in this service, they are absolutely prohibited from interfering in any of the Executive branches of the Government; thus it becoming impossible for them to form an interest separate from that of the community at large, they can have no motive whatever for betraying that of their Constituents. A Government formed on this plan, requires in the execution of it, none of those heroic virtues which we admire in the antients, and to us are known only by story. The sacrifice of our dearest interests, self-denial, and austerity of manners, are by no means necessary. Such a Government requires nothing more of its subjects than that they should study and pursue merely their own true interest and happiness. As it is adapted to the ordinary circumstances of mankind, requiring no extraordinary exertions to support it, it must of course be the more firm, secure and lasting. A Government thus founded on the broad basis of human nature, like a tree which is suffered to retain its native shape, will flourish for ages with little care or attention. But like this same tree, if distorted into a form unnatural and monstrous, will require the constant use of the pruning knife, and all the art and contrivance of a skilful operator, to counteract the efforts of nature against the violence which has been offered her.

I would not however, wish it to be thought, that it is in any degree my design to depreciate that amor patriæ, which is a sentiment so natural to the human breast, and which, when well directed, is capable of such glorious effects—but unfortunately for mankind, the majority possess it in a very gross degree. It is with them generally nothing more than a blind attachment to a party, or to the local interests of a narrow district.

Samuel Adams to Richard Henry Lee

Boston, December 3, 1787

I am to acknowledge your several Favours of the 5th and 27 of October, the one by the Post and the other by our worthy Friend Mr Gerry. The Session of our General Court which lasted six Weeks, and my Station there requiring my punctual & constant Attendance, prevented my considering the *new* Constitution as it is already called, so closely as was necessary for me before I should venture an Opinion.

I confess, as I enter the Building I stumble at the Threshold. I meet with a National Government, instead of a fœderal Union of Sovereign States. I am not able to conceive why the Wisdom of the Convention led them to give the Preference to the former before the latter. If the several States in the Union are to become one entire Nation, under one Legislature, the Powers of which shall extend to every Subject of Legislation, and its Laws be supreme & controul the whole, the Idea of Sovereignty in these States must be lost. Indeed I think, upon such a Supposition, those Sovereignties ought to be eradicated from the Mind; for they would be Imperia in Imperio justly deemd a Solecism in Politicks, & they would be highly dangerous, and destructive of the Peace Union and Safety of the Nation. And can this National Legislature be competent to make Laws for the *free* internal Government of one People, living in Climates so remote and whose "Habits & particular Interests" are and probably always will be so different. Is it to be expected that General Laws can be adapted to the Feelings of the more Eastern & the more Southern Parts of so extensive a Nation? It appears to me difficult if practicable. Hence then may we not look for Discontent, Mistrust, Disaffection to Government and frequent Insurrections, which will require standing Armies to suppress them in one Place & another where they may happen to arise. Or if Laws could be made, adapted to the local Habits Feelings, Views & Interests of those distant Parts, would they not cause Jealousies of Partiality in Government which would excite Envy and other malignant Passions productive of Wars and fighting. But should we continue distinct sovereign States, confederated for the Purposes of mutual Safety and Happiness, each contributing to the fœderal Head such a Part of its Sovereignty as would render the Government fully adequate to those Purposes and *no more*, the People would govern themselves more easily, the Laws of each State being well adapted to its own Genius & Circumstances, and the Liberties of the United States would be more secure than they can be, as I humbly conceive, under the proposed new Constitution. You are sensible, Sir, that the Seeds of Aristocracy began to spring even before the Conclusion of our Struggle for the natural Rights of Men. Seeds which like a Canker Worm lie at the Root of free Governments. So great is the Wickedness of some Men, & the stupid Servility of others, that one would be almost inclined to conclude that Communities cannot be free. The few haughty Families, think *They* must govern. The Body of the People tamely consent & submit to be their Slaves. This unravels the Mystery of Millions being enslaved by the few! But I must desist—My weak hand prevents my proceeding further at present. I will send you my poor Opinion of the political Structure at another Time. In the Interim oblige me with your Letters; & present mine & Mrs A's best Regards to your Lady & Family, Colo Francis, Mr A. L. if with you, & other Friends.

P.S. As I thought it a Piece of Justice I have venturd to say that I had often heard from the best Patriots from Virginia that Mr G Mason was an early active & able Advocate for the Liberties of America,

A Landholder (Oliver Ellsworth) VII

Connecticut Courant (Hartford), December 17, 1787

To the Landholders and Farmers.

I have often admired the spirit of candour, liberality, and justice, with which the Convention began and completed the important object of their mission. "In all our deliberations on this subject," say they, "we kept steadily in our view, that which appears to us the greatest interest of every true American, the consolidation of our union, in which is involved our prosperity, felicity, safety, perhaps our national existence. This important consideration, seriously and deeply impressed on our minds, led each state in the Convention to be less rigid on points of inferior magnitude, than might otherwise have been expected; and thus the Constitution which we now present, is the result of a spirit of amity, and of that mutual deference and concession, which the peculiarity of our political situation rendered indispensable."

Let us, my fellow citizens, take up this constitution with the same spirit of candour and liberality; consider it in all its parts; consider the important advantages which may be derived from it, and the fatal consequences which will probably follow from rejecting it. If any objections are made against it, let us obtain full information on the subject, and then weigh these objections in the balance of cool impartial reason. Let us see, if they be not wholly groundless; But if upon the whole they appear to have some weight, let us consider well, whether they be so important, that we ought on account of them to reject the whole constitution. Perfection is not the lot of human institutions; that which has the most excellencies and fewest faults, is the best that we can expect.

Some very worthy persons, who have not had great advantages for information, have objected against that clause in the constitution, which provides, that *no religious Test shall ever be required as a qualification to any office or public trust under the United States.* They have been afraid that this clause is unfavourable to religion. But, my countrymen, the sole purpose and effect of it is to exclude persecution, and to secure to you the important right of religious liberty. We are almost the only people in the world, who have a full enjoyment of this important right of human nature. In our country every man has a right to worship God in that way which is most agreeable to his own conscience. If he be a good and peaceable citizen, he is liable to no penalties or incapacities on account of his religious sentiments; or in other words, he is not subject to persecution.

But in other parts of the world, it has been, and still is, far different. Systems of religious error have been adopted, in times of ignorance. It has been the interest of tyrannical kings, popes, and prelates, to maintain these errors. When the clouds of ignorance began to vanish, and the people grew more enlightened, there was no other way to keep them in error, but to prohibit their altering their religious opinions by severe persecuting laws. In this way persecution became general throughout Europe. It was the universal opinion that one religion must be established by law; and that all, who differed in their religious opinions, must suffer the vengeance of persecution. In pursuance of this opinion, when popery was abolished in England, and the church of England was established in its stead, severe penalties were inflicted upon all who dissented from the established church. In the time of the civil wars, in the reign of Charles I. the presbyterians got the upper hand, and inflicted legal penalties upon all who differed from them in their sentiments respecting religious doctrines and discipline. When Charles II. was restored, the church of England was likewise restored, and the presbyterians and other dissenters were laid under legal penalties and incapacities. It was in this reign, that a religious test was established as a qualification for office; that is, a law was made requiring all officers civil and military (among other things) to receive the Sacrament of the Lord's Supper, according to the usage of the church of England, written six months after their admission to office, under the penalty of 500l. and disability to hold the office. And by another statute of the same reign, no person was capable of being elected to any office relating to the government of any city or corporation, unless, within a twelvemonth before, he had received the Sacrament according to the rites of the church of England. The pretence for making these severe laws, by which all but church-men were made incapable of any office civil or military, was to exclude the papists; but the real design was to exclude the prot-estant dissenters. From this account of test-laws, there arises an unfavourable presumption against them. But if we consider the nature of them and the effects which they are calculated to produce, we shall find that they are useless, tyrannical, and peculiarly unfit for the people of this country.

A religious test is an act to be done, or profession to be made, relating to religion (such as partaking of the sacrament according to certain rites and forms, or declaring one's belief of certain doctrines,) for the purpose of determining, whether his religious opinions are such, that he is admissible to a public office. A test in favour of any one denomination of christians would be to the last degree absurd in the United States. If it were in favour of either congregationalists, presbyterians, epis-copalions, baptists, or quakers; it would incapacitate more than three fourths of the American citizens for any public office; and thus degrade them from the rank of freemen. There needs no argument to prove that the majority of our citizens would never submit to this indignity.

If any test-act were to be made, perhaps the least exception-able would be one, requiring all persons appointed to office, to declare, at the time of their admission, their belief in the being of a God, and in the divine authority of the scriptures. In favour of such a test, it may be said, that one who believes these great truths, will not be so likely to violate his obliga-tions to his country, as one who disbelieves them; we may have greater confidence in his integrity. But I answer: His making a declaration of such a belief is no security at all. For suppose him to be an unprincipled man, who believes neither the word nor the being of a God; and to be governed merely by selfish motives; how easy it is for him to dissemble? how easy is it for him to make a public declaration of his belief in the creed which the law prescribes; and excuse himself by calling it a mere formality? This is the case with the test-laws and creeds in England. The most abandoned characters partake of the sacra-ment, in order to qualify themselves for public employments. The clergy are obliged by law to administer the ordinance unto them; and thus prostitute the most sacred office of religion; for it is a civil right in the party to receive the sacrament. In that country, subscribing to the thirty-nine articles is a test for admission into holy orders. And it is a fact, that many of the clergy do this; when at the same time, they totally disbelieve several of the doctrines contained in them. In short, test-laws are utterly ineffectual; they are no security at all; because men of loose principles will, by an external compliance, evade them. If they exclude any persons, it will be honest men, men of principle, who will rather suffer an injury, than act contrary to the dictates of their consciences. If we mean to have those appointed to public offices, who are sincere friends to religion; we the people who appoint them, must take care to choose such characters; and not rely upon such cob-web barriers as test-laws are.

But to come to the true principle, by which this question ought to be determined: The business of civil government is to protect the citizen in his rights, to defend the community from hostile powers, and to promote the general welfare. Civil government has no business to meddle with the private opinions of the people. If I demean myself as a good citizen, I am accountable, not to man, but to God, for the religious opinions which I embrace, and the manner in which I worship the supreme being. If such had been the universal sentiments of mankind, and they had acted accordingly, persecution, the bane of truth and nurse of error, with her bloody axe and flaming hand, would never have turned so great a part of the world into a field of blood.

But while I assert the right of religious liberty; I would not deny that the civil power has a right, in some cases, to interfere in matters of religion. It has a right to prohibit and punish gross immoralities and impieties; because the open practice of these is of evil example and public detriment. For this reason, I heartily approve of our laws against drunkenness, profane swearing, blasphemy, and professed atheism. But in this state, we have never thought it expedient to adopt a test-law; and yet I sincerely believe we have as great a proportion of religion and morality, as they have in England, where every person who holds a public office, must be either a saint by law, or a hypocrite by practice. A test-law is the parent of hypocrisy, and the offspring of error and the spirit of persecution. Legislatures have no right to set up an inquisition, and examine into the private opinions of men. Test-laws are useless and ineffectual, unjust and tyrannical; therefore the Convention have done wisely in excluding this engine of persecution, and providing that no religious test shall ever be required.

Publius (Alexander Hamilton)
The Federalist No. 23

New-York Packet, December 18, 1787

To the People of the State of New-York.

The necessity of a Constitution, at least equally energetic with the one proposed, to the preservation of the Union, is the point, at the examination of which we are now arrived.

This enquiry will naturally divide itself into three branches—the objects to be provided for by a Fœderal Government—the quantity of power necessary to the accomplishment of those objects—the persons upon whom that power ought to operate. Its distribution and organization will more properly claim our attention under the succeeding head.

The principal purposes to be answered by Union are these—The common defence of the members—the preservation of the public peace as well against internal convulsions as external attacks—the regulation of commerce with other nations and between the States—the superintendence of our intercourse, political and commercial, with foreign countries.

The authorities essential to the care of the common defence are these—to raise armies—to build and equip fleets—to prescribe rules for the government of both—to direct their operations—to provide for their support. These powers ought to exist without limitation: *Because it is impossible to foresee or define the extent and variety of national exigencies, or the correspondent extent & variety of the means which may be necessary to satisfy them.* The circumstances that endanger the safety of nations are infinite; and for this reason no constitutional shackles can wisely be imposed on the power to which the care of it is committed. This power ought to be co-extensive with all the possible combinations of such circumstances; and ought to be under the direction of the same councils, which are appointed to preside over the common defence.

This is one of those truths, which to a correct and unprejudiced mind, carries its own evidence along with it; and may be obscured, but cannot be made plainer by argument or reasoning. It rests upon axioms as simple as they are universal. The *means* ought to be proportioned to the *end*; the persons, from whose agency the attainment of any *end* is expected, ought to possess the *means* by which it is to be attained.

Whether there ought to be a Fœderal Government intrusted with the care of the common defence, is a question in the first instance open to discussion; but the moment it is decided in the affirmative, it will follow, that that government ought to be cloathed with all the powers requisite to the complete execution of its trust. And unless it can be shewn, that the circumstances which may affect the public safety are reducible within certain determinate limits; unless the contrary of this position can be fairly and rationally disputed, it must be admitted, as a necessary consequence, that there can be no limitation of that authority, which is to provide for the defence and protection of the community, in any matter essential to its efficiency; that is, in any matter essential to the *formation, direction* or *support* of the NATIONAL FORCES.

Defective as the present Confederation has been proved to be, this principle appears to have been fully recognized by the framers of it; though they have not made proper or adequate provision for its exercise. Congress have an unlimited discretion to make requisitions of men and money—to govern the army and navy—to direct their operations. As their requisitions were made constitutionally binding upon the States, who are in fact under the most solemn obligations to furnish the supplies required of them, the intention evidently was, that the United States should command whatever resources were by them judged requisite to "the common defence and general welfare." It was presumed that a sense of their true interests, and a regard to the dictates of good faith, would be found sufficient pledges for the punctual performance of the duty of the members to the Fœderal Head.

The experiment has, however demonstrated, that this expectation was ill founded and illustory; and the observations made under the last head, will, I imagine, have sufficed to convince the impartial and discerning, that there is an absolute necessity for an entire change in the first principles of the system: That if we are in earnest about giving the Union energy and duration, we must abandon the vain project of legislating upon the

States in their collective capacities: We must extend the laws of the Fœderal Government to the individual citizens of America: We must discard the fallacious scheme of quotas and requisitions, as equally impracticable and unjust. The result from all this is, that the Union ought to be invested with full power to levy troops; to build and equip fleets, and to raise the revenues, which will be required for the formation and support of an army and navy, in the customary and ordinary modes practiced in other governments.

If the circumstances of our country are such, as to demand a compound instead of a simple, a confederate instead of a sole government, the essential point which will remain to be adjusted, will be to discriminate the OBJECTS, as far as it can be done, which shall appertain to the different provinces or departments of power; allowing to each the most ample authority for fulfilling the objects committed to its charge. Shall the Union be constituted the guardian of the common safety? Are fleets and armies and revenues necessary to this purpose? The government of the Union must be empowered to pass all laws, and to make all regulations which have relation to them. The same must be the case, in respect to commerce, and to every other matter to which its jurisdiction is permitted to extend. Is the administration of justice between the citizens of the same State, the proper department of the local governments? These must possess all the authorities which are connected with this object, and with every other that may be allotted to their particular cognizance and direction. Not to confer in each case a degree of power, commensurate to the end, would be to violate the most obvious rules of prudence and propriety, and improvidently to trust the great interests of the nation to hands, which are disabled from managing them with vigour and success.

Who so likely to make suitable provisions for the public defence, as that body to which the guardianship of the public safety is confided—which, as the center of information, will best understand the extent and urgency of the dangers that threaten—as the representative of the WHOLE will feel itself most deeply interested in the preservation of every part—which, from the responsibility implied in the duty assigned to it, will be most sensibly impressed with the necessity of proper exertions—and which, by the extension of its authority throughout the States, can alone establish uniformity and concert in the plans and measures, by which the common safety is to be secured? Is there not a manifest inconsistency in devolving upon the Fœderal Government the care of the general defence, and leaving in the State governments the *effective* powers, by which it is to be provided for? Is not a want of co-operation the infallible consequence of such a system? And will not weakness, disorder, an undue distribution of the burthens and calamities of war, an unnecessary and intolerable increase of expence, be its natural and inevitable concomitants? Have we not had unequivocal experience of its effects in the course of the revolution, which we have just accomplished?

Every view we may take of the subject, as candid enquirers after truth, will serve to convince us, that it is both unwise and dangerous to deny the Fœderal Government an unconfined authority, as to all those objects which are intrusted to its management. It will indeed deserve the most vigilant and careful attention of the people, to see that it be modelled in such a manner, as to admit of its being safely vested with the requisite powers. If any plan which has been, or may be offered to our consideration, should not, upon a dispassionate inspection, be found to answer this description, it ought to be rejected. A government, the Constitution of which renders it unfit to be trusted with all the powers, which a free people *ought to delegate to any government,* would be an unsafe and improper depository of the NATIONAL INTERESTS, wherever THESE can with propriety be confided, the co-incident powers may safely accompany them. This is the true result of all just reasoning upon the subject And the adversaries of the plan, promulgated by the Convention, ought to have confined themselves to showing that the internal structure of the proposed government, was such as to render it unworthy of the confidence of the people. They ought not to have wandered into inflammatory declamations, and unmeaning cavils about the extent of the powers. The POWERS are not too extensive for the OBJECTS of Fœderal administration, or in other words, for the management of our NATIONAL INTERESTS; nor can any satisfactory argument be framed to shew that they are chargeable with such an excess. If it be true, as has been insinuated by some of the writers on the other side, that the difficulty arises from the nature of the thing, and that the extent of the country will not permit us to form a government, in which such ample powers can safely be reposed, it would prove that we ought to contract our views, and resort to the expedient of separate Confederacies, which will move within more practicable spheres. For the absurdity must continually stare us in the face of confiding to a government, the direction of the most essential national interests, without daring to trust it with the authorities which are indispensable to their proper and efficient management. Let us not attempt to reconcile contradictions, but firmly embrace a rational alternative.

I trust, however, that the impracticability of one general system cannot be shewn. I am greatly mistaken, if any thing of weight, has yet been advanced of this tendency; and I flatter myself, that the observations which have been made in the course of these papers, have sufficed to place the reverse of that position in as clear a light as any matter still in the womb of time and experience can be susceptible of. This at all events must be evident, that the very difficulty itself drawn from the extent of the country, is the strongest argument in favor of an energetic government; for any other can certainly never preserve the Union of so large an empire. If we embrace the tenets of those, who oppose the adoption of the proposed Constitution, as the standard of our political creed, we cannot fail to verify the gloomy doctrines, which predict the impracticability of a national system, pervading the entire limits of the present Confederacy.

PUBLIUS.

Brutus VII

New York Journal, January 3, 1788

The result of our reasoning in the two preceeding numbers is this, that in a confederated government, where the powers are divided between the general and the state government, it is essential to its existence, that the revenues of the country, without which no government can exist, should be divided between them, and so apportioned to each, as to answer their respective exigencies, as far as human wisdom can effect such a division and apportionment.

It has been shewn, that no such allotment is made in this constitution, but that every source of revenue is under the controul of the Congress; it therefore follows, that if this system is intended to be a complex and not a simple, a confederate and not an entire consolidated government, it contains in it the sure seeds of its own dissolution.—One of two things must happen—Either the new constitution will become a mere *nudum pactum*, and all the authority of the rulers under it be cried down, as has happened to the present confederation—Or the authority of the individual states will be totally supplanted, and they will retain the mere form without any of the powers of government.—To one or the other of these issues, I think, this new government, if it is adopted, will advance with great celerity.

It is said, I know, that such a separation of the sources of revenue, cannot be made without endangering the public safety—"unless (says a writer) it can be shewn that the circumstances which may affect the public safety are reducible within certain determinate limits; unless the contrary of this position can be fairly and rationally disputed: it must be admitted as a necessary consequence, that there can be no limitation of that authority which is to provide for the defence and protection of the community, &c."*

*Federalist, No. 23.

The pretended demonstration of this writer will instantly vanish, when it is considered, that the *protection and defence* of the community is not intended to be entrusted *solely* into the hands of the general government, and by his own confession it ought not to be. It is true this system commits to the general government the protection and defence of the community against foreign force and invasion, against piracies and felonies on the high seas, and against insurrection among ourselves. They are also authorised to provide for the administration of justice in certain matters of a general concern, and in some that I think are not so. But it ought to be left to the state governments to provide for the protection and defence of the citizen against the hand of private violence, and the wrongs done or attempted by individuals to each other—Protection and defence against the murderer, the robber, the thief, the cheat, and the unjust person, is to be derived from the respective state governments.—The just way of reasoning therefore on this subject is this, the general government is to provide for the protection and defence of the community against foreign attacks, &c. they therefore ought to have authority sufficient to effect this, so far as is consistent with the providing for our internal protection and defence. The state governments are entrusted with the care of administring justice among its citizens, and the management of other internal concerns, they ought therefore to retain power adequate to the end. The preservation of internal peace and good order, and the due administration of law and justice, ought to be the first care of every government.—The happiness of a people depends infinitely more on this than it does upon all that glory and respect which nations acquire by the most brilliant martial atchievements— and I believe history will furnish but few examples of nations who have duly attended to these, who have been subdued by foreign invaders. If a proper respect and submission to the laws prevailed over all orders of men in our country; and if a spirit of public and private justice, œconomy and industry influenced the people, we need not be under any apprehensions but what they would be ready to repel any invasion that might be made on the country. And more than this, I would not wish from them—A defensive war is the only one I think justifiable—I do not make these observations to prove, that a government ought not to be authorised to provide for the protection and defence of a country against external enemies, but to shew that this is not the most important, much less the only object of their care.

The European governments are almost all of them framed, and administered with a view to arms, and war, as that in which their chief glory consists; they mistake the end of government—it was designed to save mens lives, not to destroy them. We ought to furnish the world with an example of a great people, who in their civil institutions hold chiefly in view, the attainment of virtue, and happiness among ourselves. Let the monarchs in Europe, share among them the glory of depopulating countries, and butchering thousands of their innocent citizens, to revenge private quarrels, or to punish an insult offered to a wife, a mistress, or a favorite: I envy them not the honor, and I pray heaven this country may never be ambitious of it. The czar Peter the great, acquired great glory by his arms; but all this was nothing, compared with the true glory which he obtained, by civilizing his rude and barbarous subjects, diffusing among them knowledge, and establishing, and cultivating the arts of life: by the former he desolated countries, and drenched the earth with human blood: by the latter he softened the ferocious nature of his people, and pointed them to the means of human happiness. The most important end of government then, is the proper direction of its internal police, and œconomy; this is the province of the state governments, and it is evident, and is indeed admitted, that these ought to be under their controul. Is it not then preposterous, and in the highest degree absurd, when the state governments are vested with powers so essential to the peace and good order of society, to take from them the means of their own preservation?

The idea, that the powers of congress in respect to revenue ought to be unlimited, "because the circumstances which may affect the public safety are not reducible to certain determinate limits," is novel, as it relates to the government of the united states. The inconveniencies which resulted from the feebleness of the present confederation was discerned, and felt soon after its adoption. It was soon discovered, that a power to require money, without either the authority or means to enforce a collection of it, could not be relied upon either to provide for the common defence, the discharge of the national debt, or for support of government. Congress therefore, so early as February 1781, recommended to the states to invest them with a power to levy an impost of five per cent ad valorem, on all imported goods, as a fund to be appropriated to discharge the debts already contracted, or which should hereafter be contracted for the support of the war, to be continued until the debts should be fully and finally discharged. There is not the most distant idea held out in this act, that an unlimited power to collect taxes, duties and excises was necessary to be vested in the united states, and yet this was a time of the most pressing danger and distress. The idea then was, that if certain definite funds were assigned to the union, which were certain in their natures, productive, and easy of collection, it would enable them to answer their engagements, and provide for their defence, and the impost of five per cent was fixed upon for the purpose.

This same subject was revived in the winter and spring of 1783, and after a long consideration of the subject, and many schemes were proposed; the result was, a recommendation of the revenue system of April 1783; this system does not suggest an idea that it was necessary to grant the United States unlimitted authority in matters of revenue. A variety of amendments were proposed to this system, some of which are upon the journals of Congress, but it does not appear that any of them proposed to invest the general government with discretionary power to raise money. On the contrary, all of them limit them to certain definite objects, and fix the bounds over which they could not pass. This recommendation was passed at the conclusion of the war, and was founded on an estimate of the whole national debt. It was computed, that one million and an half of dollars, in addition to the impost, was a sufficient sum to pay the annual interest of the debt, and gradually to abolish the principal.—Events have proved that their estimate was sufficiently liberal, as the domestic debt appears upon its being adjusted to be less than it was computed, and since this period a considerable portion of the principal of the domestic debt has been discharged by the sale of the western lands. It has been constantly urged by Congress, and by individuals, ever since, until lately, that had this revenue been appropriated by the states, as it was recommended, it would have been adequate to every exigency of the union. Now indeed it is insisted, that all the treasures of the country are to be under the controul of that body, whom we are to appoint to provide for our protection and defence against foreign enemies. The debts of the several states, and the support of the governments of them are to trust to fortune and accident. If the union should not have occasion for all the money they can raise, they will leave a portion for the state, but this must be a matter of mere grace and favor. Doctrines like these would not have been listened to by any state in the union, at a time when we were pressed on every side by a powerful enemy, and were called upon to make greater exertions than we have any reason to expect we shall ever be again. The ability and character of the convention, who framed the proferred constitution, is sounded forth and reiterated by every declaimer and writer in its favor, as a powerful argument to induce its adoption. But are not the patriots who guided our councils in the perilous times of the war, entitled to equal respect. How has it happened, that none of these perceived a truth, which it is pretended is capable of such clear demonstration, that the power to raise a revenue should be deposited in the general government without limitation? Were the men so dull of apprehension, so incapable of reasoning as not to be able to draw the inference? The truth is, no such necessity exists. It is a thing practicable, and by no means so difficult as is pretended, to limit the powers of the general government in respect to revenue, while yet they may retain reasonable means to provide for the common defence.

It is admitted, that human wisdom cannot foresee all the variety of circumstances that may arise to endanger the safety of nations—and it may with equal truth be added, that the power of a nation, exerted with its utmost vigour, may not be equal to repel a force with which it may be assailed, much less may it be able, with its ordinary resources and power, to oppose an extraordinary and unexpected attack;—but yet every nation may form a rational judgment, what force will be competent to protect and defend it, against any enemy with which it is probable it may have to contend. In extraordinary attacks, every country must rely upon the spirit and special exertions of its inhabitants—and these extraordinary efforts will always very much depend upon the happiness and good order the people experience from a wise and prudent administration of their internal government. The states are as capable of making a just estimate on this head, as perhaps any nation in the world.—We have no powerful nation in our neighbourhood; if we are to go to war, it must either be with the Aboriginal natives, or with European nations. The first are so unequal to a contest with this whole continent, that they are rather to be dreaded for the depredations they may make on our frontiers, than for any impression they will ever be able to make on the body of the country. Some of the European nations, it is true, have provinces bordering upon us, but from these, unsupported by their European forces, we have nothing to apprehend; if any of them should attack us, they will have to transport their armies across the atlantic, at immense expence, while we should defend ourselves in our own country, which abounds with every necessary of life. For defence against any assault, which there is any probability will be made upon us, we may easily form an estimate.

I may be asked to point out the sources, from which the general government could derive a sufficient revenue, to answer the demands of the union. Many might be suggested, and for my part, I am not disposed to be tenacious of my own opinion on the subject. If the object be defined with precision, and will operate to make the burden fall any thing nearly equal on the different parts of the union, I shall be satisfied.

There is one source of revenue, which it is agreed, the general government ought to have the sole controul of. This is an impost upon all goods imported from foreign countries. This would, of itself, be very productive, and would be collected with ease and certainty.—It will be a fund too, constantly encreasing—for our commerce will grow, with the productions of the country; and these, together with our consumption of foreign goods, will encrease with our population. It is said, that the impost will not produce a sufficient sum to satisfy the demands of the general government; perhaps it would not. Let some other then, equally well defined, be assigned them:—that this is practicable is certain, because such particular objects were proposed by some members of Congress when the revenue system of April 1783, was agitated in that body. It was then moved, that a tax at the rate of ____ ninetieths of a dollar on surveyed land, and a house tax of half a dollar on a house, should be granted to the United States. I do not mention this, because I approve of raising a revenue in this mode. I believe such a tax would be difficult in its collection, and inconvenient in its operation. But it shews, that it has heretofore been the sense of some of those, who now contend, that the general government should have unlimited authority in matters of revenue, that their authority should be definite and limitted on that head.—My own opinion is. that the objects from which the general government should have authority to raise a revenue, should be of such a nature, that the tax should be raised by simple laws, with few officers, with certainty and expedition, and with the least interference with the internal police of the states.—Of this nature is the impost on imported goods—and it appears to me that a duty on exports, would also be of this nature—and therefore, for ought I can discover, this would be the best source of revenue to grant the general government. I know neither the Congress nor the state legislatures will have authority under the new constitution to raise a revenue in this way. But I cannot perceive the reason of the restriction. It appears to me evident, that a tax on articles exported, would be as nearly equal as any that we can expect to lay, and it certainly would be collected with more ease and less expence than any direct tax. I do not however, contend for this mode, it may be liable to well founded objections that have not occurred to me. But this I do contend for, that some mode is practicable, and that limits must be marked between the general government, and the states on this head, or if they be not, either the Congress in the exercise of this power, will deprive the state legislatures of the means of their existence, or the states by resisting the constitutional authority of the general government, will render it nugatory.

Publius (Alexander Hamilton)
The Federalist No. 30

New-York Packet, December 28, 1787

To the People of the State of New-York.

It has been already observed, that the Fœderal Government ought to possess the power of providing for the support of the national forces; in which proposition was intended to be included the expence of raising troops, of building and equiping fleets, and all other expences in any wise connected with military arrangements and operations. But these are not the only objects to which the jurisdiction of the Union, in respect to revenue, must necessarily be empowered to extend—It must embrace a provision for the support of the national civil list—for the payment of the national debts contracted, or that may be contracted—and in general for all those matters which will call for disbursements out of the national treasury. The conclusion is, that there must be interwoven in the frame of the government, a general power of taxation in one shape or another.

Money is with propriety considered as the vital principle of the body politic; as that which sustains its life and motion, and enables it to perform its most essential functions. A complete power therefore to procure a regular and adequate supply of it, as far as the resources of the community will permit, may be regarded as an indispensable ingredient in every constitution. From a deficiency in this particular, one of two evils must ensue; either the people must be subjected to continual plunder as a substitute for a more eligible mode of supplying the public wants, or the government must sink into a fatal atrophy, and in a short course of time perish.

In the Ottoman or Turkish empire, the sovereign, though in other respects absolute master of the lives and fortunes of his subjects, has no right to impose a new tax. The consequence is, that he permits the Bashaws or Governors of provinces to pillage the people without mercy; and in turn squeezes out of them the sums of which he stands in need to satisfy his own exigencies and those of the State. In America, from a like cause, the government of the Union has gradually dwindled into a state of decay, approaching nearly to annihilation. Who can doubt that the happiness of the people in both countries would be promoted by competent authorities in the proper hands, to provide the revenues which the necessities of the public might require?

The present confederation, feeble as it is, intended to repose in the United States, an unlimited power of providing for the pecuniary wants of the Union. But proceeding upon an erroneous principle, it has been done in such a manner as entirely to have frustrated the intention. Congress by the articles which compose that compact (as has been already stated) are authorised to ascertain and call for any sums of money necessary, in their judgment, to the service of the United States; and their requisitions, if conformable to the rule of apportionment, are in every constitutional sense obligatory upon the States. These have no right to question the propriety of the demand—no discretion beyond that of devising the ways and means of furnishing the sums demanded. But though this be strictly and truly the case; though the assumption of such a right be an infringement of the articles of Union; though it may seldom or never have been avowedly claimed, yet in practice it has been constantly exercised; and would continue to be so, as long as the revenues of the confederacy should remain dependent on the intermediate agency of its members. What the consequences of this system have been, is within the knowledge of every man, the least conversant in our public affairs, and has been amply unfolded in different parts of these inquiries. It is this which has chiefly contributed to reduce us to a situation which affords ample cause, both of mortification to ourselves, and of triumph to our enemies.

What remedy can there be for this situation but, in a change of the system, which has produced it? In a change of the fallacious and delusive system of quotas and requisitions? What substitute can there be imagined for this *ignis fatuus* in finance, but that of permitting the national government to raise its own revenues by the ordinary methods of taxation, authorised in every well ordered constitution of civil government? Ingenious men may declaim with plausibility on any subject; but no human ingenuity can point out any other expedient to rescue us from the inconveniences and embarrassments, naturally resulting from defective supplies of the public treasury.

The more intelligent adversaries of the new constitution admit the force of this reasoning; but they qualify their admission by a distinction between what they call *internal* and *external* taxation. The former they would reserve to the State governments; the latter, which they explain into commercial imposts, or rather duties on imported articles, they declare themselves willing to concede to the Fœderal Head. This distinction, however, would violate that fundamental maxim of good sense and sound policy, which dictates that every POWER ought to be proportionate to its OBJECT; and would still leave the General Government in a kind of tutelage to the State governments, inconsistent with every idea of vigor or efficiency. Who can pretend that commercial imposts are or would be alone equal to the present and future exigencies of the Union? Taking into the account the existing debt, foreign and domestic, upon any plan of extinguishment, which a man moderately impressed with the importance of public justice and public credit could approve, in addition to the establishments, which all parties will acknowledge to be necessary, we could not reasonably flatter ourselves, that this resource alone, upon the most improved scale, would even suffice for its present necessities. Its future necessities admit not of calculation or limitation; and upon the principle, more than once adverted to, the power of making provision for them as they arise, ought to be equally unconfined. I believe it may be regarded as a position, warranted by the history of mankind, that *in the usual progress of things, the necessities of a nation in every stage of its existence will be found at least equal to its resources.*

To say that deficiencies may be provided for by requisitions upon the States, is on the one hand, to acknowledge that this system cannot be depended upon; and on the other hand, to depend upon it for every thing beyond a certain limit. Those who have carefully attended to its vices and deformities as they have been exhibited by experience, or delineated in the course of these papers, must feel an invincible repugnancy to trusting the national interests, in any degree, to its operation. Its inevitable tendency, whenever it is brought into activity, must be to enfeeble the Union and sow the seeds of discord and contention between the Fœderal Head and its members, and

between the members themselves. Can it be expected that the
deficiencies would be better supplied in this mode, than the
total wants of the Union have heretofore been supplied, in
the same mode? It ought to be recollected, that if less will be
required from the States, they will have proportionably less
means to answer the demand. If the opinions of those who
contend for the distinction which has been mentioned, were
to be received as evidence of truth, one would be led to conclude that there was some known point in the œconomy of
national affairs, at which it would be safe to stop, and say, thus
far the ends of public happiness will be promoted by supplying the wants of government, and all beyond this is unworthy
of our care or anxiety. How is it possible that a government
half supplied and always necessitous, can fulfil the purposes of
its institution—can provide for the security of—advance the
prosperity—or support the reputation of the commonwealth?
How can it ever possess either energy or stability, dignity or
credit, confidence at home or respectability abroad? How can
its administration be any thing else than a succession of expedients temporising, impotent, disgraceful? How will it be able
to avoid a frequent sacrifice of its engagements to immediate
necessity? How can it undertake or execute any liberal or enlarged plans of public good?

Let us attend to what would be the effects of this situation
in the very first war in which we should happen to be engaged.
We will presume for argument sake, that the revenue arising
from the impost duties answer the purposes of a provision for
the public debt, and of a peace establishment for the Union.
Thus circumstanced, a war breaks out. What would be the
probable conduct of the government in such an emergency?
Taught by experience that proper dependence could not be
placed on the success of requisitions unable by its own authority to lay hold of fresh resources, and urged by considerations
of national danger, would it not be driven to the expedient of
diverting the funds already appropriated from their proper objects to the defence of the State? It is not easy to see how a step
of this kind could be avoided; and if it should be taken, it is evident that it would prove the destruction of public credit at the
very moment that it was become essential to the public safety.
To imagine that at such a crisis credit might be dispensed with,
would be the extreme of infatuation. In the modern system of

war, nations the most wealthy are obliged to have recourse to large loans. A country so little opulent as ours, must feel this necessity in a much stronger degree. But who would lend to a government that prefaced its overtures for borrowing, by an act which demonstrated that no reliance could be placed on the steadiness of its measures for paying? The loans it might be able to procure, would be as limited in their extent as burthensome in their conditions. They would be made upon the same principles that usurers commonly lend to bankrupt and fraudulent debtors; with a sparing hand, and at enormous premiums.

It may perhaps be imagined, that from the scantiness of the resources of the country, the necessity of diverting the established funds in the case supposed, would exist; though the national government should possess an unrestrained power of taxation. But two considerations will serve to quiet all apprehension on this head; one is, that we are sure the resources of the community in their full extent, will be brought into activity for the benefit of the Union; the other is, that whatever deficiencies there may be, can without difficulty be supplied by loans.

The power of creating new funds upon new objects of taxation by its own authority, would enable the national government to borrow, as far as its necessities might require. Foreigners as well as the citizens of America, could then reasonably repose confidence in its engagements; but to depend upon a government, that must itself depend upon thirteen other governments for the means of fulfilling its contracts, when once its situation is clearly understood, would require a degree of credulity, not often to be met with in the pecuniary transactions of mankind, and little reconcileable with the usual sharp-sightedness of avarice.

Reflections of this kind, may have trifling weight with men, who hope to see realized in America, the halcyon scenes of the poetic or fabulous age; but to those who believe we are likely to experience a common portion of the vicissitudes and calamities, which have fallen to the lot of other nations, they must appear entitled to serious attention. Such men must behold the actual situation of their country with painful solicitude, and deprecate the evils which ambition or revenge might, with too much facility, inflict upon it.

PUBLIUS.

PART 4:
SLAVERY AND LIBERTY

L UTHER MARTIN of Maryland had been one of the Convention's more vocal delegates, though he left halfway through. In a speech to the Maryland assembly in late November 1787 Martin accused the Constitution's proponents of plotting to obliterate the states. His inside story of the nationalists' plot was published as a twelve-part newspaper series and then as a pamphlet titled *The Genuine Information*. He blasted the Constitution for prohibiting the federal government from blocking the slave trade, as well as for preventing the states from regulating commerce. An anonymous poet in South Carolina charged that Americans' rights would vanish when "thirteen states are moulded into one," and blamed John Adams for proposing this new system. Congress and the President, the poet warned, were masks for Parliament and King. **Noah Webster**, lawyer, journalist, and author of a spelling book, supported ratification, and ridiculed those opponents who thought a Bill of Rights essential. Bills of Rights, he argued, limited the power of kings, but why should an elected government's powers be limited? An unchangeable declaration of rights would enslave future generations. *Brutus XI* feared that the Supreme Court would control the national legislature, and through its rulings would silently and imperceptibly subvert the legislative, executive, and judicial powers of the states. Writing as *Civis*, South Carolina physician, politician, and historian David Ramsay extolled the Constitution's benefits to the southern states. Ramsay argued that under the new system the North was no more likely to dominate the Union than Charleston was to dominate South Carolina under its state constitution. James Madison in **Federalist 39** argued that the new system was republican, and both federal and national in character. In **Federalist 54**, Madison explained why the Constitution counted enslaved people as three-fifths of a person for purposes of apportioning representation, thereby giving slaveholding states more seats in Congress. The laws of the southern states, he said, treated slaves as both property and persons, but if the laws were to treat them wholly as persons, then they would have to be counted equally with whites in determining representation.

Luther Martin
The Genuine Information VIII

Maryland Gazette (Baltimore), January 22, 1788

Mr. MARTIN's *Information to the House of Assembly, continued.*

It was urged that by this system, we were giving the general government full and absolute power to regulate commerce, under which general power it would have a right to *restrain*, or *totally prohibit* the *slave trade*—it must appear to the world absurd and disgraceful to the last degree, that we should *except* from the exercise of that power, the *only branch of commerce*, which is *unjustifiable in its nature*, and *contrary* to the *rights* of *mankind*—That on the contrary, we ought *rather to prohibit expressly* in our *constitution*, the *further importation* of *slaves*; and to *authorize* the general government from time to time, to make such regulations as should be thought most advantageous for the *gradual abolition* of *slavery*, and the *emancipation* of the *slaves* which are already in the States.

That *slavery* is *inconsistent* with the *genius* of *republicanism*, and has a tendency to *destroy* those *principles* on which it is *supported*, as it *lessens the sense* of the *equal rights* of *mankind*, and habituates us to *tyranny* and *oppression*.—It was further urged, that by this system of government, every State is to be protected both from *foreign invasion* and from *domestic insurrections*; that from this consideration, it was of the *utmost importance* it should have a power to restrain the importation of slaves, since in *proportion* as the number of slaves were encreased in any State, in the *same* proportion the State is *weakened* and *exposed* to foreign invasion, or domestic insurrection, and *by so much the less* will it be able to protect itself against *either*; and therefore will by so much the more, want aid from, and be a burthen to, the union.—It was further said, that as in this system we were giving the general government a power under the idea of national character, or national interest, to regulate even our *weights* and *measures*, and have prohibited all possibility of *emitting paper money*, and *passing instalment laws, &c.*—It must appear still more extraordinary, that we should prohibit the government from interfering with the slave trade, than which *nothing* could so *materially affect* both our *national honour* and *interest.*—These reasons influenced me both on the committee and in convention, most decidedly to oppose and vote against the clause, as it now makes a part of the system.

You will perceive, Sir, not only that the general government is prohibited from interfering in the slave trade *before* the year eighteen hundred and eight, but that there is no provision in the constitution that it shall *afterwards* be prohibited, nor any security that such prohibition will ever take place—and I think there is great reason to believe that if the importation of slaves is permitted until the year eighteen hundred and eight, it will not be prohibited afterwards—At *this time* we do not generally hold this commerce in so *great* abhorrence as we have done.— When our *own* liberties were at stake, we *warmly* felt for the *common rights of men*—The danger being thought to be past, which threatened ourselves, we are daily growing *more insensible* to those rights—In those States who have restrained or prohibited the importation of slaves, it is only done by legislative acts which may be repealed—When those States find that they must in their *national character* and *connection* suffer in the *disgrace,* and share in the *inconveniences* attendant upon that detestable and iniquitous traffic, they may be desirous also to share in the *benefits* arising from it, and the odium attending it will be greatly effaced by the sanction which is given to it in the general government.

By the next paragraph, the general government is to have a *power* of *suspending* the *habeas corpus act,* in cases of *rebellion* or *invasion.*

As the State governments have a power of suspending the habeas corpus act, in those cases, it was said there could be no good reason for giving such a power to the general government, since whenever the *State* which is invaded or in which an insurrection takes place, finds its safety requires it, *it* will make use of that power—*And* it was urged, that if we gave this power to the general government, it would be an engine of oppression in its hands, since whenever a State should oppose its views, however arbitrary and unconstitutional, and refuse submission to them, the general government may declare it to be *an act of rebellion*, and suspending the habeas corpus act, may *seize* upon the persons of those *advocates of freedom*, who have had *virtue* and *resolution* enough to excite the opposition, and may *imprison* them during its pleasure in the *remotest* part of the union, so that a citizen of Georgia might be *bastiled* in the furthest part of New-Hampshire—or a citizen of New-Hampshire in the furthest extreme to the south, cut off from their family, their friends, and their every connection—These considerations induced me, Sir, to give my negative also to this clause.

In this same section there is a provision that no preference shall be given to the ports of one State over another, and that vessels bound to or from one State shall not be obliged to enter, clear or pay duties in another.—This provision, as well as that which relates to the uniformity of impost duties and excises, was introduced, Sir, by the delegation of this State.—Without such a provision it would have been in the power of the general government to have compelled all ships sailing into, or out of the Chesapeak, to clear and enter at Norfolk or some port in Virginia—a regulation which would be extremely injurious to our commerce, but which would if considered merely as to the interest of the union, perhaps not be thought unreasonable, since it would render the collection of the revenue arising from commerce more certain and less expensive.

But, Sir, as the system is now reported, the general government have a *power* to *establish what ports they please in each State*, and to ascertain at what ports in every State ships shall clear and enter in such State, a power which *may* be so used as to *destroy* the *effect* of that provision, since by it may be established a port in such a place as shall be so *inconvenient* to the State as to render it *more eligible* for their shipping to clear and enter in *another* than in their *own State*; suppose, for instance the general government should determine that all ships which cleared or entered in Maryland should clear and enter at George-Town, on Potowmack, it would oblige all the ships which sailed from, or was bound to, any other part of Maryland, to clear or enter in some port in *Virginia*. To prevent such a use of the power which the general government now has of *limiting the number of ports* in a State, and *fixing the place* or *places where they shall be*, we endeavoured to obtain a provision that the general government should only, in the first instance, have authority to ascertain the *number* of ports proper to be established in each State, and transmit information thereof to the several States, the legislatures of which, respectively, should have the power to fix the *places* where those ports should be, according to their idea of what would be most *advantageous* to the *commerce* of their State, and most for the *ease* and *convenience* of their *citizens*; and that the general government should not interfere in the establishment of the *places*, unless the legislature of the State should neglect or refuse so to do; but we could not obtain this alteration.

By the tenth section, every State is *prohibited* from *emitting bills of credit*—As it was reported by the committee of detail, the States were *only* prohibited from emitting them *without the consent of Congress*; but the convention was so *smitten* with the *paper money dread*, that they insisted the prohibition should be *absolute*. It was my opinion, Sir, that the States ought not to be *totally deprived of the right to emit bills of credit*, and that as we had *not given* an *authority* to the *general government* for that purpose, it was the *more necessary* to *retain* it in the *States*—I considered that *this State*, and *some others*, have *formerly received great benefit* from paper emissions, and that if public and private credit should once more be restored, such emissions may *hereafter* be *equally advantageous*; and further, that it is impossible to foresee that events may not take place which shall render paper money of *absolute necessity*; and it was my opinion, if this power was not to be exercised by a State without the permission of the general government, it ought to be satisfactory even to those who were the *most haunted* by the apprehensions of paper money; I, therefore, thought it my duty to vote against this part of the system.

The same section also, puts it out of the power of the States, to make any thing but gold and silver coin a tender in payment of debts, or to pass any law impairing the obligation of contracts.

I considered, Sir, that there might be times of such *great public calamities* and *distress*, and of such *extreme scarcity* of *specie* as should render it the *duty* of a government for the *preservation* of even the *most valuable part* of its citizens in some measure to interfere in their favour, by passing laws *totally* or *partially stopping* the courts of justice—or authorising the debtor to pay by *instalments*, or by delivering up his property to his creditors at a *reasonable* and *honest* valuation.—The times have been such as to render regulations of this kind necessary in most, or all of the States, to prevent the *wealthy creditor* and the *monied* man from *totally* destroying the *poor* though even *industrious* debtor—*Such times* may *again* arrive.—I therefore, voted against depriving the States of this power, a power which I am decided they ought to possess, but which I admit ought only to be exercised on very important and urgent occasions.—I apprehend, Sir, the principal cause of complaint among the people at large is, the public and private debt with which they are oppressed, and which, in the present scarcity of cash, threatens them with destruction, unless they can obtain so much indulgence in point of time that by industry and frugality they may extricate themselves.

This *government proposed*, I apprehend so *far from removing* will greatly *encrease* those complaints, since grasping in its all powerful hand the citizens of the respective States, it will by the imposition of the variety of *taxes, imposts, stamps, excises* and *other duties, squeeze* from them the little money they may acquire, the hard earnings of their industry, as you would squeeze the juice from an orange, till not a drop more can be extracted, and then let *loose* upon them, their *private creditors,* to whose *mercy* it *consigns* them, by *whom* their property is to be *seized upon* and *sold* in this *scarcity* of *specie at a sheriffs sale,* where nothing but *ready cash* can be received for a *tenth part* of its *value,* and *themselves* and their *families* to be consigned to *indigence* and *distress,* without *their governments* having a *power* to *give them a moment's indulgence,* however *necessary* it might be, and however *desirous* to grant them aid.

By this same section, every State is also prohibited from laying any imposts, or duties on imports or exports, without the permission of the general government.—It was urged, that as almost all sources of taxation were given to Congress it would be but reasonable to leave the States the power of bringing revenue into their treasuries, by laying a duty on exports if they should think proper, which might be so *light* as not to injure or discourage industry, and yet might be productive of considerable revenue—Also, that there might be cases in which it would be proper, for the purpose of encouraging manufactures, to lay duties to prohibit the exportation of raw materials, and even in addition to the duties laid by Congress on *imports* for the sake of *revenue*, to lay a duty to discourage the importation of particular articles into a State, or to enable the *manufacturer here* to supply us on as *good terms* as they could be obtained from a *foreign market*; however, the most we could obtain was, that this power might be exercised by the States with, and *only* with the consent of Congress, and subject to its controul—And so anxious were they to seize on *every shilling* of our money for the general government, that they insisted *even* the *little revenue* that might thus arise, should not be appropriated to the use of the respective States where it was collected, but should be paid into the treasury of the United States; and accordingly it is so determined.

Giles Hickory (Noah Webster) I

American Magazine (New York), December 1787

One of the principal objections to the new Federal Constitution is, that it contains no *Bill of Rights*. This objection, I
presume to assert, is founded on ideas of government that are
totally false. Men seem determined to adhere to old prejudices,
and reason *wrong*, because our ancestors reasoned *right*. A Bill
of Rights against the encroachments of Kings and Barons, or
against any power independent of the people, is perfectly in-
telligible; but a Bill of Rights against the encroachments of an
elective Legislature, that is, against our *own* encroachments on
ourselves, is a curiosity in government.

One half the people who read books, have so little ability
to apply what they read to their own practice, that they had
better not read at all. The English nation, from which we descended, have been gaining their liberties, inch by inch, by
forcing concessions from the crown and the Barons, during
the course of six centuries. *Magna Charta*, which is called
the palladium of English liberty, was dated in 1215, and the
people of England were not represented in Parliament till the
year 1265. Magna Charta established the rights of the Barons
and the clergy against the encroachments of royal prerogative;
but the commons or people were hardly noticed in that deed.
There was but one clause in their favor, which stipulated that,
"no villain or rustic should, by any fine, be bereaved of his
carts, plows and instruments of husbandry." As for the rest,
they were considered as a part of the property belonging to an
estate, and were transferred, as other moveables, at the will of
their owners. In the succeeding reign, they were permitted to
send Representatives to Parliament; and from that time have
been gradually assuming their proper degree of consequence
in the British Legislature. In such a nation, every law or statute
that defines the powers of the crown, and circumscribes them
within determinate limits, must be considered as a barrier to
guard popular liberty. Every acquisition of freedom must be
established as a *right*, and solemnly recognized by the supreme

power of the nation; lest it should be again resumed by the crown under pretence of ancient prerogative; For this reason, the habeas corpus act passed in the reign of Charles 2d, the statute of the 2d of William and Mary, and many others which are declaratory of certain privileges, are justly considered as the pillars of English freedom.

These statutes are however not esteemed because they are unalterable; for the same power that enacted them, can at any moment repeal them; but they are esteemed, because they are barriers erected by the Representatives of the nation, against a power that exists independent of their own choice.

But the same reasons for such declaratory constitutions do not exist in America, where the supreme power is *the people in their Representatives*. The *Bills of Rights*, prefixed to several of the constitutions of the United States, if considered as assigning the reasons of our separation from a foreign government, or as solemn declarations of right against the encroachments of a foreign jurisdiction, are perfectly rational, and were doubtless necessary. But if they are considered as barriers against the encroachments of our own Legislatures, or as constitutions unalterable by posterity, I venture to pronounce them nugatory, and to the last degree, absurd.

In our governments, there is no power of legislation, independent of the people; no power that has an interest detached from that of the public; consequently there is no power existing against which it is necessary to guard. While our Legislatures therefore remain elective, and the rulers have the same interest in the laws, as the subjects have, the rights of the people will be perfectly secure without any declaration in their favor.

But this is not the principal point. I undertake to prove that a standing *Bill of Rights* is *absurd*, because no constitutions, in a free government, can be unalterable. The present generation have indeed a right to declare what *they* deem a *privilege*; but they have no right to say what the *next* generation shall deem a privilege. A State is a supreme corporation that never dies. Its powers, when it acts for itself, are at all times, equally extensive; and it has the same right to *repeal* a law this year, as it had to *make* it the last. If therefore our posterity are bound by our constitutions, and can neither amend nor annul them, they are to all intents and purposes our slaves.

But it will be enquired, have we then no right to say, that trial by jury, the liberty of the press, the habeas corpus writ and other invaluable privileges, shall never be infringed nor destroyed? By no means. We have the same right to say that lands shall descend in a particular mode to the heirs of the deceased proprietor, and that such a mode shall never be altered by future generations, as we have to pass a law that the trial by jury shall never be abridged. The right of Jury-trial, which we deem invaluable, may in future cease to be a privilege; or other modes of trial more satisfactory to the people, may be devised. Such an event is neither impossible nor improbable. Have we then a right to say that our posterity shall not be judges of their own circumstances? The very attempt to make *perpetual* constitutions, is the assumption of a right to control the opinions of future generations; and to legislate for those over whom we have as little authority as we have over a nation in Asia. Nay we have as little right to say that trial by jury shall be perpetual, as the English, in the reign of Edward the Confessor, had, to bind their posterity forever to decide causes by fiery Ordeal, or single combat. There are perhaps many laws and regulations, which from their consonance to the eternal rules of justice, will always be good and conformable to the sense of a nation. But most institutions in society, by reason of an unceasing change of circumstances, either become altogether improper or require amendment; and every nation has at all times, the right of judging of its circumstances and determining on the propriety of changing its laws.

The English writers talk much of the omnipotence of Parliament; and yet they seem to entertain some scruples about their right to change particular parts of their constitution. I question much whether Parliament would not hesitate to change, on any occasion, an article of Magna Charta. Mr. Pitt, a few years ago, attempted to reform the mode of representation in Parliament. Immediately an uproar was raised against the measure, as *unconstitutional*. The representation of the kingdom, when first established, was doubtless equal and wise; but by the increase of some cities and boroughs and the depopulation of others, it has become extremely *unequal*. In some boroughs there is scarcely an elector left to enjoy its privileges. If the nation feels no great inconvenience from this change of circumstances, under the old mode of representation, a reform is unnecessary. But if such a change has produced any national evils of magnitude enough to be felt, the present form of electing the Representatives of the nation, however *constitutional*, and venerable for its antiquity, may at any time be amended, if it should be the sense of Parliament. The *expediency* of the alteration must always be a matter of opinion; but all scruples as to the *right* of making it are totally groundless.

Magna Charta may be considered as a contract between two parties, the King and the Barons, and no contract can be altered but by the consent of both parties. But whenever any article of that deed or contract shall become inconvenient or oppressive, the King, Lords and Commons may either amend or annul it at pleasure.

The same reasoning applies to each of the United States, and to the Federal Republic in general. But an important question will arise from the foregoing remarks, which must be the subject of another paper.

Publius (James Madison)
The Federalist No. 39

Independent Journal (New York), January 16, 1788

To the People of the State of New-York.

The last paper having concluded the observations which were meant to introduce a candid survey of the plan of government reported by the Convention, we now proceed to the execution of that part of our undertaking. The first question that offers itself is, whether the general form and aspect of the government be strictly republican? It is evident that no other form would be reconcileable with the genius of the people of America; with the fundamental principles of the revolution; or with that honorable determination, which animates every votary of freedom, to rest all our political experiments on the capacity of mankind for self-government. If the plan of the Convention therefore be found to depart from the republican character, its advocates must abandon it as no longer defensible.

What then are the distinctive characters of the republican form? Were an answer to this question to be sought, not by recurring to principles, but in the application of the term by political writers, to the constitutions of different States, no satisfactory one would ever be found. Holland, in which no particle of the supreme authority is derived from the people, has passed almost universally under the denomination of a republic. The same title has been bestowed on Venice, where absolute power over the great body of the people, is exercised in the most absolute manner, by a small body of hereditary nobles. Poland, which is a mixture of aristocracy and of monarchy in their worst forms, has been dignified with the same appellation. The government of England which has one republican branch only, combined with a hereditery aristocracy and monarchy, has with equal impropriety been frequently placed on the list of republics. These examples, which are nearly as dissimilar to each other as to a genuine republic, shew the extreme inaccuracy with which the term has been used in political disquisitions.

If we resort for a criterion, to the different principles on which different forms of government are established, we may define a republic to be, or at least may bestow that name on, a government which derives all its powers directly or indirectly from the great body of the people; and is administered by persons holding their offices during pleasure, for a limited period, or during good behaviour. It is *essential* to such a government, that it be derived from the great body of the society, not from an inconsiderable proportion, or a favored class of it; otherwise a handful of tyrannical nobles, exercising their oppressions by a delegation of their powers, might aspire to the rank of republicans, and claim for their government the honorable title of republic. It is *sufficient* for such a government, that the persons administering it be appointed, either directly or indirectly, by the people; and that they hold their appointments by either of the tenures just specified; otherwise every government in the United States, as well as every other popular government that has been or can be well organized or well executed, would be degraded from the republican character. According to the Constitution of every State in the Union, some or other of the officers of government are appointed indirectly only by the people. According to most of them the chief magistrate himself is so appointed. And according to one, this mode of appointment is extended to one of the co-ordinate branches of the legislature. According to all the Constitutions also, the tenure of the highest offices is extended to a definite period, and in many instances, both within the legislative and executive departments, to a period of years. According to the provisions of most of the constitutions, again, as well as according to the most respectable and received opinions on the subject, the members of the judiciary department are to retain their offices by the firm tenure of good behaviour.

On comparing the Constitution planned by the Convention, with the standard here fixed, we perceive at once that it is in the most rigid sense conformable to it. The House of Representatives, like that of one branch at least of all the State Legislatures, is elected immediately by the great body of the people. The Senate, like the present Congress, and the Senate of Maryland, derives its appointment indirectly from the people. The President is indirectly derived from the choice of the people, according to the example in most of the States. Even the judges, with all other officers of the Union, will, as in the several States, be the choice, though a remote choice, of the people themselves. The duration of the appointments is equally conformable to the republican standard, and to the model of the State Constitutions. The House of Representatives is periodically elective as in all the States: and for the period of two years as in the State of South-Carolina. The Senate is elective for the period of six years; which is but one year more than the period of the Senate of Maryland; and but two more than of the Senates of New-York and Virginia. The President is to continue in office for the period of four years; as in New-York and Delaware, the chief magistrate is elected for three years, and in South-Carolina for two years. In the other States the election is annual. In several of the States however, no constitutional provision is made for the impeachment of the Chief Magistrate. And in Delaware and Virginia, he is not impeachable till out of office. The President of the United States is impeachable at any time during his continuance in office. The tenure by which the Judges are to hold their places, is, as it unquestionably ought to be, that of good behaviour. The tenure of the ministerial offices generally will be a subject of legal regulation, conformably to the reason of the case, and the example of the State Constitutions.

Could any further proof be required of the republican complextion of this system, the most decisive one might be found in its absolute prohibition of titles of nobility, both under the Federal and the State Governments; and in its express guarantee of the republican form to each of the latter.

But it was not sufficient, say the adversaries of the proposed Constitution, for the Convention to adhere to the republican form. They ought, with equal care, to have preserved the *federal* form, which regards the union as a *confederacy* of sovereign States; instead of which, they have framed a *national* government, which regards the union as a *consolidation* of the States. And it is asked by what authority this bold and radical innovation was undertaken. The handle which has been made of this objection requires, that it should be examined with some precision.

Without enquiring into the accuracy of the distinction on which the objection is founded, it will be necessary to a just estimate of its force, first to ascertain the real character of the government in question; secondly, to enquire how far the Convention were authorised to propose such a government; and thirdly, how far the duty they owed to their country, could supply any defect of regular authority.

First. In order to ascertain the real character of the government it may be considered in relation to the foundation on which it is to be established; to the sources from which its ordinary powers are to be drawn; to the operation of those powers; to the extent of them; and to the authority by which future changes in the government are to be introduced.

On examining the first relation, it appears on one hand that the Constitution is to be founded on the assent and ratification of the people of America, given by deputies elected for the special purpose; but on the other that this assent and ratification is to be given by the people, not as individuals composing one entire nation; but as composing the distinct and independent States to which they respectively belong. It is to be the assent and ratification of the several States, derived from the supreme authority in each State, the authority of the people themselves. The act therefore establishing the Constitution, will not be a *national* but a *federal* act.

That it will be a federal and not a national act, as these terms are understood by the objectors, the act of the people as forming so many independent States, not as forming one aggregate nation, is obvious from this single consideration that it is to result neither from the decision of a *majority* of the people of the Union, nor from that of a *majority* of the States. It must result from the *unanimous* assent of the several States that are parties to it, differing no other wise from their ordinary assent than in its being expressed, not by the legislative authority, but by that of the people themselves. Were the people regarded in this transaction as forming one nation, the will of the majority of the whole people of the United States, would bind the minority; in the same manner as the majority in each State must bind the minority; and the will of the majority must be determined either by a comparison of the individual votes; or by considering the will of a majority of the States, as evidence of the will of a majority of the people of the United States. Neither of these rules has been adopted. Each State in ratifying the Constitution, is considered as a sovereign body independent of all others, and only to be bound by its own voluntary act. In this relation then the new Constitution will, if established, be a *federal* and not a *national* Constitution.

The next relation is to the sources from which the ordinary powers of government are to be derived. The house of representatives will derive its powers from the people of America, and the people will be represented in the same proportion, and on the same principle, as they are in the Legislature of a particular State. So far the Government is *national* not *federal.* The Senate on the other hand will derive its powers from the States, as political and co-equal societies; and these will be represented on the principle of equality in the Senate, as they now are in the existing Congress. So far the government is *federal,* not *national.* The executive power will be derived from a very compound source. The immediate election of the President is to be made by the States in their political characters. The votes allotted to them, are in a compound ratio, which considers them partly as distinct and co-equal societies; partly as unequal members of the same society. The eventual election, again is to be made by that branch of the Legislature which consists of the national representatives; but in this particular act, they are to be thrown into the form of individual delegations from so many distinct and co-equal bodies politic. From this aspect of the Government, it appears to be of a mixed character presenting at least as many *federal* as *national* features.

The difference between a federal and national Government as it relates to the *operation of the Government* is supposed to consist in this, that in the former, the powers operate on the political bodies composing the confederacy, in their political capacities: In the latter, on the individual citizens, composing the nation, in their individual capacities. On trying the Constitution by this criterion, it falls under the *national,* not the *federal* character; though perhaps not so compleatly, as has been understood. In several cases and particularly in the trial of controversies to which States may be parties, they must be viewed and proceeded against in their collective and political capacities only. So far the national countenance of the Government on this side seems to be disfigured by a few federal features. But this blemish is perhaps unavoidable in any plan; and the operation of the Government on the people in their individual capacities, in its ordinary and most essential proceedings, may on the whole designate it in this relation a *national* Government.

But if the Government be national with regard to the *operation* of its powers, it changes its aspect again when we contemplate it in relation to the *extent* of its powers. The idea of a national Government involves in it, not only an authority over the individual citizens; but an indefinite supremacy over all persons and things, so far as they are objects of lawful Government. Among a people consolidated into one nation, this supremacy is compleatly vested in the national Legislature. Among communities united for particular purposes, it is vested partly in the general, and partly in the municipal Legislatures. In the former case, all local authorities are subordinate to the supreme; and may be controuled, directed or abolished by it at pleasure. In the latter the local or municipal authorities form distinct and independent portions of the supremacy, no more subject within their respective spheres to the general authority, than the general authority is subject to them, within its own sphere. In this relation then the proposed Government cannot be deemed a *national* one; since its jurisdiction extends to certain enumerated objects only, and leaves to the several States a residuary and inviolable sovereignty over all other objects. It is true that in controversies relating to the boundary between the two jurisdictions, the tribunal which is ultimately to decide, is to be established under the general Government. But this does not change the principle of the case. The decision is to be impartially made, according to the rules of the Constitution; and all the usual and most effectual precautions are taken to secure this impartiality. Some such tribunal is clearly essential to prevent an appeal to the sword, and a dissolution of the compact; and that it ought to be established under the general, rather than under the local Governments; or to speak more properly, that it could be safely established under the first alone, is a position not likely to be combated.

If we try the Constitution by its last relation, to the authority by which amendments are to be made, we find it neither wholly *national*, nor wholly *federal*. Were it wholly national, the supreme and ultimate authority would reside in the *majority* of the people of the Union; and this authority would be competent at all times, like that of a majority of every national society, to alter or abolish its established Government. Were it wholly federal on the other head, the concurrence of each State in the Union would be essential to every alteration that would be binding on all. The mode provided by the plan of the Convention is not founded on either of these principles. In requiring more than a majority, and particularly, in computing the proportion by *States*, not by *citizens*, it departs from the *national*, and advances towards the *federal* character: In rendering the concurrence of less than the whole number of States sufficient, it loses again the *federal*, and partakes of the *national* character.

The proposed Constitution therefore is in strictness neither a national nor a federal constitution; but a composition of both. In its foundation, it is federal, not national; in the sources from which the ordinary powers of the Government are drawn, it is partly federal, and partly national: in the operation of these powers, it is national, not federal: In the extent of them again, it is federal, not national: And finally, in the authoritative mode of introducing amendments, it is neither wholly federal, nor wholly national.

On the New Constitution

State Gazette of South Carolina (Charleston), January 28, 1788

In evil hour his pen 'squire Adams drew
Claiming dominion to his well born few:
In the gay circle of St. James's plac'd
He wrote, and, writing, has his work disgrac'd.
Smit with the splendor of a British King
The crown prevail'd, so once despis'd a thing!
Shelburne and Pitt approv'd of all he wrote,
While Rush and Wilson echo back his note.

Tho' British armies could not here prevail
Yet British politics shall turn the scale;—
In five short years of Freedom weary grown
We quit our plain republics for a throne;
Congress and *President* full proof shall bring,
A mere disguise for Parliament and King.

A standing army!—curse the plan so base;
A despot's safety—Liberty's disgrace.—
Who sav'd these realms from Britain's bloody hand,
Who, but the generous rustics of the land;
That free-born race, inur'd to every toil,
Who tame the ocean and subdue the soil,
Who tyrants banish'd from this injur'd shore
Domestic traitors may expel once more.

Ye, who have bled in Freedom's sacred cause,
Ah, why desert her maxims and her laws?
When *thirteen* states are moulded into *one*
Your rights are vanish'd and your honors gone;
The form of Freedom shall alone remain,
As Rome had Senators when she hugg'd the chain.

Sent to revise your systems—not to change—
Sages have done what Reason deems most strange:

Some alterations in our fabric we
Calmly propos'd, and hoped at length to see—
Ah, how deceived!—these heroes in renown
Scheme for themselves—and pull the fabric down—
Bid in its place Columbia's tomb-stone rise
Inscrib'd with these sad words—*Here Freedom lies!*

Brutus XI

New York Journal, January 31, 1788

The nature and extent of the judicial power of the United States, proposed to be granted by this constitution, claims our particular attention.

Much has been said and written upon the subject of this new system on both sides, but I have not met with any writer, who has discussed the judicial powers with any degree of accuracy. And yet it is obvious, that we can form but very imperfect ideas of the manner in which this government will work, or the effect it will have in changing the internal police and mode of distributing justice at present subsisting in the respective states, without a thorough investigation of the powers of the judiciary and of the manner in which they will operate. This government is a complete system, not only for making, but for executing laws. And the courts of law, which will be constituted by it, are not only to decide upon the constitution and the laws made in pursuance of it, but by officers subordinate to them to execute all their decisions. The real effect of this system of government, will therefore be brought home to the feelings of the people, through the medium of the judicial power. It is, moreover, of great importance, to examine with care the nature and extent of the judicial power, because those who are to be vested with it, are to be placed in a situation altogether unprecedented in a free country. They are to be rendered totally independent, both of the people and the legislature, both with respect to their offices and salaries. No errors they may commit can be corrected by any power above them, if any such power there be, nor can they be removed from office for making ever so many erroneous adjudications.

The only causes for which they can be displaced, is, conviction of treason, bribery, and high crimes and misdemeanors.

This part of the plan is so modelled, as to authorise the courts, not only to carry into execution the powers expressly given, but where these are wanting or ambiguously expressed, to supply what is wanting by their own decisions.

That we may be enabled to form a just opinion on this subject, I shall, in considering it,

1st. Examine the nature and extent of the judicial powers—and

2d. Enquire, whether the courts who are to exercise them, are so constituted as to afford reasonable ground of confidence, that they will exercise them for the general good.

With a regard to the nature and extent of the judicial powers, I have to regret my want of capacity to give that full and minute explanation of them that the subject merits. To be able to do this, a man should be possessed of a degree of law knowledge far beyond what I pretend to. A number of hard words and technical phrases are used in this part of the system, about the meaning of which gentlemen learned in the law differ.

Its advocates know how to avail themselves of these phrases. In a number of instances, where objections are made to the powers given to the judicial, they give such an explanation to the technical terms as to avoid them.

Though I am not competent to give a perfect explanation of the powers granted to this department of the government, I shall yet attempt to trace some of the leading features of it, from which I presume it will appear, that they will operate to a total subversion of the state judiciaries, if not, to the legislative authority of the states.

In article 3d, sect. 2d, it is said, "The judicial power shall extend to all cases in law and equity arising under this constitution, the laws of the United States, and treaties made, or which shall be made, under their authority, &c."

The first article to which this power extends, is, all cases in law and equity arising under this constitution.

What latitude of construction this clause should receive, it is not easy to say. At first view, one would suppose, that it meant no more than this, that the courts under the general government should exercise, not only the powers of courts of law, but also that of courts of equity, in the manner in which those powers are usually exercised in the different states. But this cannot be the meaning, because the next clause authorises the courts to take cognizance of all cases in law and equity arising under the laws of the United States; this last article, I conceive, conveys as much power to the general judicial as any of the state courts possess.

The cases arising under the constitution must be different from those arising under the laws, or else the two clauses mean exactly the same thing.

The cases arising under the constitution must include such, as bring into question its meaning, and will require an explanation of the nature and extent of the powers of the different departments under it.

This article, therefore, vests the judicial with a power to resolve all questions that may arise on any case on the construction of the constitution, either in law or in equity.

1st. They are authorised to determine all questions that may arise upon the meaning of the constitution in law. This article vests the courts with authority to give the constitution a legal construction, or to explain it according to the rules laid down for construing a law.—These rules give a certain degree of latitude of explanation. According to this mode of construction, the courts are to give such meaning to the constitution as comports best with the common, and generally received acceptation of the words in which it is expressed, regarding their ordinary and popular use, rather than their grammatical propriety. Where words are dubious, they will be explained by the context. The end of the clause will be attended to, and the words will be understood, as having a view to it; and the words will not be so understood as to bear no meaning or a very absurd one.

2d. The judicial are not only to decide questions arising upon the meaning of the constitution in law, but also in equity.

By this they are empowered, to explain the constitution according to the reasoning spirit of it, without being confined to the words or letter.

"From this method of interpreting laws (says Blackstone) by the reason of them, arises what we call equity;" which is thus defined by Grotius, "the correction of that, wherein the law, by reason of its universality, is deficient; for since in laws all cases cannot be foreseen, or expressed, it is necessary, that when the decrees of the law cannot be applied to particular cases, there should some where be a power vested of defining those circumstances, which had they been foreseen the legislator would have expressed; and these are the cases, which according to Grotius, lex non exacte definit, sed arbitrio boni viri permittet."

The same learned author observes, "That equity, thus depending essentially upon each individual case, there can be no established rules and fixed principles of equity laid down, without destroying its very essence, and reducing it to a positive law."

From these remarks, the authority and business of the courts of law, under this clause, may be understood.

They will give the sense of every article of the constitution, that may from time to time come before them. And in their decisions they will not confine themselves to any fixed or established rules, but will determine, according to what appears to them, the reason and spirit of the constitution. The opinions of the supreme court, whatever they may be, will have the force of law; because there is no power provided in the constitution, that can correct their errors, or controul their adjudications. From this court there is no appeal. And I conceive the legislature themselves, cannot set aside a judgment of this court, because they are authorised by the constitution to decide in the last resort. The legislature must be controuled by the constitution, and not the constitution by them. They have therefore no more right to set aside any judgment pronounced upon the construction of the constitution, than they have to take from the president, the chief command of the army and navy, and commit it to some other person. The reason is plain; the judicial and executive derive their authority from the same source, that the legislature do theirs; and therefore in all cases, where the constitution does not make the one responsible to, or controulable by the other, they are altogether independent of each other.

The judicial power will operate to effect, in the most certain, but yet silent and imperceptible manner, what is evidently the tendency of the constitution:—I mean, an entire subversion of the legislative, executive and judicial powers of the individual states. Every adjudication of the supreme court, on any question that may arise upon the nature and extent of the general government, will affect the limits of the state jurisdiction. In proportion as the former enlarge the exercise of their powers, will that of the latter be restricted.

That the judicial power of the United States, will lean strongly in favour of the general government, and will give such an explanation to the constitution, as will favour an extension of its jurisdiction, is very evident from a variety of considerations.

1st. The constitution itself strongly countenances such a mode of construction. Most of the articles in this system, which convey powers of any considerable importance, are conceived in general and indefinite terms, which are either equivocal, ambiguous, or which require long definitions to unfold the extent of their meaning. The two most important powers committed to any government, those of raising money, and of raising and keeping up troops, have already been considered, and shewn to be unlimitted by any thing but the discretion of the legislature. The clause which vests the power to pass all laws which are proper and necessary, to carry the powers given into execution, it has been shewn, leaves the legislature at liberty, to do every thing, which in their judgment is best. It is said, I know, that this clause confers no power on the legislature, which they would not have had without it—though I believe this is not the fact, yet, admitting it to be, it implies that the constitution is not to receive an explanation strictly, according to its letter; but more power is implied than is expressed. And this clause, if it is to be considered, as explanatory of the extent of the powers given, rather than giving a new power, is to be understood as declaring, that in construing any of the articles conveying power, the spirit, intent and design of the clause, should be attended to, as well as the words in their common acceptation.

This constitution gives sufficient colour for adopting an equitable construction, if we consider the great end and design it professedly has in view—there appears from its preamble to be, "to form a more perfect union, establish justice, insure domestic tranquillity, provide for the common defence, promote the general welfare, and secure the blessings of liberty to ourselves and posterity." The design of this system is here expressed, and it is proper to give such a meaning to the various parts, as will best promote the accomplishment of the end; this idea suggests itself naturally upon reading the preamble, and will countenance the court in giving the several articles such a sense, as will the most effectually promote the ends the constitution had in view—how this manner of explaining the constitution will operate in practice, shall be the subject of future enquiry.

2d. Not only will the constitution justify the courts in inclining to this mode of explaining it, but they will be interested in using this latitude of interpretation. Every body of men invested with office are tenacious of power; they feel interested, and hence it has become a kind of maxim, to hand down their offices, with all its rights and privileges, unimpared to their successors; the same principle will influence them to extend their power, and increase their rights; this of itself will operate strongly upon the courts to give such a meaning to the constitution in all cases where it can possibly be done, as will enlarge the sphere of their own authority. Every extension of the power of the general legislature, as well as of the judicial powers, will increase the powers of the courts; and the dignity and importance of the judges, will be in proportion to the extent and magnitude of the powers they exercise. I add, it is highly probable the emolument of the judges will be increased, with the increase of the business they will have to transact and its importance. From these considerations the judges will be interested to extend the powers of the courts, and to construe the constitution as much as possible, in such a way as to favour it; and that they will do it, appears probable.

3d. Because they will have precedent to plead, to justify them in it. It is well known, that the courts in England, have by their own authority, extended their jurisdiction far beyond the limits set them in their original institution, and by the laws of the land.

The court of exchequer is a remarkable instance of this. It was originally intended principally to recover the king's debts, and to order the revenues of the crown. It had a common law jurisdiction, which was established merely for the benefit of the king's accomptants. We learn from Blackstone, that the proceedings in this court are grounded on a writ called quo minus, in which the plaintiff suggests, that he is the king's farmer or debtor, and that the defendant hath done him the damage complained of, by which he is less able to pay the king. These suits, by the statute of Rutland, are expressly directed to be confined to such matters as specially concern the king, or his ministers in the exchequer. And by the articuli super cartas, it is enacted, that no common pleas be thenceforth held in the exchequer contrary to the form of the great charter: but now any person may sue in the exchequer. The surmise of being debtor to the king being matter of form, and mere words of course; and the court is open to all the nation.

When the courts will have a precedent before them of a court which extended its jurisdiction in opposition to an act of the legislature, is it not to be expected that they will extend theirs, especially when there is nothing in the constitution expressly against it? and they are authorised to construe its meaning, and are not under any controul?

This power in the judicial, will enable them to mould the government, into almost any shape they please.—The manner in which this may be effected we will hereafter examine.

Civis (David Ramsay) to the Citizens of South Carolina

Columbian Herald (Charleston, S.C.), February 4, 1788

Friends, Countrymen, and Fellow Citizens, You have at this time a new federal constitution proposed for your consideration. The great importance of the subject demands your most serious attention. To assist you in forming a right judgment on this matter, it will be proper to consider,

1st. It is the manifest interest of these states to be united. External wars among ourselves would most probably be the consequence of disunion. Our local weakness particularly proves it to be for the advantage of South-Carolina to strengthen the federal government; for we are inadequate to secure ourselves from more powerful neighbours.

2d. If the thirteen states are to be united in reality, as well as in name, the obvious principle of the union should be, that the Congress or general government, should have power to regulate all general concerns. In a state of nature, each man is free and may do what he pleases; but in society, every individual must sacrifice a part of his natural rights; the minority must yield to the majority, and the collective interest must controul particular interests. When thirteen persons constitute a family, each should forego every thing that is injurious to the other twelve. When several families constitute a parish, or county, each may adopt any regulations it pleases with regard to its domestic affairs, but must be abridged of that liberty in other cases, where the good of the whole is concerned.

When several parishes, counties or districts form a state, the separate interests of each must yield to the collective interest of the whole. When thirteen states combine in one government, the same principles must be observed. These relinquishments of natural rights, are not real sacrifices: each person, county or state, gains more than it loses, for it only gives up a right of injuring others, and obtains in return aid and strength to secure itself in the peaceable enjoyment of all remaining rights. If then we are to be an united people, and the obvious ground

of union must be, that all continental concerns should be managed by Congress—let us by these principles examine the new
constitution. Look over the 8th section, which enumerates the
powers of Congress, and point out one that is not essential on
the before recited principles of union. The first is a power to lay
and collect taxes, duties, imposts and excises, to pay the debts,
and provide for the common defence and general welfare of
the United States.

When you authorised Congress to borrow money, and to
contract debts for carrying on the late war, you could not intend to abridge them of the means of paying their engagements, made on your account. You may observe, that their
future power is confined to provide for the *common defence*
and *general welfare* of the United States. If they apply money
to any other purposes, they exceed their powers. The people
of the United States who pay, are to be judges how far their
money is properly applied. It would be tedious to go over all
the powers of Congress, but it would be easy to shew that
they all may be referred to this single principle, "that the general concerns of the union ought to be managed by the general
government." The opposers of the constitution, cannot shew
a single power delegated to Congress, that could be spared
consistently with the welfare of the whole, nor a single one
taken from the states, but such as can be more advantageously
lodged in the general government, than in that of the separate
states.

For instance—the states cannot emit money; this is not intended to prevent the emission of paper money, but only of
state paper money. Is not this an advantage? To have thirteen
paper currencies in thirteen states is embarrassing to commerce, and eminently so to travellers. It is obviously our interest, either to have no paper, or such as will circulate from
Georgia to New-Hampshire. Take another instance—the Congress are authorised to provide and maintain a navy—Our sea
coast in its whole extent needs the protection thereof; but if
this was to be done by the states, they who build ships, would
be more secure than they who do not. Again, if the local legislatures might build ships of war at pleasure, the Eastern would
have a manifest superiority over the Southern states. Observe
how much better this business is referred to the regulations of

Congress. A common navy, paid out of the common treasury, and to be disposed of by the united voice of a majority for the common defence of the weaker as well as of the stronger states, is promised, and will result from the federal constitution. Suffer not yourselves to be imposed on by declamation. Ask the man who objects to the powers of Congress two questions. Is it not necessary that the supposed dangerous power be lodged somewhere? and secondly, where can it be lodged consistently with the general good, so well as in the general government? Decide for yourselves on these obvious principles of union.

It has been objected, that the eastern states have an advantage in their representation in Congress. Let us examine this objection—the four eastern states send seventeen members to the house of representatives, but Georgia, South-Carolina, North-Carolina and Virginia, send twenty-three. The six northern states send twenty-seven, the six southern thirty. In both cases we have a superiority;—but, say the objectors, add Pennsylvania to the northern states, and there is a majority against us. It is obvious to reply, add Pennsylvania to the Southern states, and they have a majority. The objection amounts to no more than that seven are more than six. It must be known to many of you, that the Southern states, from their vast extent of uncultivated country, are daily receiving new settlers; but in New-England their country is so small, and their land so poor, that their inhabitants are constantly emigrating. As the rule of representation in Congress is to vary with the number of inhabitants, our influence in the general government will be constantly increasing. In fifty years, it is probable that the Southern states will have a great ascendency over the Eastern. It has been said that thirty-five men, not elected by yourselves, may make laws to bind you. This objection, if it has any force, tends to the destruction of your state government. By our constitution, sixty-nine make a quorum, of course, thirty-five members may make a law to bind all the people of South-Carolina.— Charleston, and any one of the neighbouring parishes send collectively thirty-six members; it is therefore possible, in the absence of all others, that three of the lower parishes might legislate for the whole country. Would this be a valid objection against your own constitution? It certainly would not—neither is it against the proposed federal plan. Learn from it this useful lesson—insist on the constant attendance of your members, both in the state assembly, and Continental Congress: your representation in the latter, is as numerous in a relative proportion with the other states as it ought to be. You have a thirteenth part in both houses; and you are not, on principles of equality, entitled to more.

It has been objected, that the president, and two-thirds of the senate, though not of your election, may make treaties binding on this state. Ask these objectors—do you wish to have any treaties? They will say yes.—Ask then who can be more properly trusted with the power of making them, than they to whom the convention have referred it? Can the state legislatures? They would consult their local interests—Can the Continental House of Representatives? When sixty-five men can keep a secret, they may. Observe the cautious guards which are placed around your interests. Neither the senate nor president can make treaties by their separate authority.—They must both concur.—This is more in your favor than the footing on which you now stand. The delegates in Congress of nine states, without your consent can not bind you;—by the new constitution there must be two thirds of the members present, and also the president, in whose election you have a vote. Two thirds are to the whole nearly as nine to thirteen. If you are not wanting to yourselves by neglecting to keep up the states compliment of senators, your situation with regard to preventing the controul of your local interests by the Northern states, will be better under the proposed constitution than now it is under the existing confederation.

It has been said, we will have a navigation act, and be restricted to American bottoms, and that high freight will be the consequence. We certainly ought to have a navigation act, and we assuredly ought to give a preference, though not a monopoly, to our own shipping.

If this state is invaded by a maritime force, to whom can we apply for immediate aid?—To Virginia and North-Carolina? Before they can march by land to our assistance, the country may be over run. The Eastern states, abounding in men and in ships, can sooner relieve us, than our next door neighbours. It is therefore not only our duty, but our interest, to encourage their shipping. They have sufficient resources on a few months notice, to furnish tonnage enough to carry off all your exports; and they can afford, and doubtless will undertake to be your carriers on as easy terms as you now pay for freight in foreign bottoms.

On this subject, let us consider what we have gained, & also what they have lost by the revolution. We have gained a free trade with all the world, and consequently a higher price for our commodities, it may be said, and so have they; but they who reply in this manner, ought to know, that there is an amazing difference in our favor: their country affords no valuable exports, and of course the privilege of a free trade is to them of little value, while our staple commodity commands a higher price than was usual before the war. We have also gained an exemption from quit rents, to which the eastern states were not subjected. Connecticut and Rhode-Island were nearly as free before the revolution as since. They had no royal governor or councils to control them, or to legislate for them. Massachusetts and New-Hampshire were much nearer independence in their late constitutions than we were. The eastern states, by the revolution, have been deprived of a market for their fish, of their carrying-trade, their ship building, and almost of every thing but their liberties.

As the war has turned out so much in our favor, and so much against them, ought we to begrudge them the carrying of our produce, especially when it is considered, that by encouraging their shipping, we increase the means of our own defence. Let us examine also the federal constitution, by the principle of reciprocal concession. We have laid a foundation for a navigation act.—This will be a general good; but particularly so to our northern brethren. On the other hand, they have agreed to change the federal rule of paying the continental debt, according to the value of land as laid down in the confederation, for a new principle of apportionment, to be founded on the numbers of inhabitants in the several states respectively. This is an immense concession in our favor. Their land is poor; our's rich; their numbers great; our's small; labour with them is done by white men, for whom they pay an equal share; while five of our negroes only count as equal to three of their whites. This will make a difference of many thousands of pounds in settling our continental accounts. It is farther objected, that they have stipulated for a right to prohibit the importation of negroes after 21 years. On this subject observe, as they are bound to protect us from domestic violence, they think we ought not to increase our exposure to that evil, by an unlimited importation of slaves. Though Congress may forbid the importation of negroes after 21 years, it does not follow that they will. On the other hand, it is probable that they will not. The more rice we make, the more business will be for their shipping: their interest will therefore coincide with our's. Besides, we have other sources of supply—the importations of the ensuing 20 years, added to the natural increase of those we already have, and the influx from our northern neighbours, who are desirous of getting rid of their slaves, will afford a sufficient number for cultivating all the lands in this state.

Let us suppose the union to be dissolved by the rejection of the new constitution, what would be our case? The United States owe several millions of dollars to France, Spain, and Holland. If an efficient government is not adopted, which will provide for the payment of our debt, especially of that which is due to foreigners—who will be the losers? Most certainly the southern states. Our exports, as being the most valuable, would be the first objects of capture on the high seas; or descents would be made on our defenceless coasts, till the creditors of the United States had paid themselves at the expence of this weaker part of the union. Let us also compare the present confederation, with the proposed constitution. The former can neither protect us at home, nor gain us respect abroad: it cannot secure the payment of our debts, nor command the resources of our country, in case of danger. Without money, without a navy, or the means of even supporting an army of our own citizens in the field, we lie at the mercy of every invader; our sea port towns may be laid under contribution, and our country ravaged.

By the new constitution, you will be protected with the force of the union, against domestic violence and foreign invasion. You will have a navy to defend your coasts.—The respectable figure you will make among the nations, will so far command the attention of foreign powers, that it is probable you will soon obtain such commercial treaties, as will open to your vessels the West-Indian islands, and give life to your expiring commerce.

In a country like our's, abounding with free men all of one rank, where property is equally diffused, where estates are held in fee simple, the press free, and the means of information common; tyranny cannot readily find admission under any form of government; but its admission is next to impossible, under one where the people are the source of all power, and elect either mediately by their representatives, or immediately by themselves the whole of their rulers.

Examine the new constitution with candor and liberality. Indulge no narrow prejudices to the disadvantage of your brethren of the other states; consider the people of all the thirteen states, as a band of brethren, speaking the same language, professing the same religion, inhabiting one undivided country, and designed by heaven to be one people. Consent that what regards all the states should be managed by that body which represents all of them; be on your guard against the misrepresentations of men who are involved in debt; such may wish to see the constitution rejected, because of the following clause "no state shall emit bills of credit, make any thing but gold and silver coin, a tender in payment of debts, pass any *expost facto* law, or law impairing the obligation of contracts." This will doubtless bear hard on debtors who wish to defraud their creditors, but it will be of real service to the honest part of the community. Examine well the characters & circumstances of men who are averse to the new constitution. Perhaps you will find that the above recited clause is the real ground of the opposition of some of them, though they may artfully cover it with a splendid profession of zeal for state privileges and general liberty.

On the whole, if the proposed constitution is not calculated to better your country, and to secure to you the blessings for which you have so successfully contended, reject it: but if it is an improvement on the present confederation, and contains within itself the principles of farther improvement suited to future circumstances, join the mighty current of federalism, and give it your hearty support. You were among the first states that formed an independent constitution; be not among the last in accepting and ratifying the proposed plan of federal government; it is your sheet anchor; and without it, independence may prove a curse.

Publius (James Madison)
The Federalist No. 54

New-York Packet, February 12, 1788

To the People of the State of New-York.

The next view which I shall take of the House of Representatives, relates to the apportionment of its members to the several States, which is to be determined by the same rule with that of direct taxes.

It is not contended that the number of people in each State ought not to be the standard for regulating the proportion of those who are to represent the people of each State. The establishment of the same rule for the apportionment of taxes, will probably be as little contested; though the rule itself in this case, is by no means founded on the same principle. In the former case, the rule is understood to refer to the personal rights of the people, with which it has a natural and universal connection. In the latter, it has reference to the proportion of wealth, of which it is in no case a precise measure, and in ordinary cases a very unfit one. But notwithstanding the imperfection of the rule as applied to the relative wealth and contributions of the States, it is evidently the least exceptionable among the practicable rules; and had too recently obtained the general sanction of America, not to have found a ready preference with the Convention.

All this is admitted, it will perhaps be said: But does it follow from an admission of numbers for the measure of representation, or of slaves combined with free citizens, as a ratio of taxation, that slaves ought to be included in the numerical rule of representation? Slaves are considered as property, not as persons. They ought therefore to be comprehended in estimates of taxation which are founded on property, and to be excluded from representation which is regulated by a census of persons. This is the objection, as I understand it, stated in its full force. I shall be equally candid in stating the reasoning which may be offered on the opposite side.

We subscribe to the doctrine, might one of our southern brethren observe, that representation relates more immediately

to persons, and taxation more immediately to property, and we
join in the application of this distinction to the case of our
slaves. But we must deny the fact that slaves are considered
merely as property, and in no respect whatever as persons. The
true state of the case is, that they partake of both these qualities; being considered by our laws, in some respects, as persons,
and in other respects, as property. In being compelled to labor
not for himself, but for a master; in being vendible by one
master to another master; and in being subject at all times to
be restrained in his liberty, and chastised in his body, by the
capricious will of another, the slave may appear to be degraded
from the human rank, and classed with those irrational ani-
mals, which fall under the legal denomination of property. In
being protected on the other hand in his life & in his limbs,
against the violence of all others, even the master of his labor
and his liberty; and in being punishable himself for all violence committed against others, the slave is no less evidently
regarded by the law as a member of the society; not as a part of
the irrational creation; as a moral person, not as a mere article
of property. The Fœderal Constitution therefore, decides with
great propriety on the case of our slaves, when it views them
in the mixt character of persons and of property. This is in
fact their true character. It is the character bestowed on them
by the laws under which they live; and it will not be denied that
these are the proper criterion; because it is only under the pretext that the laws have transformed the negroes into subjects
of property, that a place is disputed them in the computation
of numbers; and it is admitted that if the laws were to restore
the rights which have been taken away, the negroes could no
longer be refused an equal share of representation with the
other inhabitants.

This question may be placed in another light. It is agreed on
all sides, that numbers are the best scale of wealth and taxation,
as they are the only proper scale of representation. Would the
Convention have been impartial or consistent, if they had rejected the slaves from the list of inhabitants when the shares of
representation were to be calculated; and inserted them on the
lists when the tariff of contributions was to be adjusted? Could
it be reasonably expected that the southern States would concur in a system which considered their slaves in some degree as

men, when burdens were to be imposed, but refused to consider them in the same light when advantages were to be conferred? Might not some surprize also be expressed that those who reproach the southern States with the barbarous policy of considering as property a part of their human brethren, should themselves contend that the government to which all the States are to be parties, ought to consider this unfortunate race more compleatly in the unnatural light of property, than the very laws of which they complain!

It may be replied perhaps that slaves are not included in the estimate of representatives in any of the States possessing them. They neither vote themselves, nor increase the votes of their masters. Upon what principle then ought they to be taken into the fœderal estimate of representation? In rejecting them altogether, the Constitution would in this respect have followed the very laws which have been appealed to, as the proper guide.

This objection is repelled by a single observation. It is a fundamental principle of the proposed Constitution, that as the aggregate number of representatives allotted to the several States, is to be determined by a fœderal rule founded on the aggregate number of inhabitants, so the right of choosing this allotted number in each State is to be exercised by such part of the inhabitants, as the State itself may designate. The qualifications on which the right of suffrage depend, are not perhaps the same in any two States. In some of the States the difference is very material. In every State, a certain proportion of inhabitants are deprived of this right by the Constitution of the State, who will be included in the census by which the Fœderal Constitution apportions the representatives. In this point of view, the southern States might retort the complaint, by insisting, that the principle laid down by the Convention required that no regard should be had to the policy of particular States towards their own inhabitants; and consequently, that the slaves as inhabitants should have been admitted into the census according to their full number, in like manner with other inhabitants, who by the policy of other States, are not admitted to all the rights of citizens. A rigorous adherence however to this principle is waved by those who would be gainers by it. All that they ask is, that equal moderation be shewn on the other side. Let the case of the slaves be considered as it is in truth a peculiar one. Let the compromising expedient of the Constitution be mutually adopted, which regards them as inhabitants, but as debased by servitude below the equal level of free inhabitants, which regards the *slave* as divested of two fifths of the *man*.

After all may not another ground be taken on which this article of the Constitution, will admit of a still more ready defence. We have hitherto proceeded on the idea that representation related to persons only, and not at all to property. But is it a just idea? Government is instituted no less for protection of the property, than of the persons of individuals. The one as well as the other, therefore may be considered as represented by those who are charged with the government. Upon this principle it is, that in several of the States, and particularly in the State of New-York, one branch of the government is intended more especially to be the guardian of property, and is accordingly elected by that part of the society which is most interested in this object of government. In the Fœderal Constitution, this policy does not prevail. The rights of property are committed into the same hands with the personal rights. Some attention ought therefore to be paid to property in the choice of those hands.

For another reason the votes allowed in the Fœderal Legislature to the people of each State, ought to bear some proportion to the comparative wealth of the States. States have not like individuals, an influence over each other arising from superior advantages of fortune. If the law allows an opulent citizen but a single vote in the choice of his representative, the respect and consequence which he derives from his fortunate situation, very frequently guide the votes of others to the objects of his choice; and through this imperceptible channel the rights of property are conveyed into the public representation. A State possesses no such influence over other States. It is not probable that the richest State in the confederacy will ever influence the choice of a single representative in any other State. Nor will the representatives of the larger and richer States, possess any other advantage in the Fœderal Legislature over the representatives of other States, than what may result from their superior number alone; as far therefore as their superior wealth and weight may justly entitle them to any advantage, it ought to be secured to them by a superior share of representation. The new

Constitution is in this respect materially different from the existing confederation, as well as from that of the United Netherlands, and other similar confederacies. In each of the latter the efficacy of the fœderal resolutions depends on the subsequent and voluntary resolutions of the States composing the Union. Hence the States, though possessing an equal vote in the public councils, have an unequal influence, corresponding with the unequal importance of these subsequent and voluntary resolutions. Under the proposed Constitution, the fœderal acts will take effect without the necessary intervention of the individual States. They will depend merely on the majority of votes in the Fœderal Legislature, and consequently each vote whether proceeding from a larger or a smaller State, or a State more or less wealthy or powerful, will have an equal weight and efficacy; in the same manner as the votes individually given in a State Legislature, by the representatives of unequal counties or other districts, have each a precise equality of value and effect; or if there be any difference in the case, it proceeds from the difference in the personal character of the individual representative, rather than from any regard to the extent of the district from which he comes.

Such is the reasoning which an advocate for the southern interests might employ on this subject: And although it may appear to be a little strained in some points, yet on the whole, I must confess, that it fully reconciles me to the scale of representation, which the Convention have established.

In one respect the establishment of a common measure for representation and taxation will have a very salutary effect. As the accuracy of the census to be obtained by the Congress, will necessarily depend in a considerable degree on the disposition, if not the co-operation of the States, it is of great importance that the States should feel as little bias as possible to swell or to reduce the amount of their numbers. Were their share of representation alone to be governed by this rule they would have an interest in exaggerating their inhabitants. Were the rule to decide their share of taxation alone, a contrary temptation would prevail. By extending the rule to both objects, the States will have opposite interests, which will controul and balance each other; and produce the requisite impartiality.

PART 5:
THE FUTURE OF THE
AMERICAN REPUBLIC

IF MEN were angels, Madison wrote in **Federalist 51**, no government would be necessary, but in a government of men, ambition would have to be restrained. Madison argued that the multiplicity of interests in the federal republic of the United States would make it difficult for majorities to oppress minorities, and the separation of powers in the government would make it difficult for any one branch to overwhelm the others. Ambition would counteract ambition. *Brutus XII* disputed this, arguing that the Supreme Court would interpret the Constitution "according to its spirit and reason, and not to confine themselves to its letter," and would tell state legislatures what kinds of laws might be adopted. *Brutus XV* argued that the Supreme Court would use its power to abolish the state governments—an end, he claimed, that some advocates of the Constitution privately desired. Hamilton argued in **Federalist 78** that the judiciary was actually the least dangerous branch. **Harry Innes**, attorney general in the Kentucky district of Virginia, feared that the Constitution would destroy the western country by allowing the eastern states to stifle westward migration and prevent trade on the Mississippi. Innes also feared that the federal judiciary would favor the East. He opposed ratification in Virginia's 1788 convention. Nominated to run against Madison for a seat in the Virginia convention, Baptist minister **John Leland** sent Madison his objections to the Constitution, particularly about what Leland saw as its threat to religious liberty. Alexander Hamilton in **Federalist 70** argued that a single executive—rather than a committee, or an executive advised by a council—was consistent with republican government and essential to good government. **George Washington** hoped that those chosen to administer the new government would have enough wisdom and virtue to restore public faith and promote national respectability. Washington thought the opposition to ratification contributed more good than evil. The opposition had brought forth "abilities" to defend the Constitution, to shed new light on the science of government, and to give a full discussion to the rights of man. All of these arguments in support of ratification, he hoped, would make a lasting impression on those who read them.

Publius (James Madison)
The Federalist No. 51

Independent Journal (New York), February 6, 1788

To the People of the State of New-York.

To what expedient then shall we finally resort for maintaining in practice the necessary partition of power among the several departments, as laid down in the constitution? The only answer that can be given is, that as all these exterior provisions are found to be inadequate, the defect must be supplied, by so contriving the interior structure of the government, as that its several constituent parts may, by their mutual relations, be the means of keeping each other in their proper places. Without presuming to undertake a full developement of this important idea, I will hazard a few general observations, which may perhaps place it in a clearer light, and enable us to form a more correct judgment of the principles and structure of the government planned by the convention.

In order to lay a due foundation for that separate and distinct exercise of the different powers of government, which to a certain extent, is admitted on all hands to be essential to the preservation of liberty, it is evident that each department should have a will of its own; and consequently should be so constituted, that the members of each should have as little agency as possible in the appointment of the members of the others. Were this principle rigorously adhered to, it would require that all the appointments for the supreme executive, legislative, and judiciary magistracies, should be drawn from the same fountain of authority, the people, through channels, having no communication whatever with one another. Perhaps such a plan of constructing the several departments would be less difficult in practice than it may in contemplation appear. Some difficulties however, and some additional expence, would attend the execution of it. Some deviations therefore from the principle must be admitted. In the constitution of the judiciary department in particular, it might be inexpedient to insist rigorously on the principle; first, because peculiar qualifications being essential in the members, the primary consideration ought to be to select that mode of choice, which best secures these qualifications; secondly, because the permanent tenure by which the appointments are held in that department, must soon destroy all sense of dependence on the authority conferring them.

It is equally evident that the members of each department should be as little dependent as possible on those of the others, for the emoluments annexed to their offices. Were the executive magistrate, or the judges, not independent of the legislature in this particular, their independence in every other would be merely nominal.

But the great security against a gradual concentration of the several powers in the same department, consists in giving to those who administer each department, the necessary constitutional means, and personal motives, to resist encroachments of the others. The provision for defence must in this, as in all other cases, be made commensurate to the danger of attack. Ambition must be made to counteract ambition. The interest of the man must be connected with the constitutional rights of the place. It may be a reflection on human nature, that such devices should be necessary to controul the abuses of government. But what is government itself but the greatest of all reflections on human nature? If men were angels, no government would be necessary. If angels were to govern men, neither external nor internal controuls on government would be necessary. In framing a government which is to be administered by men over men, the great difficulty lies in this: You must first enable the government to controul the governed; and in the next place, oblige it to controul itself. A dependence on the people is no doubt the primary controul on the government; but experience has taught mankind the necessity of auxiliary precautions.

This policy of supplying by opposite and rival interests, the defect of better motives, might be traced through the whole system of human affairs, private as well as public. We see it particularly displayed in all the subordinate distributions of power; where the constant aim is to divide and arrange the several offices in such a manner as that each may be a check on the other; that the private interest of every individual, may be a centinel over the public rights. These inventions of prudence cannot be less requisite in the distribution of the supreme powers of the state.

But it is not possible to give to each department an equal power of self defence. In republican government the legislative authority, necessarily, predominates. The remedy for this inconveniency is, to divide the legislature into different branches; and to render them by different modes of election, and different principles of action, as little connected with each other, as the nature of their common functions, and their common dependence on the society, will admit. It may even be necessary to guard against dangerous encroachments by still further precautions. As the weight of the legislative authority requires that it should be thus divided, the weakness of the executive may require, on the other hand, that it should be fortified. An absolute negative, on the legislature, appears at first view to be the natural defence with which the executive magistrate should be armed. But perhaps it would be neither altogether safe, nor alone sufficient. On ordinary occasions, it might not be exerted with the requisite firmness; and on extraordinary occasions, it might be perfidiously abused. May not this defect of an absolute negative be supplied, by some qualified connection between this weaker department, and the weaker branch of the stronger department, by which the latter may be led to support the constitutional rights of the former, without being too much detached from the rights of its own department?

If the principles on which these observations are founded be just, as I persuade myself they are, and they be applied as a criterion, to the several state constitutions, and to the federal constitution, it will be found that if the latter does not perfectly correspond with them, the former are infinitely less able to bear such a test.

There are moreover two considerations particularly applicable to the federal system of America, which place that system in a very interesting point of view.

First. In a single republic, all the power surrendered by the people, is submitted to the administration of a single government; and usurpations are guarded against by a division of the government into distinct and separate departments. In the compound republic of America, the power surrendered by the people, is first divided between two distinct governments, and then the portion allotted to each, subdivided among distinct and separate departments. Hence a double security arises to the rights of the people. The different governments will controul each other; at the same time that each will be controuled by itself.

Second. It is of great importance in a republic, not only to guard the society against the oppression of its rulers; but to guard one part of the society against the injustice of the other part. Different interests necessarily exist in different classes of citizens. If a majority be united by a common interest, the rights of the minority will be insecure. There are but two methods of providing against this evil: The one by creating a will in the community independent of the majority, that is, of the society itself; the other by comprehending in the society so many separate descriptions of citizens, as will render an unjust combination of a majority of the whole, very improbable, if not impracticable. The first method prevails in all governments possessing an hereditary or self appointed authority. This at best is but a precarious security; because a power independent of the society may as well espouse the unjust views of the major, as the rightful interests, of the minor party, and may possibly be turned against both parties. The second method will be exemplified in the federal republic of the United States. Whilst all authority in it will be derived from and dependent on the society, the society itself will be broken into so many parts, interests and classes of citizens, that the rights of individuals or of the minority, will be in little danger from interested combinations of the majority. In a free government, the security for civil rights must be the same as that for religious rights. It consists in the one case in the multiplicity of interests, and in the other, in the multiplicity of sects. The degree of security in both cases will depend on the number of interests and sects; and this may be presumed to depend on the extent of country and number of people comprehended under the same government. This view of the subject must particularly recommend a proper federal system to all the sincere and considerate friends of republican government: Since it shews that in exact proportion as the territory of the union may be formed into more circumscribed confederacies or states, oppressive combinations

of a majority will be facilitated, the best security under the republican form, for the rights of every class of citizens, will be
diminished; and consequently, the stability and independence
of some member of the government, the only other security,
must be proportionally increased. Justice is the end of government. It is the end of civil society. It ever has been, and ever
will be pursued, untill it be obtained, or untill liberty be lost in
the pursuit. In a society under the forms of which the stronger faction can readily unite and oppress the weaker, anarchy
may as truly be said to reign, as in a state of nature where the
weaker individual is not secured against the violence of the
stronger: And as in the latter state even the stronger individuals
are prompted by the uncertainty of their condition, to submit
to a government which may protect the weak as well as themselves: So in the former state, will the more powerful factions
or parties be gradually induced by a like motive, to wish for a
government which will protect all parties, the weaker as well as
the more powerful. It can be little doubted, that if the state of
Rhode Island was separated from the confederacy, and left to
itself, the insecurity of rights under the popular form of government within such narrow limits, would be displayed by such
reiterated oppressions of factious majorities, that some power
altogether independent of the people would soon be called for
by the voice of the very factions whose misrule had proved the
necessity of it. In the extended republic of the United States,
and among the great variety of interests, parties and sects
which it embraces, a coalition of a majority of the whole society
could seldom take place on any other principles than those of
justice and the general good; and there being thus less danger
to a minor from the will of the major party, there must be less
pretext also, to provide for the security of the former, by introducing into the government a will not dependent on the latter;
or in other words, a will independent of the society itself. It is
no less certain than it is important, notwithstanding the contrary opinions which have been entertained, that the larger the
society, provided it lie within a practicable sphere, the more
duly capable it will be of self government. And happily for the
republican cause, the practicable sphere may be carried to a
very great extent, by a judicious modification and mixture of
the *federal principle*.

Brutus XII

New York Journal, February 7 and 14, 1788

In my last, I shewed, that the judicial power of the United
States under the first clause of the second section of article
eight, would be authorized to explain the constitution, not
only according to its letter, but according to its spirit and intention; and having this power, they would strongly incline
to give it such a construction as to extend the powers of the
general government, as much as possible, to the diminution,
and finally to the destruction, of that of the respective states.

I shall now proceed to shew how this power will operate in
its exercise to effect these purposes. In order to perceive the
extent of its influence, I shall consider,

First. How it will tend to extend the legislative authority.

Second. In what manner it will increase the jurisdiction of
the courts, and

Third. The way in which it will diminish, and destroy, both
the legislative and judicial authority of the United States.

First. Let us enquire how the judicial power will effect an
extension of the legislative authority.

Perhaps the judicial power will not be able, by direct and
positive decrees, ever to direct the legislature, because it is not
easy to conceive how a question can be brought before them in
a course of legal discussion, in which they can give a decision,
declaring, that the legislature have certain powers which they
have not exercised, and which, in consequence of the determination of the judges, they will be bound to exercise. But
it is easy to see, that in their adjudications they may establish
certain principles, which being received by the legislature, will
enlarge the sphere of their power beyond all bounds.

It is to be observed, that the supreme court has the power,
in the last resort, to determine all questions that may arise in
the course of legal discussion, on the meaning and construction of the constitution. This power they will hold under the
constitution, and independent of the legislature. The latter can
no more deprive the former of this right, than either of them,

or both of them together, can take from the president, with the advice of the senate, the power of making treaties, or appointing ambassadors.

In determining these questions, the court must and will assume certain principles, from which they will reason, in forming their decisions. These principles, whatever they may be, when they become fixed, by a course of decisions, will be adopted by the legislature, and will be the rule by which they will explain their own powers. This appears evident from this consideration, that if the legislature pass laws, which, in the judgment of the court, they are not authorised to do by the constitution, the court will not take notice of them; for it will not be denied, that the constitution is the highest or supreme law. And the courts are vested with the supreme and uncontroulable power, to determine, in all cases that come before them, what the constitution means; they cannot, therefore, execute a law, which, in their judgment, opposes the constitution, unless we can suppose they can make a superior law give way to an inferior. The legislature, therefore, will not go over the limits by which the courts may adjudge they are confined. And there is little room to doubt but that they will come up to those bounds, as often as occasion and opportunity may offer, and they may judge it proper to do it. For as on the one hand, they will not readily pass laws which they know the courts will not execute, so on the other, we may be sure they will not scruple to pass such as they know they will give effect, as often as they may judge it proper.

From these observations it appears, that the judgment of the judicial, on the constitution, will become the rule to guide the legislature in their construction of their powers.

What the principles are, which the courts will adopt, it is impossible for us to say; but taking up the powers as I have explained them in my last number, which they will possess under this clause, it is not difficult to see, that they may, and probably will, be very liberal ones.

We have seen, that they will be authorized to give the constitution a construction according to its spirit and reason, and not to confine themselves to its letter.

To discover the spirit of the constitution, it is of the first importance to attend to the principal ends and designs it has in view. These are expressed in the preamble, in the following words, viz. "We, the people of the United States, in order to form a more perfect union, establish justice, insure domestic tranquility, provide for the common defence, promote the general welfare, and secure the blessings of liberty to ourselves and our posterity, do ordain and establish this constitution," &c. If the end of the government is to be learned from these words, which are clearly designed to declare it, it is obvious it has in view every object which is embraced by any government. The preservation of internal peace—the due administration of justice—and to provide for the defence of the community, seems to include all the objects of government; but if they do not, they are certainly comprehended in the words, "to provide for the general welfare." If it be further considered, that this constitution, if it is ratified, will not be a compact entered into by states, in their corporate capacities, but an agreement of the people of the United States, as one great body politic, no doubt can remain, but that the great end of the constitution, if it is to be collected from the preamble, in which its end is declared, is to constitute a government which is to extend to every case for which any government is instituted, whether external or internal. The courts, therefore, will establish this as a principle in expounding the constitution, and will give every part of it such an explanation, as will give latitude to every department under it, to take cognizance of every matter, not only that affects the general and national concerns of the union, but also of such as relate to the administration of private justice, and to regulating the internal and local affairs of the different parts.

Such a rule of exposition is not only consistent with the general spirit of the preamble, but it will stand confirmed by considering more minutely the different clauses of it.

The first object declared to be in view is, "To form a perfect union." It is to be observed, it is not an union of states or bodies corporate; had this been the case the existence of the state governments, might have been secured. But it is a union of the people of the United States considered as one body, who are to ratify this constitution, if it is adopted. Now to make a union of this kind perfect, it is necessary to abolish all inferior governments, and to give the general one compleat legislative, executive and judicial powers to every purpose. The courts therefore will establish it as a rule in explaining the constitution. To give it such a construction as will best tend to perfect the union or take from the state governments every power of either making or executing laws. The second object is "to establish justice." This must include not only the idea of instituting the rule of justice, or of making laws which shall be the measure or rule of right, but also of providing for the application of this rule or of administering justice under it. And under this the courts will in their decisions extend the power of the government to all cases they possibly can, or otherwise they will be restricted in doing what appears to be the intent of the constitution they should do, to wit, pass laws and provide for the execution of them, for the general distribution of justice between man and man. Another end declared is "to insure domestic tranquility." This comprehends a provision against all private breaches of the peace, as well as against all public commotions or general insurrections; and to attain the object of this clause fully, the government must exercise the power of passing laws on these subjects, as well as of appointing magistrates with authority to execute them. And the courts will adopt these ideas in their expositions. I might proceed to the other clause, in the preamble, and it would appear by a consideration of all of them separately, as it does by taking them together, that if the spirit of this system is to be known from its declared end and design in the preamble, its spirit is to subvert and abolish all the powers of the state government, and to embrace every object to which any government extends.

As it sets out in the preamble with this declared intention, so it proceeds in the different parts with the same idea. Any person, who will peruse the 8th section with attention, in which most of the powers are enumerated, will perceive that they either expressly or by implication extend to almost every thing about which any legislative power can be employed. But if this equitable mode of construction is applied to this part of the constitution; nothing can stand before it.

This will certainly give the first clause in that article a construction which I confess I think the most natural and grammatical one, to authorise the Congress to do any thing which in their judgment will tend to provide for the general welfare, and this amounts to the same thing as general and unlimited powers of legislation in all cases.

(To be continued.)

(Continued from last Thursday's paper.)

This same manner of explaining the constitution, will fix a meaning, and a very important one too, to the 12th clause of the same section, which authorises the Congress to make all laws which shall be proper and necessary for carrying into effect the foregoing powers, &c. A voluminous writer in favor of this system, has taken great pains to convince the public, that this clause means nothing: for that the same powers expressed in this, are implied in other parts of the constitution. Perhaps it is so, but still this will undoubtedly be an excellent auxilliary to assist the courts to discover the spirit and reason of the constitution, and when applied to any and every of the other clauses granting power, will operate powerfully in extracting the spirit from them.

I might instance a number of clauses in the constitution, which, if explained in an *equitable* manner, would extend the powers of the government to every case, and reduce the state legislatures to nothing; but, I should draw out my remarks to an undue length, and I presume enough has been said to shew, that the courts have sufficient ground in the exercise of this power, to determine, that the legislature have no bounds set to them by this constitution, by any supposed right the legislatures of the respective states may have, to regulate any of their local concerns.

I proceed, 2d, To inquire, in what manner this power will increase the jurisdiction of the courts.

I would here observe, that the judicial power extends, expressly, to all civil cases that may arise save such as arise between citizens of the same state, with this exception to those of that description, that the judicial of the United States have cognizance of cases between citizens of the same state, claiming lands under grants of different states. Nothing more, therefore, is necessary to give the courts of law, under this constitution, complete jurisdiction of all civil causes, but to comprehend cases between citizens of the same state not included in the foregoing exception.

I presume there will be no difficulty in accomplishing this. Nothing more is necessary than to set forth, in the process, that the party who brings the suit is a citizen of a different state from the one against whom the suit is brought, & there can be little doubt but that the court will take cognizance of the matter, & if they do, who is to restrain them? Indeed, I will freely confess, that it is my decided opinion, that the courts ought to take cognizance of such causes, under the powers of the constitution. For one of the great ends of the constitution is, "to establish justice." This supposes that this cannot be done under the existing governments of the states; and there is certainly as good reason why individuals, living in the same state, should have justice, as those who live in different states. Moreover, the constitution expressly declares that "the citizens of each state shall be entitled to all the privileges and immunities of citizens in the several states." It will therefore be no fiction, for a citizen of one state to set forth, in a suit, that he is a citizen of another; for he that is entitled to all the privileges and immunities of a country, is a citizen of that country. And in truth, the citizen of one state will, under this constitution, be a citizen of every state.

But supposing that the party, who alledges that he is a citizen of another state, has recourse to fiction in bringing in his suit, it is well known, that the courts have high authority to plead, to justify them in suffering actions to be brought before them by such fictions. In my last number I stated, that the court of exchequer tried all causes in virtue of such a fiction. The court of king's bench, in England, extended their jurisdiction in the same way. Originally, this court held pleas, in civil cases, only of trespasses and other injuries alledged to be committed *vi et armis*. They might likewise, says Blackstone, upon the division of the *aula regia*, have originally held pleas of any other civil action whatsoever (except in real actions which are now very seldom in use) provided the defendant was an officer of the court, or in the custody of the marshall or prison-keeper of this court, for breach of the peace, &c. In process of time, by a fiction, this court began to hold pleas of any personal action whatsoever; it being surmised, that the defendant has been arrested for a supposed trespass that "he has never committed, and being thus in the custody of the marshall of the court, the plaintiff is at liberty to proceed against him, for any other personal injury: which surmise of being in the marshall's custody, the defendant is not at liberty to dispute." By a much less fiction, may the pleas of the courts of the United States extend to cases between citizens of the same state. I shall add no more on this head, but proceed briefly to remark, in what way this power will diminish and destroy both the legislative and judicial authority of the states.

It is obvious that these courts will have authority to decide upon the validity of the laws of any of the states, in all cases where they come in question before them. Where the constitution gives the general government exclusive jurisdiction, they will adjudge all laws made by the states, in such cases, void *ab initio*. Where the constitution gives them concurrent jurisdiction, the laws of the United States must prevail, because they are the supreme law. In such cases, therefore, the laws of the state legislatures must be repealed, restricted, or so construed, as to give full effect to the laws of the union on the same subject. From these remarks it is easy to see, that in proportion as the general government acquires power and jurisdiction, by the liberal construction which the judges may give the constitution, will those of the states lose its rights, until they become so trifling and unimportant, as not to be worth having. I am much mistaken, if this system will not operate to effect this with as much celerity, as those who have the administration of it will think prudent to suffer it. The remaining objections to the judicial power shall be considered in a future paper.

Harry Innes to John Brown

Danville, Kentucky, February 20, 1788

I returned late last evening from Fayette & found Mr. Lacasagne here on his way to Philadelphia. I have snatched up my pen to let you know that I am not altogether thoughtless of you; this letter should be more full but the bearer sets out early this morning & I am obliged to curtail it. I wrote you via Richmond very fully on the subject of your business & what I thought the Court would probably do at the March Term. I have nothing to add on that head but to assure you that everything in my power shall be done for the benefit of yours and your clients interest.

The subject of the Federal Constitution begins to engross the attention of the people & I am endeavoring to bring about a convention on that important subject big with the fate of Kentucky & the Western Country. The objections which have been generally made to the eastward are of a general nature and appear to affect the general interest of United America; they are of too much importance to be looked over. I need not repeat them here as they have often appeared in the Public Print, but my Dr. Sir. the adoption of that Constitution would be the destruction of our young & flourishing country which I shall endeavor to point out concisely to you, viz: All commercial regulations "are to be vested in the General Congress". Our interests and the interests of the Eastern states are so diametrically opposite to each other that there cannot be a ray of hope left to the Western Country to suppose that when once that interest clashes we shall have justice done us. There is no such idea as justice in a Political society when the interests of 59/60 are to be injured thereby and that this will be the case as soon as we have the liberty of exportation, is self evident. Is there an article that the Eastern States can export except Fish oil & rice that we shall not abound in. I say not one. So long therefore as Congress hath this sole power & a majority have the right of deciding on those grand questions we cannot expect to enjoy the navigation of the Mississippi, but another evil equally great will arise from the same point. If ever we are a great and happy people, it must arise from our industry and attention to manufactories. This desirable end can never be brought about so long as the state Legislatures have the power of prohibiting imports, can we suppose that Congress will indulge us with a partial import when we must otherwise procure all our resources from the Eastward, the consequence of which is that we will be impoverished and the Eastern States will draw all our wealth and emigration will totally cease.

The most particular objection is the power of the Judiciary if our separation takes place, there will probably arise disputes between the Citizens of New Jersey, Pennsylvania, Delaware, Maryland, Virginia, & North Carolina and the Citizens of Kentucky; it is hardly to be supposed that each of the Citizens of these States as may have disputes with the Citizens of Kentucky will sue in Kentucky we shall be drawn away to the Federal Court and the Citizens from Kentucky away from their local habitations will nine times out of ten fall a sacrifice to their contests.

There are with me three insurmountable objections to the New Constitution. I wish to see a convention of the people on the subject & to remonstrate against it through the convention of Virginia & if that cannot be done, at least to address. Our local situation must justify any measures which may be adopted upon this occasion, certain that if the Constitution is adopted by us that we shall be the mere vassals of the Congress and the consequences to me are horrible and dreadful.

I would write more, but am obliged to conclude but before I lay down my pen must observe that the Indians continue hostile. 25 horses were taken in the latter end of January when the earth was covered 5 inches of snow. Will Congress do anything for us. Let us hear from you as soon as possible. Mr. Lacasagne will stay some time in Philadelphia & hath promised me to inform you of his lodgings, & to undertake to forward any letter you may send to his care. Mr. Al Parker of Lexington will leave Philadelphia the beginning of April. We have had a most severe winter, which is not ended. I know of no changes among your acquaintances here. We are all well.

Joseph Spencer to James Madison, Enclosing John Leland's Objections

Orange County, Virginia, February 28, 1788

The Federal Constitution, has it Enimyes in Orange as well as in other parts, Col. Thos. Barber offers as a Candedit for our March Election, he is as grate an Enimy to it as he posably can be, & if not as grate as any it has, as grate as his abiliteys will alow him to be, which if our County men admired his Politickes no more than I do, the Constitution would have but Little to fear from that Quarter, but his unwared Labours riding his Carquits & the Instrements he makes use of to Obtain his Election, misrepresents things in such Horred carrecters that the weker clas of the people are much predegessed agains it. by which meens he has many which as yet, appears grately in favour of him, amoungs his Friends appears, in a General way the Baptus's, the Prechers of that Society are much alarm'd fearing relegious liberty is not Sufficiently secur'd thay pretend to other objections but that I think is the principle objection, could that be removed by sum one Caperable of the Task. I think thay would become friends to it, that body of people has become very formible in pint of Elections, as I can think of no Gentln. of my Acquaintance so Suitible to the Task as your Self. I have taken the liberty to Request it of you, several of your Conections in Orange Joines me in oppinion, thinking it would answer a Valuable purpus for I am Cartain that pople relye much on your integerity & Candure, Mr. Leeland & Mr. Bledsoe and Sanders are the most publick men of that Society in Orange, therefore as Mr. Leeland Lyes in your Way home from Fredricksburg to Orange would advise you'l call on him & spend a few Howers in his Company, in Clos'd youl receive his objections, which was Sent by me to, Barber, a Coppy I tooke, this copy was first Design'd for Capt Walker, but as I hoped youl be in this state in a few days thought proper to Send it to you, by which means youl be made Acquainted with their objections & have time to Consider them should you think it an Object worth yr Attention, my fears are that Except

you & yr friends do Exerte yr Selves Very much youl not obtain
yr Election in Orange Such are the predegeses of the people for
in short there is nothing so Vile, but what the Constitution is
Charged with, hope to See you in Orange in a few days

According, to your request, I have send you my objections
to the *Fœderal Constitution*, which are as follows,

1st. There is no Bill Rights, whenever Number of men enter into a State of Socity, a Number of individual Rights must
be given up to Socity, but there should always be a memorial
of those not surrendred, otherwise every natural & domestic
Right becomes alianable, which raises Tyranny at once, & this
is as necessary in one Form of Goverment as in another—

2nd. There is a Contradiction in the Constitution, we are
first inform'd that all Legislative Powers therein granted shall
be Vested in a Congress, composed of *two houses*, & yet afterwards all the power that lies between a Majority two thirds,
which is one Sixth part, is taken from these *two Houses*, and
given to one man, who is not only chosen two removes from
the people, but also the head of the executive Department—

3rd. The House of Representatives is the only free, direct
Representation of the body of the people, & yet in Treaties
which are to be some of the Supreme Laws of the Land, this
House has no Voice—

4th. The time place & Manner of chusing the Members of
the Lower house is intirely at the Mercy of Congress, if they
Appoint Pepin or Japan, or their ten Miles Square for the place,
no man can help it.—how can Congress guarantee to each
state a republican form of Government, when every principle
of Republicanism is Sapped—

5th. The Senators are chosen for Six years, & when they are
once Chosen, they are impeachable to nun but themselves, No
Counterpoize is left in the hands of the People, or even in
Legislative Bodys to check them, Vote as they will, there they
sit, paying themselves at Pleasure—

6th I utterly oppose any Division in Legislative Body, the
more Houses, the more parties,—the more they are Divided;
the more the Wisdom is Scattered, sometimes one house may
prevent the Error of another & the same stands true of twenty

Houses But the Question is, whether they do more good then harm the Business is cartainly thereby retarded & the Expence inhansed

7th. We are not informed whether Votes in all cases in the lower house are to be by Members or by States,—I Question wheather a man could find out the Riddle by plowing with Sampsons Heifer, if each Member is not to have a Vote why are they to be chosen according to the Numbers of Inhabitants, & why should Virginia be at ten-times the Expence of Deleware for the same power, if the Votes are always to be by States, why is it not Expressed as in the choise of a President, in cartain Cases, If each member is to have a Vote, Why is it Expressed concarning Senators, & not Concarning Representatives, this Blank appears to me, to be designed, to encourage the Small States with hops of Equality, & the Large States with Hopes of Superiority—

8ly. We have no assurance that the liberty of the press will be allowed under this Constitution—

9ly. We have been always taught that it was dangerous Mixing the Legislative & Executive powers together in the same body of People but in this Constitution, we are taught better, or worse—

10ly. What is dearest of all—*Religious Liberty*, is not Sufficiently Secured, No religious test is required as a Qualification to fill any office under the United States, but if a Majority of Congress with the presedent favour one Systom more then another, they may oblige all others to pay to the Support of their System as Much as they please, & if Oppression dose not ensue, it will be owing to the Mildness of Administration & not to any Constitutional defense, & if the Manners of People are so far Corrupted, that they cannot live by republican principles, it is Very Dangerous leaving religious Liberty at their Marcy—

Publius (Alexander Hamilton)
The Federalist No. 70

Independent Journal (New York), March 15, 1788

To the People of the State of New-York.

There is an idea, which is not without its advocates, that a vigorous executive is inconsistent with the genius of republican government. The enlightened well wishers to this species of government must at least hope that the supposition is destitute of foundation; since they can never admit its truth, without at the same time admitting the condemnation of their own principles. Energy in the executive is a leading character in the definition of good government. It is essential to the protection of the community against foreign attacks: It is not less essential to the steady administration of the laws, to the protection of property against those irregular and high handed combinations, which sometimes interrupt the ordinary course of justice to the security of liberty against the enterprises and assaults of ambition, of faction and of anarchy. Every man the least conversant in Roman story knows how often that republic was obliged to take refuge in the absolute power of a single man, under the formidable title of dictator, as well against the intrigues of ambitious individuals, who aspired to the tyranny, and the seditions of whole classes of the community, whose conduct threatened the existence of all government, as against the invasions of external enemies, who menaced the conquest and destruction of Rome.

There can be no need however to multiply arguments or examples on this head. A feeble executive implies a feeble execution of the government. A feeble execution is but another phrase for a bad execution: And a government ill executed, whatever it may be in theory, must be in practice a bad government.

Taking it for granted, therefore, that all men of sense will agree in the necessity of an energetic executive; it will only remain to inquire, what are the ingredients which constitute this energy—how far can they be combined with those other ingredients which constitute safety in the republican sense? And how far does this combination characterise the plan, which has been reported by the convention?

The ingredients, which constitute energy in the executive, are first unity, secondly duration, thirdly an adequate provision for its support, fourthly competent powers.

The circumstances which constitute safety in the republican sense are, 1st. a due dependence on the people, secondly a due responsibility.

Those politicians and statesmen, who have been the most celebrated for the soundness of their principles, and for the justness of their views, have declared in favor of a single executive and a numerous legislature. They have with great propriety considered energy as the most necessary qualification of the former, and have regarded this as most applicable to power in a single hand; while they have with equal propriety considered the latter as best adapted to deliberation and wisdom, and best calculated to conciliate the confidence of the people and to secure their privileges and interests.

That unity is conducive to energy will not be disputed. Decision, activity, secrecy, and dispatch will generally characterise the proceedings of one man, in a much more eminent degree, than the proceedings of any greater number; and in proportion as the number is increased, these qualities will be diminished.

This unity may be destroyed in two ways; either by vesting the power in two or more magistrates of equal dignity and authority; or by vesting it ostensibly in one man, subject in whole or in part to the controul and co-operation of others, in the capacity of counsellors to him. Of the first the two consuls of Rome may serve as an example; of the last we shall find examples in the constitutions of several of the states. New-York and New-Jersey, if I recollect right, are the only states, which have entrusted the executive authority wholly to single men.* Both these methods of destroying the unity of the executive have their partisans; but the votaries of an executive council are the most numerous. They are both liable, if not to equal,

*New-York has no council except for the single purpose of appointing to offices; New-Jersey has a council, whom the governor may consult. But I think from the terms of the constitution their resolutions do not bind him.

to similar objections; and may in most lights be examined in conjunction.

The experience of other nations will afford little instruction on this head. As far however as it teaches any thing, it teaches us not to be inamoured of plurality in the executive. We have seen that the Achæans on an experiment of two Prætors, were induced to abolish one. The Roman history records many instances of mischiefs to the republic from the dissentions between the consuls, and between the military tribunes, who were at times substituted to the consuls. But it gives us no specimens of any peculiar advantages derived to the state, from the circumstance of the plurality of those magistrates. That the dissentions between them were not more frequent, or more fatal, is matter of astonishment; until we advert to the singular position in which the republic was almost continually placed and to the prudent policy pointed out by the circumstances of the state, and pursued by the consuls, of making a division of the government between them. The Patricians engaged in a perpetual struggle with the Plebeians for the preservation of their antient authorities and dignities; the consuls, who were generally chosen out of the former body, were commonly united by the personal interest they had in the defence of the privileges of their order. In addition to this motive of union, after the arms of the republic had considerably expanded the bounds of its empire, it became an established custom with the consuls to divide the administration between themselves by lot; one of them remaining at Rome to govern the city and its environs; the other taking the command in the more distant provinces. This expedient must no doubt have had great influence in preventing those collisions and rivalships, which might otherwise have embroiled the peace of the republic.

But quitting the dim light of historical research, and attaching ourselves purely to the dictates of reason and good sense, we shall discover much greater cause to reject than to approve the idea of plurality in the executive, under any modification whatever.

Wherever two or more persons are engaged in any common enterprize or pursuit, there is always danger of difference of opinion. If it be a public trust or office in which they are cloathed with equal dignity and authority, there is peculiar

danger of personal emulation and even animosity. From either
and especially from all these causes, the most bitter dissentions
are apt to spring. Whenever these happen, they lessen the respectability, weaken the authority, and distract the plans and
operations of those whom they divide. If they should unfortunately assail the supreme executive magistracy of a country,
consisting of a plurality of persons, they might impede or frustrate the most important measures of the government, in the
most critical emergencies of the state. And what is still worse,
they might split the community into the most violent and ir-
reconcilable factions, adhering differently to the different individuals who composed the magistracy.

Men often oppose a thing merely because they have had no
agency in planning it, or because it may have been planned
by those whom they dislike. But if they have been consulted
and have happened to disapprove, opposition then becomes in
their estimation an indispensable duty of self love. They seem
to think themselves bound in honor, and by all the motives
of personal infallibility to defeat the success of what has been
resolved upon, contrary to their sentiments. Men of upright,
benevolent tempers have too many opportunities of remarking with horror, to what desperate lengths this disposition is
sometimes carried, and how often the great interests of society
are sacrificed to the vanity, to the conceit and to the obstinacy
of individuals, who have credit enough to make their passions
and their caprices interesting to mankind. Perhaps the question
now before the public may in its consequences afford melancholy proofs of the effects of this despicable frailty, or rather
detestable vice in the human character.

Upon the principles of a free government, inconveniencies
from the source just mentioned must necessarily be submitted to in the formation of the legislature; but it is unnecessary
and therefore unwise to introduce them into the constitution of the executive. It is here too that they may be most
pernicious. In the legislature, promptitude of decision is oftener an evil than a benefit. The differences of opinion, and
the jarrings of parties in that department of the government,
though they may sometimes obstruct salutary plans, yet often
promote deliberations and circumspection; and serve to check
excesses in the majority. When a resolution too is once taken,

the opposition must be at an end. That resolution is a law, and resistance to it punishable. But no favourable circumstances palliate or atone for the disadvantages of dissention in the executive department. Here they are pure and unmixed. There is no point at which they cease to operate. They serve to embarrass and weaken the execution of the plan or measure, to which they relate, from the first step to the final conclusion of it. They constantly counteract those qualities in the executive, which are the most necessary ingredients in its composition, vigour and expedition, and this without any counterballancing good. In the conduct of war, in which the energy of the executive is the bulwark of the national security, every thing would be to be apprehended from its plurality.

It must be confessed that these observations apply with principal weight to the first case supposed, that is to a plurality of magistrates of equal dignity and authority; a scheme the advocates for which are not likely to form a numerous sect: But they apply, though not with equal, yet with considerable weight, to the project of a council, whose concurrence is made constitutionally necessary to the operations of the ostensible executive. An artful cabal in that council would be able to distract and to enervate the whole system of administration. If no such cabal should exist, the mere diversity of views and opinions would alone be sufficient to tincture the exercise of the executive authority with a spirit of habitual feebleness and delatoriness.

But one of the weightiest objections to a plurality in the executive, and which lies as much against the last as the first plan, is that it tends to conceal faults, and destroy responsibility. Responsibility is of two kinds, to censure and to punishment. The first is the most important of the two; especially in an elective office. Man, in public trust, will much oftener act in such a manner as to render him unworthy of being any longer trusted, than in such a manner as to make him obnoxious to legal punishment. But the multiplication of the executive adds to the difficulty of detection in either case. It often becomes impossible, amidst mutual accusations, to determine on whom the blame or the punishment of a pernicious measure, or series of pernicious measures ought really to fall. It is shifted from one to another with so much dexterity, and under such plausible appearances, that the public opinion is left in suspense about the real author. The circumstances which may have led to any national miscarriage or misfortune are sometimes so complicated, that where there are a number of actors who may have had different degrees and kinds of agency, though we may clearly see upon the whole that there has been mismanagement, yet it may be impracticable to pronounce to whose account the evil which may have been incurred is truly chargeable.

"I was overruled by my council. The council were so divided in their opinions, that it was impossible to obtain any better resolution on the point." These and similar pretexts are constantly at hand, whether true or false. And who is there that will either take the trouble or incur the odium of a strict scrutiny into the secret springs of the transaction? Should there be found a citizen zealous enough to undertake the unpromising task, if there happen to be a collusion between the parties concerned, how easy is it to cloath the circumstances with so much ambiguity, as to render it uncertain what was the precise conduct of any of those parties?

In the single instance in which the governor of this state is coupled with a council, that is in the appointment to offices, we have seen the mischiefs of it in the view now under consideration. Scandalous appointments to important offices have been made. Some cases indeed have been so flagrant, that ALL PARTIES have agreed in the impropriety of the thing. When enquiry has been made, the blame has been laid by the governor on the members of the council; who on their part have charged it upon his nomination: While the people remain altogether at a loss to determine by whose influence their interests have been committed to hands so unqualified, and so manifestly improper. In tenderness to individuals, I forbear to descend to particulars.

It is evident from these considerations, that the plurality of the executive tends to deprive the people of the two greatest securities they can have for the faithful exercise of any delegated power; first, the restraints of public opinion, which lose their efficacy as well on account of the division of the censure attendant on bad measures among a number, as on account of the uncertainty on whom it ought to fall; and secondly, the opportunity of discovering with facility and clearness the misconduct of the persons they trust, in order either to their removal from office, or to their actual punishment, in cases which admit of it.

In England the king is a perpetual magistrate; and it is a maxim, which has obtained for the sake of the public peace, that he is unaccountable for his administration, and his person sacred. Nothing therefore can be wiser in that kingdom than to annex to the king a constitutional council, who may be responsible to the nation for the advice they give. Without this there would be no responsibility whatever in the executive department; an idea inadmissible in a free government. But even there the king is not bound by the resolutions of his council, though they are answerable for the advice they give. He is the absolute master of his own conduct, in the exercise of his office; and may observe or disregard the council given to him at his sole discretion.

But in a republic, where every magistrate ought to be personally responsible for his behaviour in office, the reason which in the British constitution dictates the propriety of a council not only ceases to apply, but turns against the institution. In the monarchy of Great-Britain, it furnishes a substitute for the prohibited responsibility of the chief magistrate; which serves in some degree as a hostage to the national justice for his good behaviour. In the American republic it would serve to destroy, or would greatly diminish the intended and necessary responsibility of the chief magistrate himself.

The idea of a council to the executive, which has so generally obtained in the state constitutions, has been derived from that maxim of republican jealousy, which considers power as safer in the hands of a number of men than of a single man. If the maxim should be admitted to be applicable to the case, I should contend that the advantage on that side would not counterballance the numerous disadvantages on the opposite side. But I do not think the rule at all applicable to the executive power. I clearly concur in opinion in this particular with a writer whom the celebrated Junius pronounces to be "deep, solid and ingenious," that, "the executive power is more easily confined when it is one:"*

---

*De Lome.

That it is far more safe there should be a single object for the jealousy and watchfulness of the people; and in a word that all multiplication of the executive is rather dangerous than friendly to liberty.

A little consideration will satisfy us, that the species of security sought for in the multiplication of the executive is unattainable. Numbers must be so great as to render combination difficult; or they are rather a source of danger than of security. The united credit and influence of several individuals must be more formidable to liberty than the credit and influence of either of them separately. When power therefore is placed in the hands of so small a number of men, as to admit of their interests and views being easily combined in a common enterprise, by an artful leader, it becomes more liable to abuse and more dangerous when abused, than if it be lodged in the hands of one man; who from the very circumstance of his being alone will be more narrowly watched and more readily suspected, and who cannot unite so great a mass of influence as when he is associated with others. The Decemvirs of Rome, whose name denotes their number,* were more to be dreaded in their usurpation than any ONE of them would have been. No person would think of proposing an executive much more numerous than that body, from six to a dozen have been suggested for the number of the council. The extreme of these numbers is not too great for an easy combination; and from such a combination America would have more to fear, than from the ambition of any single individual A council to a magistrate, who is himself responsible for what he does, are generally nothing better than a clog upon his good intentions; are often the instruments and accomplices of his bad, and are almost always a cloak to his faults.

I forbear to dwell upon the subject of expence; though it be evident that if the council should be numerous enough to answer the principal end, aimed at by the institution, the salaries of the members, who must be drawn from their homes to reside at the seat of government, would form an item in the catalogue of public expenditures, too serious to be incurred for an object of equivocal utility.

*Ten.

I will only add, that prior to the appearance of the constitution, I rarely met with an intelligent man from any of the states, who did not admit as the result of experience, that the UNITY of the Executive of this state was one of the best of the distinguishing features of our constitution.

PUBLIUS.

Brutus XV

New York Journal, March 20, 1788

(Continued.)

I said in my last number, that the supreme court under this constitution would be exalted above all other power in the government, and subject to no controul. The business of this paper will be to illustrate this, and to shew the danger that will result from it. I question whether the world ever saw, in any period of it, a court of justice invested with such immense powers, and yet placed in a situation so little responsible. Certain it is, that in England, and in the several states, where we have been taught to believe, the courts of law are put upon the most prudent establishment, they are on a very different footing.

The judges in England, it is true, hold their offices during their good behaviour, but then their determinations are subject to correction by the house of lords; and their power is by no means so extensive as that of the proposed supreme court of the union.—I believe they in no instance assume the authority to set aside an act of parliament under the idea that it is inconsistent with their constitution. They consider themselves bound to decide according to the existing laws of the land, and never undertake to controul them by adjudging that they are inconsistent with the constitution—much less are they vested with the power of giving an *equitable* construction to the constitution.

The judges in England are under the controul of the legislature, for they are bound to determine according to the laws passed by them. But the judges under this constitution will controul the legislature, for the supreme court are authorised in the last resort, to determine what is the extent of the powers of the Congress; they are to give the constitution an explanation, and there is no power above them to sit aside their judgment. The framers of this constitution appear to have followed that of the British, in rendering the judges independent, by granting them their offices during good behaviour, without following the constitution of England, in instituting a tribunal in which their errors may be corrected; and without adverting to this, that the judicial under this system have a power which is above the legislative, and which indeed transcends any power before given to a judicial by any free government under heaven.

I do not object to the judges holding their commissions during good behaviour. I suppose it a proper provision provided they were made properly responsible. But I say, this system has followed the English government in this, while it has departed from almost every other principle of their jurisprudence, under the idea, of rendering the judges independent; which, in the British constitution, means no more than that they hold their places during good behaviour, and have fixed salaries, they have made the judges *independent*, in the fullest sense of the word. There is no power above them, to controul any of their decisions. There is no authority that can remove them, and they cannot be controuled by the laws of the legislature. In short, they are independent of the people, of the legislature, and of every power under heaven. Men placed in this situation will generally soon feel themselves independent of heaven itself. Before I proceed to illustrate the truth of these assertions, I beg liberty to make one remark—Though in my opinion the judges ought to hold their offices during good behaviour, yet I think it is clear, that the reasons in favour of this establishment of the judges in England, do by no means apply to this country.

The great reason assigned, why the judges in Britain ought to be commissioned during good behaviour, is this, that they may be placed in a situation, not to be influenced by the crown, to give such decisions, as would tend to increase its powers and prerogatives. While the judges held their places at the will and pleasure of the king, on whom they depended not only for their offices, but also for their salaries, they were subject to every undue influence. If the crown wished to carry a favorite point, to accomplish which the aid of the courts of law was necessary, the pleasure of the king would be signified to the judges. And it required the spirit of a martyr, for the judges to determine contrary to the king's will.—They were absolutely dependent upon him both for their offices and livings. The king, holding his office during life, and transmitting it to his posterity as an inheritance, has much stronger inducements to increase the prerogatives of his office than those who hold their offices for stated periods, or even for life. Hence the English nation gained a great point, in favour of liberty. When they obtained the appointment of the judges, during good behaviour, they got from the crown a concession, which deprived it of one of the most powerful engines with which it might enlarge the boundaries of the royal prerogative and encroach on the liberties of the people. But these reasons do not apply to this country, we have no hereditary monarch; those who appoint the judges do not hold their offices for life, nor do they descend to their children. The same arguments, therefore, which will conclude in favor of the tenor of the judge's offices for good behaviour, lose a considerable part of their weight when applied to the state and condition of America. But much less can it be shewn, that the nature of our government requires that the courts should be placed beyond all account more independent, so much so as to be above controul.

I have said that the judges under this system will be *independent* in the strict sense of the word: To prove this I will shew— That there is no power above them that can controul their decisions, or correct their errors There is no authority that can remove them from office for any errors or want of capacity, or lower their salaries, and in many cases their power is superior to that of the legislature.

1st. There is no power above them that can correct their errors or controul their decisions—The adjudications of this court are final and irreversible, for there is no court above them to which appeals can lie, either in error or on the merits.—In this respect it differs from the courts in England, for there the house of lords is the highest court, to whom appeals, in error, are carried from the highest of the courts of law.

2d. They cannot be removed from office or suffer a dimunition of their salaries, for any error in judgement or want of capacity.

It is expressly declared by the constitution,—"That they shall at stated times receive a compensation for their services which shall not be diminished during their continuance in office."

The only clause in the constitution which provides for the removal of the judges from offices, is that which declares, that "the president, vice-president, and all civil officers of the United States, shall be removed from office, on impeachment for, and conviction of treason, bribery, or other high crimes and misdemeanors." By this paragraph, civil officers, in which the judges are included, are removable only for crimes. Treason and bribery are named, and the rest are included under the general terms of high crimes and misdemeanors.—Errors in judgement, or want of capacity to discharge the duties of the office, can never be supposed to be included in these words, *high crimes and misdemeanors.* A man may mistake a case in giving judgment, or manifest that he is incompetent to the discharge of the duties of a judge, and yet give no evidence of corruption or want of integrity. To support the charge, it will be necessary to give in evidence some facts that will shew, that the judges commited the error from wicked and corrupt motives.

3d. The power of this court is in many cases superior to that of the legislature. I have shewed, in a former paper, that this court will be authorised to decide upon the meaning of the constitution, and that, not only according to the natural and obvious meaning of the words, but also according to the spirit and intention of it. In the exercise of this power they will not be subordinate to, but above the legislature. For all the departments of this government will receive their powers, so far as they are expressed in the constitution, from the people immediately, who are the source of power. The legislature can only exercise such powers as are given them by the constitution, they cannot assume any of the rights annexed to the judicial, for this plain reason, that the same authority which vested the legislature with their powers, vested the judicial with theirs— both are derived from the same source, both therefore are equally valid, and the judicial hold their powers independently of the legislature, as the legislature do of the judicial.—The supreme court then have a right, independent of the legislature, to give a construction to the constitution and every part of it, and there is no power provided in this system to correct their construction or do it away. If, therefore, the legislature pass any laws, inconsistent with the sense the judges put upon the constitution, they will declare it void; and therefore in this respect their power is superior to that of the legislature. In England the judges are not only subject to have their decisions set aside by the house of lords, for error, but in cases where they give an explanation to the laws or constitution of the country, contrary to the sense of the parliament, though the parliament will not set aside the judgement of the court, yet, they have authority, by a new law, to explain a former one, and by this means to prevent a reception of such decisions. But no such power is in the legislature. The judges are supreme—and no law, explanatory of the constitution, will be binding on them.

From the preceding remarks, which have been made on the judicial powers proposed in this system, the policy of it may be fully developed.

I have, in the course of my observation on this constitution, affirmed and endeavored to shew, that it was calculated to abolish entirely the state governments, and to melt down the states into one entire government, for every purpose as well internal and local, as external and national. In this opinion the opposers of the system have generally agreed—and this has been uniformly denied by its advocates in public. Some individuals, indeed, among them, will confess, that it has this tendency, and scruple not to say, it is what they wish; and I will venture to predict, without the spirit of prophecy, that if it is adopted without amendments, or some such precautions as will ensure amendments immediately after its adoption, that the same gentlemen who have employed their talents and abilities with such success to influence the public mind to adopt this plan, will employ the same to persuade the people, that it will be for their good to abolish the state governments as useless and burdensome.

Perhaps nothing could have been better conceived to facilitate the abolition of the state governments than the constitution of the judicial. They will be able to extend the limits of the general government gradually, and by insensible degrees, and to accomodate themselves to the temper of the people. Their decisions on the meaning of the constitution will commonly take place in cases which arise between individuals, with which the public will not be generally acquainted; one adjudication will form a precedent to the next, and this to a following one. These cases will immediately affect individuals only; so that a series of determinations will probably take place before even the people will be informed of them. In the mean time all the art and address of those who wish for the change will be employed to make converts to their opinion. The people will be told, that their state officers, and state legislatures are a burden and expence without affording any solid advantage, for that all the laws passed by them, might be equally well made by the general legislature. If to those who will be interested in the change, be added, those who will be under their influence, and such who will submit to almost any change of government, which they can be persuaded to believe will ease them of taxes, it is easy to see, the party who will favor the abolition of the state governments would be far from being inconsiderable.— In this situation, the general legislature, might pass one law after another, extending the general and abridging the state jurisdictions, and to sanction their proceedings would have a course of decisions of the judicial to whom the constitution has committed the power of explaining the constitution.—If the states remonstrated, the constitutional mode of deciding upon the validity of the law, is with the supreme court, and neither people, nor state legislatures, nor the general legislature can remove them or reverse their decrees.

Had the construction of the constitution been left with the legislature, they would have explained it at their peril; if they exceed their powers, or sought to find, in the spirit of the constitution, more than was expressed in the letter, the people from whom they derived their power could remove them, and do themselves right; and indeed I can see no other remedy that the people can have against their rulers for encroachments of this nature. A constitution is a compact of a people with their rulers; if the rulers break the compact, the people have a right and ought to remove them and do themselves justice; but in order to enable them to do this with the greater facility, those whom the people chuse at stated periods, should have the power in the last resort to determine the sense of the compact; if they determine contrary to the understanding of the people, an appeal will lie to the people at the period when the rulers are to be elected, and they will have it in their power to remedy the evil; but when this power is lodged in the hands of men independent of the people, and of their representatives, and who are not, constitutionally, accountable for their opinions, no way is left to controul them but *with a high hand and an outstretched arm.*

Publius (Alexander Hamilton) The Federalist No. 78

New York, May 28, 1788

To the People of the State of New-York.

We proceed now to an examination of the judiciary department of the proposed government.

In unfolding the defects of the existing confederation, the utility and necessity of a federal judicature have been clearly pointed out. It is the less necessary to recapitulate the considerations there urged; as the propriety of the institution in the abstract is not disputed: The only questions which have been raised being relative to the manner of constituting it, and to its extent. To these points therefore our observations shall be confined.

The manner of constituting it seems to embrace these several objects—1st. The mode of appointing the judges—2d. The tenure by which they are to hold their places—3d. The partition of the judiciary authority between different courts, and their relations to each other.

First. As to the mode of appointing the judges: This is the same with that of appointing the officers of the union in general, and has been so fully discussed in the two last numbers, that nothing can be said here which would not be useless repetition.

Second. As to the tenure by which the judges are to hold their places: This chiefly concerns their duration in office; the provisions for their support; and the precautions for their responsibility.

According to the plan of the convention, all the judges who may be appointed by the United States are to hold their offices *during good behaviour*, which is conformable to the most approved of the state constitutions; and among the rest, to that of this state. Its propriety having been drawn into question by the adversaries of that plan, is no light symptom of the rage for objection which disorders their imaginations and judgments. The standard of good behaviour for the continuance in office of the judicial magistracy is certainly one of the most valuable of the modern improvements in the practice of government. In a monarchy it is an excellent barrier to the despotism of the prince: In a republic it is a no less excellent barrier to the encroachments and oppressions of the representative body. And it is the best expedient which can be devised in any government, to secure a steady, upright and impartial administration of the laws.

Whoever attentively considers the different departments of power must perceive, that in a government in which they are separated from each other, the judiciary, from the nature of its functions, will always be the least dangerous to the political rights of the constitution; because it will be least in a capacity to annoy or injure them. The executive not only dispenses the honors, but holds the sword of the community. The legislature not only commands the purse, but prescribes the rules by which the duties and rights of every citizen are to be regulated. The judiciary on the contrary has no influence over either the sword or the purse, no direction either of the strength or of the wealth of the society, and can take no active resolution whatever. It may truly be said to have neither FORCE nor WILL, but merely judgment; and must ultimately depend upon the aid of the executive arm even for the efficacy of its judgments.

This simple view of the matter suggests several important consequences. It proves incontestibly that the judiciary is beyond comparison the weakest of the three departments of power;* that it can never attack with success either of the other two; and that all possible care is requisite to enable it to defend itself against their attacks. It equally proves, that though individual oppression may now and then proceed from the courts of justice, the general liberty of the people can never be endangered from that quarter; I mean, so long as the judiciary remains truly distinct from both the legislative and executive. For I agree that "there is no liberty, if the power of judging be not separated from the legislative and executive powers."†

---

*The celebrated Montesquieu speaking of them says, "of the three powers above mentioned, the JUDICIARY is next to nothing." Spirit of Laws, vol. I, page 186.

†Idem. page 181.

And it proves, in the last place, that as liberty can have nothing to fear from the judiciary alone, but would have every thing to fear from its union with either of the other departments; that as all the effects of such an union must ensue from a dependence of the former on the latter, notwithstanding a nominal and apparent separation; that as from the natural feebleness of the judiciary, it is in continual jeopardy of being overpowered, awed or influenced by its coordinate branches; and that as nothing can contribute so much to its firmness and independence, as permanency in office, this quality may therefore be justly regarded as an indispensable ingredient in its constitution; and in a great measure as the citadel of the public justice and the public security.

The complete independence of the courts of justice is peculiarly essential in a limited constitution. By a limited constitution I understand one which contains certain specified exceptions to the legislative authority; such for instance as that it shall pass no bills of attainder, no *ex post facto* laws, and the like. Limitations of this kind can be preserved in practice no other way than through the medium of the courts of justice; whose duty it must be to declare all acts contrary to the manifest tenor of the constitution void. Without this, all the reservations of particular rights or privileges would amount to nothing.

Some perplexity respecting the right of the courts to pronounce legislative acts void, because contrary to the constitution, has arisen from an imagination that the doctrine would imply a superiority of the judiciary to the legislative power. It is urged that the authority which can declare the acts of another void, must necessarily be superior to the one whose acts may be declared void. As this doctrine is of great importance in all the American constitutions, a brief discussion of the grounds on which it rests cannot be unacceptable.

There is no position which depends on clearer principles, than that every act of a delegated authority, contrary to the tenor of the commission under which it is exercised, is void. No legislative act therefore contrary to the constitution can be valid. To deny this would be to affirm that the deputy is greater than his principal; that the servant is above his master; that the representatives of the people are superior to the people themselves; that men acting by virtue of powers may do not only what their powers do not authorise, but what they forbid.

If it be said that the legislative body are themselves the constitutional judges of their own powers, and that the construction they put upon them is conclusive upon the other departments, it may be answered, that this cannot be the natural presumption, where it is not to be collected from any particular provision in the constitution. It is not otherwise to be supposed that the constitution could intend to enable the representatives of the people to substitute their *will* to that of their constituents. It is far more rational to suppose that the courts were designed to be an intermediate body between the people and the legislature, in order, among other things, to keep the latter within the limits assigned to their authority. The interpretation of the laws is the proper and peculiar province of the courts. A constitution is in fact, and must be, regarded by the judges as a fundamental law. It therefore belongs to them to ascertain its meaning as well as the meaning of any particular act proceeding from the legislative body. If there should happen to be an irreconcileable variance between the two, that which has the superior obligation and validity ought of course to be preferred; or in other words, the constitution ought to be preferred to the statute, the intention of the people to the intention of their agents.

Nor does this conclusion by any means suppose a superiority of the judicial to the legislative power. It only supposes that the power of the people is superior to both; and that where the will of the legislature declared in its statutes, stands in opposition to that of the people declared in the constitution, the judges ought to be governed by the latter, rather than the former. They ought to regulate their decisions by the fundamental laws, rather than by those which are not fundamental.

This exercise of judicial discretion in determining between two contradictory laws, is exemplified in a familiar instance. It not uncommonly happens, that there are two statutes existing at one time, clashing in whole or in part with each other, and neither of them containing any repealing clause or expression. In such a case, it is the province of the courts to liquidate and fix their meaning and operation: So far as they can by any fair construction be reconciled to each other; reason and law conspire to dictate that this should be done: Where this is impracticable, it becomes a matter of necessity to give effect to one, in exclusion of the other. The rule which has obtained in the courts for determining their relative validity is that the last in order of time shall be preferred to the first. But this is mere rule of construction, not derived from any positive law, but from the nature and reason of the thing. It is a rule not enjoined upon the courts by legislative provision, but adopted by themselves, as consonant to truth and propriety, for the direction of their conduct as interpreters of the law. They thought it reasonable, that between the interfering acts of an *equal* authority, that which was the last indication of its will, should have the preference.

But in regard to the interfering acts of a superior and subordinate authority, of an original and derivative power, the nature and reason of the thing indicate the converse of that rule as proper to be followed. They teach us that the prior act of a superior ought to be prefered to the subsequent act of an inferior and subordinate authority; and that, accordingly, whenever a particular statute contravenes the constitution, it will be the duty of the judicial tribunals to adhere to the latter, and disregard the former.

It can be of no weight to say, that the courts on the pretence of a repugnancy, may substitute their own pleasure to the constitutional intentions of the legislature. This might as well happen in the case of two contradictory statutes; or it might as well happen in every adjudication upon any single statute. The courts must declare the sense of the law; and if they should be disposed to exercise *will* instead of *judgment*, the consequence would equally be the substitution of their pleasure to that of the legislative body. The observation, if it proved any thing, would prove that there ought to be no judges distinct from that body.

If then the courts of justice are to be considered as the bulwarks of a limited constitution against legislative encroachments, this consideration will afford a strong argument for the permanent tenure of judicial offices, since nothing will contribute so much as this to that independent spirit in the judges, which must be essential to the faithful performance of so arduous a duty.

This independence of the judges is equally requisite to guard
the constitution and the rights of individuals from the effects
of those ill humours which the arts of designing men, or the
influence of particular conjunctures, sometimes disseminate
among the people themselves, and which, though they speedily give place to better information and more deliberate reflection, have a tendency in the mean time to occasion dangerous
innovations in the government, and serious oppressions of
the minor party in the community. Though I trust the friends
of the proposed constitution will never concur with its enemies* in questioning that fundamental principle of republican
government, which admits the right of the people to alter or
abolish the established constitution whenever they find it inconsistent with their happiness; yet it is not to be inferred from
this principle, that the representatives of the people, whenever
a momentary inclination happens to lay hold of a majority of
their constituents incompatible with the provisions in the existing constitution, would on that account be justifiable in a violation of those provisions; or that the courts would be under
a greater obligation to connive at infractions in this shape, than
when they had proceeded wholly from the cabals of the representative body. Until the people have by some solemn and
authoritative act annulled or changed the established form, it
is binding upon themselves collectively, as well as individually;
and no presumption, or even knowledge of their sentiments,
can warrant their representatives in a departure from it, prior
to such an act. But it is easy to see that it would require an
uncommon portion of fortitude in the judges to do their duty
as faithful guardians of the constitution, where legislative invasions of it had been instigated by the major voice of the
community.

But it is not with a view to infractions of the constitution
only that the independence of the judges may be an essential
safeguard against the effects of occasional ill humours in the society. These sometimes extend no farther than to the injury of
the private rights of particular classes of citizens, by unjust and
partial laws. Here also the firmness of the judicial magistracy

*Vide Protest of the minority of the convention of Pennsylvania, Martin's
speech, &c.

is of vast importance in mitigating the severity, and confining the operation of such laws. It not only serves to moderate the immediate mischiefs of those which may have been passed, but it operates as a check upon the legislative body in passing them; who, perceiving that obstacles to the success of an iniquitous intention are to be expected from the scruples of the courts, are in a manner compelled by the very motives of the injustice they meditate, to qualify their attempts. This is a circumstance calculated to have more influence upon the character of our governments, than but few may be aware of. The benefits of the integrity and moderation of the judiciary have already been felt in more states than one; and though they may have displeased those whose sinister expectations they may have disappointed, they must have commanded the esteem and applause of all the virtuous and disinterested. Considerate men of every description ought to prize whatever will tend to beget or fortify that temper in the courts; as no man can be sure that he may not be tomorrow the victim of a spirit of injustice, by which he may be a gainer to-day. And every man must now feel that the inevitable tendency of such a spirit is to sap the foundations of public and private confidence, and to introduce in its stead, universal distrust and distress.

That inflexible and uniform adherence to the rights of the constitution and of individuals, which we perceive to be indispensable in the courts of justice, can certainly not be expected from judges who hold their offices by a temporary commission. Periodical appointments, however regulated, or by whomsoever made, would in some way or other be fatal to their necessary independence. If the power of making them was committed either to the executive or legislature, there would be danger of an improper complaisance to the branch which possessed it; if to both, there would be an unwillingness to hazard the displeasure of either; if to the people, or to persons chosen by them for the special purpose, there would be too great a disposition to consult popularity, to justify a reliance that nothing would be consulted but the constitution and the laws.

There is yet a further and a weighty reason for the permanency of the judicial offices; which is deducible from the nature of the qualifications they require. It has been frequently

remarked with great propriety, that a voluminous code of laws
is one of the inconveniences necessarily connected with the
advantages of a free government. To avoid an arbitrary discretion in the courts, it is indispensable that they should be
bound down by strict rules and precedents, which serve to define and point out their duty in every particular case that comes
before them; and it will readily be conceived from the variety
of controversies which grow out of the folly and wickedness
of mankind, that the records of those precedents must unavoidably swell to a very considerable bulk, and must demand
long and laborious study to acquire a competent knowledge of
them. Hence it is that there can be but few men in the society,
who will have sufficient skill in the laws to qualify them for
the stations of judges. And making the proper deductions for
the ordinary depravity of human nature, the number must be
still smaller of those who unite the requisite integrity with the
requisite knowledge. These considerations apprise us, that the
government can have no great option between fit characters;
and that a temporary duration in office, which would naturally discourage such characters from quitting a lucrative line of
practice to accept a seat on the bench, would have a tendency
to throw the administration of justice into hands less able, and
less well qualified to conduct it with utility and dignity. In the
present circumstances of this country, and in those in which it
is likely to be for a long time to come, the disadvantages on this
score would be greater than they may at first sight appear; but
it must be confessed that they are far inferior to those which
present themselves under the other aspects of the subject.

Upon the whole there can be no room to doubt that the
convention acted wisely in copying from the models of those
constitutions which have established *good behaviour* as the tenure of their judicial offices in point of duration; and that so far
from being blameable on this account, their plan would have
been inexcuseably defective f it had wanted this important
feature of good government. The experience of Great Britain affords an illustrious comment on the excellence of the
institution.

PUBLIUS.

George Washington to John Armstrong

Dear Sir,

From some cause or other which I do not know your favor of the 20th of February did not reach me till very lately. This must apologize for its not being sooner acknowledged. Altho Colo. Blain forgot to call upon me for a letter before he left Philadelphia, yet I wrote a few lines to you previous to my departure from that place; whether they ever got to your hands or not you best know.

I well remember the observation you made in your letter to me of last year, "that my domestic retirement must suffer an interruption." This took place, notwithstanding it was utterly repugnant to my feelings, my interest and my wishes; I sacrificed every private consideration and personal enjoyment to the earnest and pressing solicitations of those who saw and knew the alarming situation of our public concerns, and had no other end in view but to promote the interest of their Country; and conceiving that under those circumstances, and at so critical a moment, an absolute refusal to act, might, on my part, be construed as a total dereliction of my Country, if imputed to no worse motives. Altho' you say the same motives induce you to think that another tour of duty of this kind will fall to my lot, I cannot but hope that you will be disappointed, for I am so wedded to a state of retirement; and find the occupations of a rural life so congenial; with my feelings, that to be drawn unto public at the advanced age, would be a sacrifice that could admit of no compensation.

Your remarks on the impressions which will be made on the manners and sentiments of the people by the example of those who are first called to act under the proposed Government are very Just; and I have no doubt but (if the proposed Constitution obtains) those persons who are chosen to administer it will have wisdom enough to discern the influence which their examples as rulers and legislators may have on the body of the people, and will have virtue enough to pursue that line of conduct which will most conduce to the happiness of their

Country; and as the first transactions of a nation, like those of an individual upon his enterance into life, make the deepest impression and are to form the leading traits in its character, they will undoubtedly pursue those measures which will best tend to the restoration of public and private faith and of consequence promote our national respectibility and individual welfare.

That the proposed Constitution will admit of amendments is acknowledged by its warmest advocates but to make such amendments as may be proposed by the several States the condition of its adoption would, in my opinion amount to a compleat rejection of it; for upon examination of the objections which are made by the opponents in different States and the amendments which have been proposed, it will be found that what would be a favourite object with one State is the very thing which is strenuously opposed by another; the truth is, men are too apt to be swayed by local prejudices, and those who are so fond of amendments which have the particular interest of their own State in view cannot extend their ideas to the general welfare of the Union—they do not consider that for every sacrifice which they make they receive an ample compensation by the sacrifices which are made by other States for their benefit—and that those very things which they give up will operate to their advantage through the medium of the general interest. In addition to these considerations it should be remembered that a constitutional door is open for such amendments as shall be thought necessary by nine States. When I reflect upon these circumstances I am surprized to find that any person who is acquainted with the critical state of our public affairs, and knows the variety of views, interests, feelings and prejudices which must be consulted and conciliated in framing a general Government for these States, and how little propositions in themselves so opposite to each other, will tend to promote that desireable an end, can wish to make amendments the ultimatum for adopting the offered system.

I am very glad to find that the opposition in your State, however formidable it has been represented, is, generally speaking, composed of such characters as cannot have an extensive influence; their fort, as well as that of those of the same class in other States seems to lie in misrepresentation, and a desire to inflame the passions and to alarm the fears by noisy declamation rather than to convince the understanding by some arguments or fair and impartial statements—Baffled in their attacks upon the constitution they have attempted to vilify and debase the Characters who formed it, but even here I trust they will not succeed. Upon the whole I doubt whether the opposition to the Constitution will not ultimately be productive of more good than evil; it has called forth, in its defence, abilities (which would not perhaps have been otherwise exerted) that have thrown new lights upon the science of Government, they have given the rights of man a full and fair discussion, and have explained them in so clear and forcible a manner as cannot fail to make a lasting impression upon those who read the best publications on the subject, and particularly the pieces under the signiture of Publius. There will be a greater weight of abilities opposed to the system in the convention of this State than there has been in any other, but notwithstanding the unwearied pains which have been taken, and the vigorous efforts which will be made in the Convention to prevent its adoption, I have not the smallest doubt but it will obtain here.

I am sorry to hear that the College in your neighbourhood is in so declining a state as you represent it, and that it is likely to suffer a farther injury by the loss of Dr Nisbet whom you are afraid you shall not be able to support in a proper manner on account of the scarcity of Cash which prevents parents from sending their Children hither. This is one of the numerous evils which arise from the want of a general regulating power, for in a Country like this where equal liberty is enjoyed, where every man may reap his own harvest, which by proper attention will afford him much more that what is necessary for his own consumption, and where there is so ample a field for every mercantile and mechanical exertion, if there cannot be money found to answer the common purposes of education, not to mention the necessary commercial circulation, it is evident that there is something amiss in the ruling political power which requires a steady, regulating and energetic hand to connect and control. That money is not to be had, every mans experience tells him, and the great fall in the price of property is an unequivocal, and melancholy proof of it; when, if that property was well secured—faith and Justice well preserved—a stable government well administered—and confidence restored, the tide of population and wealth would flow to us, from every part of the Globe; and, with a due sense of the blessing, make us the happiest people upon earth. with sentiments of very great esteem and regard I am Dr Sir &c.

Go. Washington

PART 6:
THE STATE
RATIFYING CONVENTIONS

THE CONSTITUTION called for elected state conventions to ratify, or reject, the new system. When nine states had ratified, the
Constitution would take effect. This would bypass the state legislatures, which might be hostile to the system that would take away state
power. More importantly, conventions would express the sovereign
will of the people of each state. Opponents hoped to keep nine states
from ratifying, and ultimately have another convention to draw up a
different Constitution. In December 1787, conventions in Delaware,
New Jersey, and Georgia ratified unanimously. In **Pennsylvania**,
though, opponents challenged each clause of the Constitution, and
particularly criticized the lack of a Bill of Rights. Supporters of the
Constitution continued to insist that a Bill of Rights was unnecessary,
if not unwise. The supporters knew they had enough votes to ratify,
and did so by a vote of 46 to 23 on December 12. Rioting broke
out in Carlisle, and twenty-one members of the convention minority
printed their reasons for opposing ratification, with a list of changes
they would insist upon before supporting the Constitution.

In **Massachusetts**, the next large state to hold a convention,
delegates met in Boston on January 9, 1788, the same day that the
Connecticut convention voted to ratify, 128–40. Like Pennsylvania's,
Massachusetts's convention was closely divided. After three weeks of
debates, supporters realized that Massachusetts might reject the Constitution, which would be fatal to its chances. They compromised.
Rather than insisting that amendments were unnecessary, if not dangerous, they agreed that once the Constitution took effect, Congress
would recommend amendments. Governor John Hancock, who had
been elected to chair the convention but had not previously attended,
spoke for the first time on January 31, urging ratification and presenting nine drafted amendments Massachusetts would support after
ratification. Samuel Adams, a prominent opponent of ratification,
supported Hancock's proposal, and the Massachusetts convention
ratified, 187 to 168.

Subsequent state conventions also proposed amendments, to be
added after the Constitution had been ratified. Maryland and **South**

Carolina ratified in the spring of 1788 with little controversy. But Rhode Island rejected the Constitution in a popular referendum, 239 in favor, 2,711 against, and New Hampshire Federalists realized when their convention met in February that they might be outvoted, so they moved to adjourn until summer; the motion carried 56 to 51.

Eight states had ratified by June when conventions met in New Hampshire, Virginia, and New York. Governor Clinton presided at **New York**'s convention in Poughkeepsie, where Melancton Smith, a successful lawyer, merchant, and landowner, led the opponents, and Alexander Hamilton, John Jay, and Robert Livingston led the outnumbered Federalists. Ratification in **Virginia** was also in doubt. Patrick Henry, Virginia's most powerful politician and the era's greatest orator, led the opponents, who also included George Mason and James Monroe. Madison led the supporters, sometimes speaking so quietly he was inaudible, though John Marshall, who attended the convention as a Federalist delegate, later called Madison the most persuasive speaker he had ever heard. As Virginia and New York debated each clause of the Constitution, New Hampshire ratified, 57 to 47, recommending a dozen amendments to be added later. Not knowing that New Hampshire, the ninth state, had ratified, Virginia voted to ratify, 89 to 79, on June 25, while also recommending the subsequent adoption of amendments. When news that Virginia and New Hampshire had ratified reached New York on July 2, 1788, the Poughkeepsie debate continued, with New York considering conditional ratification, or even maintaining the right to secede, before voting at the end of July to ratify, 30 to 27.

In August the **North Carolina** convention rejected the Constitution, with 83 delegates in favor and 183 opposed. Nonetheless, eleven states had ratified, which meant that the government created by the Constitution would go into operation in the spring of 1789.

PENNSYLVANIA RATIFYING CONVENTION

James Wilson: Opening Address

November 24, 1787

Mr. WILSON. As the only member of this respectable body, who had the honor of a seat in the late Fœderal Convention, it is peculiarly my duty Mr. President, to submit to your consideration, the general principles that have produced the national Constitution, which has been framed and proposed by the assembled delegates of the United States, and which must finally stand or fall by the concurrent decision of this Convention, and of others acting upon the same subject, under similar powers and authority. To frame a Government for a single city or State, is a business both in its importance and facility, widely different from the task entrusted to the Fœderal Convention, whose prospects were extended not only to thirteen Independent and Sovereign States, some of which in territorial jurisdiction, population, and resource, equal the most respectable nations of Europe, but likewise to innumerable States yet unformed, and to myriads of citizens who in future ages shall inhabit the vast uncultivated regions of the continent. The duties of that body therefore, were not limitted to local or partial considerations, but to the formation of a plan commensurate with a great and valuable portion of the globe.

I confess, Sir, that the magnitude of the object before us, filled our minds with awe and apprehension. In Europe the opening and extending the navigation of a single river, has been deemed an act of imperial merit and importance; but how insignificant does it seem when we contemplate the scene that nature here exhibits, pouring forth the Potowmack, the Rapahannock, the Susquehanna, and other innumerable rivers, to dignify, adorn, and enrich our soil. But the magnitude of the object was equalled by the difficulty of accomplishing it,

259

when we considered the uncommon dexterity and address that were necessary to combat and reconcile the jarring interests that seemed naturally to prevail, in a country, which presenting a coast of 1500 miles to the Atlantic, is composed of 13 distinct and Independant States, varying essentially in their situation and dimensions, and in the number and habits of their citizens. Their interests too, in some respects really different, and in many apparently so; but whether really or apparently, such is the constitution of the human mind, they make the same impression, and are prosecuted with equal vigour and perseverance. Can it then be a subject for surprize that with the sensations indispensably excited by so comprehensive and so arduous an undertaking, we should for a moment yield to despondency, and at length, influenced by the spirit of conciliation, resort to mutual concession, as the only means to obtain the great end for which we were convened? Is it a matter of surprize that where the springs of dissension were so numerous, and so powerful, some force was requisite to impel them to take, in a collected state, a direction different from that which separately they would have pursued?

There was another reason, that in this respect, encreased the difficulties of the Fœderal Convention—the different tempers and dispositions of the people for whom they acted. But, however widely they may differ upon other topics, they cordially agree in that keen and elevated sense of freedom and independence, which has been manifested in their united and successful opposition to one of the most powerful kingdoms of the world. Still it was apprehended by some, that their abhorrence of constraint, would be the source of objection and opposition; but, I confess, that my opinion, formed upon a knowledge of the good sense, as well as the high spirit of my Constituents, made me confident that they would esteem that government to be the best, which was best calculated eventually to establish and secure the dignity and happiness of their country. Upon this ground, I have occasionally supposed that my constituents have asked the reason for my assent to the several propositions contained in the plan before us. My answer, tho' concise, is a candid, and, I think a satisfactory one—because I thought them right; and thinking them right, it would be a poor compliment indeed to presume they could be disagreeable to my

Constituents—a presumption that might occasion a retort to which I wish not to expose myself, as it would again be asked, "is this the opinion you entertain of those who have confided in your judgment? From what ground do you infer that a vote right in itself would be disagreeable to us?" and it might with justice be added, "this sentiment evinces that you deserved not the trust which we reposed in you." No Sir!—I have no right to imagine that the reflected rays of delegated power can displease by a brightness that proves the superior splendor of the luminary from which they proceed.

The extent of country for which the New Constitution was required, produced another difficulty in the business of the Fœderal Convention. It is the opinion of some celebrated writers, that to a small territory, the democratical, to a midling territory, (as Montesquieu has termed it) the monarchical, and, to an extensive territory, the despotic form of government, is best adapted. Regarding then, the wide and almost unbounded jurisdiction of the United States, at first view, the hand of despotism seemed necessary to controul, connect, and protect it; and hence the chief embarrasment arose. For, we knew that, although our Constituents would chearfully submit to the legislative restraints of a free government, they would spurn at every attempt to shackle them with despotic power.

In this dilemma, a Fœderal Republic naturally presented itself to our observation, as a species of government which secured all the internal advantages of a republic, at the same time that it maintained the external dignity and force of a monarchy. The definition of this form of government may be found in Montesquieu, who says, I believe, that it consists in assembling distinct societies, which are consolidated into a new body, capable of being encreased by the addition of other members;—an expanding quality peculiarly fitted to the circumstances of America.

But, while a Fœderal Republic, removed one difficulty, it introduced another, since there existed not any precedent to assist our deliberations; for, though there are many single governments, both ancient and modern, the history and principles of which are faithfully preserved, and well understood, a perfect confederation of independent states is a system hitherto unknown. The Swiss Cantons, which have often been mentioned in that light, cannot properly be deemed a Fœderal Republic, but merely a system of United States. The United Netherlands are also an assemblage of states; yet, as their proceedings are not the result of their combined decisions, but of the decisions of each state individually, their association is evidently wanting in that quality which is essential to constitute a Fœderal Republic. With respect to the Germanic Body, its members are of so disproportionate a size, their separate governments and jurisdictions so different in nature and extent, the general purpose and operation of their union so indefinite and uncertain, and the exterior power of the House of Austria so prevalent, that little information could be obtained or expected from that quarter. Turning then to ancient history, we find the Achæan and Lycian leagues, and the Amphyctionic council bearing a superficial resemblance to a Fœderal Republic; but of all these, the accounts which have been transmitted to us, are too vague and imperfect to supply a tolerable theory, and they are so destitute of that minute detail from which practical knowledge may be derived, that they must now be considered rather as subjects of curiosity, than of use or information.

Government, indeed, taken as a science, may yet be considered in its infancy; and with all its various modifications, it has hitherto been the result of force, fraud, or accident. For, after the lapse of six thousand years since the creation of the world, America now presents the first instance of a people assembled to weigh deliberately and calmly, and to decide leisurely and peacably, upon the form of government by which they will bind themselves and their posterity. Among the ancients, three forms of government seem to have been correctly known, the Monarchical, Aristocratical, and Democratical; but their knowledge did not extend beyond those simple kinds, though much pleasing ingenuity has occasionally been exercised, in tracing a resemblance of mixed government in some ancient institutions, particularly between them and the British Constitution. But, in my opinion, the result of these ingenious refinements does more honor to the moderns in discovering, than to the ancients in forming the similitude. In the work of Homer, it is supposed by his enthusiastic commentators, the seeds of every science are to be found; but, in truth, they are first observed in subsequent discoveries, and then the fond imagination transplants them to the book. Tacitus, who lived towards the close of that period, which is called ancient, who had read the history of all antecedent and cotemporary governments, who was perfectly competent to judge of their nature, tendency, and quality, Tacitus considers a mixed government as a thing rather to be wished than expected; and, if ever it did occur, it was his opinion, that it could not last long. One fact, however, is certain, that the ancients had no idea of representation, that essential to every system of wise, good, and efficient government. It is surprising, indeed, how very imperfectly, at this day, the doctrine of representation is understood in Europe. Even Great-Britain, which boasts a superior knowledge of the subject, and is generally supposed to have carried it into practice, falls far short of its true and genuine principles. For, let us enquire, does representation pervade the constitution of that country? No. Is it either immediately or remotely the source of the executive power? No. For it is not any part of the British constitution, as practised at this time, that the king derives his authority from the people. Formerly that authority was claimed by hereditary or divine right; and even at the revolution, when the government was essentially improved, no other principle was recognized, but that of an original contract between the sovereign and the people—a contract which rather excludes than implies the doctrine of representation. Again; Is the judicial system of England grounded on representation? No. For the judges are appointed by the king, and he, as we have already observed, derives not his majesty or power from the people. Lastly, then, let us review the legislative body of that nation, and even there, though we find representation operating as a check, it cannot be considered as a pervading principle. The lords, acting with hereditary right, or under an authority immediately communicated by regal prerogative, are not the representatives of the people, and yet they, as well as the sovereign, possess a negative power in the paramount business of legislation. Thus the vital principle of the British constitution is confined to a narrow corner, and the world has left to America the glory and happiness of forming a government, where representation shall at once supply the basis and the cement of the superstructure. For, representation, Sir, is the true chain between the people, and those to whom they entrust the administration of the government; and, though it may consist of many links, its strength and brightness, never should be impaired. Another, and perhaps the most important obstacle to the proceedings of the Fœderal Convention, arose in drawing the line between the national and the individual governments of the states.

On this point a general principle readily occurred, that whatever object was confined in its nature and operation to a particular State, ought to be subject to the separate government of the States, but whatever in its nature and operation extended beyond a particular State, ought to be comprehended within the Fœderal jurisdiction. The great difficulty, therefore, was the application of this general principle, for it was found impracticable to enumerate and distinguish the various objects to which it extended, and as the mathematics, only, are capable of demonstration, it ought not to be thought extraordinary that the Convention could not develope a subject, involved in such endless perplexity. If however, the proposed constitution should be adopted, I trust that in the theory there will be found such harmony, and in the practice such mutual confidence between the national and individual governments, that every sentiment of jealousy and apprehension will be effectually destroyed. But Sir, permit me to ask, whether on the ground of a union, the individual or the national government ought most to be trusted? For my part, I think it more natural to presume that the interest of each would be pursued by the whole, than the reverse of the proposition, that the several States would prefer the interest of the confederated body; for in the general government each is represented, but in the separate governments, only the separate States.

These difficulties, Mr. President, which embarrassed the Fœderal Convention, are not represented to enhance the merit of surmounting them, but with a more important view, to shew how unreasonable it is to expect that the plan of government, should correspond with the wishes of all the States, of all the citizens of any one state, or of all the citizens of the United continent. I remember well, Sir, the effect of those surrounding difficulties in the late Convention. At one time the great and interesting work seemed to be at a stand, at another it proceeded with energy and rapidity, and when at last, it was accomplished, many respectable members beheld it with wonder and admiration. But having pointed out the obstacles which they had to encounter, I shall now beg leave to direct your attention, to the end which the Convention proposed.

Our wants, imperfections, and weakness, Mr. President, naturally incline us to society; but it is certain, society cannot exist without some restraints. In a state of nature each individual has a right, uncontrouled, to act as his pleasure or his interest may prevail, but it must be observed that this licence extends to every individual, and hence the state of nature is rendered insupportable, by the interfering claims, and the consequent animosities of men, who are independant of every power and influence, but their passions and their will. On the other hand, in entering into the social compact, though the individual parts with a portion of his natural rights, yet, it is evident that he gains more by the limitation of the liberty of others, than he loses by the limitation of his own,—so that in truth, the aggregate of liberty is more in society, than it is in a state of nature.

It is then, Sir, a fundamental principle of society, that the welfare of the whole shall be pursued and not of a part, and the measures necessary to the good of the community, must consequently be binding upon the individuals that compose it. This principle is universally allowed to be just with respect to single governments, and there are instances in which it applies with equal force to independent Communities; for the situation and circumstances of states may make it as necessary for them, as for individuals, to associate. Hence, Mr. President, the important question arises—are such the situation and circumstances of the American States?

At this period, America has it in her power to adopt either of the following modes of Government: She may dissolve the individual sovereignty of the States, and become one consolidated empire; She may be divided into thirteen separate, independant, and unconnected Commonwealths; she may be erected into two or more confederacies; or, lastly, she may become one comprehensive Fœderal Republic.

Allow me, Sir, to take a short view of each of these suppositions. Is it probable that the dissolution of the State governments, and the establishment of one consolidated empire, would be eligible in its nature, and satisfactory to the people in its administration? I think not, as I have given reasons to shew that so extensive a territory could not be governed, connected, and preserved, but by the Supremacy of despotic power. All the exertions of the most potent Emperors of Rome were not capable of keeping that Empire together, which in extent was far inferior to the dominion of America. Would an independent, an unconnected situation, without any associating head, be advantageous or satisfactory? The consequences of this system would at one time expose the States to foreign insult and depredations, and, at another, to internal jealousy, contention, and war. Then let us consider the plan of two or more confederacies which has often been suggested, and which certainly presents some aspects more inviting than either of the preceeding modes, since the subjects of strife would not be so numerous, the strength of the confederates would be greater, and their interests more united. But even here when we fairly weigh the advantages and the disadvantages, we shall find the last greatly preponderating; the expences of government would be considerably multiplied, the seeds of rivalship and animosity would spring up, and spread the calamities of war and tumult through the country; for tho' the sources of rancour might be diminished, their strength, and virulence would probably be increased.

Of these three species of government, however, I must observe, that they obtained no advocates in the Fœderal Convention, nor can I presume that they will find advocates here, or in any of our sister states. The general sentiment in that body, and, I believe, the general sentiment of the citizens of America, is expressed in the motto which some of them have chosen, UNITE OR DIE; and while we consider the extent of the country, so intersected and almost surrounded with navigable rivers, so separated and detached from the rest of the world, it is natural to presume that Providence has designed us for an united people, under one great political compact. If this is a just and reasonable conclusion, supported by the wishes of the people, the Convention did right in proposing a single confederated Republic. But in proposing it, they were necessarily lead, not only to consider the situation, circumstances, and interests of one, two, or three states, but of the collective body; and as it is essential to society, that the welfare of the whole should be preferred to the accommodation of a part, they followed the same rule in promoting the national advantages of the Union, in preference to the separate advantages of the States. A principle of candor, as well as duty, lead to this conduct; for, as I have said before, no government, either single or confederated can exist, unless private and individual rights are subservient to the public and general happiness of the nation. It was not alone the state of Pennsylvania, however important she may be as a constituent part of the union, that could influence the deliberations of a Convention, formed by a delegation from all the United States, to devise a government adequate to their common exigencies, and impartial in its influence and operation. In the spirit of union, inculcated by the nature of their commission, they framed the constitution before us, and in the same spirit, they submit it to the candid consideration of their constituents.

Having made some remarks upon the nature and principles of civil society, I shall now take a cursory notice of civil liberty, which is essential to the well-being of civil government. The definition of civil liberty is, briefly, that portion of natural liberty which men resign to the government, and which then produces more happiness, than it would have produced if retained by the individuals who resign it;—still however leaving to the human mind, the full enjoyment of every privilege that is not incompatible with the peace and order of society. Here I am easily lead to the consideration of another species of liberty, which has not yet received a discriminating name, but which I will venture to term Fœderal liberty. This, Sir, consists in the agregate of the civil liberty which is surrendered by each state to the national government; and the same principles that operate in the establishment of a single society, with respect to the rights reserved or resigned by the individuals that compose it, will justly apply in the case of a confederation of distinct and Independent States.

These observations have been made, Mr. President, in order to preface a representation of the state of the union, as it appeared to the late Convention. We all know, and we have all felt, that the present system of confederation is inadequate to the government and the exigencies of the United States. Need I describe the contrasted scene which the revolution has presented to our view? On the one hand, the arduous struggle in the cause of liberty terminated by a glorious and triumphant peace; on the other, contention and poverty at home, discredit and disgrace abroad. Do we not remember what high expectations were formed by others and by ourselves, on the return of peace? And have those honorable expectations from our national character, been realized? No!—What then has been the cause of disappointment? Has America lost her magnanimity or perseverance? no. Has she been subdued by any high handed invasion of her liberties? still I answer no; for, dangers of that kind were no sooner seen, than they were repelled. But the evil has stolen in from a quarter little suspected, and the rock of Freedom, which stood firm against the attacks of a foreign foe, has been sapped and undermined by the licentiousness of our own citizens. Private calamity, and public anarchy have prevailed; and even the blessing of Independency has been scarcely felt or understood by a people who have dearly atchieved it.

Shall I, Sir, be more particular in this lamentable history? The commencement of peace, was likewise the commencement of our distresses and disgrace. Devoid of power, we could neither prevent the excessive importations which lately deluged the country, nor even raise from that excess a contribution to the public revenue; devoid of importance, we were unable to command a sale for our commodities in a foreign market; devoid of credit, our public securities were melting in the hands of their deluded owners, like snow before the Sun; devoid of dignity, we were inadequate to perform treaties on our own part, or to compel a performance on the part of a contracting nation. In short, Sir, the tedious tale disgusts me, and I fondly hope, it is unnecessary to proceed. The years of languor are over. We have seen dishonor and destruction, it is true, but we have at length penetrated the cause, and are now anxious to obtain the cure. The cause need not be specified by a recapitulation of facts; every act of Congress, and the proceedings of every State are replete with proofs in that respect, and all point to the weakness and imbecility of the existing Confederation; while the loud and concurrent voice of the people proclaims an efficient national government to be the only cure. Under these impressions, and with these views, the late Convention were appointed and met; the end which they proposed to accomplish, being to frame one national and efficient government, in which the exercise of beneficence, correcting the jarring interests of every part, should pervade the whole, and by which the peace, freedom, and happiness of the United States should be permanently ensured. The principles and means that were adopted by the Convention to obtain that end, are now before us, and will become the great object of our discussion. But on this point, as upon others, permit me to make a few general observations.

In all governments, whatever is their form, however they may be constituted, there must be a power established, from which there is no appeal—and which is therefore called absolute, supreme, and uncontroulable. The only question is, where that power is lodged?—a question that will receive different answers from the different writers on the subject. Sir William Blackstone says, it resides in the omnipotence of the British Parliament, or in other words, corresponding with the practice of that country, it is whatever the British Parliament pleases to do: So that when that body was so base and treacherous to the rights of the people as to transfer the legislative authority to Henry the eighth, his exercising that authority by proclamations and edicts, could not strictly speaking be termed unconstitutional, for under the act of Parliament his will was made the law, and therefore, his will became in that respect the constitution itself. But were we to ask some politicians who have taken a faint and inaccurate view of our establishments, where does this supreme power reside in the United States? They would probably answer, in their Constitutions. This however, tho' a step nearer to the fact, is not a just opinion; for, in truth, it remains and flourishes with the people; and under the influence of that truth we, at this moment, sit, deliberate and speak. In other countries, indeed the revolutions of government are connected with war, and all its concomitant calamities. But with us, they are considered as the means of obtaining a superior knowledge of the nature of government, and of accomplishing its end. That the supreme power therefore, should be vested in the people, is, in my judgment, the great panacea of human politics. It is a power paramount to every constitution, inalienable in its nature, and indefinite in its extent. For, I insist, if there are errors in government the people have the right not only to correct and amend them, but likewise totally to change and reject its form; and under the operation of that right, the citizens of the United States can never be wretched beyond retrieve, unless they are wanting to themselves.

Then let us examine, Mr. President, the three species of simple governments, which, as I have already mentioned, are the monarchical, aristocratical and democratical. In a monarchy, the supreme power is vested in a single person: in an aristocracy, it is possessed by a body, not formed upon the principle of representation, but enjoying their station by descent, by election among themselves, or in right of some personal or territorial qualification; and, lastly, in a democracy, it is inherent in the people, and is either exercised by themselves or by their representatives. Each of these systems has its advantages, and its disadvantages. The advantages of a monarchy are strength, dispatch, and unity: its disadvantages are expence, tyranny, and war. The advantages of an aristocracy are experience, and the wisdom resulting from education: its disadvantages are the disention of the governors, and the oppression of the people. The advantages of a democracy are liberty, caution, industry, fidelity, and an opportunity of bringing forward the talents and abilities of the citizens, without regard to birth or fortune: its disadvantages are disention and imbecility, for the assent of many being required, their exertions will be feeble, and their councils too soon discovered.

To obtain all the advantages, and to avoid all the inconveniences of these governments, was the leading object of the late Convention. Having therefore considered the formation and principles of other systems, it is natural to enquire, of what description is the Constitution before us? In its principles, Sir, it is purely democratical; varying indeed, in its form, in order to admit all the advantages, and to exclude all the disadvantages which are incidental to the known and established constitutions of government. But when we take an extensive and accurate view of the streams of power that appear through this great and comprehensive plan, when we contemplate the variety of their directions, the force and dignity of their currents, when we behold them intersecting, embracing, and surrounding the vast possessions and interests of the Continent, and when we see them distributing on all hands, beauty, energy and riches, still, however numerous and wide their courses, however diversified and remote the blessings they diffuse, we shall be able to trace them all to one great and noble source, THE PEOPLE.

Such, Mr. President, are the general observations with which I have thought it necessary to trouble you. In discussing the distinct propositions of the Fœderal Plan, I shall have occasion to apply them more particularly to that subject, but at present, I shall conclude with requesting the pardon of the Convention for having so long intruded upon their patience.

James Wilson and John Smilie Debate the Need for a Bill of Rights

November 28, 1787

Mr. Wilson. Mr. President, we are repeatedly called upon to give some reason why a bill of rights has not been annexed to the proposed plan. I not only think that enquiry is at this time unnecessary and out of order, but I expect, at least, that those who desire us to shew why it was omitted, will furnish some arguments to shew that it ought to have been inserted; for the proof of the affirmative naturally falls upon them. But the truth is, Sir, that this circumstance, which has since occasioned so much clamour and debate, never struck the mind of any member in the late convention 'till, I believe, within three days of the dissolution of that body, and even then, of so little account was the idea, that it passed off in a short conversation, without introducing a formal debate, or assuming the shape of a motion. For, Sir, the attempt to have thrown into the national scale an instrument in order to evince that any power not mentioned in the constitution was reserved, would have been spurned at as an insult to the common understanding of mankind. In civil government it is certain, that bills of rights are unnecessary and useless, nor can I conceive whence the contrary notion has arisen. Virginia has no bill of rights, and will it be said that her constitution was the less free?

Mr. Smilie. I beg leave to observe, Mr. President, that although it has not been inserted in the printed volume of state constitutions, yet I have been assured by Mr. Mason, that Virginia has a bill of rights.

Mr. Wilson. I do not rely upon the information of Mr. Mason, or of any other gentleman on a question of this kind, but I refer to the authenticity of the volume which contains the state constitutions, and in that Virginia has no bill of rights. But, Sir, has South Carolina no security for her liberties? that state has no bill of rights. Are the citizens of the Eastern shore

of the Delaware more secured in their freedom, or more enlightened on the subject of government than the citizens of
the western shore? New Jersey has no bill of rights; New-York
has none; Connecticut has none, and Rhode-Island has none.
Thus, Sir, it appears from the example of other states, as well
as from principle, that a bill of rights is neither an essential
nor a necessary instrument in framing a system of government,
since liberty may exist and be as well secured without it. But
it was not only unnecessary, but on this occasion, it was found
impracticable; for who will be bold enough to undertake to
enumerate all the rights of the people? and when the attempt
to enumerate them is made, it must be remembered that if the
enumeration is not complete, every thing not expressly mentioned will be presumed to be purposely omitted. So it must
be with a bill of rights, and an omission in stating the powers
granted to the government, is not so dangerous as an omission
in recapitulating the rights reserved by the people. We have
already seen the origin of magna charta, and tracing the subject
still further, we find the petition of rights claiming the liberties
of the people, according to the laws and statutes of the realm,
of which the great charter was the most material; so that here
again recourse is had to the old source from which their liberties are derived, the grant of the king. It was not 'till the
revolution that the subject was placed upon a different footing,
and even then the people did not claim their liberties as an inherent right, but as the result of an original contract between
them and the sovereign. Thus, Mr. President, an attention to
the situation of England, will shew that the conduct of that
country in respect to bills of rights, cannot furnish an example
to the inhabitants of the United States, who by the revolution
have regained all their natural rights, and possess their liberty
neither by grant nor contract. In short, Sir, I have said that
a bill of rights would have been improperly annexed to the
federal plan, and for this plain reason, that it would imply that
whatever is not expressed was given, which is not the principle
of the proposed constitution.

Mr. Smilie. The arguments which have been urged, Mr.
President, have not in my opinion, satisfactorily shewn that
a bill of rights would have been an improper, nay, that it is

not a necessary appendage to the proposed system. As it has been denied that Virginia possesses a bill of rights, I shall on that subject only observe, that Mr. Mason, a gentleman certainly of great information and integrity, has assured me that such a thing does exist, and I am persuaded, I shall be able at a future period to lay it before the convention. But, Sir, the state of Delaware has a bill of rights, and I believe one of the honourable members (Mr. M'Kean) who now contests the necessity and propriety of that instrument, took a very conspicuous part in the formation of the Delaware government. It seems however that the members of the federal convention were themselves convinced, in some degree, of the expediency and propriety of a bill of rights, for we find them expressly declaring that the writ of Habeas Corpus and the trial by jury in criminal cases shall not be suspended or infringed. How does this indeed agree with the maxim that whatever is not given is reserved? Does it not rather appear from the reservation of these two articles that every thing else, which is not specified, is included in the powers delegated to the government? This, sir, must prove the necessity of a full and explicit declaration of rights; and when we further consider the extensive, the undefined powers vested in the administrators of this system, when we consider the system itself as a great political compact between the governors and the governed, a plain, strong, and accurate, criterion by which the people might at once determine when, and in what instance, their rights were violated, is a preliminary, without which this plan ought not to be adopted. So loosely, so inaccurately are the powers which are enumerated in this constitution defined, that it will be impossible, without a test of that kind, to ascertain the limits of authority, and to declare when government has degenerated into oppression. In that event the contest will arise between the people and the rulers: "You have exceeded the powers of your office, you have oppressed us," will be the language of the suffering citizens. The answer of the government will be short—"We have not exceeded our power: you have no test by which you can prove it." Hence, Sir, it will be impracticable to stop the progress of tyranny, for there will be no check but the people, and their exertions must be futile and uncertain; since it will be difficult indeed, to communicate to them, the violation that has been committed, and their proceedings will be neither system-atical nor unanimous. It is said, however, that the difficulty of framing a bill of rights was insurmountable: but, Mr. Presi-dent, I can not agree in this opinion. Our experience, and the numerous precedents before us, would have furnished a very sufficient guide. At present there is no security, even for the rights of conscience, and under the sweeping force of the sixth article, every principle of a bill of rights, every stipulation for the most sacred and invaluable privileges of man, are left at the mercy of government.

Benjamin Rush Speaks
Against a Bill of Rights

November 30, 1787

Doctor Rush. I believe, Mr. President, that of all the treaties which have ever been made, William Penn's was the only one, which was contracted without parchment; and I believe, likewise, it is the only one that has ever been faithfully adhered to. As it has happened with treaties, so, Sir, has it happened with bills of rights, for never yet has one been made which has not, at some period or other, been broken. The celebrated magna charta of England was broken over and over again, and these infractions gave birth to the petition of rights. If, indeed, the government of that country has not been violated for the last hundred years, as some writers have said, it is not owing to charters or declarations of rights, but to the balance which has been introduced and established in the legislative body. The constitution of Pennsylvania, Mr. President, is guarded by an oath, which every man employed in the administration of the public business, is compelled to take; and yet, sir, examine the proceedings of the council of censors, and you will find innumerable instances of the violation of that constitution, committed equally by its friends and enemies. In truth then, there is no security but in a pure and adequate representation; the checks and all the other desiderata of government, are nothing but political error without it, and with it, liberty can never be endangered. While the honorable convention, who framed this system, were employed in their work, there are many gentlemen who can bear testimony that my only anxiety was upon the subject of representation; and when I beheld a legislature constituted of two branches, and in so excellent a manner, either directly or indirectly, elected by the people, and amenable to them, I confess, Sir, that here I chearfully reposed all my hopes and confidence of safety. Civilians having taught us, Mr. President, that occupancy was the origin of property, I think, it may likewise be considered as the origin of liberty; and as we enjoy all our natural rights from a pre occupancy, antecedent to the social state, in entering into that state, whence shall they be said to be derived? would it not be absurd to frame a formal declaration that our natural rights are acquired from ourselves? and would it not be a more rediculous solecism to say, that they are the gift of those rulers whom we have created, and who are invested by us with every power they possess? Sir, I consider it as an honor to the late convention, that this system has not been disgraced with a bill of rights; though I mean not to blame, or reflect upon those states, which have encumbered their constitutions with that idle and superfluous instrument. One would imagine however, from the arguments of the opposition that this government was immediately to be administered by foreigners,—strangers to our habits and opinions, and unconnected with our interests and prosperity. These apprehensions, Sir, might have been excused while we were contending with Great Britain; but, at this time, they are applicable to all governments, as well as that under consideration; and the arguments of the honorable members are, indeed, better calculated for an Indian council fire, than the meridian of this refined and enlightened convention.

James Wilson on the Slave-Trade Clause

Much fault has been found with the mode of expression, used in the first clause of the ninth section of the first article. I believe I can assign a reason, why that mode of expression was used, and why the term slave was not directly admitted in this constitution;—and as to the manner of laying taxes, this is not the first time that the subject has come into the view of the United States, and of the legislatures of the several states. The gentleman (Mr. Findley) will recollect, that in the present congress, the quota of the fœderal debt, and general expences, was to be in proportion to the value of LAND, and other enumerated property, within the states. After trying this for a number of years, it was found on all hands, to be a mode that could not be carried into execution. Congress were satisfied of this, and in the year 1783, recommended, in conformity with the powers they possess'd under the articles of confederation, that the quota should be according to the number of free people, including those bound to servitude, and excluding Indians not taxed. These were the very expressions used in 1783, and the fate of this recommendation was similar to all their other resolutions. It was not carried into effect, but it was adopted by no fewer than eleven, out of thirteen states; and it can not but be matter of surprise, to hear gentlemen, who agreed to this very mode of expression at that time, come forward and state it as an objection on the present occasion. It was natural, sir, for the late convention, to adopt the mode after it had been agreed to by eleven states, and to use the expression, which they found had been received as unexceptionable before. With respect to the clause, restricting congress from prohibiting the migration or importation of such persons, as any of the states now existing, shall think proper to admit, prior to the year 1808. The honorable gentleman says, that this clause is not only dark, but intended to grant to congress, for that time, the power to admit the importation of slaves. No such thing was intended; but I will tell you what was done, and it give me high pleasure, that so much was done. Under the present confederation, the states may admit the importation of slaves as long as they please; but by this article after the year 1808, the congress will have power to prohibit such importation, notwithstanding the disposition of any state to the contrary. I consider this as laying the foundation for banishing slavery out of this country; and though the period is more distant than I could wish, yet it will produce the same kind, gradual change, which was pursued in Pennsylvania. It is with much satisfaction I view this power in the general government, whereby they may lay an interdiction on this reproachful trade; but an immediate advantage is also obtained, for a tax or duty may be imposed on such importation, not exceeding ten dollars for each person; and, this sir, operates as a partial prohibition; it was all that could be obtained, I am sorry it was no more; but from this I think there is reason to hope, that yet a few years, and it will be prohibited altogether; and in the mean time, the new states which are to be formed, will be under the control of congress in this particular; and slaves will never be introduced amongst them. The gentleman says, that it is unfortunate in another point of view; it means to prohibit the introduction of white people from Europe, as this tax may deter them from coming amongst us; a little impartiality and attention will discover the care that the convention took in selecting their language. The words are, the *migration or* IMPORTATION of such persons, &c. shall not be prohibited by congress prior to the year 1808, but a tax or duty may be imposed on such IMPORTATION; it is observable here, that the term migration is dropped, when a tax or duty is mentioned; so that congress have power to impose the tax, only on those imported.

Robert Whitehill Replies to Wilson
on the Slave-Trade Clause

December 3, 1787

Mr. PRESIDENT,

It has been said that Congress will have power, by the new constitution, to lay an impost on the *importation* of slaves, into these states; but that they will have no power to impose any tax upon the *migration* of Europeans. Do the gentlemen, sir, mean to insult our understandings, when they assert this? Or are they ignorant of the English language? If, because of their ignorance, they are at a loss, I can easily explain this clause for them—The words "*migration*" and "*importation*," sir, being *connected* by the *disjunctive* conjunction "*or*," certainly mean either migration, or importation; either the one, or the other; or both. Therefore, when we say "a tax may be laid upon such *importation*," we mean, either upon the *importation*, or *migration*; or upon both; for, because they are *joined together*, in the first instance, by the *disjunctive* conjunction *or*, they are both synonimous terms for the same thing—therefore, "*such importation*," because the *comparative* word, *such*, is used, means both importation, and migration.

Dissent of the Minority
of the Pennsylvania Convention

Pennsylvania Packet (Philadelphia), December 18, 1787

The Address and Reasons of Dissent of the Minority
of the Convention of the State of Pennsylvania
to their Constituents.

It was not until after the termination of the late glorious contest, which made the people of the United States an independent nation, that any defect was discovered in the present confederation. It was formed by some of the ablest patriots in America. It carried us successfully through the war; and the virtue and patriotism of the people, with their disposition to promote the common cause, supplied the want of power in Congress.

The requisition of Congress for the five *per cent.* impost was made before the peace, so early as the first of February, 1781, but was prevented taking effect by the refusal of one state; yet it is probable every state in the union would have agreed to this measure at that period, had it not been for the extravagant terms in which it was demanded. The requisition was new moulded in the year 1783, and accompanied with an additional demand of certain supplementary funds for 25 years. Peace had now taken place, and the United States found themselves labouring under a considerable foreign and domestic debt, incurred during the war. The requisition of 1783 was commensurate with the interest of the debt, as it was then calculated; but it has been more accurately ascertained since that time. The domestic debt has been found to fall several millions of dollars short of the calculation, and it has lately been considerably diminished by large sales of the western lands. The states have been called on by Congress annually for supplies until the general system of finance proposed in 1783 should take place.

It was at this time that the want of an efficient federal government was first complained of, and that the powers vested in Congress were found to be inadequate to the procuring of the benefits that should result from the union. The impost was granted by most of the states, but many refused the supplementary funds; the annual requisitions were set at nought by some of the states, while others complied with them by legislative acts, but were tardy in their payments, and Congress found themselves incapable of complying with their engagements, and supporting the federal government. It was found that our national character was sinking in the opinion of foreign nations. The Congress could make treaties of commerce, but could not enforce the observance of them. We were suffering from the restrictions of foreign nations, who had shackled our commerce, while we were unable to retaliate: and all now agreed that it would be advantageous to the union to enlarge the powers of Congress; that they should be enabled in the amplest manner to regulate commerce, and to lay and collect duties on the imports throughout the United States. With this view a convention was first proposed by Virginia, and finally recommended by Congress for the different states to appoint deputies to meet in convention, "for the purposes of revising and amending the present articles of confederation, so as to make them adequate to the exigencies of the union." This recommendation the legislatures of twelve states complied with so hastily as not to consult their constituents on the subject; and though the different legislatures had no authority from their constituents for the purpose, they probably apprehended the necessity would justify the measure; and none of them extended their ideas at that time further than "revising and amending the present articles of confederation." Pennsylvania by the act appointing deputies expressly confined their powers to this object; and though it is probable that some of the members of the assembly of this state had at that time in contemplation to annihilate the present confederation, as well as the constitution of Pennsylvania, yet the plan was not sufficiently matured to communicate it to the public.

The majority of the legislature of this commonwealth, were at that time under the influence of the members from the city of Philadelphia. They agreed that the deputies sent by them to convention should have no compensation for their services, which determination was calculated to prevent the election of any member who resided at a distance from the city. It was in vain for the minority to attempt electing delegates to the convention, who understood the circumstances, and the feelings of the people, and had a common interest with them. They found a disposition in the leaders of the majority of the house to chuse themselves and some of their dependants. The minority attempted to prevent this by agreeing to vote for some of the leading members, who they knew had influence enough to be appointed at any rate, in hopes of carrying with them some respectable citizens of Philadelphia, in whose principles and integrity they could have more confidence; but even in this they were disappointed, except in one member: the eighth member was added at a subsequent session of the assembly.

The Continental convention met in the city of Philadelphia at the time appointed. It was composed of some men of excellent characters; of others who were more remarkable for their ambition and cunning, than their patriotism; and of some who had been opponents to the independence of the United States. The delegates from Pennsylvania were, six of them, uniform and decided opponents to the constitution of this commonwealth. The convention sat upwards of four months. The doors were kept shut, and the members brought under the most solemn engagements of secrecy.* Some of those who opposed their going so far beyond their powers, retired, hopeless, from the convention, others had the firmness to refuse signing the plan altogether; and many who did sign it, did it not as a system they wholly approved, but as the best that could be then obtained, and notwithstanding the time spent on this subject, it is agreed on all hands to be a work of haste and accommodation.

Whilst the gilded chains were forging in the secret conclave, the meaner instruments of despotism without, were busily employed in alarming the fears of the people with dangers which did not exist, and exciting their hopes of greater advantages from the expected plan than even the best government on earth could produce.

The proposed plan had not many hours issued forth from the womb of suspicious secrecy, until such as were prepared for the purpose, were carrying about petitions for people to sign, signifying their approbation of the system, and requesting

---

*The Journals of the conclave are still concealed.

the legislature to call a convention. While every measure was taken to intimidate the people against opposing it, the public papers teemed with the most violent threats against those who should dare to think for themselves, and *tar and feathers* were liberally promised to all those who would not immediately join in supporting the proposed government be it what it would. Under such circumstances petitions in favour of calling a convention were signed by great numbers in and about the city, before they had leisure to read and examine the system, many of whom, now they are better acquainted with it, and have had time to investigate its principles, are heartily opposed to it. The petitions were speedily handed into the legislature.

Affairs were in this situation when on the 28th of September last a resolution was proposed to the assembly by a member of the house who had been also a member of the federal convention, for calling a state convention, to be elected within *ten* days for the purpose of examining and adopting the proposed constitution of the United States, though at this time the house had not received it from Congress. This attempt was opposed by a minority, who after offering every argument in their power to prevent the precipitate measure, without effect, absented themselves from the house as the only alternative left them, to prevent the measure taking place previous to their constituents being acquainted with the business—That violence and outrage which had been so often threatened was now practised; some of the members were seized the next day by a mob collected for the purpose, and forcibly dragged to the house, and there detained by force whilst the quorum of the legislature, *so formed*, compleated their resolution. We shall dwell no longer on this subject, the people of Pennsylvania have been already acquainted therewith. We would only further observe that every member of the legislature, previously to taking his seat, by solemn oath or affirmation, declares, "that he will not do or consent to any act or thing whatever that shall have a tendency to lessen or abridge their rights and privileges, as declared in the constitution of this state." And that constitution which they are so solemnly sworn to support cannot legally be altered but by a recommendation of the council of censors, who alone are authorised to propose alterations and amendments, and even these must be published at least *six months*, for the consideration of the people.—The proposed system of government for the United States, if adopted, will alter and may annihilate the constitution of Pennsylvania; and therefore the legislature had no authority whatever to recommend the calling a convention for that purpose. This proceeding could not be considered as binding on the people of this commonwealth. The house was formed by violence, some of the members composing it were detained there by force, which alone would have vitiated any proceedings, to which they were otherwise competent; but had the legislature been legally formed, this business was absolutely without their power.

In this situation of affairs were the subscribers elected members of the convention of Pennsylvania. A convention called by a legislature in direct violation of their duty, and composed in part of members, who were compelled to attend for that purpose, to consider of a constitution proposed by a convention of the United States, who were not appointed for the purpose of framing a new form of government, but whose powers were expressly confined to altering and amending the present articles of confederation.—Therefore the members of the continental convention in proposing the plan acted as individuals, and not as deputies from Pennsylvania.* The assembly who called the state convention acted as individuals, and not as the legislature of Pennsylvania; nor could they or the convention chosen on their recommendation have authority to do any act or thing, that can alter or annihilate the constitution of Pennsylvania (both of which will be done by the new constitution) nor are their proceedings in our opinion, at all binding on the people.

The election for members of the convention was held at so early a period and the want of information was so great, that some of us did not know of it until after it was over, and we have reason to believe that great numbers of the people of Pennsylvania have not yet had an opportunity of sufficiently

---

*The continental convention in direct violation of the 13th article of the confederation, have declared, "that the ratification of nine states shall be sufficient for the establishment of this constitution, between the states so ratifying the same."—Thus has the plighted faith of the states been sported with! They had solemnly engaged that the confederation now subsisting should be inviolably preserved by each of them, and the union thereby formed, should be perpetual, unless the same should be altered by mutual consent.

examining the proposed constitution.—We apprehend that no change can take place that will affect the internal government or constitution of this commonwealth, unless a majority of the people should evidence a wish for such a change; but on examining the number of votes given for members of the present state convention, we find that of upwards of *seventy thousand* freemen who are intitled to vote in Pennsylvania, the whole convention has been elected by about *thirteen thousand* voters, and though *two thirds* of the members of the convention have thought proper to ratify the proposed constitution, yet those *two thirds* were elected by the votes of only *six thousand and eight hundred* freemen.

In the city of Philadelphia and some of the eastern counties, the junto that took the lead in the business agreed to vote for none but such as would solemnly promise to adopt the system in *toto*, without exercising their judgment. In many of the counties the people did not attend the elections as they had not an opportunity of judging of the plan. Others did not consider themselves bound by the call of a set of men who assembled at the state-house in Philadelphia, and assumed the name of the legislature of Pennsylvania; and some were prevented from voting, by the violence of the party who were determined at all events to force down the measure. To such lengths did the tools of despotism carry their outrage, that in the night of the election for members of convention, in the city of Philadelphia, several of the subscribers (being then in the city to transact your business) were grossly abused, ill-treated and insulted while they were quiet in their lodgings, though they did not interfere, nor had any thing to do with the said election, but, as they apprehend, because they were supposed to be adverse to the proposed constitution, and would not tamely surrender those sacred rights, which you had committed to their charge.

The convention met, and the same disposition was soon manifested in considering the proposed constitution, that had been exhibited in every other stage of the business. We were prohibited by an express vote of the convention, from taking any question on the separate articles of the plan, and reduced to the necessity of adopting or rejecting *in toto*.—'Tis true the majority permitted us to debate on each article, but restrained us from proposing amendments.—They also determined not to permit us to enter on the minutes our reasons of dissent against any of the articles, nor even on the final question our reasons of dissent against the whole. Thus situated we entered on the examination of the proposed system of government, and found it to be such as we could not adopt, without, as we conceived, surrendering up your dearest rights. We offered our objections to the convention, and opposed those parts of the plan, which, in our opinion, would be injurious to you, in the best manner we were able; and closed our arguments by offering the following propositions to the convention.

1. The right of conscience shall be held inviolable; and neither the legislative, executive nor judicial powers of the United States shall have authority to alter, abrogate, or infringe any part of the constitution of the several states, which provide for the preservation of liberty in matters of religion.

2. That in controversies respecting property, and in suits between man and man, trial by jury shall remain as heretofore, as well in the federal courts, as in those of the several states.

3. That in all capital and criminal prosecutions, a man has a right to demand the cause and nature of his accusation, as well in the federal courts, as in those of the several states; to be heard by himself and his counsel; to be confronted with the accusers and witnesses; to call for evidence in his favor, and a speedy trial by an impartial jury of his vicinage, without whose unanimous consent, he cannot be found guilty, nor can he be compelled to give evidence against himself; and that no man be deprived of his liberty, except by the law of the land or the judgment of his peers.

4. That excessive bail ought not to be required, nor excessive fines imposed, nor cruel nor unusual punishments inflicted.

5. That warrants unsupported by evidence, whereby any officer or messenger may be commanded or required to search suspected places, or to seize any person or persons, his or their property, not particularly described, are grievous and oppressive, and shall not be granted either by the magistrates of the federal government or others.

6. That the people have a right to the freedom of speech, of writing and publishing their sentiments, therefore, the freedom of the press shall not be restrained by any law of the United States.

7. That the people have a right to bear arms for the defence of themselves and their own state, or the United States, or for the purpose of killing game; and no law shall be passed for disarming the people or any of them, unless for crimes committed, or real danger of public injury from individuals; and as standing armies in the time of peace are dangerous to liberty, they ought not to be kept up: and that the military shall be kept under strict subordination to and be governed by the civil powers.

8. The inhabitants of the several states shall have liberty to fowl and hunt in seasonable times, on the lands they hold, and on all other lands in the United States not inclosed, and in like manner to fish in all navigable waters, and others not private property, without being restrained therein by any laws to be passed by the legislature of the United States.

9. That no law shall be passed to restrain the legislatures of the several states from enacting laws for imposing taxes, except imposts and duties on goods imported or exported, and that no taxes, except imposts and duties upon goods imported and exported, and postage on letters shall be levied by the authority of Congress.

10. That the house of representatives be properly increased in number; that elections shall remain free; that the several states shall have power to regulate the elections for senators and representatives, without being controuled either directly or indirectly by any interference on the part of the Congress; and that elections of representatives be annual.

11. That the power of organizing, arming and disciplining the militia (the manner of disciplining the militia to be prescribed by Congress) remain with the individual states, and that Congress shall not have authority to call or march any of the militia out of their own state, without the consent of such state, and for such length of time only as such state shall agree.

That the sovereignty, freedom and independency of the several states shall be retained, and every power, jurisdiction and right which is not by this constitution expressly delegated to the United States in Congress assembled.

12. That the legislative, executive, and judicial powers be kept separate; and to this end that a constitutional council be appointed, to advise and assist the president, who shall be

responsible for the advice they give, hereby the senators would be relieved from almost constant attendance; and also that the judges be made completely independent.

13. That no treaty which shall be directly opposed to the existing laws of the United States in Congress assembled, shall be valid until such laws shall be repealed, or made conformable to such treaty; neither shall any treaties be valid which are in contradiction to the constitution of the United States, or the constitutions of the several states.

14. That the judiciary power of the United States shall be confined to cases affecting ambassadors, other public ministers and consuls; to cases of admiralty and maritime jurisdiction; to controversies to which the United States shall be a party; to controversies between two or more states—between a state and citizens of different states—between citizens claiming lands under grants of different states; and between a state or the citizens thereof and foreign states, and in criminal cases, to such only as are expressly enumerated in the constitution, & that the United States in Congress assembled, shall not have power to enact laws, which shall alter the laws of descents and distribution of the effects of deceased persons, the titles of lands or goods, or the regulation of contracts in the individual states.

After reading these propositions, we declared our willingness to agree to the plan, provided it was so amended as to meet those propositions, or something similar to them: and finally moved the convention to adjourn, to give the people of Pennsylvania time to consider the subject, and determine for themselves; but these were all rejected, and the final vote was taken, when our duty to you induced us to vote against the proposed plan, and to decline signing the ratification of the same.

During the discussion we met with many insults, and some personal abuse; we were not even treated with decency, during the sitting of the convention, by the persons in the gallery of the house; however, we flatter ourselves that in contending for the preservation of those invaluable rights you have thought proper to commit to our charge, we acted with a spirit becoming freemen, and being desirous that you might know the principles which actuated our conduct, and being

prohibited from inserting our reasons of dissent on the minutes of the convention, we have subjoined them for your consideration, as to you alone we are accountable. It remains with
you whether you will think those inestimable privileges, which
you have so ably contended for, should be sacrificed at the
shrine of despotism, or whether you mean to contend for them
with the same spirit that has so often baffled the attempts of an
aristocratic faction, to rivet the shackles of slavery on you and
your unborn posterity.

Our objections are comprised under three general heads of
dissent, viz.

WE Dissent, first, because it is the opinion of the most celebrated writers on government, and confirmed by uniform experience, that a very extensive territory cannot be governed on
the principles of freedom, otherwise than by a confederation
of republics, possessing all the powers of internal government;
but united in the management of their general, and foreign
concerns.

If any doubt could have been entertained of the truth of the
foregoing principle, it has been fully removed by the concession of *Mr. Wilson*, one of the majority on this question; and
who was one of the deputies in the late general convention. In
justice to him, we will give his own words; they are as follows,
viz. "The extent of country for which the new constitution
was required, produced another difficulty in the business of the
federal convention. It is the opinion of some celebrated writers, that to a small territory, the democratical; to a middling
territory (as Montesquieu has termed it) the monarchial; and
to an extensive territory, the despotic form of government is
best adapted. Regarding then the wide and almost unbounded
jurisdiction of the United States, at first view, the hand of
despotism seemed necessary to controul, connect, and protect
it; and hence the chief embarrassment rose. For, we know that,
altho' our constituents would chearfully submit to the legislative restraints of a free government, they would spurn at every
attempt to shackle them with despotic power."—And again in
another part of his speech he continues.—"Is it probable that
the dissolution of the state governments, and the establishment of one *consolidated empire* would be eligible in its nature,
and satisfactory to the people in its administration? I think not,

as I have given reasons to shew that so extensive a territory could not be governed, connected, and preserved, but by the *supremacy of despotic power*. All the exertions of the most potent emperors of Rome were not capable of keeping that empire together, which in extent was far inferior to the dominion of America."

We dissent, secondly, because the powers vested in Congress by this constitution, must necessarily annihilate and absorb the legislative, executive, and judicial powers of the several states, and produce from their ruins one consolidated government, which from the nature of things will be *an iron handed despotism*, as nothing short of the supremacy of despotic sway could connect and govern these United States under one government.

As the truth of this position is of such decisive importance, it ought to be fully investigated, and if it is founded to be clearly ascertained; for, should it be demonstrated, that the powers vested by this constitution in Congress, will have such an effect as necessarily to produce one consolidated government, the question then will be reduced to this short issue, viz. whether satiated with the blessings of liberty; whether repenting of the folly of so recently asserting their unalienable rights, against foreign despots at the expence of so much blood and treasure, and such painful and arduous struggles, the people of America are now willing to resign every privilege of freemen, and submit to the dominion of an absolute government, that will embrace all America in one chain of despotism; or whether they will with virtuous indignation, spurn at the shackles prepared for them, and confirm their liberties by a conduct becoming freemen.

That the new government will not be a confederacy of states, as it ought, but one consolidated government, founded upon the destruction of the several governments of the states, we shall now shew.

The powers of Congress under the new constitution, are complete and unlimited over the *purse* and the *sword*, and are perfectly independent of, and supreme over, the state governments; whose intervention in these great points is entirely destroyed. By virtue of their power of taxation, Congress may command the whole, or any part of the property of the people.

They may impose what imposts upon commerce; they may impose what land taxes, poll taxes, excises, duties on all written instruments, and duties on every other article that they may judge proper; in short, every species of taxation, whether of an external or internal nature is comprised in section the 8th, of article the 1st, viz. "The Congress shall have power to lay and collect taxes, duties, imposts, and excises, to pay the debts, and provide for the common defence and general welfare of the United States."

As there is no one article of taxation reserved to the state governments, the Congress may monopolise every source of revenue, and thus indirectly demolish the state governments, for without funds they could not exist, the taxes, duties and excises imposed by Congress may be so high as to render it impracticable to levy further sums on the same articles; but whether this should be the case or not, if the state governments should presume to impose taxes, duties or excises, on the same articles with Congress, the latter may abrogate and repeal the laws whereby they are imposed, upon the allegation that they interfere with the due collection of their taxes, duties or excises, by virtue of the following clause, part of section 8th, article 1st. viz. "To make all laws which shall be necessary and proper for carrying into execution the foregoing powers, and all other powers vested by this constitution in the government of the United States, or in any department or officer thereof."

The Congress might gloss over this conduct by construing every purpose for which the state legislatures now lay taxes, to be for the "*general welfare*," and therefore as of their jurisdiction.

And the supremacy of the laws of the United States is established by article 6th, viz. "That this constitution and the laws of the United States, which shall be made in pursuance thereof, and *all treaties* made, or which shall be made, under the authority of the United States, shall be the *supreme law* of the *land*; and *the judges in every state shall be bound thereby; any thing in the constitution or laws of any state to the contrary notwithstanding*." It has been alledged that the words "pursuant to the constitution," are a restriction upon the authority of Congress; but when it is considered that by other sections they are invested with every efficient power of government, and which may be exercised to the absolute destruction of the state governments, without any violation of even the forms of the constitution, this seeming restriction, as well as every other restriction in it, appears to us to be nugatory and delusive; and only introduced as a blind upon the real nature of the government. In our opinion, "pursuant to the constitution," will be co-extensive with the *will* and *pleasure* of Congress, which, indeed, will be the only limitation of their powers.

We apprehend that two co-ordinate sovereignties would be a solecism in politics. That therefore as there is no line of distinction drawn between the general, and state governments; as the sphere of their jurisdiction is undefined, it would be contrary to the nature of things, that both should exist together, one or the other would necessarily triumph in the fullness of dominion. However the contest could not be of long continuance, as the state governments are divested of every means of defence, and will be obliged by "the supreme law of the land" *to yield at discretion.*

It has been objected to this total destruction of the state governments, that the existence of their legislatures is made essential to the organization of Congress; that they must assemble for the appointment of the senators and president general of the United States. True, the state legislatures may be continued for some years, as boards of appointment, merely, after they are divested of every other function, but the framers of the constitution foreseeing that the people will soon be disgusted with this solemn mockery of a government without power and usefulness, have made a provision for relieving them from the imposition, in section 4th, of article 1st, viz. "The times, places, and manner of holding elections for senators and representatives, shall be prescribed in each state by the legislature thereof; *but the Congress may at any time, by law make or alter such regulations; except as to the place of chusing senators.*"

As Congress have the controul over the time of the appointment of the president general, of the senators and of the representatives of the United States, they may prolong their existence in office, for life, by postponing the time of their election and appointment, from period to period, under various pretences, such as an apprehension of invasion, the factious disposition of the people, or any other plausible pretence that the occasion may suggest; and having thus obtained life-estates in the government, they may fill up the vacancies themselves, by their controul over the mode of appointment; with this exception in regard to the senators, that as the place of appointment for them, must, by the constitution, be in the particular state, they may depute some body in the respective states, to fill up the vacancies in the senate, occasioned by death, until they can venture to assume it themselves. In this manner, may the only restriction in this clause be evaded. By virtue of the foregoing section, when the spirit of the people shall be gradually broken; when the general government shall be firmly established, and when a numerous standing army shall render opposition vain, the Congress may compleat the system of despotism, in renouncing all dependance on the people, by continuing themselves, and children in the government.

The celebrated *Montesquieu*, in his Spirit of Laws, vol. 1, page 12th, says, "That in a democracy there can be no exercise of sovereignty, but by the suffrages of the people, which are their will; now the sovereigns will is the sovereign himself; the laws therefore, which establish the right of suffrage, are fundamental to this government. In fact, it is as important to regulate in a republic in what manner, by whom, and concerning what suffrages are to be given, as it is in a monarchy to know who is the prince, and after what manner he ought to govern." The *time, mode* and *place* of the election of representatives, senators and president general of the United States, ought not to be under the controul of Congress, but fundamentally ascertained and established.

The new constitution, consistently with the plan of consolidation, contains no reservation of the rights and privileges of the state governments, which was made in the confederation of the year 1778, by article the 2d, viz. "That each state retains its sovereignty, freedom and independence, and every power, jurisdiction and right, which is not by this confederation expressly delegated to the United States in Congress assembled."

The legislative power vested in Congress by the foregoing recited sections, is so unlimited in its nature; may be so comprehensive and boundless in its exercise, that this alone would be amply sufficient to annihilate the state governments, and swallow them up in the grand vortex of general empire.

The judicial powers vested in Congress are also so various and extensive, that by legal ingenuity they may be extended to every case, and thus absorb the state judiciaries, and when we consider the decisive influence that a general judiciary would have over the civil polity of the several states, we do not hesitate to pronounce that this power, unaided by the legislative, would effect a consolidation of the states under one government.

The powers of a court of equity, vested by this constitution, in the tribunals of Congress; powers which do not exist in Pennsylvania, unless so far as they can be incorporated with jury trial, would, in this state, greatly contribute to this event. The rich and wealthy suitors would eagerly lay hold of the infinite mazes, perplexities and delays, which a court of chancery, with the appellate powers of the supreme court in fact as well as law would furnish him with, and thus the poor man being plunged in the bottomless pit of legal discussion, would drop his demand in despair.

In short, consolidation pervades the whole constitution. It begins with an annunciation that such was the intention. The main pillars of the fabric correspond with it, and the concluding paragraph is a confirmation of it. The preamble begins with the words, "We the people of the United States," which is the style of a compact between individuals entering into a state of society, and not that of a confederation of states. The other features of consolidation, we have before noticed.

Thus we have fully established the position, that the powers vested by this constitution in Congress, will effect a consolidation of the states under one government, which even the advocates of this constitution admit, could not be done without the sacrifice of all liberty.

3. We dissent, Thirdly, Because if it were practicable to govern so extensive a territory as these United States includes, on the plan of a consolidated government, consistent with the principles of liberty and the happiness of the people, yet the construction of this constitution is not calculated to attain the object, for independent of the nature of the case, it would of itself, necessarily produce a despotism, and that not by the

usual gradations, but with the celerity that has hitherto only attended revolutions effected by the sword.

To establish the truth of this position, a cursory investigation of the principles and form of this constitution will suffice.

The first consideration that this review suggests, is the omission of a BILL OF RIGHTS ascertaining and fundamentally establishing those unalienable and personal rights of men, without the full, free, and secure enjoyment of which there can be no liberty, and over which it is not necessary for a good government to have the controul. The principal of which are the rights of conscience, personal liberty by the clear and unequivocal establishment of the writ of *habeas corpus*, jury trial in criminal and civil cases, by an impartial jury of the vicinage or county; with the common law proceedings, for the safety of the accused in criminal prosecutions and the liberty of the press, that scourge of tyrants; and the grand bulwark of every other liberty and, privilege; the stipulations heretofore made in favor of them in the state constitutions, are entirely superceded by this constitution.

The legislature of a free country should be so formed as to have a competent knowledge of its constitutents, and enjoy their confidence. To produce these essential requisites, the representation ought to be fair, equal, and sufficiently numerous, to possess the same interests, feelings, opinions, and views, which the people themselves would possess, were they all assembled; and so numerous as to prevent bribery and undue influence, and so responsible to the people, by frequent and fair elections, as to prevent their neglecting or sacrificing the views and interests of their constitutents, to their own pursuits.

We will now bring the legislature under this constitution to the test of the foregoing principles, which will demonstrate, that it is deficient in every essential quality of a just and safe representation.

The house of representatives is to consist of 65 members; that is one for about every 50,000 inhabitants, to be chosen every two years. Thirty-three members will form a quorum for doing business; and 17 of these, being the majority, determine the sense of the house.

The senate, the other constituent branch of the legislature, consists of 26 members, being *two* from each state, appointed by their legislatures every six years—fourteen senators make a quorum; the majority of whom, eight, determines the sense of that body: except in judging on impeachments, or in making treaties, or in expelling a member, when two thirds of the senators present, must concur.

The president is to have the controul over the enacting of laws, so far as to make the concurrence of *two* thirds of the representatives and senators present necessary, if he should object to the laws.

Thus it appears that the liberties, happiness, interests, and great concerns of the whole United States, may be dependent upon the integrity, virtue, wisdom, and knowledge of 25 or 26 men.—How unadequate and unsafe a representation! Inadequate, because the sense and views of 3 or 4 millions of people diffused over so extensive a territory comprising such various climates, products, habits, interests, and opinions, cannot be collected in so small a body; and besides, it is not a fair and equal representation of the people even in proportion to its number, for the smallest state has as much weight in the senate as the largest, and from the smallness of the number to be chosen for both branches of the legislature; and from the mode of election and appointment, which is under the controul of Congress; and from the nature of the thing, men of the most elevated rank in life, will alone be chosen. The other orders in the society, such as farmers, traders, and mechanics, who all ought to have a competent number of their best informed men in the legislature, will be totally unrepresented.

The representation is unsafe, because in the exercise of such great powers and trusts, it is so exposed to corruption and undue influence, by the gift of the numerous places of honor and emolument, at the disposal of the executive; by the arts and address of the great and designing; and by direct bribery.

The representation is moreover inadequate and unsafe, because of the long terms for which it is appointed, and the mode of its appointment, by which Congress may not only controul the choice of the people, but may so manage as to divest the people of this fundamental right, and become self-elected.

The number of members in the house of representatives *may* be encreased to one for every 30,000 inhabitants. But when we consider, that this cannot be done without the consent of the senate, who from their share in the legislative, in the executive, and judicial departments, and permanency of appointment, will be the great efficient body in this government, and whose weight and predominancy would be abridged by an increase of the representatives, we are persuaded that this is a circumstance that cannot be expected. On the contrary, the number of representatives will probably be continued at 65, although the population of the country may swell to treble what it now is; unless a revolution should effect a change.

We have before noticed the judicial power as it would effect a consolidation of the states into one government; we will now examine it, as it would affect the liberties and welfare of the people, supposing such a government were practicable and proper.

The judicial power, under the proposed constitution, is founded on the well-known principles of the *civil law*, by which the judge determines both on law and fact, and appeals are allowed from the inferior tribunals to the superior, upon the whole question; so that *facts* as well as *law*, would be re-examined, and even new facts brought forward in the court of appeals; and to use the words of a very eminent Civilian—"The cause is many times another thing before the court of appeals, than what it was at the time of the first sentence."

That this mode of proceeding is the one which must be adopted under this constitution, is evident from the following circumstances:—1st. That the trial by jury, which is the grand characteristic of the common law, is secured by the constitution, only in criminal cases.—2d. That the appeal from both *law* and *fact* is expressly established, which is utterly inconsistent with the principles of the common law, and trials by jury. The only mode in which an appeal from law and fact can be established, is, by adopting the principles and practice of the civil law; unless the United States should be drawn into the absurdity of calling and swearing juries, merely for the purpose of contradicting their verdicts, which would render juries contemptible and worse than useless.—3d. That the courts to be established would decide on all cases *of law and equity*, which is a well known characteristic of the civil law, and these courts would have conusance not only of the laws of the United

States and of treaties, and of cases affecting ambassadors, but of all cases of *admiralty and maritime jurisdiction*, which last are matters belonging exclusively to the civil law, in every nation in Christendom.

Not to enlarge upon the loss of the invaluable right of trial by an unbiassed jury, so dear to every friend of liberty, the monstrous expence and inconveniences of the mode of proceeding to be adopted, are such as will prove intolerable to the people of this country. The lengthy proceedings of the civil law courts in the chancery of England, and in the courts of Scotland and France, are such that few men of moderate fortune can endure the expence of; the poor man must therefore submit to the wealthy. Length of purse will too often prevail against right and justice. For instance, we are told by the learned judge *Blackstone*, that a question only on the property of an *ox*, of the value of *three* guineas, originating under the civil law proceedings in Scotland, after many interlocutory orders and sentences below, was carried at length from the court of sessions, the highest court in that part of Great Britain, by way of *appeal* to the house of lords, where the question of law and fact was finally determined. He adds, that no pique or spirit could in the court of king's bench or common pleas at Westminster, have given continuance to such a cause for a tenth part of the time, nor have cost a twentieth part of the expence. Yet the costs in the courts of king's bench and common pleas in England, are infinitely greater than those which the people of this country have ever experienced. We abhor the idea of losing the transcendant privilege of trial by jury, with the loss of which, it is remarked by same learned author, that in Sweden, the liberties of the commons were extinguished by an aristocratic senate: and that *trial by jury* and the liberty of the people went out together. At the same time we regret the intolerable delay, the enormous expences and infinite vexation to which the people of this country will be exposed from the voluminous proceedings of the courts of civil law, and especially from the appellate jurisdiction, by means of which a man may be drawn from the utmost boundaries of this extensive country to the seat of the supreme court of the nation to contend, perhaps with a wealthy and powerful adversary. The consequence of this establishment will be an absolute confirmation of the power of aristocratical influence in the courts of justice; for the common people will not be able to contend or struggle against it.

Trial by jury in criminal cases may also be excluded by declaring that the libeller for instance shall be liable to an action of debt for a specified sum; thus evading the common law prosecution by indictment and trial by jury. And the common course of proceeding against a ship for breach of revenue laws by information (which will be classed among civil causes) will at the civil law be within the resort of a court, where no jury intervenes. Besides, the benefit of jury trial, in cases of a criminal nature, which cannot be evaded, will be rendered of little value, by calling the accused to answer far from home; there being no provision that the trial be by a jury of the neighbourhood or country. Thus an inhabitant of Pittsburgh, on a charge of crime committed on the banks of the Ohio, may be obliged to defend himself at the side of the Delaware, and so *vice versa*. To conclude this head: we observe that the judges of the courts of Congress would not be independent, as they are not debarred from holding other offices, during the pleasure of the president and senate, and as they may derive their support in part from fees, alterable by the legislature.

The next consideration that the constitution presents, is the undue and dangerous mixture of the powers of government: the same body possessing legislative, executive, and judicial powers. The senate is a constituent branch of the legislature, it has judicial power in judging on impeachments, and in this case unites in some measure the characters of judge and party, as all the principal officers are appointed by the president-general, with the concurrence of the senate and therefore they derive their offices in part from the senate. This may biass the judgments of the senators, and tend to screen great delinquents from punishment. And the senate has, moreover, various and great executive powers, viz. in concurrence with the president-general, they form treaties with foreign nations, that may controul and abrogate the constitutions and laws of the several states. Indeed, there is no power, privilege or liberty of the state governments, or of the people, but what may be affected by virtue of this power. For all treaties, made by them, are to be the "supreme law of the land; any thing in the constitution or laws of any state, to the contrary notwithstanding."

And this great power may be exercised by the president and 10 senators (being two-thirds of 14, which is a quorum of that body). What an inducement would this offer to the ministers of foreign powers to compass by bribery *such concessions* as could not otherwise be obtained. It is the unvaried usage of all free states, whenever treaties interfere with the positive laws of the land, to make the intervention of the legislature necessary to give them operation. This became necessary, and was afforded by the parliament of Great-Britain, in consequence of the late commercial treaty between that kingdom and France.—As the senate judges on impeachments, who is to try the members of the senate for the abuse of this power! And none of the great appointments to office can be made without the consent of the senate.

Such various, extensive, and important powers combined in one body of men, are inconsistent with all freedom; the celebrated Montesquieu tells us, that "when the legislative and executive powers are united in the same person, or in the same body of magistrates, there can be no liberty, because apprehensions may arise, lest the same monarch or *senate* should enact tyrannical laws, to execute them in a tyrannical manner."

"Again, there is no liberty, if the power of judging be not separated from the legislative and executive powers. Were it joined with the legislative, the life and liberty of the subject would be exposed to arbitrary controul; for the judge would then be legislator. Were it joined to the executive power, the judge might behave with all the violence of an oppressor. There would be an end of every thing, were the same man, or the same body of the nobles, or of the people, to exercise those three powers; that of enacting laws; that of executing the public resolutions; and that of judging the crimes or differences of individuals."

The president general is dangerously connected with the senate; his coincidence with the views of the ruling junto in that body, is made essential to his weight and importance in the government, which will destroy all independency and purity in the executive department, and having the power of pardoning without the concurrence of a council, he may skreen from punishment the most treasonable attempts that may be made on the liberties of the people, when instigated by his coadjutors in the senate. Instead of this dangerous and improper mixture of the executive with the legislative and judicial, the supreme executive powers ought to have been placed in the president, with a small independent council, made personally responsible for every appointment to office or other act, by having their opinions recorded; and that without the concurrence of the majority of the quorum of this council, the president should not be capable of taking any step.

We have before considered internal taxation, as it would effect the destruction of the state governments, and produce one consolidated government. We will now consider that subject as it affects the personal concerns of the people.

The power of direct taxation applies to every individual, as congress, under this government, is expressly vested with the authority of laying a capitation or poll tax upon every person to any amount. This is a tax that, however oppressive in its nature, and unequal in its operation, is certain as to its produce and simple in its collection; it cannot be evaded like the objects of imposts or excise, and will be paid, because all that a man hath will he give for his head. This tax is so congenial to the nature of despotism, that it has ever been a favorite under such governments. Some of those who were in the late general convention from this state, have long laboured to introduce a poll-tax among us.

The power of direct taxation will further apply to every individual as congress may tax land, cattle, trades, occupations, &c. to any amount, and every object of internal taxation is of that nature, that however oppressive, the people will have but this alternative, either to pay the tax, or let their property be taken, for all resistance will be vain. The standing army and select militia would enforce the collection.

For the moderate exercise of this power, there is no controul left in the state governments, whose intervention is destroyed. No relief, or redress of grievances can be extended, as heretofore, by them. There is not even a declaration of RIGHTS to which the people may appeal for the vindication of their wrongs in the court of justice. They must therefore, implicitly, obey the most arbitrary laws, as the worst of them will be pursuant to the principles and form of the constitution, and that strongest of all checks upon the conduct of administration, *responsibility to the people*, will not exist in this government. The permanency of the appointments of senators and representatives, and the controul the congress have over their election, will place them independent of the sentiments and resentment of the people, and the administration having a greater interest in the government than in the community, there will be no consideration to restrain them from oppression and tyranny. In the government of this state, under the old confederation, the members of the legislature are taken from among the people, and their interests and welfare are so inseparably connected with those of their constituents, that they can derive no advantage from oppressive laws and taxes, for they would suffer in common with their fellow citizens; would participate in the burthens they impose on the community, as they must return to the common level, after a short period; and notwithstanding every exertion of influence, every means of corruption, a necessary rotation excludes them from permanency in the legislature.

This large state is to have but ten members in that Congress which is to have the liberty, property and dearest concerns of every individual in this vast country at absolute command and even these ten persons, who are to be our only guardians; who are to supercede the legislature of Pennsylvania, will not be of the choice of the people, nor amenable to them. From the mode of their election and appointment they will consist of the lordly and high-minded; of men who will have no congenial feelings with the people, but a perfect indifference for, and contempt of them; they will consist of those harpies of power, that prey upon the very vitals; that riot on the miseries of the community. But we will suppose, although in all probability it may never be realized in fact, that our deputies in Congress have the welfare of their constituents at heart, and will exert themselves in their behalf, what security could even this afford; what relief could they extend to their oppressed constituents? To attain this, the majority of the deputies of the twelve other states in Congress must be alike well disposed; must alike forego the sweets of power, and relinquish the pursuits of ambition, which from the nature of things is not to be expected. If the people part with a responsible representation in the legislature, founded upon fair, certain and frequent elections, they have nothing left they can call their own. Miserable is the lot of that people whose every concern depends on the WILL and PLEASURE of their rulers. Our soldiers will become Janissaries, and our officers of government Bashaws; in short, the system of despotism will soon be compleated.

From the foregoing investigation, it appears that the Congress under this constitution will not possess the confidence of the people, which is an essential requisite in a good government; for unless the laws command the confidence and respect of the great body of the people, so as to induce them to support them, when called on by the civil magistrate, they must be executed by the aid of a numerous standing army, which would be inconsistent with every idea of liberty; for the same force that may be employed to compel obedience to good laws, might and probably would be used to wrest from the people their constitutional liberties. The framers of this constitution appear to have been aware of this great deficiency; to have been sensible that no dependence could be placed on the people for their support: but on the contrary, that the government must be executed by force. They have therefore made a provision for this purpose in a permanent STANDING ARMY, and a MILITIA that may be subjected to as strict discipline and government.

A standing army in the hands of a government placed so independent of the people, may be made a fatal instrument to overturn the public liberties; it may be employed to enforce the collection of the most oppressive taxes, and to carry into execution the most arbitrary measures. An ambitious man who may have the army at his devotion, may step up into the throne, and seize upon absolute power.

The absolute unqualified command that Congress have over the militia may be made instrumental to the destruction of all liberty, both public and private; whether of a personal, civil or religious nature.

First, the personal liberty of every man probably from sixteen to sixty years of age, may be destroyed by the power Congress have in organizing and governing of the militia. As militia they may be subjected to fines to any amount, levied in a military manner; they may be subjected to corporal punishments of the most disgraceful and humiliating kind, and to death itself, by the sentence of a court martial: To this our young men will be more immediately subjected, as a select militia, composed of them, will best answer the purposes of government.

Secondly, The rights of conscience may be violated, as there is no exemption of those persons who are conscientiously scrupulous of bearing arms. These compose a respectable proportion of the community in the state. This is the more remarkable, because even when the distresses of the late war, and the evident disaffection of many citizens of that description, inflamed our passions, and when every person, who was obliged to risque his own life, must have been exasperated against such as on any account kept back from the common danger, yet even then, when outrage and violence might have been expected, the rights of conscience were held sacred.

At this momentous crisis, the framers of our state constitution made the most express and decided declaration and stipulations in favour of the rights of conscience: but now when no necessity exists, those dearest rights of men are left insecure.

Thirdly, The absolute command of Congress over the milita may be destructive of public liberty; for under the guidance of an arbitrary government, they may be made the unwilling instruments of tyranny. The militia of Pennsylvania may be marched to New England or Virginia to quell an insurrection occasioned by the most galling oppression, and aided by the standing army, they will no doubt be successful in subduing their liberty and independency; but in so doing, although the magnanimity of their minds will be extinguished, yet the meaner passions of resentment and revenge will be increased, and these in turn will be the ready and obedient instruments of despotism to enslave the others; and that with an irritated vengeance. Thus may the militia be made the instruments of crushing the last efforts of expiring liberty, of riveting the chains of despotism on their fellow citizens, and on one another. This power can be exercised not only without violating the constitution, but in strict conformity with it; it is calculated for this express purpose, and will doubtless be executed accordingly.

As this government will not enjoy the confidence of the people, but be executed by force, it will be a very expensive and burthensome government. The standing army must be numerous, and as a further support, it will be the policy of this government to multiply officers in every department: judges, collectors, tax-gatherers, excisemen and the whole host of revenue officers will swarm over the land, devouring the hard earnings of the industrious. Like the locusts of old, impoverishing and desolating all before them.

We have not noticed the smaller, nor many of the considerable blemishes, but have confined our objections to the great and essential defects; the main pillars of the constitution: which we have shewn to be inconsistent with the liberty and happiness of the people, as its establishment will annihilate the state governments, and produce one consolidated government, that will eventually and speedily issue in the supremacy of despotism.

In this investigation, we have not confined our views to the interests or welfare of this state, in preference to the others. We have overlooked all local circumstances—we have considered this subject on the broad scale of the general good: we have asserted the cause of the present and future ages: the cause of liberty and mankind.

Nathaniel Breading
John Smilie
Richard Baird
Adam Orth
John A. Hanna
John Whitehill
John Harris
Robert Whitehill
John Reynolds
Jonathan Hoge
Nicholas Lutz
John Ludwig
Abraham Lincoln
John Bishop
Joseph Heister
Joseph Powel
James Martin
William Findley
John Baird
James Edgar
William Todd.

MASSACHUSETTS RATIFYING CONVENTION

Fisher Ames on Biennial Elections and the "Volcano" of Democracy

January 15, 1788

Mr. AMES. I do not regret, Mr. President, that we are not unanimous upon this question. I do not consider the diversity of sentiment which prevails, as an impediment in our way to the discovery of truth. In order that we may think alike upon this subject at last, we shall be compelled to discuss it, by ascending to the principles upon which the doctrine of representation is grounded.

Without premeditation, in a situation so novel, and awed by the respect which I feel for this venerable assembly, I distrust extremely my own feelings, as well as my competency to prosecute this inquiry. With the hope of an indulgent hearing, I will attempt to proceed. I am sensible, sir, that the doctrine of frequent elections, has been sanctified by antiquity; and is still more endeared to us by our recent experience, and uniform habits of thinking. Gentlemen have expressed their zealous partiality for it. They consider this as a leading question in the debate, and that the merits of many other parts of the constitution are involved in the decision. I confess, sir, and I declare that my zeal for frequent elections, is not inferior to their own. I consider it as one of the first securities for popular liberty, in which its very essence may be supposed to reside. But how shall we make the best use of this pledge and instrument of our safety? A right principle, carried to an extreme, becomes useless. It is apparent that a delegation for a very short term, as for a single day, would defeat the design of representation. The election in that case would not seem to the people to be of any importance, and the person elected would think as lightly of his appointment. The other extreme is equally to be avoided.

An election for a very long term of years, or for life, would remove the member too far from the controul of the people, would be dangerous to liberty, and in fact repugnant to the purposes of the delegation. The truth as usual, is placed somewhere between the extremes, and I believe is included in this proposition: The term of election must be so long, that the representative may understand the interests of the people, and yet so limited, that his fidelity may be secured by a dependence upon their approbation.

Before I proceed to the application of this rule, I cannot forbear to premise some remarks upon two opinions, which have been suggested.

Much has been said about the people divesting themselves of power, when they delegate it to representatives; and that all representation is to their disadvantage, because it is but an image, a copy, fainter and more imperfect than the original, the people, in whom the light of power is primary and unborrowed, which is only reflected by their delegates.—I cannot agree to either of these opinions.—The representation of the people is something more than the people. I know, sir, but one purpose which the people can effect without delegation, and that is, to destroy a government. That they cannot erect a government is evinced by our being thus assembled, on their behalf. The people must govern by a majority, with whom all power resides. But how is the sense of this majority to be obtained? It has been said that a pure democracy is the best government for a small people who may assemble in person. It is of small consequence to discuss it, as it would be inapplicable to the great country we inhabit. It may be of some use in this argument, however, to consider, that it would be very burdensome, subject to faction and violence, decisions would often be made by surprise, in the precipitancy of passion, by men who either understand nothing, or care nothing about the subject; or by interested men, or those who vote for their own indemnity. It would be a government not by laws, but by men. Such were the paltry democracies of Greece and Asia Minor, so much extolled, and so often proposed as a model for our imitation. I desire to be thankful, that our people are not under any temptation, to adopt the advice. I think it will not be denied, that the people are gainers by the election of representatives. They may destroy, but they cannot exercise the powers of government, in person; but by their servants, *they* govern—they do not renource their power—they do not sacrifice their rights—they become the true sovereigns of the country when they delegate that power, which they cannot use themselves, to their trustees.

I know, sir, that the people talk about the liberty of nature, and assert that we divest ourselves of a portion of it, when we enter into society. This is declamation against matter of fact. We cannot live without society; and as to liberty, how can I be said to enjoy that which another may take from me, when he pleases. The liberty of one depends not so much on the removal of all restraint, from him, as on the due restraint upon the liberty of others. Without such restraint, there can be no liberty—liberty is so far from being endangered or destroyed by this, that it is extended and secured. For I said, that we do not enjoy that, which another may take from us. But civil liberty cannot be taken from us, when any one may please to invade it: For we have the strength of the society of our side.

I hope, sir, that these reflections, will have some tendency to remove the ill impressions which are made by proposing to divest the people of their power.

That they may never be divested of it, I repeat that I am in favour of frequent elections. They who commend annual elections, are desired to consider, that the question is, whether biennial elections are a defect in the constitution: For it does not follow, because annual elections are safe, that biennial are dangerous: For both may be good. Nor is there any foundation for the fears of those, who say that if we who have been accustomed to chuse for one year only, now extend it to two, the next stride will be to five, or seven years, and the next for term of life: For this article, with all its supposed defects, is in favour of liberty. Being inserted in the constitution, it is not subject to be repealed by law. We are sure that it is the worst of the case.

It is a fence against ambitious encroachments, too high and too strong to be passed: In this respect, we have greatly the advantage of the people of England and of all the world. The law which limits their parliaments, is liable to be repealed.

I will not defend this article, by saying that it was a matter of compromise in the federal Convention: It has my entire approbation as it stands. I think that we ought to prefer, in this article, biennial elections to annual, and my reasons for this opinion, are drawn from these sources.

From the extent of the country to be governed.

The objects of their legislation.

And the more perfect security of our liberty.

It seems obvious, that men who are to collect in Congress from this great territory, perhaps from the bay of Fundy, or from the banks of the Ohio, and the shore of Lake Superiour, ought to have a longer term in office, than the delegates of a single state, in their own legislature. It is not by riding post to and from Congress, that a man can acquire a just knowledge of the true interests of the union. This term of election, is inapplicable to the state of a country, as large as Germany, or as the Roman empire in the zenith of its power.

If we consider the objects of their delegation, little doubt will remain. It is admitted that annual elections may be highly fit for the state legislature. Every citizen grows up with a knowledge of the local circumstances of the state. But the business of the federal government will be very different. The objects of their power are few and national. At least two years in office will be necessary to enable a man to judge of the trade and interests of states which he never saw. The time I hope, will come, when this excellent country will furnish food, and freedom, (which is better than food, which is the food of the soul) for fifty millions of happy people. Will any man say that the national business can be understood in one year?

Biennial elections appear to me, sir, an essential security to liberty. These are my reasons.

Faction and enthusiasm are the instruments by which popular governments are destroyed. We need not talk of the power of an aristocracy. The people when they lose their liberties are cheated out of them. They nourish factions in their bosoms, which will subsist so long as abusing their honest credulity shall be the means of acquiring power. A democracy is a volcano, which conceals the fiery materials of its own destruction. These will produce an eruption, and carry desolation in their way. The people always mean right, and if time is allowed for reflection and information, they will do right. I would not have the first wish, the momentary impulse of the publick mind, become law. For it is not always the sense of the people, with whom, I admit, that all power resides. On great questions, we first hear the loud clamours of passion, artifice and faction. I consider biennial elections as a security that the sober, second thought of the people shall be law. There is a calm review of publick transactions, which is made by the citizens who have families and children, the pledges of their fidelity. To provide for popular liberty, we must take care that measures shall not be adopted without due deliberation. The member chosen for two years will feel some independence in his seat. The factions of the day will expire before the end of his term.

The people will be proportionally attentive to the merits of a candidate. Two years will afford opportunity to the member to deserve well of them, and they will require evidence that he has done it.

But, sir, the representatives are the grand inquisition of the union. They are by impeachment to bring great offenders to justice. One year will not suffice to detect guilt, and to pursue it to conviction: therefore they will escape, and the balance of the two branches will be destroyed, and the people oppressed with impunity. The senators will represent the sovereignty of the states. The representatives are to represent the people. The offices ought to bear some proportion in point of importance. This will be impossible if they are chosen for one year only.

Will the people then blind the eyes of their own watchmen? Will they bind the hands which are to hold the sword for their defence? Will they impair their own power, by an unreasonable jealousy of themselves?

For these reasons I am clearly of opinion, that the article is entitled to our approbation as it stands: and as it has been demanded, why annual elections were not preferred to biennial, permit me to retort the question, and to inquire in my turn, what reason can be given why, if annual elections are good, biennial elections are not better?

The enquiry in the latter part of Mr. Ames's speech, being directed to the Hon. Mr. ADAMS—that gentleman said, he only made the inquiry for information, and that he had heard sufficient to satisfy himself of its propriety.

An Exchange on the Powers of Congress and Its Probable Corruption

The 4th section still under deliberation.

Hon. Mr. TURNER. Mr. President, I am pleased with the ingenuity, of some gentlemen in defence of this section. I am so impressed with the love of our liberty so dearly bought, that I heartily acquiesce in compulsory laws, for the people ought to be obliged to attend to their interest. But I do not wish to give Congress a power which they can abuse; and, I wish to know whether such a power is not contained in this section? I think it is. I now proceed, sir, to the consideration of an idea, that Congress may alter the place for chusing representatives in the general Congress—they may order that it may be at the extremity of a state, and by their influence, may there prevail that persons may be chosen, who otherwise would not; by reason that a part of the qualified voters in part of the state, would be so incommoded thereby, as to be debarred from their right as much as if they were bound at home. If so, such a circumstance would militate against the constitution, which allows every man to vote. Altering the *place* will put it so far in the power of Congress, as that the representatives chosen will not be the true and genuine representatives of the people, but creatures of the Congress; and so far as they are so, so far are the people deprived of their rights, and the choice will be made in an irregular and unconstitutional manner. When this alteration is made by Congress—may we not suppose whose re-election will be provided for? Would it not be for those who were chosen before? The great law of self preservation will prevail. It is true, they might, one time in an hundred, provide for a friend, but most commonly for themselves. But, however honourable the convention may be who proposed this article, I think it is a genuine power for Congress to perpetuate themselves—a power that cannot be unexceptionally exercised in any case whatever:—Knowing the numerous arts, that designing men are prone to, to secure their election, and

MASSACHUSETTS CONVENTION, JAN. 1788   313

perpetuate themselves, it is my hearty wish that a rotation may be provided for. I respect and revere the convention who proposed this constitution. In order that the power given to Congress may be more palatable, some gentlemen are pleased to hold up the idea, that we may be blessed with sober, solid, upright men in Congress. I wish that we may be favoured with such rulers; but I fear they will not all, if most be the best moral or political characters. It gives me pain, and I believe it gives pain to others, thus to characterize the country in which I was born. I will endeavour to guard against any injurious reflections against my fellow citizens. But they must have their true characters, and if I represent them wrong, I am willing to make concessions. I think that the operation of paper money, and the practice of privateering, have produced a gradual decay of morals—introduced pride—ambition—envy—lust of power—produced a decay of patriotism, and the love of commutative justice; and I am apprehensive these are the invariable concommitants of the luxury, in which we are unblessedly involved, almost to our total destruction. In the lower ranks of people, luxury and avarice operate to the want of publick duty and the payment of debts. These demonstrate the necessity of an energetick government: As people become more luxurious, they become more incapacitated of governing themselves. And are we not so? A like people, a like prince: But suppose it should so happen, that the administrators of this constitution should be preferable to the corrupt mass of the people, in point of manners, morals, and rectitude. power will give a keen edge to the principles I have mentioned. Ought we not, then, to put all checks and controuls on governours for the publick safety: therefore, instead of giving Congress powers they *may* not abuse, we ought to withold our hands from granting such, as *must* be abused if exercised. This is a general observation. But to the point: At the time of the restoration, the people of England were so vexed, harassed and worn down, by the *anarchical* and confused state of the nation, owing to the commonwealth not being well digested, that they took an opposite career; they run mad with loyalty, and would have given Charles any thing he could have asked—Pardon me, sir, if I say I feel the want of an energetick government, and the dangers to which this dear country is reduced, as much as any citizen of the United States; but I cannot prevail on myself to adopt a government, which wears the face of power, without examining it. Relinquishing an *hair's breadth* in a constitution is a great deal; for by small degrees has liberty in all nations, been wrested from the hands of the people. I know great powers are necessary to be given to Congress, but I wish they may be well guarded.

Judge SUMNER, remarking on Gen. *Thompson*'s frequent exclamation of "*O! my country!*" expressed from an apprehension that the Constitution would be adopted, said, *that* expression might be used with greater propriety, should this Convention reject it. The Hon. Gentleman then proceeded to demonstrate the necessity of the 4th sect.—the absurdity of the *supposition*, that Congress would remove the places of election to remote parts of the States;—combated the idea, that Congress would, when chosen, act as bad as possible—and concluded by asking, if a war should take place, (and it was supposable) if France and Holland should send an army to collect the millions of livres they have lent us in the time of our distresses, and that army should be in possession of the seat of government of any particular State, (as was the case when Lord *Cornwallis* ravaged Carolina) and the state legislature could not appoint the elections, is not a power to provide for such elections necessary to be lodged in the general Congress?

Mr. WIDGERY denied the statement of Dr. *Jarvis* (that every 30,000 persons can elect one representative) to be just, as the Constitution provides, that the number *shall not exceed* one to every 30,000—it did not follow, he thought that the 30,000 *shall* elect one. But admitting that they have a right to chuse one—we will suppose Congress should order an election to be in Boston in January, and from the scarcity of money, &c. not a fourth part could attend—would not three quarters of the people be deprived of their right?

Rev. Mr. WEST. I rise to express my astonishment at the arguments of some gentlemen against this section!—They have only started *possible* objections—I wish the gentlemen would shew us, that what they so much deprecate is *probable*. Is it probable that we shall choose men to ruin us? Are we to object to all governments; and because power *may* be abused, shall we be reduced to anarchy and a state of nature? What hinders our state legislatures from abusing their power? They may violate the Constitution—they may levy taxes oppressive and intolerable, to the amount of all our property. An argument which proves too much, it is said, proves nothing. Some say, Congress may remove the place of elections to the State of South-Carolina; this is inconsistent with the words of the Constitution, which says, "*that the elections shall be prescribed in each State by the legislature thereof*," &c. and that representation shall be apportioned according to numbers; it will frustrate the end of the Constitution—and is a reflection on the gentlemen who formed it. Can we, sir, suppose them so wicked, so vile, as to recommend an article so dangerous: Surely gentlemen who argue these *possibilities*, shew they have a very weak cause. That we may all be free from passions, prepossessions and party spirit, I sincerely hope, otherwise reason will have no effect. I hope there are none here but who are open to conviction, as it is the sured method to gain the suffrage of our consciences. The Hon. Gentleman from Scituate has told us, that the people of England, at the restoration, *on account of the inconveniencies of the confused state of the Commonwealth, run mad with loyalty*. If the gentleman means to apply this to us, we ought to adopt this Constitution—for if the people are *running mad* after an energetick government, it is best to stop now, as by his rule they may run further and get a worse one; therefore the gentleman's arguments turn right against himself. Is it possible that imperfect man can make a perfect Constitution. Is it possible that a frame of government can be devised by such weak and frail creatures, but what must savour of that weakness? Though there are some things that I do not like in this Constitution, yet I think it necessary that it should be adopted. For may we not rationally conclude, that the persons we shall cause to administer it, will be in general good men?

Gen. THOMPSON. Mr. President, I have frequently heard of the abilities and fame of the learned and reverend gentleman last speaking, and now I am witness to them: but, sir, one thing surprizes me—it is, to hear the worthy gentleman insinuate that our federal rulers would undoubtedly be *good men*, and that therefore, we have little to fear from their being intrusted with all power—This, sir, is quite contrary to the common language of the clergy, who are continually representing mankind as reprobate and deceitful, and that we really grow worse and worse day after day. I really believe we do, sir, and I make no doubt to prove it before I sit down, from the old testament. When I consider the man that slew the lion and the bear, and that he was a man after *God's own heart*; when I consider his son, blessed with *all wisdom*—and the errors they fell into, I extremely doubt the infallibility of human nature. Sir, I suspect my own heart, and I shall suspect our rulers.

Dr. HOLTEN thought this paragraph necessary to a complete system of government. [*But the Hon. gentleman spoke so low that we could not hear him distinctly throughout.*]

Capt. SNOW. It has been said, Mr. President, that there is too much power delegated to Congress, by the section under consideration—I doubt it; I think power the hinge on which the whole Constitution turns. Gentlemen have talked about Congress moving the place of elections from Georgia to the Mohawk river, but I never can believe it. I will venture to conjecture we shall have some honest men in our Congress. We read that there were two who brought a *good report*, Caleb and Joshua—Now, if there are but two in Congress who are honest men, and Congress should attempt to do what the gentlemen say they will, (which will be *high treason*) they will bring a *report* of it—and I stand ready to leave my wife and family—sling my knapsack—travel westward—to cut their heads off. I, sir, since the war, have had commerce with six different nations of the globe, and I have enquired in what estimation America is held—and if I may believe good, honest, credible men, I find this country held in the same light by foreign nations, as a well behaved negro is, in a gentleman's family. Suppose, Mr. President, I had a chance to make a good voyage, but I tie my Captain up to such strict orders, that he can go to no other island to sell my vessel, although there is a certainty of his doing well: the consequence is, he returns, but makes a bad voyage, because he had not power enough to act his judgment: (for honest men do right:) Thus, sir, Congress cannot save us from destruction, because we tie their hands and give them no power; (I think people have lost their privileges by not improving them) and I like this power being vested in Congress as well as any paragraph in the Constitution: for as the man is accountable for his conduct, I think there is no danger. Now,

Mr. President, to take all things into consideration, something more must be said, to convince me to the contrary.

[*Several other gentlemen went largely into the debate on the 4th section, which those in favour of it demonstrated to be necessary:* first, *as it may be used to correct a negligence in elections:* secondly, *as it will prevent the dissolution of the government by designing and refractory states:* thirdly, *as it will operate as a check, in favour of the people, against any designs of the federal Senate, and their constituents, the state legislatures, to deprive the people of their right of election: and* fourthly, *as it provides a remedy for the evil, should any state, by invasion, or other cause, not have it in its power to appoint a place, where the citizens thereof may meet to chuse their federal representatives. Those against it urged, that the power is unlimitted and unnecessary.*——]

Amos Singletary and Jonathan Smith on "Leviathan" and on the Danger of Anarchy

Hon. Mr. SINGLETARY. Mr. President, I should not have troubled the Convention again, if some gentlemen had not called upon them that were on the stage in the beginning of our troubles, in the year 1775. I was one of them—I have had the honour to be a member of the court all the time, Mr. President, and I say, that if any body had proposed such a Constitution as this, in that day, it would have been thrown away at once—it would not have been looked at. We contended with Great-Britain—some said for a three-penny duty on tea, but it was not that—it was because they claimed a right to tax us and bind us in all cases whatever. And does not this Constitution do the same? does it not take away all we have—all our property? does it not lay *all* taxes, duties, imposts and excises? and what more have we to give? They tell us Congress won't lay dry taxes upon us, but collect all the money they want by impost. I say there has always been a difficulty about impost. Whenever the General Court was a going to lay an impost they would tell us it was more than trade could bear, that it hurt the fair trader, and encouraged smuggling; and there will always be the same objection; they won't be able to raise money enough by impost and then they will lay it on the land, and take all we have got. These lawyers, and men of learning, and monied men, that talk so finely and gloss over matters so smoothly, to make us poor illiterate people swallow down the pill, expect to get into Congress themselves; they expect to be the managers of this Constitution and get all the power and all the money into their own hands, and then they will swallow up all us little folks, like the great *Leviathan*, Mr. President, yes, just as the whale swallowed up *Jonah*. This is what I am afraid of; but I won't say any more at present, but reserve the rest to another opportunity.

Hon. Mr. SMITH. Mr. President, I am a plain man and get my living by the plough. I am not used to speak in publick, but I beg your leave to say a few words to my brother plough-joggers in this house. I have lived in a part of the country where I have known the worth of good government by the want of it. There was a black cloud that rose in the east last winter, and spread over the west.—[*Here Mr.* Widgery *interrupted. Mr. President, I wish to know what the gentleman means by the* east.] I mean, sir, the county of Bristol; the cloud rose there and burst upon us, and produced a dreadful effect. It brought on a state of *anarchy*, and that leads to *tyranny*. I say it brought anarchy. People that used to live peaceably, and were before good neighbours, got distracted and took up arms against government. [*Here Mr.* Kingsley *called to order, and asked what had the history of last winter to do with the Constitution? Several gentlemen, and among the rest the Hon. Mr.* Adams, *said the gentleman was in order—let him go on in his own way.*] I am a going, Mr. President, to shew you, my brother farmers, what were the effects of anarchy, that you may see the reasons why I wish for good government. People, I say took up arms, and then if you went to speak to them, you had the *musket of death* presented to your breast. They would rob you of your property, threaten to burn your houses; oblige you to be on your guard night and day; alarms spread from town to town; families were broke up; the tender mother would cry, O my son is among them! What shall I do for my child! Some were taken captive, children taken out of their schools and carried away. Then we should hear of an *action*, and the poor prisoners were *set in the front*, to be killed by their own friends. How dreadful, how distressing was this! Our distress was so great that we should have been glad to catch at any thing that looked like a government for protection. Had any person, that was able to protect us, come and set up his standard we should all have flocked to it, even if it had been a *monarch*, and that monarch might have proved a tyrant, so that you see that anarchy leads to tyranny, and better have *one* tyrant than so many at once.

Now, Mr. President, when I saw this Constitution, I found that it was a cure for these disorders. It was just such a thing as we wanted. I got a copy of it and read it over and over. I had been a member of the Convention to form our own state Constitution, and had learnt something of the checks and balances of power, and I found them all here. I did not go to any lawyer, to ask his opinion, we have no lawyer in our town, and we do well enough without. I formed my own opinion, and was pleased with this Constitution. My honourable old daddy there (*pointing to Mr.* Singletary) won't think that I expect to be a Congress-man, and swallow up the liberties of the people. I never had any post, nor do I want one, and before I am done you will think that I don't deserve one. But I don't think the worse of the Constitution because lawyers, and men of learning and monied men, are fond of it. I don't suspect that they want to get into Congress and abuse their power. I am not of such a jealous make; they that are honest men themselves are not apt to suspect other people. I don't know why our constituents have not as good a right to be as jealous of us, as we seem to be of the Congress, and I think those gentlemen who are so very suspicious, that as soon as a man gets into power he turns rogue, had better look *at home.*

We are by this Constitution allowed to send *ten* members to Congress. Have we not more than that number fit to go? I dare say if we pick out ten, we shall have another ten left, and I hope ten times ten, and will not these be a check upon those that go; Will they go to Congress and abuse their power and do mischief, when they know that they must return and look the other ten in the face, and be called to account for their conduct? Some gentlemen think that our liberty and property is not safe in the hands of monied men, and men of learning, I am not of that mind.

Brother farmers, let us suppose a case now—suppose you had a farm of 50 acres, and your title was disputed, and there was a farm of 5000 acres joined to you that belonged to a man of learning, and his title was involved in the same difficulty; would not you be glad to have him for your friend, rather than to stand alone in the dispute? Well, the case is the same, these lawyers, these monied men, these men of learning, are all embarked in the same cause with us, and we must all swim or sink together; and shall we throw the Constitution overboard, because it does not please us alike? Suppose two or three of you had been at the pains to break up a piece of rough land, and sow it with wheat—would you let it lay waste, because you could not agree what *sort* of a fence to make? would it not be better to put up a fence that did not please every one's fancy rather than not fence it at all, or keep disputing about it, until the wild beast came in and devoured it. Some gentlemen say, don't be in a hurry—take time to consider, and don't take a leap in the dark.—I say take things in time—gather fruit when it is ripe. There is a time to sow and a time to reap; we sowed our seed when we sent men to the federal convention, now is the harvest, now is the time to reap the fruit of our labour, and if we don't do it now I am afraid we never shall have another opportunity.

Daniel Shute and William Jones
on Religious Tests

January 31, 1788

Rev. Mr. SHUTE. Mr. President—To object to the latter part of the paragraph under consideration, which excludes a religious test, is, I am sensible, very popular; for the most of men, some how, are rigidly tenacious of their own sentiments in religion, and disposed to impose them upon others as the *standard* of truth. If in my sentiments, upon the point in view, I should differ from some in this honourable body, I only wish from them the exercise of that candour, with which true religion is adapted to inspire the honest and well-disposed mind.

To establish a religious test as a qualification for offices in the proposed Federal Constitution, appears to me, sir, would be attended with injurious consequences to some individuals, and with no advantage to the *whole*.

By the injurious consequences to individuals, I mean, that some, who in every other respect, are qualified to fill some important post in government, will be excluded by their not being able to stand the religious test—which I take to be a privation of part of their civil rights.

Nor is there to me any conceivable advantage, sir, that would result in the *whole* from such a test. Unprincipled and dishonest men will not hesitate to subscribe to *any thing*, that may open the way for their advancement, and put them into a situation the better to execute their base and iniquitous designs. Honest men alone, therefore, however well qualified to serve the publick, would be excluded by it, and their country be deprived of the benefit of their abilities.

In this great and extensive empire, there is and will be a great variety of sentiments in religion among its inhabitants. Upon the plan of a religious test, the question I think must be, who shall be excluded from national trusts? Whatever answer bigotry may suggest, the dictates of candour and equity, I conceive, will be *none*.

Far from limiting my charity and confidence to men of my own denomination in religion, I suppose, and I believe, sir, that there are worthy characters among men of every other denomination—among the Quakers—the Baptists—the Church of England—the Papists—and even among those who have no other guide, in the way to virtue and heaven, than the dictates of natural religion.

I must therefore think, sir, that the proposed plan of government, in this particular, is wisely constructed: That as all have an equal claim to the blessings of the government under which they live, and which they support, so none should be excluded from them for being of any particular denomination in religion.

The presumption is, that the eyes of the people will be upon the faithful in the land, and from a regard to their own safety, will chuse for their rulers, men of known abilities—of known probity—of good moral characters. The apostle Peter tells us, that God is no respecter of persons, but in every nation he that feareth him and worketh righteousness, is *acceptable* to him—And I know of no reason, why men of such a character, in a community, of whatever denomination in religion, *ceteris paribus*, with other suitable qualifications, should not be *acceptable* to the people, and why they may not be employed, by them, with safety and advantage in the important offices of government.—The exclusion of a religious test in the proposed Constitution, therefore, clearly appears to me, sir, to be in favour of its adoption.

Colonel JONES (*Bristol*) thought, that the rulers ought to believe in God or Christ—and that however a test may be prostituted in England, yet he thought if our publick men were to be of those who had a good standing in the church, it would be happy for the United States—and that a person could not be a good man without being a good Christian.

John Hancock Proposes Ratification with Recommended Amendments

January 31, 1788

When the Convention met in the afternoon,

His Excellency the PRESIDENT observed, that a motion had been made and seconded, that this Convention do assent to, and ratify, the Constitution which had been under consideration—and that he had in the former part of the day intimated his intention of submitting a proposition to the consideration of the Convention. My motive, says he, arises from my earnest desire to this Convention, my fellow-citizens and the publick at large, that this Convention may adopt such a form of government, as may extend its good influences to every part of the United States, and advance the prosperity of the whole world. His situation, his Excellency said, had not permitted him to enter into the debates of this Convention.— It however, appeared to him necessary, from what had been advanced in them, to adopt the form of government proposed; but, observing a diversity of sentiment in the gentlemen of the Convention, he had frequently had conversation with them on the subject; and from this conversation, he was induced to propose to them, whether the introduction of some general amendments would not be attended with the happiest consequences: For that purpose he should, with the leave of the Hon. Convention, submit to their consideration a proposition, in order to remove the doubts, and quiet the apprehensions of gentlemen; and if in any degree the object should be acquired, he should feel himself perfectly satisfied. He should therefore, submit them—for he was, he said, unable to go more largely into the subject, if his abilities would permit him, relying on the candour of the Convention to bear him witness, that his wishes for a good constitution were sincere. [*His Excellency then read his proposition.*] This gentlemen, concluded his Excellency, is the proposition which I had to make; and I submit it to your consideration, with the sincere wish, that it may have a tendency to promote a spirit of union.

Samuel Adams Supports Hancock's Proposition

January 31, 1788

Hon. Mr. ADAMS. Mr. President—I feel myself happy in contemplating the idea, that many benefits will result from your Excellency's conciliatory proposition, to this commonwealth and to the United States; and I think it ought to precede the motion made by the gentleman from Newbury-Port; and to be at this time considered by the Convention. I have said, that I have had my doubts of this Constitution—I could not digest every part of it, as readily as some gentlemen; but this, sir, is my misfortune, not my fault. Other gentlemen have had their doubts, but, in my opinion the proposition submitted, will have a tendency to remove such doubts, and to conciliate the minds of the convention, and the people without doors. This subject, sir, is of the greatest magnitude, and has employed the attention of every rational man in the United States: but the minds of the people are not so well agreed on it as all of us could wish. A proposal, of this sort, coming from Massachusetts, from her importance, will have its weight. Four or five states have considered and ratified the constitution as it stands; but we know there is a diversity of opinion even in these states, and one of them is greatly agitated. If this Convention should particularize the amendments necessary to be proposed, it appears to me it must have weight in other States where Conventions have not yet met. I have observed the sentiments of gentlemen on the subject, as far as Virginia; and I have found that the objections were similar, in the news papers, and in some of the Conventions.—Considering these circumstances, it appears to me that such a measure will have the most salutary effect throughout the union.—It is of the greatest importance, that *America* should still be united in sentiment. I think I have not been heretofore unmindful of the advantage of such an union. It is essential that the people should be united in the federal government, to withstand the common enemy, and to preserve their valuable rights and liberties. We find in the great

325

State of Pennsylvania, one third of the Convention are opposed to it: should there then be large minorities in the several states, I should fear the consequences of such disunion.

Sir, there are many parts of it I esteem as highly valuable, particularly the article which empowers Congress to regulate commerce, to form treaties &c. For want of this power in our national head, our friends are grieved, and our enemies insult us. Our ambassadour at the court of London is considered as a mere cypher, instead of the representative of the United States.—Therefore it appears to me, that a power to remedy this evil should be given to Congress, and the remedy applied as soon as possible.

The only difficulty on gentlemen's minds is, whether it is best to accept this Constitution on conditional amendments, or to rely on amendments in future, as the Constitution provides. When I look over the article which provides for a revision, I have my doubts. Suppose, sir, nine states accept the Constitution without any conditions at all; and the four states should wish to have amendments, where will you find nine States to propose, and the legislatures of nine States to agree, to the introduction of amendments—Therefore it seems to me, that the expectation of amendments taking place at some future time, will be frustrated. This method, if we take it, will be the most likely to bring about the amendments, as the Conventions of New-Hampshire, Rhode-Island, New-York, Maryland, Virginia, and South-Carolina, have not yet met. I apprehend, sir, that these States will be influenced by the proposition which your Excellency has submitted, as the resolutions of Massachusetts have ever had their influence. If this should be the case, the necessary amendments would be introduced more early, and more safely. From these considerations, as your Excellency did not think it proper to make a motion, with submission, I move, that the paper read by your Excellency, be now taken under consideration, by the Convention.

John Hancock's Final Observations
"We Must All Rise or Fall Together"

February 6, 1788

GENTLEMEN,

Being now called upon to bring the subject under debate to a decision, by bringing forward the question—I beg your indulgence to close the business with a few words. I am happy that my health has been so far restored, that I am rendered able to meet my fellow-citizens, as represented in this Convention. I should have considered it was one of the most distressing misfortunes of my life, to be deprived of giving my aid and support to a system, which if amended (as I feel assured it will be) according to your proposals, cannot fail to give the people of the United States, a greater degree of political freedom, and eventually as much national dignity, as falls to the lot of any nation on the earth. I have not since I had the honour to be in this place, said much on the important subject before us: All the ideas appertaining to the system, as well those which are against as for it, have been debated upon with so much learning and ability, that the subject is quite exhausted.

But you will permit me, gentlemen, to close the whole with one or two general observations. This I request, not expecting to throw any new light upon the subject, but because it may possibly prevent uneasiness and discordance, from taking place amongst us and amongst our constituents.

That a general system of government is indispensably necessary to save our country from ruin, is agreed upon all sides. That the one now to be decided upon has its defects, all agree; But when we consider the variety of interests, and the different habits of the men it is intended for, it would be very singular to have an entire union of sentiment respecting it. Were the people of the United States to delegate the powers proposed to be given, to men who were not dependent on them frequently for elections—to men whose interests either from rank, or title, would differ from that of their fellow-citizens in common, the task of delegating authority would be vastly more difficult; but as the matter now stands, the powers reserved by the people render them secure, and until they themselves become corrupt, they will always have upright and able rulers. I give my assent to the Constitution in full confidence that the amendments proposed will soon become a part of the system—these amendments being in no wise local, but calculated to give security and ease alike to all the States, I think that all will agree to them.

Suffer me to add, that let the question be decided as it may, there can be no triumph on the one side, or chagrin on the other—Should there be a great division, every good man, every one who loves his country, will be so far from exhibiting extraordinary marks of joy, that he will sincerely lament the want of unanimity, and strenuously endeavour to cultivate a spirit of conciliation, both in Convention, and at home. The people of this Commonwealth, are a people of great light— of great intelligence in publick business—They know that we have none of us an interest separate from theirs—that it must be our happiness to conduce to theirs—and that we must all rise or fall together—They will never, therefore, forsake the first principle of society, that of being governed by the voice of the majority; and should it be that the proposed form of government should be rejected, they will zealously attempt another. Should it by the vote now to be taken be ratified, they will quietly acquiesce, and where they see a want of perfection in it, endeavour in a constitutional way to have it amended.

The question now before you is such as no nation on earth, without the limits of America, have ever had the privilege of deciding upon. As the Supreme Ruler of the Universe has seen fit to bestow upon us this glorious opportunity, let us decide upon it—appealing to him for the rectitude of our intentions— and in humble confidence that he will yet continue to bless and save our country.

The Form of the Ratification of Massachusetts

February 6, 1788

COMMONWEALTH of MASSACHUSETTS.

In convention of the delegates of the people of the commonwealth of Massachusetts, Feb. 6, 1788.

The convention having impartially discussed, and fully considered, the constitution for the United States of America, reported to Congress, by the convention of delegates from the United States, of America, and submitted to us, by a resolution of the General Court of the said commonwealth, passed the twenty fifth day of October last past; and acknowledging with grateful hearts the goodness of the Supreme Ruler of the universe, in affording the people of the United States, in the course of his Providence, an opportunity, deliberately and peaceably, without fraud or surprise, of entering into an explicit and solemn compact with each other, by assenting to and ratifying a new constitution, in order to form a more perfect union, establish justice, insure domestick tranquillity, provide for the common defence, promote the general welfare, and secure the blessings of liberty to themselves, and their posterity—DO, in the name and in behalf of the people of the commonwealth of Massachusetts, ASSENT to and RATIFY the said *constitution, for the United States of America*.

And as it is the opinion of this convention, that certain amendments and alterations in the said constitution, would remove the fears, and quiet the apprehensions of many of the good people of this commonwealth, and more effectually guard against an undue administration of the federal government, the convention do therefore recommend, that the following alterations and provisions be introduced into the said constitution:

First. That it be explicitly declared, that all powers, not expressly delegated by the aforesaid constitution, are reserved to the several states, to be by them exercised.

Secondly. That there shall be one representative to every thirty thousand persons, according to the census mentioned in the constitution, until the whole number of the representatives amounts to two hundred.

Thirdly. That Congress do not exercise the powers vested in them by the 4th sect. of the 1st art. but in cases when a state neglect or refuse to make regulations therein mentioned, or shall make regulations subversive of the rights of the people, to a free and equal representation in Congress, agreeably to the constitution.

Fourthly, That Congress do not lay direct taxes, but when the monies arising from the impost and excise are insufficient for the publick exigencies; nor then, until Congress shall have first made a requisition upon the states, to assess, levy and pay their respective proportions of such requisition, agreeably to the census fixed in the said constitution, in such way and manner as the legislature of the state shall think best,—and in such case, if any state shall neglect or refuse to pay its proportion, pursuant to such requisition, then Congress may assess and levy such states proportion, together with interest thereon, at the rate of six per cent. per annum, from the time of payment prescribed in such requisition.

Fifthly. That Congress erect no company of merchants with exclusive advantages of commerce.

Sixthly. That no person shall be tried for any crime by which he may incur an infamous punishment, or loss of life, until he be first indicted by a grand jury, except in such cases as may arise in the government and regulation of the land and naval forces.

Seventhly. The supreme judicial federal court shall have no jurisdiction of causes between citizens of different states, unless the matter in dispute, whether it concerns the reality or personality, be of the value of three thousand dollars, at the least: Nor shall the federal judicial powers extend to any actions between citizens of different states where the matter in dispute, whether it concerns the reality or personality, is not of the value of fifteen hundred dollars, at the least.

Eighthly. In civil actions, between citizens of different states, every issue of fact, arising in actions at common law, shall be tried by a jury, if the parties, or either of them, request it.

Ninthly. Congress shall, at no time, consent, that any person, holding an office of trust or profit, under the United

States, shall accept of a title of nobility, or any other title or office, from any king, prince, or foreign state.

And the Convention do, in the name and in behalf of the people of this commonwealth, enjoin it upon their representatives in Congress, at all times, until the alterations and provisions aforesaid have been considered, agreeably to the fifth article of the said constitution, to exert all their influence, and use all reasonable and legal methods to obtain a ratification of the said alterations and provisions in such manner as is provided in the said article.

And that the United States in Congress assembled may have due notice of the assent and ratification of the said constitution by this Convention—It is

RESOLVED, That the assent and ratification aforesaid be engrossed on parchment, together with the recommendation and injunction aforesaid, and with this resolution; and that his excellency JOHN HANCOCK, esquire, president, and the honourable WILLIAM CUSHING, esquire, vice-president, of this Convention, transmit the same, countersigned by the secretary of the Convention, under their hands and seals, to the United States in Congress assembled.

(Signed) JOHN HANCOCK, President,
WILLIAM CUSHING, Vice-President.

(Countersigned)

GEORGE RICHARDS MINOT, Sec'y.

SOUTH CAROLINA
RATIFYING CONVENTION

Charles Cotesworth Pinckney Explains America's Unique "Structure of Freedom"

May 14, 1788

The following Speech of the Honorable Mr. Charles Pinckney's, as delivered in the late Convention of this state, and published in the City Gazette, on the 3d inst, we have taken the liberty to re publish.

Mr. PRESIDENT,

After so much has been said with respect to the powers possessed by the late convention, to form and propose a new system—after so many observations have been made on its leading principles, as well in the house of representatives as in the conventions of other states, whose proceedings have been published, it will be as unnecessary for me again minutely to examine a subject which has been so thoroughly investigated, as it would be difficult to carry you into a field that has not been sufficiently explored.

Having, however, had the honor of being associated in the delegation from this state, and presuming on the indulgence of the house, I shall proceed to make some observations which appear to me as necessary to a full and candid discussion of the system before us. It seems to be generally confessed, that of all sciences, that of government or of politics is most difficult. In the old world, as far as the lights of history extend, from the earliest ages to the present, we find them in the constant exercise of all the forms with which the world is still furnished. We have seen among the ancients as well as the moderns— monarchies limited, and absolute aristocracies—republics of a single state, and federal unions; but notwithstanding all their experience, how imperfect at this moment is their knowledge of government? How little is the true doctrine of representation understood? How few states enjoy what we term freedom? How few governments answer these great ends of public happiness, which we seem to expect from our own?

In reviewing such of the European states as we are best acquainted with, we may with truth affirm, that there is but one among the most important, which confirms to its citizens their civil liberties or provides for the security of private rights; but as if it had been fated that we should be the first perfectly free people the world had ever seen—even the government I have alluded to, withholds from a part of its subjects the equal enjoyment of their religious liberties. How many thousands of the subjects of Great-Britain at this moment labour under civil disabilities, merely on account of their religious persuasions? To the liberal and enlightened mind the rest of Europe afford a melancholly picture of the depravity of human nature, and of the total subversion of those rights without which we should suppose no people could be happy or content.

We have been taught here to believe that all power of right belongs to THE PEOPLE—that it flows immediately from them, and is delegated to their officers for the public good—that our rulers are the servants of the people, amenable to their will, and created for their use. How different are the governments of Europe? There the people are the servants and subjects of their rulers. There merit and talents have little or no influence, but all the honors and offices of government are swallowed up by birth, by fortune, or by rank.

From the European world no precedents are to be drawn for a people who think they are capable of governing themselves. Instead of receiving instruction from them, we may with pride assert, that new as this country is in point of settlement; inexperienced as she must be upon questions of government, she still has held forth more useful lessons to the old world—she has made them more accquainted with their own rights, than they had been otherwise for centuries.—It is with pride I repeat, that old and experienced as they are, they are indebted to us for light and refinement upon points of all others the most interesting.

Had the American revolution not happened, would Ireland at this time enjoy her present rights of commerce and legislation? Would the subjects of the emperor in the Netherlands have presumed to contend for and ultimately secure the privileges they demanded? Would the parliament of Paris have resisted the edicts of their monarch, and justified this step in a language that would do honor to the freest people? Nay, I may add, would a becoming sense of liberty, and of the rights of mankind, have so generally pervaded that kingdom, had not their knowledge of America led them to the investigation? Undoubtedly not. Let it be therefore our boast, that we have already taught some of the oldest and wisest nations to explore their rights as men; and let it be our prayer, that the effects of our revolution may never cease to operate, until they have unshackled all the nations that have firmness enough to resist the fetters of despotism. Without a precedent, and with the experience of but a few years, were the convention called upon to form a system for a people, differing from all others we are acquainted with. The first knowledge necessary for us to acquire, was a knowledge of the people for whom this system was to be formed. For unless we were acquainted with their situation, their habits, opinions and resources, it would be impossible to form a government upon adequate or practicable principles. If we examine the reasons which have given rise to the distinctions of rank that at present prevail in Europe, we shall find that none of them do, or in all probability ever will, exist in the union. The only distinction that may take place is that of wealth. Riches, no doubt, will ever have their influence, and where they are suffered to increase to large amounts in a few hands, there they may become dangerous to the public; particularly when from the cheapness of labor, and from the scarcity of money, a great proportion of the people are poor. These however are dangers that I think we have very little to apprehend; for these reasons—One is from the destruction of the right of primogeniture, by which means the estates of intestates are equally to be divided among all their children—a provision no less consonant to the principles of a republican government, than it is to those of general equity and parental affection; to endeavour to raise a name by accumulating property in one branch of a family at the expence of others, *equally related and deserving*, is a vanity no *less unjust and cruel*, than dangerous to the interest of liberty; it is a practice no wise state will ever encourage or tolerate.

In the northern and eastern states such distinctions among children are seldom heard of. Laws have been long since passed in all of them destroying the right of primogeniture; and as laws never fail to have a powerful influence upon the manners of a people, we may suppose that in future an equal division of property among children will in general take place in all the states, and one means of amassing inordinate wealth in the hands of individuals be, as it ought, for ever removed.

Another reason is, that in the eastern and northern states, the landed property is nearly equally divided. Very few have large bodies, and there are few of them that have not small tracts; the greater part of the people are employed in cultivating their own lands; the rest in handicrafts and commerce. They are frugal in their manner of living, plain tables, cloathing, and furniture prevail in their houses, and expensive appearances avoided. Among the landed interest it may be truly said there are few of them rich, or few of them very poor; nor while the states are capable of supporting so many more inhabitants than they contain at present—while so vast a territory on our frontier remains uncultivated and unexplored—while the means of subsistence are so much within every man's power, are those dangerous distinctions of fortune to be expected which at present prevail in other countries.

The people of the union may be classed as follows:

Commercial men—who will be of consequence or not in the political scale, as commerce may be made an object of the attention of government. As far as I am able to judge, and presuming that proper sentiments will ultimately prevail me upon this subject, it does not appear to me that the commercial line will ever have much influence in the politics of the union. Foreign trade is one of the enemies against which we must be extremely guarded, more so than against any other, as none will ever have a more unfavorable operation.—I consider it as the root of our present public distress—as the plentiful source from which our future national calamities will flow, unless great care is taken to prevent it. Divided as we are from the old world, we should have nothing to do with their politics, and as little as possible with their commerce—they can never improve, but must inevitably corrupt us.

Another class is that of professional men, who from their education and pursuits must ever have a considerable influence, while your government retains the republican principle, and its affairs are agitated in assemblies of the people.

The third—with whom I will connect the mechanical as generally attached to them, are the landed interest, the owners and cultivators of the soil—the men attached to the truest interests of their country, from those motives which always bind and secure the affections of nations. In these consist the great body of the people; and here rests, and I hope will ever continue, all the authority of our government.

I remember once to have seen in the writings of a very celebrated author on national wealth, the following remark. "Finally, says he, there are but three ways for a nation to acquire wealth—the first is *by war*, as the Romans did in plundering their conquered neighbours—this *is robbery*; the second is in *commerce*, which is *generally cheating*; the third is agriculture, the only honest way; wherein a man receives a real increase of the seed thrown into the ground, in a kind of continual miracle, wrought by the hand of God in his favor, as a reward for his innocent life and virtuous industry."

I do not agree with him so far as to suppose that commerce is generally cheating. I think there are some kinds of commerce not only fair and valuable, but such as ought to be encouraged by government. I agree with him in this general principle, *that all the great objects of government should be subservient to the increase of agriculture, and the support of the landed interest; and that commerce should only be so far attended to, as it may serve to improve and strengthen it—that the object of a republic is to render its citizens virtuous and happy; and that an unlimited foreign commerce can seldom fail to have a contrary tendency.*

These classes compose the people of the union, and fortunately for their harmony they may be said in a great measure to be connected with and dependent upon each other.

The merchant is dependent upon the planter as the purchaser of his imports, and as furnishing him with the means of his remittances—the professional men depend upon both for employment in their respective pursuits, and are in their turn useful to both. The landholder, though the most independent of the three, is still in some measure obliged to the merchant for furnishing him *at home* with a ready sale for his productions.

From this mutual dependence, and the statement I have made respecting the situation of the people of the union, I am led to conclude, that *mediocrity of fortune* is a leading feature in our national character—that most of the causes which lead to distinctions of fortune among other nations being removed and causes of equality existing with us, which are not to be found among them, we may with safety assert, that the great body of national wealth is nearly equal in the hands of the people, among whom there are few dangerously rich, or few miserably poor—that we may congratulate ourselves with living under the blessings of a mild and equal government, which knows no distinctions but those of merit or of talents—under a government whose honors and offices are *equally open* to the exertions of *all her citizens, and which adopts virtue and worth for her own wheresoever she can find them.*

Another distinguishing feature in our union is its division into individual states, differing in extent of territory, manners, population and products.

Those who are acquainted with the eastern states; their reasons of their original migration, and the present habits and principles, well know that they are essentially different from those of the middle and southern states; that they retain all those opinions respecting religion and government which first induced their ancestors to cross the Atlantic, and that they are perhaps more purely republican in habit and sentiment than any other part of the union. The inhabitants of New York, and the eastern part of New Jersey, originally Dutch settlements, seem to have altered less than might have been expected in the course of a century. Indeed the greatest part of New-York may still be considered as a Dutch settlement, the people in the interior country generally using that language in their families, and having very little varied their ancient customs. Pennsylvania and Delaware are nearly one half inhabited by Quakers, whose passive principles upon questions of government, and rigid opinions in private life, render them extremely different from either the eastern or southern states. Maryland was originally a Roman Catholic colony, and a great number of their inhabitants, some of them the most wealthy and cultivated, are still of this persuasion. It is unnecessary for me to state the striking difference in sentiment and habit, which must always exist between the independence of the east, the Calvinists and Quakers of the middle states, and the Roman Catholics of Maryland; but striking as this is, it is not to be compared with the difference that there is between the inhabitants of the *northern and southern states*; when I say southern states, I mean Maryland and the states to the southward of her; here we may truly observe nature has drawn a strong mark of distinction in the habits and manners of the people as she has in their climates and productions—The southern citizen beholds with a kind of surprize the simple manners of the east, and is too often induced to entertain undeserved opinions of the apparent purity of the Quaker—while they in their turn seem concerned at what they term the extravagance and dissipation of their southern friends, and reprobate as an unpardonable, moral and political evil the dominion they hold over a part of the human race.

The inconveniencies which too frequently attend these differences in habits and opinions among the citizens that compose the union, are not a little encreased by the variety of their state governments; for as I have already observed, the constitutions or laws under which a people live, never fail to have a powerful effect upon their manners. We know that all the states have adhered in their forms to the republican principles, though they have differed widely in their opinions of the mode best calculated to preserve it.—In Pennsylvania and Georgia the whole powers of government are lodged in a legislative body of a single branch, over which there is no controul; nor are their executives or judicials, from their connection and necessary dependence on the legislature capable of strictly executing their respective offices. In all the other states, except Maryland, Massachusetts and New-York, they are only so far improved as to have a legislature with two branches, which compleatly involve and swallow up all the powers of their government. In neither of these are the judicial or executive placed in that firm or independent situation which can alone secure the safety of the people, or the just administration of the laws. In Maryland one branch of their legislature is a senate, chosen for *five years*, by electors chosen by the people;

the knowledge and firmness which this body have upon all occasions displayed, not only in the exercise of their legislative duties, but in withstanding and defeating such of the projects of the other house as appeared to them founded in local and personal motives, have long since convinced me that the senate of Maryland is the best model of a senate that has yet been offered to the union—that it is capable of correcting many of the vices of the other parts of their constitution, and in a great measure atoning for those defects which in common with the states I have mentioned, are but too evident in their execution—*the want of stability and independence in the judicial and executive departments.*

In Massachusetts we find the principle of legislation more improved by the revisionary power which is given to their government, and the independence of their judges.

In New York the same improvement in legislation has taken place as in Massachusetts, but here from the executive being elected by the great body of the people,—holding his office for three years, and being re-eligible—from the appointment to offices being taken from the legislature, and placed in a select council—I think their constitution upon the whole, is the best in the union. Its faults are the want of permanent salaries to their judges, and giving to their executive the nomination to offices, which is in fact giving him the appointment. It does not, however, appear to me that this can be strictly called a vice of their system, as I have always been of opinion, that the insisting upon the right to nominate, *was an usurpation* of their executives, not warranted by the letter or meaning of the constitution.

These are the outlines of their various forms, in few of which are their executive or judicial departments wisely constructed, or that solid distinction adopted between the branches of their legislature, which can alone provide for the influence of different principles in their operation.

Much difficulty was expected from the extent of country to be governed.—All the republics we read of, either in the ancient or modern world, have been extremely limited in territory— we know of none a tenth part so large as the United States. Indeed we are hardly able to determine, from the lights we are furnished with, whether the governments we have heard of under the names of republics really deserved them, or whether the ancients ever had any just or proper ideas upon the subject. Of the doctrine of representation, the fundamental of a republic, they certainly were ignorant. If they were in possession of any other safe or practicable principles, they have long since been lost and forgotten to the world. Among the other honors therefore that have been reserved for the American union, not the least inconsiderable of them, is that of defining a mixed system by which a people may govern themselves, possessing all the virtue and benefits, and avoiding all the dangers and inconveniences of the three simple forms. I have said, that the ancient confederacies, as far as we are acquainted with them, covered but an inconsiderable territory. Among the moderns, in our sense of the words, there is no such system as a confederate republic; there are indeed some small states whose interior governments are democratic, but these are too inconsiderable to afford information. The Swiss Cantons are only connected by alliances; the Germanic body is merely an association of potentates, most of them absolute in their own dominions; and as to the United Netherlands, it is such a confusion of states and assemblies, that I have always been at a loss what speces of government to term it; according to my idea of the word, it is not a republic, for I consider it as indispensible in a republic, that all authority should flow from the people. In the United Netherlands the people have no interference, either in the election of their magistrates, or the affairs of government.

From the experiment therefore never having been fairly made, opinions have been entertained, and sanctioned by high authorities, that republics are only suited to small societies. This opinion has its advocates among all those who not having a sufficient share of industry or talents to investigate for themselves, easily adopt the opinions of such authors as are supposed to have written with ability upon the subject, but I am led to believe other opinions begin to prevail.—Opinions more to be depended upon, because they result from juster principles.

We begin now to suppose that the evils of a republic—dissention, tumult and faction, are more dangerous in small societies than in large confederate states. In the first, the people are easily assembled and inflamed—are always opposed to those convulsive tumults of infatuation and enthusiasm, which often overturn all public order. In the latter, the multitude will be less imperious, and consequently less inconstant, because the extensive territory of each republic, and the number of its citizens will not permit them all to be assembled at one time, and in one place—the sphere of government being enlarged, it will not easily be in the power of factious and designing men to infect the whole people—it will give an opportunity to the more temperate and prudent part of the society to correct the licentiousness and injustice of the rest. We have strong proofs of the truth of this opinion in the examples of Rhode-Island and Massachusetts. Instances which have perhaps been critically afforded by an all merciful providence, to evince the truth of a position extremely important to our present enquiries. In the former the most contracted society in the union, we have seen their licentiousness so far prevail as to seize the reins of government, and oppress the people by laws the most infamous that have ever disgraced a civilized nation. In the latter, where the sphere was enlarged, similar attempts have been rendered abortive by the zeal and activity of those who were opposed to them.

As the constitution before you is intended to represent states as well as citizens, I have thought it necessary to make these remarks, because there are no doubt a great number of the members of this body, who from their particular pursuits have not had an opportunity of minutely investigating them; and because it will be impossible for the house fairly to determine whether the government is a proper one, or not, unless they are in some degree acquainted with the people and states for whose use it is instituted.

For a people thus situated is a government to be formed—a people who have the justest opinions of their civil and religious rights, and who have risqued every thing in defending and asserting them.

In every government there necessarily exists a power from which there is no appeal, and which for that reason may be termed absolute and uncontroulable.

The person or assembly in whom this power resides, is called the sovereign or supreme power of the state. With us the *Sovereignty of the union is in the People.*

One of the best political and moral writers* I have met with, enumerates three principal forms of government, which he says are to be regarded rather as the simple forms, by some combination and intermixture of which all actual governments are composed, than as any where existing in a pure and elementary state.

These forms are—

1st. Despotism or absolute Monarchy, where the legislature is in a single person.

2d. An Aristocracy, where the legislature is in a select assembly, the members of which either fill up by election the vacancies in their own body, or succeed to it by inheritance, property, tenure of lands, or in respect of some personal right or qualification.

3d. A Republic, where the people at large either collectively or by representation form the legislature.

The separate advantages of *Monarchy* are, unity of council, decision, secrecy, and dispatch—the military strength and energy resulting from these qualities of government: The exclusion of popular and Aristocratical contentions—the preventing by a known rule of succession all competition for the supreme power, thereby repressing the dangerous hope and intrigues of aspiring citizens.

The dangers of a *Monarchy* are, tyranny, expence, exaction, military domination, unnecessary wars,—ignorance in the governors of the interest and accomodation of the people, and a consequent deficiency of salutary regulations—want of constancy and uniformity in the rules of government, and proceeding from thence in security of person and property.

The separate advantage of an *Aristocracy* is the wisdom which may be expected from experience and education—a permanent council naturally possesses experience, and the members will always be educated with a view to the stations they are destined by their birth to occupy.

The mischiefs of an *Aristocracy* are dissentions in the ruling orders of the state—an oppression of the lower orders by the privileges of the higher, and by laws partial to the separate interests of the law makers.

*Paley, a deacon of Carlisle, 2 vols. 174 & 175.

The advantages of a *Republic* are liberty, exemption from needless restrictions—equal laws—public spirit—averseness to war—frugality—above all, the opportunities which they afford to men of every description of producing their abilities and councils to public observation, and the exciting to the service of the commonwealth the faculties of its best citizens.

The evils of a *Republic* are dissentions—tumults—faction—the attempts of ambitious citizens to possess power—the confusion and clamour which are the inevitable consequences of propounding questions of state to the discussion of large popular assemblies—the delay and disclosure of the public councils, and too often the imbecility of the laws.

A *mixed government* is composed by the combination of two or more of the simple forms above described; and in whatever proportion each form enters into the constitution of a government, in the same proportion may both the advantages and evils which have been attributed to that form, be expected.

The citizens of the United States would reprobate, with indignation, the idea of a monarchy; but the essential qualities of a monarch—unity of councils—vigor—secrecy and dispatch, are qualities essential in every government.

While therefore, we have reserved to the people *the fountain* of all power, the periodical election of their first magistrate; while we have defined his authorities, and bound them to such limits as will effectually prevent his usurping others dangerous to the general welfare; we have at the same time endeavoured to infuse into this department, that degree of vigor which will enable the president to execute the laws *with energy and dispatch*.

By constructing the senate upon rotative principles, we have removed, as will be shewn on another occasion, all danger of an *aristocratic influence*, while, by electing the members for six years, we hope that we have given to this part of the system all the advantages of an *aristocracy—wisdom—experience—and a consistency of measures*.

The house of representatives, in which the people of the union are proportionably represented, are to be biennially elected by them; those appointments are sufficiently short to render the member as dependent as he ought to be upon his constituent.

They are the moving spring of the system,—with them all grants of money are to originate—on them depend the wars we shall be engaged in—the fleets and armies we shall raise and support—the salaries we shall pay—in short, on them depend the appropriations of money, and consequently all the arrangements of government. With the powerful influence of the purse, they will be always able to restrain the usurpations of the other departments, while their own licentiousness will, in its turn, be checked and corrected by them. I trust, that when we proceed to review the system by sections, it will be found to contain all those necessary provisions and restraints, which while they enable the general government to guard and protect our common rights as a nation—to restore to us those blessings of commerce and mutual confidence which have been so long removed and impaired—will secure to us those rights, which, as the citizens of a state, will make us content and happy at home—as the citizens of the union respectable abroad.

How differently Mr. President, is this government constructed from any we have yet known among us.

In their individual capacities as citizens, the people are proportionably represented *in the house of representatives.* Here they who are to support the expences of government have purse strings in their hands. Here the people hold and feel that they possess an influence sufficiently powerful to prevent any undue attempt of the other branches; to maintain that weight in the political scale which as the source of all authority they should ever possess. Here too the states, whose existence as such we have often heard predicted as precarious, will find in the senate *the guards of their rights as political associations,* a sure protection.

On them, I mean the *state systems,* rests the general fabric; on their foundation is this magnificent structure of freedom erected—each depending upon, supporting and protecting the other, nor, so intimate is the connexion, can the one be removed without prostrating the other in ruin—like the head and the body, separate them and they die.

Far be it from me to suppose, that such an attempt should ever be made—the good sense and virtue of our country forbid the idea. To the union we will look up as to the temple of our freedom—a temple founded in the affections, and supported by the virtue of the people—here we will point out our gratitude to the author of all good, for suffering us to participate in the rights of a people who *govern themselves*. Is there at this moment a nation upon earth that enjoys this right—where the true principles of representation are understood and practised, and where all authority flows from and returns at stated periods to the people? I answer there is not. Can a government be said to be free where these rights do not exist? It cannot. On what depends the enjoyment of these rare, these inestimable privileges? On the firmness—on the power of the union to protect them.

How grateful then should we be, that at this important period—a period important, not to us alone, but to the general rights of mankind, so much harmony and concession should prevail throughout the states—that the public opinion should be so much actuated by candor and an attention to their general interests—that disdaining to be governed by the narrow motives of state policy, they have liberally determined to dedicate a part of their advantages to the support of that government from which they received them.

To the philosophic mind how new and awful an instance do the United States at present exhibit in the political world?— They exhibit, sir, the first instance of a people, who being dissatisfied with their government—unattacked by foreign force, and undisturbed by domestic uneasiness—coolly and deliberately resort to the virtue and good sense of their country for a correction of their public errors.

It must be obvious, that without a superintending government, it is impossible the liberties of this country can long be secured.

Single and unconnected, how weak and contemptible are the largest of our states—how unable to protect themselves from external or domestic insult—how incompetent to national purposes would our partial unions be?—how liable to intestine wars and confusion?—how little able to secure the blessings of peace?

Let us therefore be careful in strengthening the union—let us remember that we are bounded by vigilant and attentive neighbours, who view with a jealous eye our rise to empire.

Let us remember that we are bound in gratitude to our northern brethren to aid them in the recovery of those rights which they have lost in obtaining for us an extension of our commerce and the security of our liberties—Let us not be unmindful, that those who are weak and may expect support, must, in their turn, be ready to afford it.

We are called upon to execute an important trust—to examine the principles of the constitution before you, and, in the name of the people, to receive or reject it. I have no doubt we shall do this with attention and harmony, and flatter myself that, at the conclusion of our discussions, we shall find that it is not only expedient, but safe and honorable to adopt it.

Patrick Dollard Fears a Corrupt and Despotic Aristocracy

May 22, 1788

It being mentioned in conversation, that it would be proper to know, from gentlemen, what were the sentiments of their constituents, with regard to the new constitution. Mr. Dollard, a member from Prince Frederick's parish, made the following speech, to which his colleague Mr. Tweed added.

Mr. President,

I rise with the greatest diffidence to speak on this occasion, not only knowing myself unequal to the task, but believing this to be the most important question that ever the good people of this state were called together to deliberate upon. This constitution has been ably supported, and ingeniously glossed over by many able and respectable gentlemen in this house, whose reasoning, aided by the most accurate eloquence, might strike conviction even in the pre-determined breast, had they a good cause to support. Conscious that they have not, and also conscious of my inabilities to point out the consequences of its defects, which have in some measure been defined by able gentlemen in this house, I shall therefore confine myself within narrow bounds, that is, concisely to make known the sense and language of my constituents. The people of Prince Frederick's parish, whom I have the honor to represent, are a brave, honest and industrious people. In the late bloody contest they bore a conspicuous part, when they fought, bled and conquered, in defence of their civil rights and privileges, which they expected to transmit untainted to their posterity. They are nearly to a man opposed to this new constitution, because, they say, they have omitted to insert a bill of rights therein, ascertaining and fundamentally establishing the unalienable rights of men, without a full, free and secure enjoyment of which there can be no liberty, and over which it is not necessary that a good government should have the controul. They say, that they are by no means against vesting congress with ample and sufficient powers, but to make over to them or any set of men, their birthright comprized in Magna Charta, which this new constitution absolutely does, they can never agree to. Notwithstanding this they have the highest opinion of the virtue and abilities of the honorable gentlemen from this state, who represented us in the general convention; and also a few other distinguished characters, whose names will be transmitted with honor to future ages; but I believe at the same time, they are but mortal, and therefore liable to err; and as the virtue and abilities of those gentlemen will consequently recommend their being first employed in jointly conducting the reins of this government, they are led to believe it will commence in a moderate aristocracy, but that it will in its future operations produce a monarchy, or a corrupt and oppressive aristocracy they have no manner of doubt. Lust of dominion is natural in every soil, and the love of power and superiority is as prevailing in the United States at present as in any part of the earth; yet in this country, depraved as it is, there still remains a strong regard for liberty: an American bosom is apt to glow at the sound of it, and the splendid merit of preserving that best gift of God, which is mostly expelled every country in Europe, might stimulate indolence, and animate even luxury herself to consecrate at the altar of freedom. My constituents are highly alarmed at the large and rapid strides which this new government has taken towards despotism. They say it is big with political mischiefs, and pregnant with a greater variety of impending woes to the good people of the southern states, especially South-Carolina, than all the plagues supposed to issue from the poisonous box of Pandora. They say it is particularly calculated for the meridian of despotic aristocracy—that it evidently tends to promote the ambitious views of a few able and designing men, and enslave the rest; that it carries with it the appearance of an old phrase formerly made use of in despotic reigns, and especially by archbishop Laud in the reign of Charles the 1st, that is "*non resistance.*" They say they will resist against it—that they will not accept of it unless compelled by force of arms, which this new constitution plainly threatens; and then, they say, your standing army, like Turkish Janizaries enforcing despotic laws, must ram it down their throats with the points of Bayonets. They warn the gentlemen of this convention, as the guardians of their liberty, to beware how they will be accessary to the disposal of, or rather sacrificing their dear bought rights and privileges. This is the sense and language, Mr. President, of the people; and it is an old saying, and I believe, a very true one, that the general voice of the people is the voice of God. The general voice of the people to whom I am responsible is against it; I shall never betray the trust reposed in me by them, therefore shall give it my hearty dissent.

VIRGINIA RATIFYING CONVENTION

Patrick Henry's Opening Speech Opposing Ratification

June 4, 1788

Mr. *Henry*—Mr. Chairman.—The public mind, as well as my own, is extremely uneasy at the proposed change of Government. Give me leave to form one of the number of those who wish to be thoroughly acquainted with the reasons of this perilous and uneasy situation—and why we are brought hither to decide on this great national question. I consider myself as the servant of the people of this Commonwealth, as a centinel over their rights, liberty, and happiness. I represent their feelings when I say, that they are exceedingly uneasy, being brought from that state of full security, which they enjoyed, to the present delusive appearance of things. A year ago the minds of our citizens were at perfect repose. Before the meeting of the late Federal Convention at Philadelphia, a general peace, and an universal tranquillity prevailed in this country;—but since that period they are exceedingly uneasy and disquieted. When I wished for an appointment to this Convention, my mind was extremely agitated for the situation of public affairs. I conceive the republic to be in extreme danger. If our situation be thus uneasy, whence has arisen this fearful jeopardy? It arises from this fatal system—it arises from a proposal to change our government:—A proposal that goes to the utter annihilation of the most solemn engagements of the States. A proposal of establishing 9 States into a confederacy, to the eventual exclusion of 4 States. It goes to the annihilation of those solemn treaties we have formed with foreign nations. The present circumstances of France—the good offices rendered us by that kingdom, require our most faithful and most punctual adherence to our treaty with her. We are in alliance with the Spaniards, the Dutch, the Prussians: Those treaties bound us as thirteen States, confederated together—Yet, here is a proposal to sever that confederacy. Is it possible that we shall abandon all our treaties and national engagements?—And for what? I expected to have heard the reasons of an event so unexpected to my mind, and many others. Was our civil polity, or public justice, endangered or sapped? Was the real existence of the country threatened—or was this preceded by a mournful progression of events? This proposal of altering our Federal Government is of a most alarming nature: Make the best of this new Government—say it is composed by any thing but inspiration—you ought to be extremely cautious, watchful, jealous of your liberty; for instead of securing your rights you may lose them forever. If a wrong step be now made, the republic may be lost forever. If this new Government will not come up to the expectation of the people, and they should be disappointed—their liberty will be lost, and tyranny must and will arise. I repeat it again, and I beg Gentlemen to consider, that a wrong step made now will plunge us into misery, and our Republic will be lost. It will be necessary for this Convention to have a faithful historical detail of the facts, that preceded the session of the Federal Convention, and the reasons that actuated its members in proposing an entire alteration of Government—and to demonstrate the dangers that awaited us: If they were of such awful magnitude, as to warrant a proposal so extremely perilous as this, I must assert, that this Convention has an absolute right to a thorough discovery of every circumstance relative to this great event. And here I would make this enquiry of those worthy characters who composed a part of the late Federal Convention. I am sure they were fully impressed with the necessity of forming a great consolidated Government, instead of a confederation. That this is a consolidated Government is demonstrably clear, and the danger of such a Government, is, to my mind, very striking. I have the highest veneration for those Gentlemen,—but, Sir, give me leave to demand, what right had they to say, *We, the People.* My political curiosity, exclusive of my anxious solicitude for the public welfare, leads me to ask, who authorised them to speak the language of, *We, the People,* instead of *We, the States?* States are the characteristics, and the soul of a confederation.

If the States be not the agents of this compact, it must be one great consolidated National Government of the people of all the States. I have the highest respect for those Gentlemen who formed the Convention, and were some of them not here, I would express some testimonial of my esteem for them. America had on a former occasion put the utmost confidence in them: A confidence which was well placed: And I am sure, Sir, I would give up any thing to them; I would chearfully confide in them as my Representatives. But, Sir, on this great occasion, I would demand the cause of their conduct.—Even from that illustrious man, who saved us by his valor, I would have a reason for his conduct—that liberty which he has given us by his valor, tells me to ask this reason,—and sure I am, were he here, he would give us that reason: But there are other Gentlemen here, who can give us this information. The people gave them no power to use their name. That they exceeded their power is perfectly clear. It is not mere curiosity that actuates me—I wish to hear the real actual existing danger, which should lead us to take those steps so dangerous in my conception. Disorders have arisen in other parts of America, but here, Sir, no dangers, no insurrection or tumult, has happened—every thing has been calm and tranquil. But notwithstanding this, we are wandering on the great ocean of human affairs. I see no landmark to guide us. We are running we know not whither. Difference in opinion has gone to a degree of inflammatory resentment in different parts of the country—which has been occasioned by this perilous innovation. The Federal Convention ought to have amended the old system—for this purpose they were solely delegated: The object of their mission extended to no other consideration. You must therefore forgive the solicitation of one unworthy member, to know what danger could have arisen under the present confederation, and what are the causes of this proposal to change our Government.

Patrick Henry States His Main Objections, and James Madison Responds

June 12, 1788

Mr. *Henry.*—Mr. Chairman,—Once more I find it necessary to trespass on your patience. An Honorable Gentleman several days ago observed, that the great object of this Government, was justice. We were told before, that the greater consideration was Union. However, the consideration of justice seems to have been what influenced his mind when he made strictures on the proceedings of the Virginia Assembly. I thought the reasons of that transaction had been sufficiently explained. It is exceedingly painful to me to be objecting, but I must make a few observations. I shall not again review the catalogue of dangers which the Honorable Gentleman entertained us with. They appear to me absolutely imaginary. They have in my conception proved to be such. But sure I am, that the dangers of this system are real, when those who have no similar interests with the people of this country, are to legislate for us—when our dearest interests are left in the power of those whose advantage it may be to infringe them. How will the quotas of troops be furnished? *Hated* as requisitions are, your Federal officers cannot collect troops like dollars, and carry them in their pockets. You must make those *abominable* requisitions for them, and the scale will be in proportion to the number of your blacks, as well as your whites, unless they violate the constitutional rule of apportionment. This is not calculated to rouse the fears of the people. It is founded in truth. How oppressive and dangerous must this be to the Southern States who alone have slaves? This will render their proportion infinitely greater than that of the Northern States. It has been openly avowed that this shall be the rule. I will appeal to the judgments of the Committee, whether there be danger.—The Honorable Gentleman said, that there was no precedent for *this* American revolution. We have precedents in abundance. They have been drawn from Great-Britain. Tyranny has arisen there in the same manner in which it was introduced among

353

the Dutch. The tyranny of Philadelphia may be like the tyranny of George the IIId. I believe this similitude will be incontestibly proved before we conclude.

The Honorable Gentleman has endeavored to explain the opinion of Mr. Jefferson our common friend, into an advice to adopt this new Government. What are his sentiments? He wishes nine States to adopt, and that four States may be found somewhere to reject it? Now, Sir, I say, if we pursue his advice, what are we to do?—To prefer form to substance? For, give me leave to ask what is the substantial part of his counsel? It is, Sir, that four States should *reject*. They tell us, that from the most authentic accounts, New-Hampshire will adopt it. When I denied this, Gentlemen said they were absolutely certain of it. Where then will four States be found to reject, if we adopt it? If we do, the counsel of this enlightened and worthy countryman of ours, will be thrown away,—and for what? He wishes to secure amendments and a Bill of Rights, if I am not mistaken. I speak from the best information, and if wrong, I beg to be put right. His amendments go to that despised thing *a Bill of Rights*, and all the rights which are dear to human nature—Trial by jury, the liberty of religion, and the press, &c.—Do not Gentlemen see, that if we adopt under the idea of following Mr. Jefferson's opinion, we amuse ourselves with the shadow, while the substance is given away? If Virginia be for adoption, what States will be left, of sufficient respectability and importance, to secure amendments by their rejection? As to North Carolina it is *a poor despised place*. Its dissent will not have influence to introduce any amendments.—Where is the American spirit of liberty? Where will you find attachment to the rights of mankind, when Massachusetts the great Northern State, Pennsylvania the great middle State, and Virginia the great Southern State, shall have adopted this Government? Where will you find magnanimity enough to reject it? Should the remaining States have this magnanimity, they will not have sufficient weight to have the Government altered. This State has weight and importance. Her example will have powerful influence—Her rejection will procure amendments—Shall we by our adoption hazard the loss of amendments?—Shall we forsake that importance and respectability which our station in America commands, in

hopes that relief will come from an obscure part of the Union?
I hope my countrymen will spurn at the idea. The necessity of
amendments is universally admitted. It is a word which is re-
echoed from every part of the Continent. A majority of those
who hear me, think amendments are necessary. Policy tells us
they are necessary. Reason, self-preservation, and every idea
of propriety, powerfully urge us to secure the dearest rights of
human nature—Shall we in direct violation of these principles,
rest this security upon the uncertainty of its being obtained by
a few States more weak, and less respectable than ourselves—
and whose virtue and magnanimity may be overborne by the
example of so many adopting States?—*Poor* Rhode-Island and
North-Carolina, and even New-York, surrounded with Federal
walls on every side, may not be magnanimous enough to reject, and if they do reject it, they will have but little influence to
obtain amendments. I ask, if amendments be necessary, from
whence can they be so properly proposed as from this State?
The example of Virginia is a powerful thing, particularly with
respect to North-Carolina, whose supplies must come *through*
Virginia. Every possible opportunity of procuring amendments
is gone—Our power and political salvation is gone, if we ratify unconditionally. The important right of making treaties is
upon the most dangerous foundation. The President with a
few Senators possess it in the most unlimited manner, without
any real responsibility, if from sinister views they should think
proper to abuse it. For they may keep all their measures in the
most profound secrecy as long as they please. Were we not told
that war was the case wherein secrecy was most necessary? But
by the paper on your table, their secrecy is not limited to this
case only. It is as unlimited and unbounded as their powers.
Under the abominable veil of political secrecy and contrivance,
your most valuable rights may be sacrificed by a most corrupt
faction, without having the satisfaction of knowing who injured you. They are bound by honor and conscience to act
with integrity, but they are under no constitutional restraint.
The navigation of the Mississippi, which is of so much importance to the happiness of the people of this country, may be
lost by the operation of that paper. There are seven States now
decidedly opposed to this navigation. If it be of the highest
consequence to know who they are who shall have voted its

relinquishment, the Federal veil of secrecy will prevent that discovery. We may labor under the magnitude of our miseries without knowing or being able to punish those who produced them. I did not wish that transactions relative to treaties should when unfinished, be exposed; but that it should be known after they were concluded, who had advised them to be made, in order to secure some degree of certainty that the public interest shall be consulted in their formation.

We are told that all powers not given are reserved. I am sorry to bring forth hackneyed observations. But, Sir, important truths lose nothing of their validity or weight, by frequency of repetition. The English history is frequently recurred to by Gentlemen. Let us advert to the conduct of the people of that country. The people of England lived without a declaration of rights, till the war in the time of Charles Ist. That King made usurpations upon the rights of the people. Those rights were in a great measure before that time undefined. Power and privilege then depended on implication and logical discussion. Though the declaration of rights was obtained from that King, his usurpations cost him his life. The limits between the liberty of the people, and the prerogative of the King, were still not clearly defined. The rights of the people continued to be violated till the Steward family was banished in the year 1688. The people of England magnanimously defended their rights, banished the tyrant, and prescribed to William Prince of Orange, *by the Bill of Rights*, on what terms he should reign. And this Bill of Rights put an end to all construction and implication. Before this, Sir, the situation of the public liberty of England was dreadful. For upwards of a century the nation was involved in every kind of calamity, till the Bill of Rights put an end to all, by defining the rights of the people, and limiting the King's prerogative. Give me leave to add (if I can add any thing to so splendid an example) the conduct of the American people. They Sir, thought a *Bill of Rights* necessary. It is alledged that several States, in the formation of their governments, omitted a Bill of Rights. To this I answer, that they had the substance of a Bill of Rights contained in their Constitutions, which is the same thing. I believe that Connecticut has preserved by her Constitution her royal charter, which clearly defines and secures the great rights of mankind—Secure

to us the great important rights of humanity, and I care not in
what form it is done. Of what advantage is it to the American
Congress to take away this great and general security? I ask of
what advantage is it to the public or to Congress to drag an
unhappy debtor, not for the sake of justice, but to gratify the
malice of the plaintiff, with his witnesses to the Federal Court,
from a great distance? What was the principle that actuated
the Convention in proposing to put such dangerous powers
in the hands of any one? Why is the trial by jury taken away?
All the learned arguments that have been used on this occasion
do not prove that it is secured. Even the advocates for the plan
do not all concur in the certainty of its security. Wherefore is
religious liberty not secured? One Honorable Gentleman who
favors adoption, said that he had had his fears on the subject.
If I can well recollect, he informed us that he was perfectly satisfied by the powers of reasoning (with which he is so happily
endowed) that those fears were not well grounded. There is
many a religious man who knows nothing of argumentative
reasoning;—there are many of our most worthy citizens, who
cannot go through all the labyrinths of syllogistic argumentative deductions, when they think that the rights of conscience
are invaded. This sacred right ought not to depend on con-
structive logical reasoning. When we see men of such talents
and learning, compelled to use their utmost abilities to convince themselves that there is no danger, is it not sufficient
to make us tremble? Is it not sufficient to fill the minds of
the ignorant part of men with fear? If Gentlemen believe that
the apprehensions of men will be quieted, they are mistaken;
since our best informed men are in doubt with respect to the
security of our rights. Those who are not so well informed will
spurn at the Government. When our common citizens, who
are not possessed with such extensive knowledge and abilities,
are called upon to change their Bill of Rights, (which in plain
unequivocal terms, secures their most valuable rights and privileges) for construction and implication, will they implicitly acquiesce? Our Declaration of Rights tells us, "That all men are
by nature free and independent, &c." (Here Mr. *Henry* read
the Declaration of Rights.) Will they exchange these Rights for
logical reasons? If you had a thousand acres of land, dependent on this, would you be satisfied with logical construction?

Would you depend upon a title of so disputable a nature? The present opinions of individuals will be buried in entire oblivion when those rights will be thought of. That sacred and lovely thing Religion, ought not to rest on the ingenuity of logical deduction. Holy Religion, Sir, will be prostituted to the lowest purposes of human policy. What has been more productive of mischief among mankind than Religious disputes. Then here, Sir, is a foundation for such disputes, when it requires learning and logical deduction to perceive that religious liberty is secure. The Honorable member told us that he had doubts with respect to the judiciary department. I hope those doubts will be explained.—He told us that his object was Union. I admit that the reality of Union and not the name, is the object which most merits the attention of every friend to his country. He told you that you should hear many great *sounding words* on our side of the question. We have heard the *word Union* from him. I have heard no word so often pronounced in this House as he did this. I admit that the American Union is dear to every man—I admit that every man who has three grains of information, must know and think that Union is the best of all things. But as I said before, we must not mistake the end for the means. If he can shew that the rights of the Union are secure, we will consent. It has been sufficiently demonstrated that they are not secured. It sounds mighty prettily to Gentlemen to curse paper money and honestly pay debts. But apply to the situation of America, and you will find there are thousands and thousands of contracts, whereof equity forbids an exact literal performance. Pass that government, and you will be bound hand and foot. There was an immense quantity of depreciated continental paper money in circulation at the conclusion of the war. This money is in the hands of individuals to this day. The holders of this money may call for the nominal value, if this government be adopted. This State may be compelled to pay her proportion of that currency pound for pound. Pass this government and you will be carried to the Federal Court (if I understand that paper right) and you will be compelled to pay shilling for shilling. I doubt on the subject, at least as a public man, I ought to have doubts. A State may be sued in the Federal Court by the paper on your table. It appears to me then, that the holder of the paper money may require shilling for shilling. If there be any latent remedy to prevent this, I hope it will be discovered.

The precedent, with respect to the Union between England and Scotland, does not hold. The Union of Scotland speaks in plain and direct terms. Their privileges were particularly secured. It was expressly provided that they should retain their own particular laws. Their nobles have a right to choose Representatives to the number of sixteen.—I might thus go on and specify particulars, but it will suffice to observe generally, that their rights and privileges were expressly and unequivocally reserved.—The power of direct taxation was not given up by the Scotch people. There is no trait in that Union which will maintain their arguments. In order to do this, they ought to have proved that Scotland united without securing their rights, and afterwards got that security by subsequent amendments. Did the people of Scotland do this? No, Sir, like a sensible people, they trusted nothing to hazard. If they have but 45 members, and those be often corrupted, these defects will be greater here. The number will be smaller, and they will be consequently the more easily corrupted. Another Honorable Gentleman advises us to give this power, in order to exclude the necessity of going to war. He wishes to establish national credit I presume—and imagines that if a nation has public faith and shews a disposition to comply with her engagements, she is safe among ten thousand dangers. If the Honorable Gentleman can prove that this paper is calculated to give us public faith, I will be satisfied. But if you be in constant preparation for war, on such airy and imaginary grounds, as the mere possibility of danger, your government must be military, which will be inconsistent with the enjoyment of liberty. But, Sir, we must become formidable, and have a strong government to protect us from the British nation. Will the paper on the table prevent the attacks of the British navy, or enable us to raise a fleet equal to the British fleet? The British have the strongest fleet in Europe, and can strike any where. It is the utmost folly to conceive, that that paper can have such an operation. It will be no less so to attempt to raise a powerful fleet. With respect to requisitions, I beseech Gentlemen to consider the importance of the subject. We who are for amendments propose, (as has been frequently mentioned) that a requisition shall be made for £. 200,000 for instance, instead of direct taxation, and that if it be not complied with, then it shall be raised by direct taxes. We do not wish to have strength to refuse to pay them, but to possess the power of raising the taxes in the most easy mode for the people. But says he, you may delay us by this mode.—Let us see if there be not sufficient to counterbalance this evil. The oppression arising from taxation, is not from the amount but, from the mode—a thorough acquaintance with the condition of the people, is necessary to a just distribution of taxes. The whole wisdom of the science of Government, with respect to taxation, consists in selecting that mode of collection which will best accommodate the convenience of the people. When you come to tax a great country, you will find that ten men are too few to settle the manner of collection. One capital advantage which will result from the proposed alternative is this, that there will be necessary communications between your ten members in Congress, and your 170 Representatives here. If it goes through the hands of the latter, they will know how much the citizens *can* pay, and by looking at the paper on your table, they will know how much they *ought* to pay. No man is possessed of sufficient information to know how much we can or ought to pay.

We might also remonstrate, if by mistake or design, they should call for a greater sum than our proportion. After a remonstrance, and a free investigation between our Representatives here, and those in Congress, the error would be removed.

Another valuable thing which it will produce is, that the people will pay the taxes chearfully. It is supposed, that this would occasion a waste of time, and be an injury to public credit. This would only happen if requisitions should not be complied with. In this case the delay would be compensated by the payment of interest, which with the addition of the credit of the State to that of the General Government, would in a great measure obviate this objection. But if it had all the force which it is supposed to have, it would not be adequate to the evil of direct taxation. But there is every probability that requisitions would be then complied with. Would it not then be our interest, as well as duty, to comply? After noncompliance, there would be a general acquiescence in the exercise of this power. We are fond of giving power, at least power which is constitutional. Here is an option to pay according to your own mode, or otherwise. If you give probability fair play, you must conclude, that they would be complied with. Would the Assembly of Virginia by refusal, destroy the country and plunge the people into miseries and distress? If you give your reasoning faculty fair play, you cannot but know, that payment must be made when the consequence of a refusal would be an accumulation of inconveniences to the people. Then they say, that if requisitions be not complied with, in case of a war, the destruction of the country may be the consequence; that therefore, we ought to give the power of taxation to the Government to enable it to protect us. Would not this be another reason for complying with requisitions, to prevent the country from being destroyed? You tell us, that unless requisitions be complied with, your commerce is gone. The prevention of this also, will be an additional reason to comply.

He tells us, that responsibility is secured by direct taxation. Responsibility instead of being increased, will be lost for ever by it. In our State Government, our Representatives may be severally instructed by their constituents. There are no persons to counteract their operations. They can have no excuse for deviating from our instructions. In the General Government other men have power over the business. When oppressions may take place, our Representatives may tell us, *We contended for your interest, but we could not carry our point, because the Representatives from Massachusetts, New Hampshire, Connecticut, &c. were against us.* Thus, Sir, you may see, that there is no real responsibility. He further said, that there was such a contrariety of interests, as to hinder a consolidation. I will only make one remark—There is a variety of interests—Some of the States owe a great deal on account of paper money—Others very little—Some of the Northern States have collected and barrelled up paper money. Virginia has sent thither her cash long ago. There is little or none of the Continental paper money retained in this State. Is it not their business to appreciate this money? Yes,—and it will be your business to prevent it. But there will be a majority against you, and you will be obliged to pay your share of this money in its nominal value. It has been said by several Gentlemen, that the freeness of elections would be promoted by throwing the country into large districts. I contend, Sir, that it will have a contrary effect. It will destroy that connection that ought to subsist between the electors and the elected. If your elections be by districts instead of counties, the people will not be acquainted with the candidates. They must therefore be directed in the elections by those who know them. So that instead of a confidential connection between the electors and the elected, they will be absolutely unacquainted with each other. A common man must ask a man of influence how he is to proceed, and for whom he must vote. The elected, therefore, will be careless of the interest of the electors. It will be a common job to extort the suffrages of the common people for the most influential characters. The same men may be repeatedly elected by these means. This, Sir, instead of promoting the freedom of elections, leads us to an Aristocracy. Consider the mode of elections in England. Behold the progress of an election in an English shire. A man of an enormous fortune will spend 30,000 l. or 40,000 l. to get himself elected. This is frequently the case. Will the Honorable Gentleman say, that a poor man, as enlightened as any man in the island, has an equal chance with a rich man, to be elected? He will stand no chance though he may have the finest understanding of any man in the shire. It will be so here. Where is the chance that a poor man can come forward with the rich? The Honorable Gentleman will find that instead of supporting Democratical principles, it goes absolutely to destroy them. The State Governments, says he, will possess greater advantages than the General Government, and will consequently prevail. His opinion and mine are diametrically opposite. Bring forth the Federal allurements, and compare them with the poor contemptible things that the State Legislatures can bring forth. On the part of the State Legislatures, there are Justices of Peace and militia officers—And even these Justices and officers, are bound by oath in favour of the Constitution. A constable is the only man who is not obliged to swear paramount allegiance to this beloved Congress. On the other hand, there are rich, fat Federal emoluments—your rich, snug, fine, fat Federal offices—The number of collectors of taxes and excises will outnumber any thing from the States. Who can cope with the excisemen and taxmen? There are none in this country, that can cope with this class of men alone. But, Sir, is this the only danger? Would to Heaven that it were. If we are to ask which will last the longest—the State or the General Government, you must take an army and a navy into the account. Lay these things together, and add to the enumeration the superior abilities of those who manage the General Government. Can then the State Governments look it in the face? You dare not look it in the face now, when it is but in *embryo*. The influence of this Government will be such, that you never can get amendments; for if you propose alterations, you will affront them. Let the Honorable Gentleman consider all these things and say, whether the State Governments will last as long as the Federal Government. With respect to excises, I can never endure them. They have been productive of the most intolerable oppressions every where. Make a probable calculation of the expence attending the Legislative, Executive, and Judiciary. You will find that there must be an immense increase of taxes. We are the same mass of people we were before.—In the same circumstances—The same pockets are to pay—The expences are to be increased—What will enable us to bear this augmentation of taxes? The mere form of the Government will not do it. A plain understanding cannot conceive how the taxes can be diminished, when our expences are augmented, and the means of paying them not increased.

With respect to our tax-laws, we have purchased a little knowledge by sad experience upon the subject. Reiterated experiments have taught us what can alleviate the distresses and suit the convenience of the people. But we are now to throw away that system, by which we have acquired this knowledge, and send ten men to legislate for us.

The Honorable Gentleman was pleased to say, that the representation of the people was the vital principle of this Government. I will readily agree that it ought to be so.—But I contend that this principle is only nominally, and not substantially to be found there. We contended with the British about representation; they offered us such a representation as Congress now does. They called it a virtual representation. If you look at that paper you will find it so there. Is there but a virtual representation in the upper House? The States are represented *as States*, by two Senators each. This is virtual, not actual. They encounter you with Rhode-Island and Delaware. This is not an actual representation. What does the term representation signify? It means that a certain district—a certain association of men should be represented in the Government for *certain ends*. These ends ought not to be impeded or obstructed in any manner. Here, Sir, this populous State has not an adequate share of legislative influence. The two petty States of Rhode-Island and Delaware, which together are infinitely inferior to this State, in extent and population, have double her weight, and can counteract her interest. I say, that the representation in the Senate, as applicable to States, is not actual. Representation is not therefore the vital principle of this Government—So far it is wrong.

Rulers are the servants and agents of the people—The people are their masters—Does the new Constitution acknowledge this principle? Trial by jury is the best appendage of freedom—Does it secure this? Does it secure the other great rights of mankind? Our own Constitution preserves these principles. The Honorable Gentleman contributed to form that Constitution: The applauses so justly due to it, should, in my opinion, go to the condemnation of that paper.

With respect to the failures and errors of our Government, they might have happened in any Government.—I do not justify what merits censure, but I shall not degrade my country. As to deviations from justice, I hope they will be attributed to the errors of the head, and not to those of the heart.

The Honorable Gentleman did our Judiciary honour in saying, that they had firmness to counteract the Legislature in some cases. Yes, Sir, our Judges opposed the acts of the Legislature. We have this land mark to guide us.—They had fortitude to declare that they were the Judiciary and would oppose unconstitutional acts. Are you sure that your Federal Judiciary will act thus? Is that Judiciary so well constructed and so independent of the other branches, as our State Judiciary? Where are your land-marks in this Government? I will be bold to say you cannot find any in it. I take it as the highest encomium on this country, that the acts of the Legislature, if unconstitutional, are liable to be opposed by the Judiciary.

Then the Honorable Gentleman said, that the two Judiciaries and Legislatures, would go in a parallel line and never

interfere—That as long as each was confined to its proper objects, that there would be no danger of interference—That like
two parallel lines as long as they continued in their parallel
direction they never would meet. With submission to the Honorable Gentleman's opinion, I assert, that there is danger of
interference, because no line is drawn between the powers of
the two Governments in many instances; and, where there is
a line, there is no check to prevent the one from encroach-
ing upon the powers of the other. I therefore contend that
they must interfere, and that this interference must subvert
the State Government, as being less powerful. Unless your
Government have checks, it must inevitably terminate in the
destruction of your privileges. I will be bold to say, that the
British Government has real checks. I was attacked by Gentlemen, as if I had said that I loved the British Government better
than our own. I never said so. I said that if I were obliged to
relinquish a Republican Government, I would chuse the British Monarchy. I never gave the preference to the British or any
other Government, when compared to *that* which the Honorable Gentleman assisted to form. I was constrained to say what
I said. When two disagreeable objects present themselves to
the mind, we choose that which has the least deformity.

As to the Western Country, notwithstanding our representation in Congress, and notwithstanding any regulation that
may be made by Congress, it may be lost. The seven Northern
States are determined to give up the Mississippi. We are told
that in order to secure the navigation of that river, it was necessary to give it up twenty-five years to the Spaniards, and that
thereafter we should enjoy it forever without any interruption
from them. This argument resembles that which recommends
adopting first and then amending. I think the reverse of what
the Honorable Gentleman said on this subject. Those seven
States are decidedly against it. He tells us, that it is the policy of the whole Union to retain it. If men were wise, virtuous, and honest, we might depend on an adherence to this
policy.—Did we not know of the fallibility of human nature, we
might rely on the present structure of this Government.—
We might depend that the rules of propriety, and the general
interest of the Union would be observed. But the depraved
nature of man is well known. He has a natural biass towards his

own interest, which will prevail over every consideration, unless it be checked. It is the interest and inclination of the seven Northern States to relinquish this river. If you enable them to do so, will the mere propriety of consulting the interest of the other six States, refrain them from it? Is it imagined, that Spain will, after a peaceable possession of it for thirty years, give it up to you again? Can credulity itself hope, that the Spaniards who wish to have it for that period, wish to clear the river for you? What is it they wish?—To clear the river?—For whom? America saw the time when she had the reputation of common sense at least. Do you suppose they will restore it to you after thirty years? If you do, you depart from that rule. Common observation tells you, that it must be the policy of Spain to get it first, and then retain it forever. If you give it up, in my poor estimation, they will never voluntarily restore it. Where is the man who will believe that after clearing the river, strengthening themselves, and increasing the means of retaining it, the Spaniards will tamely surrender it?

With respect to the concurrent collections of parochial, county, and State taxes, which the Honorable Gentleman has instanced as a proof of the practicability of the concurrent collection of taxes by the General and State Governments, the comparison will not stand examination. As my honorable friend has said, these concurrent collections come from one power. They irradiate from the same center. They are not co-equal or co-extensive. There is no clashing of powers between them. Each is limited to its own particular objects, and all subordinate to one supreme controuling power—The Legislature.—The County Courts have power over the county and parish collections, and can constantly redress any injuries or oppressions committed by the collectors. Will this be the case in the Federal Courts? I hope they will not have Federal Courts in every county. If they will, the State Courts will be debased and stripped of their cognizance, and utterly abolished. Yet, if there be no power in the county to call them to account, they will more flagrantly trample on your rights. Does the Honorable Gentleman mean that the Thirteen States will have thirteen different tax-laws? Is this the expedient which is to be substituted to the unequal and unjust one of uniform taxes? If so, many horrors present themselves to my mind. They may be imaginary, but it appears to my mind to be the most abominable system that could be imagined. It will destroy every principle of responsibility: It will be destructive of that fellow-feeling, and consequent confidence, which ought to subsist between the Representatives and the represented. We shall then be taxed by those who bear no part of the taxes themselves, and who consequently will be regardless of our interest in imposing them upon us. The efforts of our ten men will avail very little when opposed by the Northern majority. If our ten men be disposed to sacrifice our interests, we cannot detect them. Under the colour of being outnumbered by the Northern Representatives, they can always screen themselves. When they go to the General Government, they may make a bargain with the Northern Delegates. They may agree to tax our citizens in any manner which may be proposed by the Northern members; in consideration of which the latter may make them some favorite concessions. The Northern States will never assent to regulations promotive of the Southern aggrandisement. Notwithstanding what Gentlemen say of the probable virtue of our Representatives, I dread the depravity of human nature. I wish to guard against it by proper checks, and trust nothing to accident or chance. I will never depend on so slender a protection as the possibility of being represented by virtuous men.

Will not thirteen different objects of taxation in the thirteen different States, involve us in an infinite number of inconveniences and absolute confusion? There is a striking difference, and great contrariety of interests between the States. They are naturally divided into carrying and productive States. This is an actual existing distinction which cannot be altered. The former are more numerous, and must prevail. What then will be the consequence of their contending interests, if the taxation of America is to go on in thirteen different shapes? This Government subjects every thing to the Northern majority. Is there not then a settled purpose to check the Southern interest? We thus put unbounded power over our property in hands not having a common interest with us. How can the Southern members prevent the adoption of the most oppressive mode of taxation in the Southern States, as there is a majority in favor of the Northern States? Sir, this is a picture so horrid, so wretched, so dreadful, that I need no longer dwell upon it.—Mr. *Henry* then concluded by remarking, that he dreaded the most iniquitous speculation and stock-jobbing, from the operation of such a system.

Mr. *Madison*,—Mr. Chairman.—Pardon me for making a few remarks on what fell from the Honorable Gentleman last up:—I am sorry to follow the example of Gentlemen in deviating from the rule of the House:—But as they have taken the utmost latitude in their objections, it is necessary that those who favor the Government should answer them.—But I wish as soon as possible to take up the subject regularly. I will therefore take the liberty to answer some observations which have been irregularly made, though they might be more properly answered when we came to discuss those parts of the Constitution to which they respectively refer.—I will, however, postpone answering some others till then.—If there be that terror in direct taxation, that the States would comply with requisitions to guard against the Federal Legislature; and if, as Gentlemen say, this State will always have it in her power to make her collections speedily and fully, the people will be compelled to pay the same amount as quickly and punctually as if raised by the General Government. It has been amply proved, that the General Government can lay taxes as conveniently to the people as the State Governments, by imitating the State systems of taxation.—If the General Government have not the power of collecting its own revenues, in the first instance, it will be still dependent on the State Governments in some measure; and the exercise of this power after refusal, will be inevitably productive of injustice and confusion, if partial compliances be made before it is driven to assume it.—Thus, Sir, without relieving the people in the smallest degree, the alternative proposed will impair the efficacy of the Government, and will perpetually endanger the tranquillity of the Union.

The honorable member's objection with respect to requisitions of troops will be fully obviated at another time.—Let it suffice now to say, that it is altogether unwarrantable, and founded upon a misconception of the paper before you. But the honorable member, in order to influence our decision, has mentioned the opinion of a citizen who is an ornament to this State. When the name of this distinguished character was introduced, I was much surprised.—Is it come to this then, that we are not to follow our own reason?—Is it proper to introduce the opinions of respectable men not within these walls?—If the opinion of an important character were to weigh on this occasion, could we not adduce a character equally great on our side?—Are we who (in the Honorable Gentleman's opinion) are not to be governed by an *erring world*, now to submit to the opinion of a citizen beyond the Atlantic? I believe that were that Gentleman now on this floor, he would be *for* the adoption of this Constitution. I wish his name had never been mentioned.—I wish every thing spoken here relative to his opinion may be suppressed if our debates should be published. I know that the delicacy of his feelings will be wounded when he will see in print what has, and may be said, concerning him on this occasion. I am in some measure acquainted with his sentiments on this subject. It is not right for me to unfold what he has informed me. But I will venture to assert, that the clause now discussed, is not objected to by Mr. Jefferson:— He approves of it, because it enables the Government to carry on its operations. He admires several parts of it, which have been reprobated with vehemence in this House. He is captivated with the equality of suffrage in the Senate, which the Honorable Gentleman (Mr. *Henry*) calls the rotten part of this Constitution. But whatever be the opinion of that illustrious citizen, considerations of personal delicacy should dissuade us from introducing it here.

The honorable member has introduced the subject of religion.—Religion is not guarded—There is no Bill of Rights declaring that religion should be secure.—Is a Bill of Rights a security for religion? Would the Bill of Rights in this State exempt the people from paying for the support of one particular sect, if such sect were exclusively established by law? If there were a majority of one sect, a Bill of Rights would be a poor protection for liberty. Happily for the States, they enjoy the utmost freedom of religion. This freedom arises from that multiplicity of sects, which pervades America, and which is the best and only security for religious liberty in any society. For where there is such a variety of sects, there cannot be a majority of any one sect to oppress and persecute the rest. Fortunately for this Commonwealth, a majority of the people are decidedly against any exclusive establishment—I believe it to be so in the other States. There is not a shadow of right in the General Government to intermeddle with religion.—Its least interference with it would be a most flagrant usurpation.—I can appeal to my uniform conduct on this subject, that I have warmly supported religious freedom.—It is better that this security should be depended upon from the General Legislature, than from one particular State. A particular State might concur in one religious project.—But the United States abound in such a vast variety of sects, that it is a strong security against religious persecution, and is sufficient to authorise a conclusion, that no one sect will ever be able to out number or depress the rest.

I will not travel over that extensive tract, which the honorable member has traversed.—I shall not now take notice of all his desultory objections.—As occasions arise I shall answer them.

It is worthy of observation on this occasion, that the Honorable Gentleman himself, seldom fails to contradict the arguments of Gentlemen on that side of the question.—For example, he strongly complains that the Federal Government from the number of its members will make an addition to the public expence, too formidable to be borne; and yet he and other Gentlemen on the same side, object that the number of Representatives is too small, though ten men are more than we are entitled to under the existing system! How can these contradictions be reconciled? If we are to adopt any efficient Government at all, how can we discover or establish such a system, if it be thus attacked?—Will it be possible to form a rational conclusion upon contradictory principles? If arguments of a contradictory nature were to be brought against the wisest and most admirable system, to the formation of which human intelligence is competent, it never could stand them.

He has accrimoniously inveighed against the Government, because such transactions as Congress think require secrecy, may be concealed—and particularly those which relate to treaties. He admits that when a treaty is forming, secrecy is proper; but urges that when actually made, the public ought to be made acquainted with every circumstance relative to it. The policy of not divulging the most important transactions, and negotiations of nations, such as those which relate to warlike arrangements and treaties, is universally admitted. The Congressional proceedings are to be occasionally published, including *all receipts and expenditures* of public money, of which no part can be used, but in consequence of appropriations made by law. This is a security which we do not enjoy under the existing system.—That part which authorises the Government to with-hold from the public knowledge what in their judgment may require secrecy, is imitated from the Confederation—that very system which the Gentleman advocates.

No treaty has been formed, and I will undertake to say, that none *will* be formed under the old system, which will secure to us the actual enjoyment of the navigation of the Mississippi. Our weakness precludes us from it. We *are* entitled to it. But it is not under an inefficient Government that we shall be able to avail ourselves fully of that right.—I most conscientiously believe, that it will be far better secured under the new Government, than the old, as we will be more able to enforce our right. The people of Kentucky will have an additional safe-guard from the change of system. The strength and respectability of the Union will secure them in the enjoyment of that right, till that country becomes sufficiently populous. When this happens they will be able to retain it in spite of every opposition.

I never can admit that seven States are disposed to surrender that navigation.—Indeed it never was the case.—Some of their most distinguished characters are decidedly opposed to its relinquishment. When its cession was proposed by the Southern States, the Northern States opposed it. They still oppose it. New-Jersey directed her Delegates to oppose it, and is strenuously against it. The same sentiments pervade Pennsylvania:—At least I am warranted to say so, from the best information which I have. Those States, added to the Southern States, would be a majority against it.

The Honorable Gentleman, to obviate the force of my observations with respect to concurrent collections of taxes under different authorities, said that there was no interference between the concurrent collections of parochial, county, and State taxes, because they all irradiated from the same centre; but that this was not the case with the General Government.—To make use of the Gentleman's own term, the concurrent collections under the authorities of the General Government and State Governments, all irradiate from the people at large. The people is their common superior. The sense of the people at large is to be the predominant spring of their actions. This is a sufficient security against interference.

Our attention was called to our commercial interest, and at the same time the landed interest was said to be in danger. If those ten men who are to be chosen, be elected by landed men, and have land themselves, can the electors have anything to apprehend?—If the commercial interest be in danger, why are we alarmed about the carrying trade?—Why is it said, that the carrying States will preponderate, if commerce be in danger?—With respect to speculation, I will remark that stock-jobbing has more or less prevailed in all countries, and ever will in some degree, notwithstanding any exertions to prevent it. If you judge from what has happened under the existing system, any change would render a melioration probable.

George Mason and James Madison
Debate the Slave-Trade Clause

June 17, 1788

Mr. *George Mason*,—Mr. Chairman.—This is a fatal section, which has created more dangers than any other.—The first clause, allows the importation of slaves for twenty years. Under the royal Government, this evil was looked upon as a great oppression, and many attempts were made to prevent it; but the interest of the African merchants prevented its prohibition. No sooner did the revolution take place, than it was thought of. It was one of the great causes of our separation from Great-Britain. Its exclusion has been a principal object of this State, and most of the States in the Union. The augmentation of slaves weakens the States; and such a trade is diabolical in itself, and disgraceful to mankind. Yet by this Constitution it is continued for twenty years. As much as I value an union of all the States, I would not admit the Southern States into the Union, unless they agreed to the discontinuance of this disgraceful trade, because it would bring weakness and not strength to the Union. And though this infamous traffic be continued, we have no security for the property of that kind which we have already. There is no clause in this Constitution to secure it; for they may lay such a tax as will amount to manumission. And should the Government be amended, still this detestable kind of commerce cannot be discontinued till after the expiration of twenty years.—For the fifth article, which provides for amendments, expressly excepts this clause I have ever looked upon this as a most disgraceful thing to America. I cannot express my detestation of it. Yet they have not secured us the property of the slaves we have already. So that "They have done what they ought not to have done, and have left undone what they ought to have done."

Mr. *Madison*,—Mr. Chairman.—I should conceive this clause to be impolitic, if it were one of those things which could be excluded without encountering greater evils.—The Southern States would not have entered into the Union of America, without the temporary permission of that trade. And if they were excluded from the Union, the consequences might be dreadful to them and to us. We are not in a worse situation than before. That traffic is prohibited by our laws, and we may continue the prohibition. The Union in general is not in a worse situation. Under the articles of Confederation, it might be continued forever: But by this clause an end may be put to it after twenty years. There is therefore an amelioration of our circumstances. A tax may be laid in the mean time; but it is limited, otherwise Congress might lay such a tax as would amount to a prohibition. From the mode of representation and taxation, Congress cannot lay such a tax on slaves as will amount to manumission. Another clause secures us that property which we now possess. At present, if any slave elopes to any of those States where slaves are free, he becomes emancipated by their laws. For the laws of the States are uncharitable to one another in this respect. But in this Constitution, "No person held to service, or labor, in one State, under the laws thereof, escaping into another, shall in consequence of any law or regulation therein, be discharged from such service or labor; but shall be delivered up on claim of the party to whom such service or labour may be due."—This clause was expressly inserted to enable owners of slaves to reclaim them. This is a better security than any that now exists. No power is given to the General Government to interpose with respect to the property in slaves now held by the States. The taxation of this State being equal only to its representation, such a tax cannot be laid as he supposes. They cannot prevent the importation of slaves for twenty years; but after that period they can. The Gentlemen from South-Carolina and Georgia argued in this manner:—"We have now liberty to import this species of property, and much of the property now possessed, has been purchased, or otherwise acquired, in contemplation of improving it by the assistance of imported slaves. What would be the consequence of hindering us from it? The slaves of Virginia would rise in value, and we would be obliged to go to your markets." I need not expatiate on this subject. Great as the evil is, a dismemberment of the Union would be worse. If those States should disunite from the other States, for not indulging them in the temporary continuance of this traffic, they might solicit and obtain aid from foreign powers.

NEW YORK RATIFYING CONVENTION

Robert R. Livingston, Melancton Smith, and John Jay Debate Aristocracy, Representation, and Corruption

June 23, 1788

Mr. Chancellor *Livingston*. The gentleman from Dutchess appears to have misapprehended some of the ideas which dropped from me: My argument was, that a republic might very properly be formed by a league of states; but that the laws of the general legislature must act, and be enforced upon individuals. I am contending for this species of government. The gentlemen who have spoken in opposition to me, have either misunderstood or perverted my meaning: But, Sir, I flatter myself, it has not been misunderstood by the convention at large.

If we examine the history of federal republics, whose legislative powers were exercised only on states, in their collective capacity; we shall find in their fundamental principles, the seeds of domestic violence and consequent annihilation. This was the principal reason why I thought the old confederation would be forever impracticable.

Much has been said, Sir, about the number which ought to compose the house of representatives, and the question has been debated with great address by the gentlemen on both sides of the house. It is agreed, that the representative body should be so small, as to prevent the disorder inseparable from the deliberations of a mob; and yet sufficiently numerous, to represent the interests of the people; and to be a safe depository of power. There is, unfortunately, no standard, by which we can determine this matter. Gentlemen who think that a hundred may be the medium, in which the advantages of regular deliberation, and the safety of the people are united, will probably be disposed to support the plan as it stands; others,

375

who imagine that no number less than three or four hundred can ensure the preservation of liberty, will contend for an alteration. Indeed, these effects depend so much upon contingency, and upon circumstances totally unconnected with the idea of number; that we ought not to be surprized at the want of a standing criterion. On so vague a subject, it is very possible that the opinions of no two gentlemen in this assembly, if they were governed by their own original reflections, would entirely coincide. I acknowledge myself one of those who suppose the number expressed in the constitution to be about the proper medium; and yet future experience may induce me to think it too small or too large. When I consider the objects and powers of the general government, I am of an opinion that one hundred men may at all times be collected, of sufficient information and integrity, to manage well the affairs of the union. Some gentlemen suppose, that to understand and provide for the general interests of commerce and manufactures, our legislatures ought to know how all commodities are produced, from the first principle of vegetation to the last polish of mechanical labour; that they ought to be minutely acquainted with all the process of all the arts: if this were true, it would be necessary, that a great part of the British house of commons should be woolen drapers: Yet, we seldom find such characters in that celebrated assembly.

As to the idea of representing the feelings of the people, I do not entirely understand it, unless by their feelings is meant their interests. They appear to me to be the same thing. But if they have feelings which do not rise out of their interests, I think they ought not to be represented. What! Shall the unjust, the selfish, the unsocial feelings be represented? Shall the vices, the infirmities, the passions of the people be represented? Government, Sir, would be a monster: Laws made to encourage virtue and maintain peace, would have a preposterous tendency to subvert the authority and outrage the principles, on which they were founded: Besides, the feelings of the people are so variable and inconstant, that our rulers should be chosen every day: People have one sort of feelings to day, another to-morrow; and the voice of the representative must be incessantly changing in correspondence with these feelings: This would be making him a political weathercock.

The honorable gentleman from Dutchess [Mr. *Smith*] who
has so copiously declaimed against all declamation, has pointed
his artillery against the rich and the great. I am not interested
in defending rich men: But what does he mean by telling us
that the rich are vicious and intemperate. Will he presume to
point out to us the class of men in which intemperance is not
to be found? Is there less intemperence in feeding on beef than
on turtle; or in drinking rum than wine? I think the gentleman does not reason from facts: If he will look round among
the rich men of his acquaintance, I fancy he will find them as
honest and virtuous as any class in the community—He says
the rich are unfeeling—I believe they are less so than the poor:
For it seems to me probable that those who are most occupied
by their own cares and distresses, have the least sympathy with
the distresses of others. The sympathy of the poor is generally
selfish; that of the rich a more disinterested emotion.

The gentleman further observes, that ambition is peculiarly
the vice of the wealthy. But, have not all classes of men their
objects of ambition? Will not a poor man contend for a constable's staff with as much assiduity and eagerness as a man of rank
will aspire to the chief magistracy? The great offices in a state
are beyond the view of the poor and ignorant man: He will
therefore contemplate a humbler office as the highest alluring
object of ambition: He will look, with equal envy, on a successful competitor; and will equally sacrifice to the attainment of
his wishes, the duty he owes to his friends or to the public. But,
says the gentleman, the rich will be always brought forward:
They will exclusively enjoy the suffrages of the people.—For
my own part, I believe that if two men of equal abilities set out
together in life, one rich, the other of small fortune, the latter
will generally take the lead in your government. The rich are
ever objects of envy; and this, more or less, operates as a bar
to their advancement. What is the fact? Let us look around
us: I might mention gentlemen in office who have not been
advanced for their wealth; I might instance in particular the
honorable gentleman who presides over this state, who was not
promoted to the chief magistracy for his riches, but his virtue.

The gentleman, sensible of the weakness of this reasoning,
is obliged to fortify it by having recourse to the phantom aristocracy. I have heard much of this. I always considered it as the

bugbear of the party. We are told, that in every country there is a natural aristocracy, and that this aristocracy consists of the rich and the great: Nay, the gentleman goes further, and ranks in this class of men, the wise, the learned, and those eminent for their talents or great virtues. Does a man possess the confidence of his fellow-citizens for having done them important services? He is an aristocrat—Has he great integrity? Such a man will be greatly trusted; he is an aristocrat. Indeed, to determine that one is an aristocrat, we need only be assured that he is a man of merit. But, I hope we have many such—I hope, Sir, we are all aristocrats. So sensible am I of that gentleman's talents, integrity and virtue, that we might at once hail him the first of the nobles, the very prince of the Senate.—But who, in the name of common sense, will he have to represent us? Not the rich; for they are sheer aristocrats. Not the learned, the wise, the virtuous, for they are all aristocrats. Who then? Why, those who are not virtuous; those who are not wise; those who are not learned: These are the men, to whom alone we can trust our liberties. He says further we ought not to choose these aristocrats, because the people will not have confidence in them; that is, the people will not have confidence in those who best deserve and most possess their confidence. He would have his government composed of other classes of men: Where will he find them? Why, he must go out into the highways, and pick up the rogue and the robber: He must go to the hedges and ditches and bring in the poor, the blind and the lame. As the gentleman has thus settled the definition of aristocracy, I trust that no man will think it a term of reproach: For who among us would not be wise? Who would not be virtuous? Who would not be above want? How, again, would he have us guard against aristocracy? Clearly by doubling the representation, and sending twelve aristocrats, instead of six. The truth is, in these republican governments we know no such ideal distinctions.—We are all equally aristocrats. Offices, emoluments, honors are open to all.

Much has been said by the gentleman about corruption: He calculates that twenty-four may give the voice of Congress.—That is, they will compose a bare majority of a bare quorum of both houses. He supposes here the most singular, and I might add, the most improbable combination of events: First, there is to be a power in the government who has the means, and whose interest it is to corrupt—Next, twenty-four men are to compose the legislature; and these twenty-four, selected by their fellow citizens as the most virtuous, are all, in violation of their oath and their real interests, to be corrupted. Then he supposes the virtuous minority inattentive, regardless of their own honor, and the good of their country; making no alarm, no struggle: A whole people, suffering the injury of a ruinous law, yet ignorant, inactive, and taking no measures to redress the grievance.

Let us take a view of the present Congress. The gentleman is satisfied with our present federal government, on the score of corruption. Here he has confidence: Though each state may delegate seven, they generally send no more than three; consequently, thirty-nine men may transact any business under the old government; while, the new legislature, which will be in all probability constantly full, will consist of ninety-one. But, say the gentlemen, our present Congress have not the same powers.—I answer they have the very same. Congress have the power of making war and peace, of levying money and raising men; they involve us in a war at their pleasure; they may negociate loans to any extent, and make unlimited demands upon the states. Here, the gentleman comes forward, and says, that the states are to carry these powers into execution; and they have the power of non-compliance. But is not every state bound to comply? What power have they to controul Congress in the exercise of those rights, which they have pledged themselves to support? It is true, they have broken, in numerous instances, the compact by which they were obligated; and they may do it again: But, will the gentleman draw an argument of security from the facility of violating their faith? Suppose there should be a majority of creditor states, under the present government; might they not combine and compel us to observe the covenant, by which we had bound ourselves?

We are told, that this constitution gives Congress the power over the purse and the sword. Sir, have not all good governments this power? Nay, does any one doubt, that under the old confederation, Congress holds the purse and the sword? How many loans did they procure, which we are bound to pay? How many men did they raise, which we were bound to maintain?

How will gentlemen say, that that body, which indeed is extremely small, can be more safely trusted than a much larger body, possessed of the same authority?—What is the ground of such entire confidence in the one—what the cause of so much jealousy of the other?

An honorable member from New-York, has viewed the subject of representation in a point of light which had escaped me; and which I think clear and conclusive. He says, that the state of Delaware must have one; and as that state will not probably increase for a long time, it will be the interest of the larger states to determine the ratio, by the number which Delaware contains. The gentlemen in opposition say, suppose Delaware contains fifty thousand, why not fix the ratio at sixty thousand? Clearly, because by this, the other states will give up a sixth part of their interests. The members of Congress, also, from a more private motive, will be induced to augment the representation. The chance of their own re-election will increase with the number of their colleagues.

It has been further observed, that the sense of the people is for a larger representation; and that this ought to govern us:— That the people generally are of opinion, that even our House of Assembly is too small.—I very much doubt this fact. As far as my observation has extended, I have found a very different sentiment prevail. It seems to be the predominant opinion, that sixty-five is fully equal, if not superior to the exigencies of our state government: And I presume, that the people have as much confidence in their Senate of twenty-four, as in their Assembly of sixty five. All these considerations have united to give my mind the most perfect conviction, that the number specified in the constitution, is fully adequate to the present wants and circumstances of our country; and that this number will be increased to the satisfaction of the most timid and jealous.

Honorable Mr. *Smith.* I did not intend to make any more observations on this article. Indeed, I have heard nothing to day, which has not been suggested before, except the polite reprimand I have received for my declamation. I should not have risen again, but to examine who proved himself the greatest declaimer. The gentleman wishes me to describe what I meant, by representing the feelings of the people. If I recollect right, I said the representative ought to understand, and govern his conduct by the true interest of the people.—I believe I stated this idea precisely. When he attempts to explain my ideas, he explains them away to nothing; and instead of answering, he distorts, and then sports with them. But he may rest assured, that in the present spirit of the Convention, to irritate is not the way to conciliate. The gentleman, by the false gloss he has given to my argument, makes me an enemy to the rich: This is not true. All I said, was, that mankind were influenced, in a great degree, by interests and prejudices:—That men, in different ranks of life, were exposed to different temptations—and that ambition was more peculiarly the passion of the rich and great. The gentleman supposes the poor have less sympathy with the sufferings of their fellow creatures; for that those who feel most distress themselves, have the least regard to the misfortunes of others:—Whether this be reasoning or declamation, let all who hear us determine. I observed that the rich were more exposed to those temptations, which rank and power hold out to view; that they were more luxurious and intemperate, because they had more fully the means of enjoyment; that they were more ambitious, because more in the hope of success. The gentleman says my principle is not true; for that a poor man will be as ambitious to be a constable, as a rich man to be a governor:—But he will not injure his country so much by the party he creates to support his ambition.

The next object of the gentleman's ridicule is my idea of an aristocracy; and he indeed has done me the honor, to rank me in the order. If then I am an aristocrat, and yet publicly caution my countrymen against the encroachments of the aristocrats, they will surely consider me as one of their most disinterested friends. My idea of aristocracy is not new:—It is embraced by many writers on government:—I would refer the gentleman for a definition of it to the honorable *John Adams*, one of our natural aristocrats. This writer will give him a description the most ample and satisfactory. But I by no means intended to carry my idea of it to such a ridiculous length as the gentleman would have me; nor will any of my expressions warrant the construction he imposes on them. My argument was, that in order to have a true and genuine representation, you must receive the middling class of people into your government—such as compose the body of this assembly. I observed, that a representation from the United States could not be so constituted, as to represent completely the feelings and interests of the people; but that we ought to come as near this object as possible. The gentlemen say, that the exactly proper number of representatives is so indeterminate and vague, that it is impossible for them to ascertain it with any precision. But surely, they are able to see the distinction between twenty and thirty. I acknowledged that a complete representation would make the legislature too numerous; and therefore, it is our duty to limit the powers, and form checks on the government, in proportion to the smallness of the number.

The honorable gentleman next animadverts on my apprehensions of corruption, and instances the present Congress, to prove an absurdity in my argument. But is this fair reasoning? There are many material checks to the operations of that body, which the future Congress will not have. In the first place, they are chosen annually:—What more powerful check! They are subject to recal: Nine states must agree to any important resolution, which will not be carried into execution, till it meets the approbation of the people in the state legislatures. Admitting what he says, that they have pledged their faith to support the acts of Congress: yet, if these be contrary to the essential interests of the people, they ought not to be acceded to for they are not bound to obey any law, which tends to destroy them.

It appears to me, that had economy been a motive for making the representation small; it might have operated more properly in leaving out some of the offices which this constitution requires. I am sensible that a great many of the common people, who do not reflect, imagine that a numerous representation involves a great expence:—But they are not aware of the real security it gives to an œconomical management in all the departments of government.

The gentleman further declared, that as far his acquaintance extended, the people thought sixty-five a number fully large enough for our State Assembly; and hence inferred, that sixty-five is to two hundred and forty thousand, as sixty-five is to three millions.—This is curious reasoning.

I feel that I have troubled the committee too long. I should not indeed have risen again upon this subject, had not my ideas been grossly misrepresented.

The honorable Mr. *Jay*. I will make a few observations on this article, Mr. Chairman, though I am sensible it may not appear very useful to travel over the field, which has been already so fully explored.

Sir, it seems to be on all sides agreed, that a strong, energetic, federal government, is necessary for the United States. It has given me pleasure to hear such declarations come from all parts of the house. If gentlemen are of this opinion, they give us to understand that such a government is the favorite object of their desire; and also that it can be instituted; That, indeed, it is both necessary and practicable; or why do they advocate it.

The gentleman last on the floor, has informed us, that according to his idea of a complete representation, the extent of our country is too great for it.—[Here he called on Mr. *Smith*, to know if he had mistaken him; who replied—My idea is not that a proper representation for a strong federal government is unattainable; but that such a representation, under the proposed constitution, is impracticable.] Sir, continued Mr. *Jay*, I now understand the gentleman in a different sense—However, what I shall say will reach equally his explanation. I take it, that no federal government is worth having, unless it can provide for the general interests of the United States. If this constitution be so formed as to answer these purposes, our object is obtained. The providing for the general interests of the Union requires certain powers in government, which the gentleman seems to be willing it should possess; that is, the important powers of war and peace. These powers are peculiarly interesting—Their operation reaches objects the most dear to the people; and every man is concerned in them. Yet; for the exercise of these powers the gentleman does not think a very large representation necessary: But, Sir, if the proposed constitution provides for a representation adequate to the purposes I have described, why not adequate to all other purposes of a federal government? The adversaries of the plan seem to consider the general government, as possessing all the minute

and local powers of the state governments. The direct inference from this, according to their principle, would be that the
federal representation should be proportionably large: In this
state, as the gentleman says, we have sixty-five: If the national
representation is to be extended in proportion, what an un-
wieldy body shall we have! If the United States contain three
millions of inhabitants, in this ratio, the Congress must consist
of more than eight hundred. But, Sir, let us examine whether
such a number is necessary or reasonable—What are the objects
of our state legislatures? Innumerable things of small moment
occupy their attention—matters of a private nature, which require much minute and local information. The objects of the
general government are not of this nature—They comprehend
the interests of the States in relation to each other, and in relation to foreign powers. Surely there are many men in this state,
fully informed of the general interests of its trade, its agriculture, its manufactures: Is any thing more than this necessary? Is
it requisite that our representatives in Congress should possess
any particular knowledge of the local interests of the county of
Suffolk, distinguished from those of Orange and Ulster? The
Senate is to be composed of men, appointed by the state legislatures: They will certainly choose those who are most distinguished for their general knowledge: I presume they will also
instruct them; that there will be a constant correspondence
supported between the senators and the state executives, who
will be able, from time to time, to afford them all that particular information, which particular circumstances may require. I
am in favour of large representations: Yet, as the minds of the
people are so various on this subject, I think it best to let things
stand as they are. The people in Massachusetts are satisfied with
two hundred: The gentlemen require three hundred: Many
others suppose either number unnecessarily large.—There is
no point on which men's opinions vary more materially. If
the matter be doubtful, and much may be rationally said on
both sides, gentlemen ought not to be very strenuous on such
points. The convention, who decided this question, took all
these different opinions into consideration, and were directed
by a kind of necessity of mutual accommodation, and by reasons of expediency: It would therefore be unfair to censure
them. Were I asked if the number corresponds exactly with

my own private judgment, I should answer, no.—But I think it is best, under our present circumstances, to acquiesce. Yet, Sir, if I could be convinced that danger would probably result from so small a number, I should certainly withhold my acquiescence—But whence will this danger arise? Sir, I am not fearful of my countrymen: We have yet known very little of corruption:—We have already experienced great distresses and difficulties: We have seen perilous times; when it was the interest of Great-Britain to hold out the most seducing temptations to every man worth gaining. I mention this as a circumstance to shew, that in case of a war with any foreign power, there can be little fear of corruption; and I mention it to the honor of the American character.—At the time I allude to, how many men had you in Congress? Generally fewer than sixty-five.

Sir, all the arguments offered on the other side serve to shew, that it will be easier to corrupt under the old, than under the new government: Such arguments, therefore, do not seem to answer the gentleman's purpose. In the federal government, as it now stands, there are but thirteen votes, though there may be sixty or seventy voices.—Now, what is the object of corruption? To gain votes. In the new government there are to be ninety-one votes. Is it easier to buy many than a few? In the present Congress, you cannot declare war, make peace, or do any other important act, without the concurrence of nine states. There are rarely more than nine present. A full Congress is an extraordinary thing. Is it necessary to declare war, or pass a requisition for money to support it? A foreign Prince says, this will be against my interest—I must prevent it—How? By having recourse to corruption. If there are eleven states on the floor, it will be necessary to corrupt three: What measure shall I take? Why, it is common for each state to have no more than two members in Congress. I will take off one, and the vote of that state is lost: I will take off three, and their most important plan is defeated. Thus in the old government, it is only necessary to bribe the few: In the new government, it is only necessary to corrupt the many. Where lies the greater security? The gentleman says, the election is annual, and you may recall your delegates when you please. But how are you to form your opinion of his conduct? He may excuse himself from acting, without giving any reason. Nay, on a particular emergency, he has only to go home, for which he may have a thousand plausible reasons to offer, and you have no mode of compelling his attendance.—To detect corruption is at all times difficult; but, under these circumstances, it appears almost impossible. I give out these hints to shew, that on the score of corruption, we have much the best chance under the new constitution: and that if we do not reach perfection, we certainly change for the better. But, Sir, suppose corruption should infect one branch of the government, for instance, the house of representatives; what a powerful check you have in the senate! You have a double security—You have two chances in your favor to one against you. The two houses will naturally be in a state of rivalship: This will make them always vigilant, quick to discern a bad measure, and ready to oppose it. Thus the chance of corruption is not only lessened by an increase of the number, but vastly diminished by the necessity of concurrence. This is the peculiar excellence of a division of the legislature.

Sir, I argue from plain facts—Here is no sophistry; no construction; no false glosses, but simple inferences from the obvious operation of things. We did not come here to carry points. If the gentleman will convince me I am wrong, I will submit. I mean to give them my ideas frankly upon the subject. If my reasoning is not good, let them shew me the folly of it. It is from this reciprocal interchange of ideas, that the truth must come out. My earnest wish is, that we may go home attended with the pleasing consciousness that we have industriously and candidly sought the truth, and have done our duty. I cannot conclude, without repeating, that though I prefer a large representation, yet considering our present situation, I see abundant reason to acquiesce in the wisdom of the general convention, and to rest satisfied, that the representation will increase in a sufficient degree, to answer the wishes of the most zealous advocates for liberty.

The hon. Mr. *Smith* rose and said. It appeared to him probable, that it would be the interest of the state having the least number of inhabitants, to make its whole number the measure of the representation: That it would be the interest of Delaware, supposing she has forty thousand, and consequently only one vote, to make this whole number the ratio: So, if she had fifty thousand, or any number under sixty thousand. The interest also of some other of the small states would correspond with hers; and thus, the representation would be reduced in proportion to the increase of Delaware. He still insisted, that the number of representatives might be diminished.

He would make one observation more, upon the gentleman's idea of corruption. His reasoning, he said, went only to prove that the present Congress might be restrained from doing good, by the wilful absence of two or three members. It was rare, he said, that the people were oppressed by a government's not doing; and little danger to liberty could flow from that source.

Melancton Smith Fears
the Federal Taxing Power

June 27, 1788

The hon. Mr. *Smith* rose.—We are now come to a part of the system, which requires our utmost attention, and most careful investigation. It is necessary that the powers vested in government should be precisely defined, that the people may be able to know whether it moves in the circle of the constitution. It is the more necessary in governments like the one under examination; because Congress here is to be considered as only part of a complex system. The state governments are necessary for certain local purposes; The general government for national purposes: The latter ought to rest on the former, not only in its form, but in its operations. It is therefore of the highest importance, that the line of jurisdiction should be accurately drawn: It is necessary, sir, in order to maintain harmony between the governments, and to prevent the constant interference which must either be the cause of perpetual differences, or oblige one to yield, perhaps unjustly, to the other. I conceive the system cannot operate well, unless it is so contrived, as to preserve harmony. If this be not done, in every contest, the weak must submit to the strong. The clause before us is of the greatest importance: It respects the very vital principle of government: The power is the most efficient and comprehensive that can be delegated; and seems in some measure to answer for all others. I believe it will appear evident, that money must be raised for the support of both governments: If therefore you give to one or the other, a power which may in its operation become exclusive; it is obvious, that one can exist only at the will of the other; and must ultimately be sacrificed. The powers of the general government extend to the raising of money, in all possible ways, except by duties on exports; to the laying taxes on imports, lands, buildings, and even on persons. The individual states in time will be allowed to raise no money at all: The United States will have a right to raise money from every quarter. The general government has moreover this advantage.

All disputes relative to jurisdiction must be decided in a federal court.

It is a general maxim, that all governments find a use for as much money as they can raise. Indeed they have commonly demands for more: Hence it is, that all, as far as we are acquainted, are in debt. I take this to be a settled truth, that they will all spend as much as their revenue; that is, will live at least up to their income. Congress will ever exercise their powers, to levy as much money as the people can pay. They will not be restrained from direct taxes, by the consideration that necessity does not require them. If they forbear, it will be because the people cannot answer their demands. There will be no possibility of preventing the clashing of jurisdictions, unless some system of accomodation is formed. Suppose taxes are laid by both governments on the same article: It seems to me impossible, that they can operate with harmony. I have no more conception that in taxation two powers can act together; than that two bodies can occupy the same place. They will therefore not only interfere; but they will be hostile to each other. Here are to be two lists of all kinds of officers—supervisors, assessors, constables, &c. imployed in this business. It is unnecessary that I should enter into a minute detail, to prove that these complex powers cannot operate peaceably together, and without one being overpowered by the other. One day, the continental collector calls for the tax; He seizes a horse: The next day, the state collector comes, procures a replevin and retakes the horse, to satisfy the state tax. I just mention this, to shew that people will not submit to such a government, and that finally it must defeat itself.

It must appear evident, that there will be a constant jarring of claims and interests. Now will the states in this contest stand any chance of success? If they will, there is less necessity for our amendment. But, consider the superior advantages of the general government: Consider their extensive, exclusive revenues; the vast sums of money they can command, and the means they thereby possess of supporting a powerful standing force. The states, on the contrary, will not have the command of a shilling, or a soldier. The two governments will be like two men contending for a certain property: The one has no interest but that which is the subject of the controversy; while the other has money enough to carry on the law-suit for twenty years. By this clause unlimited powers in taxation are given: Another clause declares, that Congress shall have power to make all laws necessary to carry the constitution into effect. Nothing therefore is left to construction; but the powers are most express. How far the state legislature will be able to command a revenue, every man, on viewing the subject, can determine. If he contemplates the ordinary operation of causes, he will be convinced that the powers of the confederacy will swallow up those of the members. I do not suppose that this effect will be brought about suddenly—As long as the people feel universally and strongly attached to the state governments, Congress will not be able to accomplish it: If they act prudently, their powers will operate and be increased by degrees. The tendency of taxation, tho' it be moderate, is to lessen the attachment of the citizens—If it becomes oppressive, it will certainly destroy their confidence. While the general taxes are sufficiently heavy, every attempt of the states to enhance them, will be considered as a tyrannical act, and the people will lose their respect and affection for a government, which cannot support itself, without the most grievous impositions upon them. If the constitution is accepted as it stands, I am convinced, that in seven years as much will be laid against the state governments, as is now said in favour of the proposed system.

Sir, I contemplate the abolition of the state constitutions as an event fatal to the liberties of America. These liberties will not be violently wrested from the people; they will be undermined and gradually consumed. On subjects of this kind we cannot be too critical. The investigation is difficult, because we have no examples to serve as guides. The world has never seen such a government over such a country. If we consult authorities in this matter, they will declare the impracticability of governing a free people, on such an extensive plan. In a country, where a portion of the people live more than twelve hundred miles from the center, I think that one body cannot possibly legislate for the whole. Can the legislature frame a system of taxation that will operate with uniform advantages? Can they carry any system into execution? Will it not give occasion for an innumerable swarm of officers, to infest our country and consume our substance? People will be subject to impositions, which they cannot support, and of which their complaints can never reach the government.

Another idea is in my mind, which I think conclusive against a simple government for the United States. It is not possible to collect a set of representatives, who are acquainted with all parts of the continent. Can you find men in Georgia who are acquainted with the situation of New-Hampshire? Who know what taxes will best suit the inhabitants; and how much they are able to bear? Can the best men make laws for a people of whom they are entirely ignorant? Sir, we have no reason to hold our state governments in contempt, or to suppose them incapable of acting wisely. I believe they have operated more beneficially than most people expected, who considered that those governments were erected in a time of war and confusion, when they were very liable to errors in their structure. It will be a matter of astonishment to all unprejudiced men hereafter, who shall reflect upon our situation, to observe to what a great degree good government has prevailed. It is true some bad laws have been passed in most of the states; but they arose more from the difficulty of the times, than from any want of honesty or wisdom. Perhaps there never was a government, which in the course of ten years did not do something to be repented of. As for Rhode-Island, I do not mean to justify her—She deserves to be condemned—If there were in the world but one example of political depravity, it would be her's: And no nation ever merited or suffered a more genuine infamy, than a wicked administration has attached to her character. Massachusetts also has been guilty of errors: and has lately been distracted by an internal convulsion. Great-Britain, notwithstanding her boasted constitution, has been a perpetual scene of revolutions and civil war—Her parliaments have been abolished: her kings have been banished and murdered. I assert that the majority of the governments in the union have operated better than any body had reason to expect: and that nothing but experience and habit is wanting, to give the state laws all the stability and wisdom necessary to make them respectable. If these things be true, I think we ought not to exchange our condition, with a hazard of losing our state constitutions. We all agree that a general government is necessary: But it ought not to go so far, as to destroy the authority of the members. We shall be unwise, to make a new experiment in so important a matter, without some known and sure grounds to go upon. The state constitutions should be the guardians of our domestic rights and interests; and should be both the support and the check of the federal government. The want of the means of raising a general revenue has been the principal cause of our difficulties. I believe no man will doubt that if our present Congress had money enough, there would be few complaints of their weakness. Requisitions have perhaps been too much condemned. What has been their actual operation? Let us attend to experience, and see if they are such poor, unproductive things, as is commonly supposed. If I calculate right, the requisitions for the ten years past, have amounted to thirty-six millions of dollars; of which twenty-four millions, or two thirds, have been actually paid. Does not this fact warrant a conclusion that some reliance is to be placed on this mode? Besides, will any gentleman say that the states have generally been able to collect more than two thirds of their taxes from the people? The delinquency of some states has arisen from the fluctuations of paper money, &c. Indeed it is my decided opinion, that no government in the difficult circumstances, which we have passed thro', will be able to realize more than two thirds of the taxes it imposes. I might suggest two other considerations which have weight with me—There has probably been more money called for, than was actually wanted, on the expectation of delinquencies; and it is equally probable, that in a short course of time the increasing ability of the country will render requisitions a much more efficient mode of raising a revenue. The war left the people under very great burthens, and oppressed with both public and private debts. They are now fast emerging from their difficulties. Many individuals without doubt still feel great inconveniences; but they will find a gradual remedy. Sir, has any country which has suffered distresses like ours, exhibited within a few years, more striking marks of improvement and prosperity? How its population has grown; How its agriculture, commerce and manufactures have been extended and improved! How many forests have been cut down; How many wastes have been cleared and cultivated; How many additions have been made to the extent and beauty of our towns and cities! I think our advancement has been rapid. In a few years, it is to be hoped, that we shall be relieved from our embarrassments; and unless new, calamities come upon us, shall be flourishing and happy. Some difficulties will ever occur in the collection of taxes by any mode whatever. Some states will pay more; some less. If New-York lays a tax, will not one county or district furnish more, another less than its proportion? The same will happen to the United States, as happens in New-York, and in every other country.—Let them impose a duty equal and uniform—those districts, where there is plenty of money, will pay punctually: Those, in which money is scarce, will be in some measure delinquent. The idea that Congress ought to have unlimited powers, is entirely novel; I never heard of it, till the meeting of this convention. The general government once called on the states, to invest them with the command of funds adequate to the exigencies of the union: but they did not ask to command all the resources of the states—They did not wish to have a controul over all the property of the people. If we now give them this controul, we may as well give up the state governments with it. I have no notion of setting the two powers at variance; nor would I give a farthing for a government, which could not command a farthing. On the whole, it appears to me probable, that unless some certain, specific source of revenue is reserved to the states, their governments, with their independence will be totally annihilated.

NORTH CAROLINA RATIFYING CONVENTION

James Iredell on the Presidency and the Pardoning Power

July 28, 1788

The second section of the second article read.

Mr. *Iredell*—Mr. Chairman, This part of the Constitution has been much objected to. The office of superintending the execution of the laws of the union, is an office of the utmost importance. It is of the greatest consequence to the happiness of the people of America, that the person to whom this great trust is delegated should be worthy of it. It would require a man of abilities and experience: It would also require a man who possessed in a high degree the confidence of his country. This being the case, it would be a great defect in forming a Constitution for the United States, if it was so constructed that by any accident an improper person could have a chance to obtain that office. The Committee will recollect, that the President is to be elected by Electors appointed by each state, according to the number of Senators and Representatives to which the state may be entitled in the Congress: That they are to meet on the same day throughout all the states, and vote by ballot for two persons, one of whom shall not be an inhabitant of the same state with themselves. These votes are afterwards to be transmitted under seal to the seat of the general government. The person who has the greatest number of votes, if it be a majority of the whole, will be the President. If more than one have a majority, and equal votes, the House of Representatives are to choose one of them. If none have a majority of votes, then the House of Representatives are to choose which of the persons they think proper, out of the five highest on the list. The person having the next greatest number of votes is to be the Vice President, unless two or more should have equal votes, in which case the Senate is to choose one of them for Vice-President. If I recollect right, these are the principal characteristics. Thus, Sir, two men will be in office at the same time. The President, who possesses in the highest degree the confidence of his country; and the Vice-President, who is thought to be the next person in the union most fit to perform this trust. Here, Sir, every contingency is provided for. No faction or combination can bring about the election. It is probable, that the choice will always fall upon a man of experienced abilities and fidelity. In all human probability, no better mode of election could have been devised.

The rest of the first section read without any observations.

Second section read.

Mr. *Iredell*—Mr. Chairman, I was in hopes that some other gentleman would have spoken to this clause. It conveys very important powers, and ought not to be passed by. I beg leave in as few words as possible to speak my sentiments upon it. I believe most of the Governors of the different states, have powers similar to those of the President. In almost every country the Executive has the command of the military forces. From the nature of the thing, the command of armies ought to be delegated to one person only. The secrecy, dispatch and decision which are necessary in military operations, can only be expected from one person. The President therefore is to command the military forces of the United States, and this power I think a proper one; at the same time it will be found to be sufficiently guarded. A very material difference may be observed between this power, and the authority of the King of Great-Britain under similar circumstances. The King of Great-Britain is not only the Commander in Chief of the land and naval forces, but has power in time of war to raise fleets and armies. He has also authority to declare war. The President has not the power of declaring war by his own authority, nor that of raising fleets and armies: These powers are vested in other hands. The power of declaring war is expressly given to Congress, that is, to the two branches of the Legislature, the Senate composed of Representatives of the state Legislatures, the House of Representatives deputed by the people at large.

They have also expressly delegated to them, the powers of raising and supporting armies, and of providing and maintaining a navy.

With regard to the militia, it must be observed, that though he has the command of them when called into the actual service of the United States, yet he has not the power of calling them out. The power of calling them out, is vested in Congress, for the purpose of executing the laws of the union. When the militia are called out for any purpose, some person must command them; and who so proper as that person who has the best evidence of his possessing the general confidence of the people? I trust therefore, that the power of commanding the militia when called forth into the actual service of the United States, will not be objected to.

The next part which says, "That he may require the opinion in writing of the principal officers," is in some degree substituted for a Council. He is only to consult them if he thinks proper. Their opinion is to be given him in writing. By this means he will be aided by their intelligence, and the necessity of their opinions being in writing, will render them more cautious in giving them, and make them responsible should they give advice manifestly improper. This does not diminish the responsibility of the President himself. They might otherwise have colluded, and opinions have been given too much under his influence.

It has been the opinion of many gentlemen, that the President should have a Council. This opinion probably has been derived from the example in England. It would be very proper for every gentleman to consider attentively, whether that example ought to be imitated by us. Altho' it be a respectable example, yet in my opinion very satisfactory reasons can be assigned for a departure from it in this Constitution.

It was very difficult, immediately on our separation from Great-Britain, to disengage ourselves entirely from ideas of government we had been used to. We had been accustomed to a Council under the old government, and took it for granted we ought to have one under the new. But examples ought not to be implicitly followed; and the reasons which prevail in Great-Britain for a Council, do not apply equally to us. In that country the executive authority is vested in a magistrate who holds it by birth-right. He has great powers and prerogatives; and it is a constitutional maxim, *that he can do no wrong*. We have experienced that he can do wrong, yet no man can say so in his own country. There are no courts to try him for any crimes; nor is there any constitutional method of depriving him of his throne. If he loses it, it must be by a general resistance of his people contrary to *forms* of law, as at the revolution which took place about a hundred years ago. It is therefore of the utmost moment in that country, that whoever is the instrument of any act of government should be personally responsible for it, since the King is not; and for the same reason, that no act of government should be exercised but by the instrumentality of some person, who can be accountable for it. Every thing therefore that the King does must be by some *advice*, and the adviser of course answerable. Under our Constitution we are much happier. No man has an authority to injure another with impunity. No man is better than his fellow-citizens, nor can pretend to any superiority over the meanest man in the country. If the President does a single act, by which the people are prejudiced, he is punishable himself, and no other man merely to screen him. If he commits any misdemeanor in office, he is impeachable, removable from office, and incapacitated to hold any office of honour, trust or profit. If he commits any crime, he is punishable by the laws of his country, and in capital cases may be deprived of his life. This being the case, there is not the same reason here for having a Council, which exists in England. It is, however, much to be desired, that a man who has such extensive and important business to perform, should have the means of some assistance to enable him to discharge his arduous employment. The advice of the principal executive officers, which he can at all times command, will in my opinion answer this valuable purpose. He can at no time want advice, if he desires it, as the principal officers will always be on the spot. Those officers from their abilities and experience, will probably be able to give as good, if not better advice, than any Counsellors would do; and the solemnity of the advice in writing, which must be preserved, would be a great check upon them.

Besides these considerations, it was difficult for the Convention to prepare a Council that would be unexceptionable. That jealousy which naturally exists between the different states, enhanced this difficulty. If a few Counsellors were to be chosen from the northern, southern or middle states, or from a few states only, undue preference might be given to those particular states from which they should come. If to avoid this difficulty, one Counsellor should be sent from each state, this would require great expence, which is a consideration at this time of much moment, especially as it is probable, that by the method proposed, the President may be equally well advised without any expence at all.

We ought also to consider, that had he a Council, by whose advice he was bound to act, his responsibility in all such cases must be destroyed. You surely would not oblige him to follow their advice, and punish him for obeying it. If called upon on any occasion of dislike, it would be natural for him to say, "You know my Council are men of integrity and ability: I could not act against their opinions, though I confess my own was contrary to theirs." This, Sir, would be pernicious. In such a situation, he might easily combine with his Council, and it might be impossible to fix a fact upon him. It would be difficult often to know, whether the President or Counsellors were most to blame. A thousand plausible excuses might be made, which would escape detection. But the method proposed in the Constitution creates no such embarrassment. It is plain and open. And the President will personally have the credit of good, or the censure of bad measures; since, though he may ask advice, he is to use his own judgment in following or rejecting it. For all these reasons I am clearly of opinion, that the clause is better as it stands than if the President were to have a Council. I think every good that can be derived from the institution of a Council, may be expected from the advice of these officers, without its being liable to the disadvantages to which it appears to me the institution of a Council would be.

Another power that he has is to grant pardons, except in cases of impeachment. I believe it is the sense of a great part of America, that this power should be exercised by their Governors. It is in several states on the same footing that it is here. It is the genius of a republican government, that the laws should be rigidly executed without the influence of favour or ill-will: That when a man commits a crime, however powerful he or his friends may be, yet he should be punished for it; and on the other hand, though he should be universally hated by his country, his real guilt alone as to the particular charge is to operate against him. This strict and scrupulous observance of justice is proper in all governments, but it is particularly indispensable in a republican one; because in such a government, the law is superior to every man, and no man is superior to another. But though this general principle be unquestionable, surely there is no gentleman in the committee, who is not aware that there ought to be exceptions to it; because there may be many instances, where though a man offends against the *letter* of the law, yet peculiar circumstances in his case may entitle him to mercy. It is impossible for any general law to foresee and provide for all possible cases that may arise, and therefore an inflexible adherence to it in every instance, might frequently be the cause of very great injustice. For this reason, such a power ought to exist somewhere; and where could it be more properly vested, than in a man who had received such strong proofs of his possessing the highest confidence of the people? This power however only refers to offences against the United States, and not against particular states. Another reason for the President possessing this authority, is this: It is often necessary to convict a man by means of his accomplices: We have sufficient experience of that in this country. A criminal would often go unpunished, were not this method to be pursued against him. In my opinion, till an accomplice's own danger is removed, his evidence ought to be regarded with great diffidence. If in civil causes of property, a witness must be entirely disinterested, how much more proper is it he should be so in cases of life and death! This power is naturally vested in the President, because it is his duty to watch over the public safety, and as that may frequently require the evidence of accomplices to bring great offenders to justice, he ought to be entrusted with the most effectual means of procuring it.

I beg leave farther to observe, that for another reason I think there is a propriety in leaving this power to the general discretion of the executive magistrate, rather than to fetter it in any manner which has been proposed. It may happen, that many men, upon plausible pretences, may be seduced into very dangerous measures against their country. They may aim by an insurrection to redress imaginary grievances, at the same time believing, upon false suggestions, that their exertions are necessary to save their country from destruction. Upon cool reflection however, they possibly are convinced of their error, and clearly see thro' the treachery and villainy of their leaders. In this situation, if the President possessed the power of pardoning, they probably would immediately throw themselves on the equity of the government, and the whole body be peaceably broke up. Thus, at a critical moment, the President might prevent perhaps a civil war. But if there was no authority to pardon, in that delicate exigency, what would be the consequence? The principle of self-preservation would prevent their parting. Would it not be natural for them to say, "We shall be punished if we disband. Were we sure of mercy we would peaceably part. But we know not that there is any chance of this. We may as well meet one kind of death as another. We may as well die in the field as at the gallows." I therefore submit to the committee, if this power be not highly necessary for such a purpose. We have seen a happy instance of the good effect of such an exercise of mercy in the state of Massachusetts, where very lately there was so formidable an insurrection. I believe a great majority of the insurgents were drawn into it by false artifices. They at length saw their error, and were willing to disband. Government, by a wise exercise of lenity, after having shewn its power, generally granted a pardon; and the whole party were dispersed. There is now as much peace in that country as in any state in the union.

A particular instance which occurs to me, shews the utility of this power very strongly. Suppose we were involved in war. It would be then necessary to know the designs of the enemy. This kind of knowledge cannot always be procured but by means of *spies*, a set of wretches whom all nations despise, but whom all employ; and as they would assuredly be used against us, a principle of self defence would urge and justify the use of them on our part. Suppose therefore the President could prevail upon a man of some importance to go over to the enemy, in order to give him secret information of his measures. He goes off privately to the enemy. He feigns resentment against his country for some ill usage, either real or pretended, and is received possibly into favour and confidence. The people would not know the purpose for which he was employed. In the mean time he secretly informs the President of the enemy's designs, and by this means, perhaps those designs are counteracted, and the country saved from destruction. After his business is executed, he returns into his own country, where the people, not knowing he had rendered them any service, are naturally exasperated against him for his supposed treason. I would ask any gentleman whether the President ought not to have the power of pardoning this man. Suppose the concurrence of the Senate, or any other body was necessary, would this obnoxious person be properly safe? We know in every country there is a strong prejudice against the executive authority. If a prejudice of this kind, on such an occasion, prevailed against the President, the President might be suspected of being influenced by corrupt motives, and the application in favour of this man be rejected. Such a thing might very possibly happen when the prejudices of party were strong, and therefore no man so clearly entitled as in the case I have supposed, ought to have his life exposed to so hazardous a contingency.

The power of impeachment is given by this Constitution, to bring great offenders to punishment. It is calculated to bring them to punishment for crimes which it is not easy to describe, but which every one must be convinced is a high crime and misdemeanor against the government. This power is lodged in those who represent the great body of the people, because the occasion for its exercise will arise from acts of great injury to the community, and the objects of it may be such as cannot be easily reached by an ordinary tribunal. The trial belongs to the Senate, lest an inferior tribunal should be too much awed by so powerful an accuser. After a trial thus solemnly conducted, it is not probable that it would happen once in a thousand times, that a man actually convicted, would be entitled to mercy; and if the President had the power of pardoning in such a case, this great check upon high officers of state would lose much of its influence. It seems therefore proper, that the general power of pardoning should be abridged in this particular instance. The punishment annexed to conviction on impeachment, can only be removal from office, and disqualification to hold any place of honour, trust or profit. But the person convicted is further liable to a trial at common law, and may receive such common law punishment as belongs to a description of such offences, if it be one punishable by that law. I hope, for the reasons I have stated, that the whole of this clause will be approved by the committee. The regulations altogether, in my opinion, are as wisely contrived as they could be. It is impossible for imperfect beings to form a perfect system. If the present one may be productive of possible inconveniences, we are not to reject it for that reason, but inquire whether any other system could be devised which would be attended with fewer inconveniences, in proportion to the advantages resulting. But we ought to be exceedingly attentive in examining, and still more cautious in deciding, lest we should condemn what may be worthy of applause, or approve of what may be exceptionable. I hope, that in the explanation of this clause, I have not improperly taken up the time of the committee.

James Iredell on Impeachment

Mr. *Iredell*—Mr. Chairman, The objections to this clause deserve great consideration. I believe it will be easy to obviate the objections against it, and that it will be found to have been necessary, for the reasons stated by the gentleman from Halifax, to vest this power in some body composed of Representatives of states, where their voices should be equal: For in this case the sovereignty of the states is particularly concerned; and the great caution of giving the states an equality of suffrage in making treaties, was for the express purpose of taking care of that sovereignty, and attending to their interests, as political bodies, in foreign negociations. It is objected to as improper, because if the President or Senate should abuse their trust, there is not sufficient responsibility, since he can only be tried by the Senate, by whose advice he acted; and the Senate cannot be tried at all. I beg leave to observe, that when any man is impeached, it must be for an error of the heart, and not of the head. God forbid, that a man in any country in the world, should be liable to be punished for want of judgment. This is not the case here. As to errors of the heart there is sufficient responsibility. Should these be committed, there is a ready way to bring him to punishment. This is a responsibility which answers every purpose that could be desired by a people jealous of their liberty. I presume that if the President, with the advice of the Senate, should make a treaty with a foreign power, and that treaty should be deemed unwise, or against the interest of the country, yet if nothing could be objected against it but the difference of opinion between them and their constituents, they could not justly be obnoxious to punishment. If they were punishable for exercising their own judgment, and not that of their constituents, no man who regarded his reputation would accept the office either of a Senator or President. Whatever mistake a man may make, he ought not to be punished for it, nor his posterity rendered infamous. But if a man be a villain, and wilfully abuses his trust, he is to be held up as a public offender, and ignominiously punished.

A public officer ought not to act from a principle of fear. Were he punishable for want of judgment, he would be continually in dread. But when he knows that nothing but real guilt can disgrace him, he may do his duty firmly if he be an honest man, and if he be not, a just fear of disgrace, may perhaps, as to the public, have nearly the effect of an intrinsic principle of virtue. According to these principles, I suppose the only instances in which the President would be liable to impeachment, would be where he had received a bribe, or had acted from some corrupt motive or other. If the President had received a bribe without the privity or knowledge of the Senate, from a foreign power, and had, under the influence of that bribe, had address enough with the Senate, by artifices and misrepresentations, to seduce their consent to a pernicious treaty—if it appeared afterwards that this was the case, would not that Senate be as competent to try him as any other persons whatsoever? Would they not exclaim against his villainy? Would they not feel a particular resentment against him for their being made the instrument of his treacherous purposes? In this situation, if any objection could be made against the Senate as a proper tribunal, it might more properly be made by the President himself, lest their resentment should operate too strongly, rather than by the public, on the ground of a supposed partiality. The President must certainly be punishable for giving false information to the Senate. He is to regulate all intercourse with foreign powers, and it is his duty to impart to the Senate every material intelligence he receives. If it should appear that he has not given them full information, but has concealed important intelligence which he ought to have communicated, and by that means induced them to enter into measures injurious to their country, and which they would not have consented to had the true state of things been disclosed to them—In this case, I ask whether, upon an impeachment for a misdemeanor upon such an account, the Senate would probably favour him? With respect to the impeachability of the Senate, that is a matter of doubt. There have been no instances of impeachment for legislative misdemeanors: And we shall find, upon examination, that the inconveniences resulting from such impeachments, would more than preponderate the advantages. There is no greater honour in the world, than being the representative of a free people—There is no trust on which the happiness of the people has a greater dependence. Yet, whoever heard of impeaching a Member of the Legislature for any legislative misconduct? It would be a great check on the public business, if a Member of the Assembly was liable to punishment for his conduct as such. Unfortunately it is the case, not only in other countries but even in this, that divisions and differences in opinion will continually arise. On many questions, there will be two or more parties. These often judge with little charity of each other, and attribute every opposition to their own system to an ill motive. We know this very well from experience; but, in my opinion, this constant suspicion is frequently unjust. I believe in general, both parties really think themselves right, and that the majority of each commonly act with equal innocence of intention. But, with the usual want of charity in these cases, how dangerous would it be to make a Member of the Legislature liable to impeachment! A mere difference of opinion might be interpreted by the malignity of party, into a deliberate, wicked action. It, therefore, appears to me at least very doubtful, whether it would be proper to render the Senate impeachable at all; especially as in the branches of executive government, where their concurrence is required, the President is the primary agent, and plainly responsible; and they in fact are but a Council to validate proper, or restrain improper, conduct in him.—But if a Senator is impeachable, it could only be for corruption, or some other wicked motive; in which case, surely those Senators who had acted from upright motives, would be competent to try him. Suppose there had been such a Council as was proposed, consisting of thirteen, one from each state, to assist the President in making treaties, &c. more general alarm would have been excited, and stronger opposition made to this Constitution, than even at present— The power of the President would have appeared more formidable, and the states would have lost one half of their security; since, instead of two Representatives, which each has now for those purposes, they would have had but one. A gentleman from New-Hanover has asked, whether it is not the practice in Great-Britain to submit treaties to Parliament, before they are esteemed valid. The King has the sole authority, by the laws of that country, to make treaties. After treaties are made, they are frequently discussed in the two Houses of Parliament; where, of late years, the most important measures of government have been narrowly examined. It is usual to move for an address of approbation; and such has been the complaisance of Parliament for a long time, that this seldom hath been with-held. Sometimes they pass an act in conformity to the treaty made: But this I believe is not for the mere purpose of confirmation, but to make alterations in a particular system, which the change of circumstances requires. The constitutional power of making treaties is vested in the crown; and the power with whom a treaty is made, considers it as binding without any act of Parliament, unless an alteration by such is provided for in the treaty itself, which I believe is sometimes the case. When the treaty of peace was made in 1763, it contained stipulations for the surrender of some islands to the French. The islands were given up, I believe, without any act of Parliament. The power of making treaties is very important, and must be vested somewhere, in order to counteract the dangerous designs of other countries, and to be able to terminate a war when it is begun. Were it known that our government was weak, two or more European powers might combine against us. Would it not be politic to have some power in this country, to obviate this danger by a treaty? If this power was injudiciously limited, the nations where the power was possessed without restriction, would have greatly the advantage of us in negociation; and every one must know, according to modern policy, of what moment an advantage in negociation is. The honourable Member from Anson said, that the accumulation of all the different branches of power in the Senate, would be dangerous. The experience of other countries shews that this fear is without foundation. What is the Senate of Great-Britain opposed to the House of Commons, although it be composed of an hereditary nobility, of vast fortunes, and entirely independent of the people? Their weight is far inferior to that of the Commons. Here is a strong instance of the accumulation of powers of the different branches of government without producing any inconvenience. That Senate, Sir, is a separate branch of the Legislature, is the great constitutional Council of the Crown,

and decides on lives and fortunes in impeachments, besides
being the ultimate tribunal for trying controversies respecting
private rights. Would it not appear that all these things should
render them more formidable than the other House? Yet the
Commons have generally been able to carry every thing before
them. The circumstance of their representing the great body of
the people, alone gives them great weight. This weight has
great authority added to it, by their possessing the right (a
right given to the people's Representatives in Congress) of exclusively originating money bills. The authority over money
will do every thing. A government cannot be supported without money. Our Representatives may at any time compel the
Senate to agree to a reasonable measure, by with-holding supplies till the measure is consented to. There was a great debate
in the Convention, whether the Senate should have an equal
power of originating money bills. It was strongly insisted by
some that they should; but at length a majority thought it un-
adviseable, and the clause was passed as it now stands. I have
reason to believe our own Representatives had a great share in
establishing this excellent regulation, and in my opinion they
deserve the public thanks for it. It has been objected, that this
power must necessarily injure the people, inasmuch as a bare
majority of the Senate might alone be assembled, and eight
would be sufficient for a decision. This is on a supposition that
many of the Senators would neglect attending. It is to be
hoped that the gentlemen who will be honored with seats in
Congress, will faithfully execute their trust, as well in attending
as in every other part of their duty. An objection of this sort,
will go against all government whatever. Possible abuse and
neglect of attendance, are objections which may be urged
against any government which the wisdom of man is able to
construct. When it is known of how much importance attendance is, no Senator would dare to incur the universal resentment of his fellow-citizens, by grossly absenting himself from
his duty. Do gentlemen mean that it ought to have been provided by the Constitution, that the whole body should attend
before particular business was done? Then it would be in the
power of a few men, by neglecting to attend, to obstruct the
public business, and possibly bring on the destruction of their
country. If this power be improperly vested, it is incumbent on

gentlemen to tell us in what body it could be more safely and properly lodged. I believe, on a serious consideration, it will be found that it was necessary, for the reasons mentioned by the gentleman from Halifax, to vest the power in the Senate or in some other body representing equally the sovereignty of the states, and that the power, as given in the Constitution, is not likely to be attended with the evils which some gentlemen apprehend. The only real security of liberty in any country, is the jealousy and circumspection of the people themselves. Let them be watchful over their rulers. Should they find a combination against their liberties, and all other methods appear insufficient to preserve them, they have, thank God, an ultimate remedy. That power which created the government, can destroy it. Should the government, on trial, be found to want amendments, those amendments can be made in a regular method, in a mode prescribed by the Constitution itself. Massachusetts, South-Carolina, New-Hampshire, and Virginia, have all proposed amendments; but they all concurred in the necessity of an immediate adoption. A constitutional mode of altering the Constitution itself, is perhaps, what has never been known among mankind before. We have this security, in addition to the natural watchfulness of the people, which I hope will never be found wanting. The objections I have answered, deserved all possible attention, and for my part I shall always respect that jealousy which arises from the love of public liberty.

Henry Abbot and James Iredell
Debate Religious Tests

Mr. *Henry Abbot*, after a short exordium which was not distinctly heard, proceeded thus—Some are afraid, Mr. Chairman, that should the Constitution be received, they would be deprived of the privilege of worshipping God according to their consciences, which would be taking from them a benefit they enjoy under the present Constitution. They wish to know if their religious and civil liberties be secured under this system, or whether the general government may not make laws infringing their religious liberties. The worthy member from Edenton mentioned sundry political reasons why treaties should be the supreme law of the land. It is feared by some people, that by the power of making treaties, they might make a treaty engaging with foreign powers to adopt the Roman catholic religion in the United States, which would prevent the people from worshipping God according to their own consciences. The worthy member from Halifax has in some measure satisfied my mind on this subject. But others may be dissatisfied. Many wish to know what religion shall be established. I believe a majority of the community are Presbyterians. I am for my part against any exclusive establishment, but if there were any, I would prefer the Episcopal. The exclusion of religious tests is by many thought dangerous and impolitic. They suppose that if there be no religious test required, Pagans, Deists and Mahometans might obtain offices among us, and that the Senate and Representatives might all be Pagans. Every person employed by the general and state governments is to take an oath to support the former. Some are desirous to know how, and by whom they are to swear, since no religious tests are required—whether they are to swear by Jupiter, Juno, Minerva, Proserpine or Pluto. We ought to be suspicious of our liberties. We have felt the effects of oppressive measures, and know the happy consequences of being jealous of our rights. I would be glad some gentleman would endeavour to obviate these objections, in order to satisfy the religious part of the society. Could I be convinced that the objections were well founded, I would then declare my opinion against the Constitution. [Mr. *Abbot* added several other observations, but spoke too low to be heard.]

Mr. *Iredell*—Mr. Chairman, Nothing is more desireable than to remove the scruples of any gentleman on this interesting subject: Those concerning religion are entitled to particular respect. I did not expect any objection to this particular regulation, which in my opinion, is calculated to prevent evils of the most pernicious consequences to society. Every person in the least conversant in the history of mankind, knows what dreadful mischiefs have been committed by religious persecutions. Under the colour of religious tests the utmost cruelties have been exercised. Those in power have generally considered all wisdom centered in themselves, that they alone had a right to dictate to the rest of mankind, and that all opposition to their tenets was profane and impious. The consequence of this intolerant spirit has been, that each church has in turn set itself up against every other, and persecutions and wars of the most implacable and bloody nature have taken place in every part of the world. America has set an example to mankind to think more modestly and reasonably; that a man may be of different religious sentiments from our own, without being a bad member of society. The principles of toleration, to the honour of this age, are doing away those errors and prejudices which have so long prevailed even in the most intolerant countries. In the Roman catholic countries, principles of moderation are adopted, which would have been spurned at a century or two ago. I should be sorry to find, when examples of toleration are set even by arbitrary governments, that this country, so impressed with the highest sense of liberty, should adopt principles on this subject, that were narrow and illiberal. I consider the clause under consideration as one of the strongest proofs that could be adduced, that it was the intention of those who formed this system, to establish a general religious liberty in America. Were we to judge from the examples of religious tests in other countries, we should be persuaded that they do not answer the purpose for which they are intended. What is the consequence of such in England? In that country no man can be a Member in the House of Commons, or hold any office under the Crown, without taking the sacrament according to the rites of the church. This in the first instance must degrade and profane a rite, which never ought to be taken but from a sincere principle of devotion. To a man of base principles, it is made a mere instrument of civil policy. The intention was to exclude all persons from offices, but the members of the church of England. Yet it is notorious, that Dissenters qualify themselves for offices in this manner, though they never conform to the church on any other occasion; and men of no religion at all, have no scruple to make use of this qualification. It never was known that a man who had no principles of religion, hesitated to perform any rite when it was convenient for his private interest. No test can bind such a one. I am therefore clearly of opinion, that such a discrimination would neither be effectual for its own purposes, nor if it could, ought it by any means to be made. Upon the principles I have stated, I confess the restriction on the power of Congress in this particular has my hearty approbation. They certainly have no authority to interfere in the establishment of any religion whatsoever, and I am astonished that any gentleman should conceive they have. Is there any power given to Congress in matters of religion? Can they pass a single act to impair our religious liberties? If they could, it would be a just cause of alarm. If they could, Sir, no man would have more horror against it than myself. Happily no sect here is superior to another. As long as this is the case, we shall be free from those persecutions and distractions with which other countries have been torn. If any future Congress should pass an act concerning the religion of the country, it would be an act which they are not authorised to pass by the Constitution, and which the people would not obey. Every one would ask, "Who authorised the government to pass such an act? It is not warranted by the Constitution, and is a barefaced usurpation." The power to make treaties can never be supposed to include a right to establish a foreign religion among ourselves, though it might authorise a toleration of others.

But it is objected, that the people of America may perhaps chuse Representatives who have no religion at all, and that Pagans and Mahometans may be admitted into offices. But how is it possible to exclude any set of men, without taking away that principle of religious freedom which we ourselves so warmly contend for? This is the foundation on which persecution has been raised in every part of the world. The people in power were always in the right, and every body else wrong. If you admit the least difference, the door to persecution is opened. Nor would it answer the purpose, for the worst part of the excluded sects would comply with the test, and the best men only be kept out of our counsels. But it is never to be supposed that the people of America will trust their dearest rights to persons who have no religion at all, or a religion materially different from their own. It would be happy for mankind if religion was permitted to take its own course, and maintain itself by the excellence of its own doctrines. The divine author of our religion never wished for its support by worldly authority. Has he not said, *that the gates of hell shall not prevail against it*? It made much greater progress for itself, than when supported by the greatest authority upon earth.

It has been asked by that respectable gentleman [Mr. Abbot] what is the meaning of that part, where it is said, that the United States shall *guarantee* to every state in the union a republican form of government, and why a *guarantee* of *religious freedom* was not included. The meaning of the guarantee provided was this—There being thirteen governments confederated, upon a republican principle, it was essential to the existence and harmony of the confederacy that each should be a republican government, and that no state should have a right to establish an aristocracy or monarchy. That clause was therefore inserted to prevent any state from establishing any government but a republican one. Every one must be convinced of the mischief that would ensue, if any state had a right to change its government to a monarchy. If a monarchy was established in any one state, it would endeavour to subvert the freedom of the others, and would probably by degrees succeed in it. This must strike the mind of every person here who recollects the history of Greece when she had confederated governments. The King of Macedon by his arts and intrigues got himself admitted a member of the Amphyctionic council, which was the superintending government of the Grecian republics, and in a short time he became master of them all. It is then necessary that the members of a confederacy should have similar governments. But consistently with this restriction the states may make what change in their own governments they think proper. Had Congress undertaken to guarantee *religious freedom*, or any particular species of it, they would then have had a pretence to interfere in a subject they have nothing to do with. Each state, so far as the clause in question does not interfere, must be left to the operation of its own principles.

There is a degree of jealousy which it is impossible to satisfy. Jealousy in a free government ought to be respected: But it may be carried to too great an extent. It is impracticable to guard against all *possible* danger of people's chusing their officers indiscreetly. If they have a right to chuse, they may make a bad choice. I met by accident with a pamphlet this morning, in which the author states as a very serious danger, that the Pope of Rome might be elected President. I confess this never struck me before, and if the author had read all the qualifications of a President, perhaps his fears might have been quieted. No man but a native, and who has resided fourteen years in America, can be chosen President. I know not all the qualifications for a Pope, but I believe he must be taken from the college of Cardinals, and probably there are many previous steps necessary before he arrives at this dignity. A native of America must have very singular good fortune, who after residing fourteen years in his own country, should go to Europe, enter into Romish orders, obtain the promotion of Cardinal, afterwards that of Pope, and at length be so much in the confidence of his own country, as to be elected President. It would be still more extraordinary if he should give up his Popedom for our Presidency. Sir, it is impossible to treat such idle fears with any degree of gravity. Why is it not objected, that there is no provision in the Constitution against electing one of the Kings of Europe President? It would be a clause equally rational and judicious.

I hope that I have in some degree satisfied the doubts of the gentleman. This article is calculated to secure universal religious liberty, by putting all sects on a level, the only way to prevent persecution. I thought nobody would have objected

to this clause, which deserves in my opinion the highest approbation. This country has already had the honour of setting an
example of civil freedom, and I trust it will likewise have the
honour of teaching the rest of the world the way to religious
freedom also. God grant both may be perpetuated to the end
of time.

The Rev. David Caldwell and Samuel Spencer Debate Religious Toleration

Mr. *Caldwell* thought that some danger might arise. He imagined it might be objected to in a political as well as in a religious view. In the first place, he said there was an invitation for Jews, and Pagans of every kind, to come among us. At some future period, said he, this might endanger the character of the United States. Moreover, even those who do not regard religion, acknowledge that the Christian religion is best calculated of all religions to make good members of society, on account of its morality. I think then, added he, that in a political view, those gentlemen who formed this Constitution, should not have given this invitation to Jews and Heathens. All those who have any religion are against the emigration of those people from the eastern hemisphere.

Mr. *Spencer* was an advocate for securing every unalienable right, and that of worshipping God according to the dictates of conscience in particular. He therefore thought that no one particular religion should be established. Religious tests, said he, have been the foundation of persecutions in all countries. Persons who are conscientious will not take the oath required by religious tests, and will therefore be excluded from offices, though equally capable of discharging them as any member of the society. It is feared, continued he, that persons of bad principles, Deists, Atheists, &c. may come into this country, and there is nothing to restrain them from being eligible to offices. He asked if it was reasonable to suppose that the people would chuse men without regarding their characters. Mr. *Spencer* then continued thus—Gentlemen urge that the want of a test admits the most vicious characters to offices. I desire to know what test could bind them. If they were of such principles, it would not keep them from enjoying those offices. On the other hand, it would exclude from offices conscientious and truly religious people, though equally capable as others. Conscientious persons would not take such an oath, and would be therefore excluded. This would be a great cause of objection to a religious test. But in this case as there is not a religious test required, it leaves religion on the solid foundation of its own inherent validity, without any connexion with temporal authority, and no kind of oppression can take place. I confess it strikes me so. I am sorry to differ from the worthy gentleman. I cannot object to this part of the Constitution. I wish every other part was as good and proper.

The Constitution

[*The footnotes in this appendix, keyed to the line number on the page, indicate portions of the Constitution that have been altered by subsequent amendment.*]

We the People of the United States, in Order to form a more perfect Union, establish Justice, insure domestic Tranquility, provide for the common defence, promote the general Welfare, and secure the Blessings of Liberty to ourselves and our Posterity, do ordain and establish this Constitution for the United States of America.

Article. I.

Section. 1. All legislative Powers herein granted shall be vested in a Congress of the United States, which shall consist of a Senate and House of Representatives.

Section. 2. The House of Representatives shall be composed of Members chosen every second Year by the People of the several States, and the Electors in each State shall have the Qualifications requisite for Electors of the most numerous Branch of the State Legislature.

No Person shall be a Representative who shall not have attained to the Age of twenty five Years, and been seven Years a Citizen of the United States, and who shall not, when elected, be an Inhabitant of that State in which he shall be chosen.

Representatives and direct Taxes shall be apportioned among the several States which may be included within this Union, according to their respective Numbers, which shall be determined by adding to the whole Number of free Persons, including those bound to Service for a Term of Years, and excluding Indians not taxed, three fifths of all other Persons. The actual Enumeration shall be made within three Years after the first Meeting of the Congress of the United States, and within every subsequent Term of ten Years, in such Manner as they shall

417.24–29 Representatives . . . other Persons.] Changed regarding representation by the Fourteenth Amendment; changed regarding taxation by the Sixteenth Amendment.

by Law direct. The Number of Representatives shall not exceed one for every thirty Thousand, but each State shall have at Least one Representative; and until such enumeration shall be made, the State of New Hampshire shall be entitled to chuse three, Massachusetts eight, Rhode-Island and Providence Plantations one, Connecticut five, New-York six, New Jersey four, Pennsylvania eight, Delaware one, Maryland six, Virginia ten, North Carolina five, South Carolina five, and Georgia three.

When vacancies happen in the Representation from any State, the Executive Authority thereof shall issue Writs of Election to fill such Vacancies.

The House of Representatives shall chuse their Speaker and other Officers; and shall have the sole Power of Impeachment.

Section. 3. The Senate of the United States shall be composed of two Senators from each State, chosen by the Legislature thereof, for six Years; and each Senator shall have one Vote.

Immediately after they shall be assembled in Consequence of the first Election, they shall be divided as equally as may be into three Classes. The Seats of the Senators of the first Class shall be vacated at the Expiration of the second Year, of the second Class at the Expiration of the fourth Year, and of the third Class at the Expiration of the sixth Year, so that one third may be chosen every second Year; and if Vacancies happen by Resignation, or otherwise, during the Recess of the Legislature of any State, the Executive thereof may make temporary Appointments until the next Meeting of the Legislature, which shall then fill such Vacancies.

No Person shall be a Senator who shall not have attained to the Age of thirty Years, and been nine Years a Citizen of the United States, and who shall not, when elected, be an Inhabitant of that State for which he shall be chosen.

The Vice President of the United States shall be President of the Senate, but shall have no Vote, unless they be equally divided.

418.15–16   chosen by the Legislature thereof,] Changed by the Seventeenth Amendment.
418.24–28   and if Vacancies . . . Vacancies.] Changed by the Seventeenth Amendment.

The Senate shall chuse their other Officers, and also a President pro tempore, in the Absence of the Vice President, or when he shall exercise the Office of President of the United States.

The Senate shall have the sole Power to try all Impeachments. When sitting for that Purpose, they shall be on Oath or Affirmation. When the President of the United States is tried, the Chief Justice shall preside: And no Person shall be convicted without the Concurrence of two thirds of the Members present.

Judgment in Cases of Impeachment shall not extend further than to removal from Office, and disqualification to hold and enjoy any Office of honor, Trust or Profit under the United States: but the Party convicted shall nevertheless be liable and subject to Indictment, Trial, Judgment and Punishment, according to Law.

Section. 4.   The Times, Places and Manner of holding Elections for Senators and Representatives, shall be prescribed in each State by the Legislature thereof; but the Congress may at any time by Law make or alter such Regulations, except as to the Places of chusing Senators.

The Congress shall assemble at least once in every Year, and such Meeting shall be on the first Monday in December, unless they shall by Law appoint a different Day.

Section. 5.   Each House shall be the Judge of the Elections, Returns and Qualifications of its own Members, and a Majority of each shall constitute a Quorum to do Business; but a smaller Number may adjourn from day to day, and may be authorized to compel the Attendance of absent Members, in such Manner, and under such Penalties as each House may provide.

Each House may determine the Rules of its Proceedings, punish its members for disorderly Behaviour, and, with the Concurrence of two thirds, expel a Member.

Each House shall keep a Journal of its Proceedings, and from time to time publish the same, excepting such Parts as may in their Judgment require Secrecy; and the Yeas and Nays

419.23   be on . . . December,] Changed by the Twentieth Amendment.

of the Members of either House on any question shall, at the Desire of one fifth of those Present, be entered on the Journal.

Neither House, during the Session of Congress, shall, without the Consent of the other, adjourn for more than three days, nor to any other Place than that in which the two Houses shall be sitting.

Section. 6. The Senators and Representatives shall receive a Compensation for their Services, to be ascertained by Law, and paid out of the Treasury of the United States. They shall in all Cases, except Treason, Felony and Breach of the Peace, be privileged from Arrest during their Attendance at the Session of their respective Houses, and in going to and returning from the same; and for any Speech or Debate in either House, they shall not be questioned in any other Place.

No Senator or Representative shall, during the Time for which he was elected, be appointed to any civil Office under the Authority of the United States which shall have been created, or the Emoluments whereof shall have been encreased during such time; and no Person holding any Office under the United States, shall be a Member of either House during his Continuance in Office.

Section. 7. All Bills for raising Revenue shall originate in the House of Representatives; but the Senate may propose or concur with Amendments as on other Bills.

Every Bill which shall have passed the House of Representatives and the Senate shall, before it become a Law, be presented to the President of the United States; If he approve he shall sign it, but if not he shall return it, with his Objections to that House in which it shall have originated, who shall enter the Objections at large on their Journal, and proceed to reconsider it. If after such Reconsideration two thirds of that House shall agree to pass the Bill, it shall be sent, together with the Objections, to the other House, by which it shall likewise be reconsidered, and if approved by two thirds of that House, it shall become a Law. But in all such Cases the Votes of both Houses shall be determined by yeas and Nays, and the Names of the Persons voting for and against the Bill shall be entered on the

Journal of each House respectively. If any Bill shall not be returned by the President within ten Days (Sundays excepted) after it shall have been presented to him, the Same shall be a Law, in like Manner as if he had signed it, unless the Congress by their Adjournment prevent its Return, in which Case it shall not be a Law.

Every Order, Resolution, or Vote to which the Concurrence of the Senate and House of Representatives may be necessary (except on a question of Adjournment) shall be presented to the President of the United States; and before the Same shall take Effect, shall be approved by him, or being disapproved by him, shall be repassed by two thirds of the Senate and House of Representatives, according to the Rules and Limitations prescribed in the Case of a Bill.

Section. 8. The Congress shall have Power To lay and collect Taxes, Duties, Imposts and Excises, to pay the Debts and provide for the common Defence and general Welfare of the United States; but all Duties, Imposts and Excises shall be uniform throughout the United States;

To borrow Money on the credit of the United States;

To regulate Commerce with foreign Nations, and among the several States, and with the Indian Tribes;

To establish an uniform Rule of Naturalization, and uniform Laws on the subject of Bankruptcies throughout the United States;

To coin Money, regulate the Value thereof, and of foreign Coin, and fix the Standard of Weights and Measures;

To provide for the Punishment of counterfeiting the Securities and current Coin of the United States;

To establish Post Offices and post Roads;

To promote the Progress of Science and useful Arts, by securing for limited Times to Authors and Inventors the exclusive Right to their respective Writings and Discoveries;

To constitute Tribunals inferior to the supreme Court;

To define and punish Piracies and Felonies committed on the high Seas, and Offences against the Law of Nations;

To declare War, grant Letters of Marque and Reprisal, and make Rules concerning Captures on Land and Water;

To raise and support Armies, but no Appropriation of Money to that Use shall be for a longer Term than two Years;

To provide and maintain a Navy;

To make Rules for the Government and Regulation of the land and naval Forces;

To provide for calling forth the Militia to execute the Laws of the Union, suppress Insurrections and repel Invasions;

To provide for organizing, arming, and disciplining, the Militia, and for governing such Part of them as may be employed in the Service of the United States, reserving to the States respectively, the Appointment of the Officers, and the Authority of training the Militia according to the discipline prescribed by Congress;

To exercise exclusive Legislation in all Cases whatsoever, over such District (not exceeding ten Miles square) as may, by Cession of particular States, and the Acceptance of Congress, become the Seat of the Government of the United States, and to exercise like Authority over all Places purchased by the Consent of the Legislature of the State in which the same shall be, for the Erection of Forts, Magazines, Arsenals, dock-Yards, and other needful Buildings; —And

To make all Laws which shall be necessary and proper for carrying into Execution the foregoing Powers, and all other Powers vested by this Constitution in the Government of the United States, or in any Department or Officer thereof.

Section. 9.   The Migration or Importation of such Persons as any of the States now existing shall think proper to admit, shall not be prohibited by the Congress prior to the Year one thousand eight hundred and eight, but a Tax or duty may be imposed on such Importation, not exceeding ten dollars for each Person.

The Privilege of the Writ of Habeas Corpus shall not be suspended, unless when in Cases of Rebellion or Invasion the public Safety may require it.

No Bill of Attainder or ex post facto Law shall be passed.

No Capitation, or other direct, Tax shall be laid, unless in

Proportion to the Census or Enumeration herein before directed to be taken.

No Tax or Duty shall be laid on Articles exported from any State.

No Preference shall be given by any Regulation of Commerce or Revenue to the Ports of one State over those of another: nor shall Vessels bound to, or from, one State, be obliged to enter, clear, or pay Duties in another.

No Money shall be drawn from the Treasury, but in Consequence of Appropriations made by Law; and a regular Statement and Account of the Receipts and Expenditures of all public Money shall be published from time to time.

No Title of Nobility shall be granted by the United States: And no Person holding any Office of Profit or Trust under them, shall, without the Consent of the Congress, accept of any present, Emolument, Office, or Title, of any kind whatever, from any King, Prince, or foreign State.

Section. 10.   No State shall enter into any Treaty, Alliance, or Confederation; grant Letters of Marque and Reprisal; coin Money; emit Bills of Credit; make any Thing but gold and silver Coin a Tender in Payment of Debts; pass any Bill of Attainder, ex post facto Law, or Law impairing the Obligation of Contracts, or grant any Title of Nobility.

No State shall, without the Consent of the Congress, lay any Imposts or Duties on Imports or Exports, except what may be absolutely necessary for executing it's inspection Laws: and the net Produce of all Duties and Imposts, laid by any State on Imports or Exports, shall be for the Use of the Treasury of the United States; and all such Laws shall be subject to the Revision and Controul of the Congress.

No State shall, without the Consent of Congress, lay any Duty of Tonnage, keep Troops, or Ships of War in time of Peace, enter into any Agreement or Compact with another State, or with a foreign Power, or engage in War, unless actually invaded, or in such imminent Danger as will not admit of delay.

422.38–423.2   No Capitation . .   taken.] Changed by the Sixteenth Amendment.

Article. II.

Section. 1. The executive Power shall be vested in a President of the United States of America. He shall hold his Office during the Term of four Years, and, together with the Vice President, chosen for the same Term, be elected, as follows

Each State shall appoint, in such Manner as the Legislature thereof may direct, a Number of Electors, equal to the whole Number of Senators and Representatives to which the State may be entitled in the Congress: but no Senator or Representative, or Person holding an Office of Trust or Profit under the United States, shall be appointed an Elector.

The Electors shall meet in their respective States and vote by Ballot for two Persons, of whom one at least shall not be an Inhabitant of the same State with themselves. And they shall make a List of all the Persons voted for, and of the Number of Votes for each; which List they shall sign and certify, and transmit sealed to the Seat of the Government of the United States, directed to the President of the Senate. The President of the Senate shall, in the Presence of the Senate and House of Representatives, open all the Certificates, and the Votes shall then be counted. The Person having the greatest Number of Votes shall be the President, if such Number be a Majority of the whole Number of Electors appointed; and if there be more than one who have such Majority, and have an equal Number of Votes, then the House of Representatives shall immediately chuse by Ballot one of them for President; and if no Person have a Majority, then from the five highest on the List the said House shall in like Manner chuse the President. But in chusing the President, the Votes shall be taken by States, the Representation from each State having one Vote; A quorum for this Purpose shall consist of a Member or Members from two thirds of the States, and a Majority of all the States shall be necessary to a Choice. In every Case, after the Choice of the President, the Person having the greatest Number of Votes of the Electors shall be the Vice President. But if there should remain two or more who have equal Votes, the Senate shall chuse from them by Ballot the Vice President.

The Congress may determine the Time of chusing the Electors, and the Day on which they shall give their Votes; which Day shall be the same throughout the United States.

No Persons except a natural born Citizen, or a Citizen of the United States, at the time of the Adoption of this Constitution, shall be eligible to the Office of President; neither shall any Person be eligible to that Office who shall not have attained to the Age of thirty five Years, and been fourteen Years a Resident within the United States.

In Case of the Removal of the President from Office, or of his Death, Resignation, or Inability to discharge the Powers and Duties of the said Office, the Same shall devolve on the Vice President, and the Congress may by Law provide for the Case of Removal, Death, Resignation or Inability, both of the President and Vice President, declaring what Officer shall then act as President, and such Officer shall act accordingly, until the Disability be removed, or a President shall be elected.

The President shall, at stated Times, receive for his Services, a Compensation, which shall neither be encreased nor diminished during the Period for which he shall have been elected, and he shall not receive within that Period any other Emolument from the United States, or any of them.

Before he enter on the Execution of his Office, he shall take the following Oath or Affirmation:—"I do solemnly swear (or affirm) that I will faithfully execute the Office of President of the United States, and will to the best of my Ability, preserve, protect and defend the Constitution of the United States."

Section. 2.   The President shall be Commander in Chief of the Army and Navy of the United States, and of the Militia of the several States, when called into the actual Service of the United States; he may require the Opinion, in writing, of the principal Officer in each of the executive Departments, upon any Subject relating to the Duties of their respective

424.14–425.2   The Electors . . . Vice President.] Changed by the Twelfth Amendment.
   425.12–19   In Case . . . elected.] Changed by the Twenty-fifth Amendment.

Offices, and he shall have Power to grant Reprieves and Pardons for Offences against the United States, except in Cases of Impeachment.

He shall have Power, by and with the Advice and Consent of the Senate, to make Treaties, provided two thirds of the Senators present concur; and he shall nominate, and by and with the Advice and Consent of the Senate, shall appoint Ambassadors, other public Ministers and Consuls, Judges of the supreme Court, and all other Officers of the United States, whose Appointments are not herein otherwise provided for, and which shall be established by Law: but the Congress may by Law vest the Appointment of such inferior Officers, as they think proper, in the President alone, in the Courts of Law, or in the Heads of Departments.

The President shall have Power to fill up all Vacancies that may happen during the Recess of the Senate, by granting Commissions which shall expire at the End of their next Session.

Section. 3.   He shall from time to time give to the Congress Information of the State of the Union, and recommend to their Consideration such Measures as he shall judge necessary and expedient; he may, on extraordinary Occasions, convene both Houses, or either of them, and in Case of Disagreement between them, with Respect to the Time of Adjournment, he may adjourn them to such Time as he shall think proper; he shall receive Ambassadors and other public Ministers; he shall take Care that the Laws be faithfully executed, and shall Commission all the Officers of the United States.

Section. 4.   The President, Vice President and all civil Officers of the United States, shall be removed from Office on Impeachment for, and Conviction of Treason, Bribery, or other high Crimes and Misdemeanors.

Article. III.

Section. 1.   The judicial Power of the United States, shall be vested in one supreme Court, and in such inferior Courts as the Congress may from time to time ordain and establish. The Judges, both of the supreme and inferior Courts, shall hold their Offices during good Behaviour, and shall, at stated Times, receive for their Services, a Compensation, which shall not be diminished during their Continuance in Office.

Section. 2. The judicial Power shall extend to all Cases, in Law and Equity, arising under this Constitution, the Laws of the United States, and Treaties made, or which shall be made, under their Authority;—to all Cases affecting Ambassadors, other public Ministers and Consuls;—to all Cases of admiralty and maritime Jurisdiction;—to Controversies to which the United States shall be a Party;—to Controversies between two or more States—between a State and Citizens of another State; —between Citizens of different States,—between Citizens of the same State claiming Lands under Grants of different States, and between a State, or the Citizens thereof, and of foreign States, Citizens or Subjects.

In all Cases affecting Ambassadors, other public Ministers and Consuls, and those in which a State shall be Party, the supreme Court shall have original Jurisdiction. In all the other Cases before mentioned, the supreme Court shall have appellate Jurisdiction, both as to Law and Fact, with such Exceptions, and under such Regulations as the Congress shall make.

The Trial of all Crimes, except in Cases of Impeachment, shall be by Jury; and such Trial shall be held in the State where the said Crimes shall have been committed; but when not committed within any State, the Trial shall be at such Place or Places as the Congress may by Law have directed.

Section. 3. Treason against the United States, shall consist only in levying War against them, or in adhering to their Enemies, giving them Aid and Comfort. No Person shall be convicted of Treason unless on the Testimony of two Witnesses to the same overt Act, or on Confession in open Court.

The Congress shall have Power to declare the Punishment of Treason, but no Attainder of Treason shall work Corruption

427.12–16 between a State . . . Subjects] Jurisdiction over suits brought against states by citizens of another state, or by foreigners, was addressed by the Eleventh Amendment.

of Blood, or Forfeiture except during the Life of the Person attainted.

Article. IV.

Section. 1.　Full Faith and Credit shall be given in each State to the public Acts, Records, and judicial Proceedings of every other State. And the Congress may by general Laws prescribe the Manner in which such Acts, Records and Proceedings shall be proved, and the Effect thereof.

Section. 2.　The Citizens of each State shall be entitled to all privileges and Immunities of Citizens in the several States.

A Person charged in any State with Treason, Felony, or other Crime, who shall flee from Justice, and be found in another State, shall on Demand of the executive Authority of the State from which he fled, be delivered up, to be removed to the State having Jurisdiction of the Crime.

No Person held to Service or Labour in one State, under the Laws thereof, escaping into another, shall, in Consequence of any Law or Regulation therein, be discharged from such Service or Labour, but shall be delivered up on Claim of the Party to whom such Service or Labour may be due.

Section. 3.　New States may be admitted by the Congress into this Union; but no new State shall be formed or erected within the Jurisdiction of any other State; nor any State be formed by the Junction of two or more States, or Parts of States, without the Consent of the Legislatures of the States concerned as well as of the Congress.

The Congress shall have Power to dispose of and make all needful Rules and Regulations respecting the Territory or other Property belonging to the United States; and nothing in this Constitution shall be so construed as to Prejudice any Claims of the United States, or of any particular State.

428.17–22　No Person . . . due.] Changed by the Thirteenth Amendment.

Section. 4. The United States shall guarantee to every State in this Union a Republican Form of Government, and shall protect each of them against Invasion; and on Application of the Legislature, or of the Executive (when the Legislature cannot be convened) against domestic Violence.

Article. V.

The Congress, whenever two thirds of both Houses shall deem it necessary, shall propose Amendments to this Constitution, or, on the Application of the Legislatures of two thirds of the several States, shall call a Convention for proposing Amendments, which, in either Case, shall be valid to all Intents and Purposes, as Part of this Constitution, when ratified by the Legislatures of three fourths of the several States, or by Conventions in three fourths thereof, as the one or the other Mode of Ratification may be proposed by the Congress; Provided that no Amendment which may be made prior to the Year One thousand eight hundred and eight shall in any Manner affect the first and fourth Clauses in the Ninth Section of the first Article; and that no State, without its Consent, shall be deprived of it's equal Suffrage in the Senate.

Article VI.

All Debts contracted and Engagements entered into, before the Adoption of this Constitution, shall be as valid against the United States under this Constitution, as under the Confederation.

This Constitution, and the Laws of the United States which shall be made in Pursuance thereof; and all Treaties made, or which shall be made, under the Authority of the United States, shall be the supreme Law of the Land; and the Judges in every State shall be bound thereby, any Thing in the Constitution or Laws of any State to the Contrary notwithstanding.

The Senators and Representatives before mentioned, and the Members of the several State Legislatures, and all executive and judicial Officers; both of the United States and of the several States, shall be bound by Oath or Affirmation, to support this Constitution; but no religious Test shall ever be required as a Qualification to any Office or public Trust under the United States.

Article. VII.

The Ratification of the Conventions of nine States, shall be sufficient for the Establishment of this Constitution between the States so ratifying the Same.

DONE in Convention by the Unanimous Consent of the States present the Seventeenth Day of September in the Year of our Lord one thousand seven hundred and Eighty seven and of the Independance of the United States of America the Twelfth In Witness whereof We have hereunto subscribed our Names,

Attest William Jackson Secretary

Go: Washington—Presidt.
and deputy from Virginia

Delaware
{
Geo: Read
Gunning Bedford junr
John Dickinson
Richard Bassett
Jaco: Broom
}

Maryland
{
James McHenry
Dan of St Thos. Jenifer
Danl Carroll
}

Virginia
{
John Blair—
James Madison Jr.
}

North Carolina
{
Wm. Blount
Richd. Dobbs Spaight.
Hu Williamson
}

South Carolina
{
J. Rutledge
Charles Cotesworth Pinckney
Charles Pinckney
Pierce Butler
}

Georgia
{
William Few
Abr Baldwin
}

New Hampshire
{
John Langdon
Nicholas Gilman
}

Massachusetts
{
Nathaniel Gorham
Rufus King
}

Connecticut
{
Wm: Saml. Johnson
Roger Sherman
}

New York . . . Alexander Hamilton

New Jersey
{
Wil: Livingston
David Brearley
Wm. Paterson.
Jona: Dayton
}

Pensylvania
{
B Franklin
Thomas Mifflin
Robt Morris
Geo. Clymer
Thos. FitzSimons
Jared Ingersoll
James Wilson
Gouv. Morris
}

ARTICLES in Addition to, and Amendment of, the Constitution of the United States of America, proposed by Congress, and ratified by the Legislatures of the several States, pursuant to the fifth Article of the original Constitution.

Article I.

Congress shall make no law respecting an establishment of religion, or prohibiting the free exercise thereof; or abridging the freedom of speech, or of the press; or the right of the people peaceably to assemble, and to petition the Government for a redress of grievances.

Article II.

A well regulated Militia, being necessary to the security of a free State, the right of the people to keep and bear Arms, shall not be infringed.

Article III.

No Soldier shall, in time of peace be quartered in any house, without the consent of the Owner, nor in time of war, but in a manner to be prescribed by law.

Article IV.

The right of the people to be secure in their persons, houses, papers, and effects, against unreasonable searches and seizures, shall not be violated, and no Warrants shall issue, but upon probable cause, supported by Oath or affirmation, and particularly describing the place to be searched, and the persons or things to be seized.

Article V.

No person shall be held to answer for a capital, or otherwise infamous crime, unless on a presentment or indictment of a Grand Jury, except in cases arising in the land or naval forces, or in the Militia, when in actual service in time of War or public danger; nor shall any person be subject for the same offence to be twice put in jeopardy of life or limb; nor shall be compelled in any criminal case to be a witness against himself, nor be deprived of life, liberty, or property, without due process of law; nor shall private property be taken for public use, without just compensation.

Article VI.

In all criminal prosecutions, the accused shall enjoy the right to a speedy and public trial, by an impartial jury of the State and district wherein the crime shall have been committed, which district shall have been previously ascertained by law, and to be informed of the nature and cause of the accusation; to be confronted with the witnesses against him; to have compulsory process for obtaining witnesses in his favor, and to have the Assistance of Counsel for his defence.

Article VII.

In Suits at common law, where the value in controversy shall exceed twenty dollars, the right of trial by jury shall be preserved, and no fact tried by a jury, shall be otherwise reexamined in any Court of the United States, than according to the rules of the common law.

Article VIII.

Excessive bail shall not be required, nor excessive fines imposed, nor cruel and unusual punishments inflicted.

Article IX.

The enumeration in the Constitution, of certain rights, shall not be construed to deny or disparage others retained by the people.

Article X.

The powers not delegated to the United States by the Constitution, nor prohibited by it to the States, are reserved to the States respectively, or to the people.

Articles I.–X. proposed to the states by Congress, September 25, 1789
Ratification completed, December 15, 1791
Ratification declared, March 1, 1792

Article XI.

The Judicial power of the United States shall not be construed to extend to any suit in law or equity, commenced or prosecuted against one of the United States by Citizens of another State, or by Citizens or Subjects of any Foreign State.

Proposed to the states by Congress, March 4, 1794
Ratification completed, February 7, 1795
Ratification declared, January 8, 1798

Article XII.

The Electors shall meet in their respective states, and vote by ballot for President and Vice-President, one of whom, at least, shall not be an inhabitant of the same state with themselves; they shall name in their ballots the person voted for as President, and in distinct ballots the person voted for as Vice-President, and they shall make distinct lists of all persons voted for as President, and of all persons voted for as Vice-President, and of the number of votes for each, which lists they shall sign and certify, and transmit sealed to the seat of the government of the United States, directed to the President of the Senate;—The President of the Senate shall, in the presence of the Senate and House of Representatives, open all the certificates and the votes shall then be counted;—The person having the greatest number of votes for President, shall be the President, if such number be a majority of the whole number of Electors appointed; and if no person have such majority, then from the persons having the highest numbers not exceeding three on the list of those voted for as President, the House of Representatives shall choose immediately, by ballot, the President. But in choosing the President, the votes shall be taken by states, the representation from each state having one vote; a quorum for this purpose shall consist of a member or members from two-thirds of the states, and a majority of all the states shall be necessary to a choice. And if the House of Representatives shall not choose a President whenever the right of choice shall devolve upon them, before the fourth day of March next following, then the Vice-President shall act as President, as in the case of the death or other constitutional disability of the President.—The person having the greatest number of votes as Vice-President, shall be the Vice-President, if such number be a majority of the whole number of Electors appointed, and if no person have a majority, then from the two highest numbers on the list, the Senate shall choose the Vice-President; a quorum for the purpose shall consist of two-thirds of the whole number of Senators, and a majority of the whole number shall be necessary to a choice. But no person constitutionally ineligible to the office of President shall be eligible to that of Vice-President of the United States.

Proposed to the states by Congress, December 9, 1803
Ratification completed, June 15, 1804
Ratification declared, September 25, 1804

Article XIII.

SECTION 1.   Neither slavery nor involuntary servitude, except as a punishment for crime whereof the party shall have been duly convicted, shall exist within the United States, or any place subject to their jurisdiction.

SECTION 2.   Congress shall have power to enforce this article by appropriate legislation.

Proposed to the states by Congress, January 31, 1865
Ratification completed, December 6, 1865
Ratification declared, December 18, 1865

Article XIV.

SECTION 1.   All persons born or naturalized in the United States, and subject to the jurisdiction thereof, are citizens of the United States and of the State wherein they reside. No

434.3–8 And if . . . President.—] Changed by the Twentieth Amendment.

State shall make or enforce any law which shall abridge the privileges or immunities of citizens of the United States; nor shall any State deprive any person of life, liberty, or property, without due process of law; nor deny to any person within its jurisdiction the equal protection of the laws.

SECTION 2.   Representatives shall be apportioned among the several States according to their respective numbers, counting the whole number of persons in each State, excluding Indians not taxed. But when the right to vote at any election for the choice of electors for President and Vice President of the United States, Representatives in Congress, the Executive and Judicial officers of a State, or the members of the Legislature thereof, is denied to any of the male inhabitants of such State, being twenty-one years of age, and citizens of the United States, or in any way abridged, except for participation in rebellion, or other crime, the basis of representation therein shall be reduced in the proportion which the number of such male citizens shall bear to the whole number of male citizens twenty-one years of age in such State.

SECTION 3.   No person shall be a Senator or Representative in Congress, or elector of President and Vice President, or hold any office, civil or military, under the United States, or under any State, who, having previously taken an oath, as a member of Congress, or as an officer of the United States, or as a member of any State legislature, or as an executive or judicial officer of any State, to support the Constitution of the United States, shall have engaged in insurrection or rebellion against the same, or given aid or comfort to the enemies thereof. But Congress may by a vote of two-thirds of each House, remove such disability.

SECTION 4.   The validity of the public debt of the United States, authorized by law, including debts incurred for payment of pensions and bounties for services in suppressing insurrection or rebellion, shall not be questioned. But neither the United States nor any State shall assume or pay any debt or obligation incurred in aid of insurrection or rebellion against

435.13–14   male inhabitants . . . twenty-one years of age] Regarding voting rights and sex, see the Nineteenth Amendment; regarding voting rights and age, see the Twenty-sixth Amendment.

the United States, or any claim for the loss or emancipation of any slave; but all such debts, obligations and claims shall be held illegal and void.

SECTION 5. The Congress shall have power to enforce, by appropriate legislation, the provisions of this article.

Proposed to the states by Congress, June 13, 1866
Ratification completed, July 9, 1868
Ratification declared, July 28, 1868

Article XV.

SECTION 1. The right of citizens of the United States to vote shall not be denied or abridged by the United States or by any State on account of race, color, or previous condition of servitude.

SECTION 2. The Congress shall have power to enforce this article by appropriate legislation.

Proposed to the states by Congress, February 26, 1869
Ratification completed, February 3, 1870
Ratification declared, March 30, 1870

Article XVI.

The Congress shall have power to lay and collect taxes on incomes, from whatever source derived, without apportionment among the several States, and without regard to any census or enumeration.

Proposed to the states by Congress, July 12, 1909
Ratification completed, February 3, 1913
Ratification declared, February 25, 1913

Article XVII.

The Senate of the United States shall be composed of two Senators from each State, elected by the people thereof, for six years; and each Senator shall have one vote. The electors in each State shall have the qualifications requisite for electors of the most numerous branch of the State legislatures.

When vacancies happen in the representation of any State in the Senate, the executive authority of such State shall issue writs of election to fill such vacancies: *Provided*, That the legislature of any State may empower the executive thereof to make temporary appointments until the people fill the vacancies by election as the legislature may direct.

This amendment shall not be so construed as to affect the election or term of any Senator chosen before it becomes valid as part of the Constitution.

Proposed to the states by Congress, May 13, 1912
Ratification completed, April 8, 1913
Ratification declared, May 31, 1913

Article XVIII.

SECTION 1. After one year from the ratification of this article the manufacture, sale, or transportation of intoxicating liquors within, the importation thereof into, or the exportation thereof from the United States and all territory subject to the jurisdiction thereof for beverage purposes is hereby prohibited.

SEC. 2. The Congress and the several States shall have concurrent power to enforce this article by appropriate legislation.

SEC. 3. This article shall be inoperative unless it shall have been ratified as an amendment to the Constitution by the legislatures of the several States, as provided in the Constitution, within seven years from the date of the submission hereof to the States by the Congress.

Proposed to the states by Congress, December 18, 1917
Ratification completed, January 16, 1919
Ratification declared, January 29, 1919

Article XIX.

The right of citizens of the United States to vote shall not be denied or abridged by the United States or by any State on account of sex.

Congress shall have power to enforce this article by appropriate legislation.

Proposed to the states by Congress, June 4, 1919
Ratification completed, August 18, 1920
Ratification declared, August 26, 1920

437.10–22 Article XVIII. . . . Congress] Repealed by the Twenty-first Amendment.

Article XX.

SECTION 1.   The terms of the President and Vice President shall end at noon on the 20th day of January, and the terms of Senators and Representatives at noon on the 3d day of January, of the years in which such terms would have ended if this article had not been ratified; and the terms of their successors shall then begin.

SEC. 2.   The Congress shall assemble at least once in every year, and such meeting shall begin at noon on the 3d day of January, unless they shall by law appoint a different day.

SEC. 3.   If, at the time fixed for the beginning of the term of the President, the President elect shall have died, the Vice President elect shall become President. If a President shall not have been chosen before the time fixed for the beginning of his term, or if the President elect shall have failed to qualify, then the Vice President elect shall act as President until a President shall have qualified; and the Congress may by law provide for the case wherein neither a President elect nor a Vice President elect shall have qualified, declaring who shall then act as President, or the manner in which one who is to act shall be selected, and such person shall act accordingly until a President or Vice President shall have qualified.

SEC. 4.   The Congress may by law provide for the case of the death of any of the persons from whom the House of Representatives may choose a President whenever the right of choice shall have devolved upon them, and for the case of the death of any of the persons from whom the Senate may choose a Vice President whenever the right of choice shall have devolved upon them.

SEC. 5.   Sections 1 and 2 shall take effect on the 15th day of October following the ratification of this article.

SEC. 6.   This article shall be inoperative unless it shall have been ratified as an amendment to the Constitution by the legislatures of three-fourths of the several States within seven years from the date of its submission.

Proposed to the states by Congress, March 2, 1932
Ratification completed, January 23, 1933
Ratification declared, February 6, 1933

Article XXI.

SECTION 1. The eighteenth article of amendment to the Constitution of the United States is hereby repealed.

SECTION 2. The transportation or importation into any State, Territory, or possession of the United States for delivery or use therein of intoxicating liquors, in violation of the laws thereof, is hereby prohibited.

SECTION 3. This article shall be inoperative unless it shall have been ratified as an amendment to the Constitution by conventions in the several States, as provided in the Constitution, within seven years from the date of the submission hereof to the States by the Congress.

Proposed to the states by Congress, February 20, 1933
Ratification completed, December 5, 1933
Ratification declared, December 5, 1933

Article XXII.

SECTION 1. No person shall be elected to the office of the President more than twice, and no person who has held the office of President, or acted as President, for more than two years of a term to which some other person was elected President shall be elected to the office of the President more than once. But this Article shall not apply to any person holding the office of President when this Article was proposed by the Congress, and shall not prevent any person who may be holding the office of President, or acting as President, during the term within which this Article becomes operative from holding the office of President or acting as President during the remainder of such term.

SEC. 2. This article shall be inoperative unless it shall have been ratified as an amendment to the Constitution by the legislatures of three-fourths of the several States within seven years from the date of its submission to the States by the Congress.

Proposed to the states by Congress, March 21, 1947
Ratification completed, February 27, 1951
Ratification declared, March 1, 1951

Article XXIII.

SECTION 1. The District constituting the seat of Government of the United States shall appoint in such manner as the Congress may direct:

A number of electors of President and Vice President equal to the whole number of Senators and Representatives in Congress to which the District would be entitled if it were a State, but in no event more than the least populous State; they shall be in addition to those appointed by the States, but they shall be considered, for the purposes of the election of President and Vice President, to be electors appointed by a State; and they shall meet in the District and perform such duties as provided by the twelfth article of amendment.

SEC. 2. The Congress shall have power to enforce this article by appropriate legislation.

Proposed to the states by Congress, June 17, 1960
Ratification completed, March 29, 1961
Ratification declared, April 3, 1961

Article XXIV.

SECTION 1. The right of citizens of the United States to vote in any primary or other election for President or Vice President, for electors for President or Vice President, or for Senator or Representative in Congress, shall not be denied or abridged by the United States or any State by reason of failure to pay any poll tax or other tax.

SEC. 2. The Congress shall have power to enforce this article by appropriate legislation.

Proposed to the states by Congress, August 27, 1962
Ratification completed, January 23, 1964
Ratification declared, February 4, 1964

Article XXV.

SECTION 1. In case of the removal of the President from office or of his death or resignation, the Vice President shall become President.

SEC. 2. Whenever there is a vacancy in the office of the Vice President, the President shall nominate a Vice President who shall take office upon confirmation by a majority vote of both Houses of Congress.

SEC. 3.   Whenever the President transmits to the President pro tempore of the Senate and the Speaker of the House of Representatives his written declaration that he is unable to discharge the powers and duties of his office, and until he transmits to them a written declaration to the contrary, such powers and duties shall be discharged by the Vice President as Acting President.

SEC. 4.   Whenever the Vice President and a majority of either the principal officers of the executive departments or of such other body as Congress may by law provide, transmit to the President pro tempore of the Senate and the Speaker of the House of Representatives their written declaration that the President is unable to discharge the powers and duties of his office, the Vice President shall immediately assume the powers and duties of the office as Acting President.

Thereafter, when the President transmits to the President pro tempore of the Senate and the Speaker of the House of Representatives his written declaration that no inability exists, he shall resume the powers and duties of his office unless the Vice President and a majority of either the principal officers of the executive department or of such other body as Congress may by law provide, transmit within four days to the President pro tempore of the Senate and the Speaker of the House of Representatives their written declaration that the President is unable to discharge the powers and duties of his office. Thereupon Congress shall decide the issue, assembling within forty-eight hours for that purpose if not in session. If the Congress, within twenty-one days after receipt of the latter written declaration, or, if Congress is not in session, within twenty-one days after Congress is required to assemble, determines by two-thirds vote of both Houses that the President is unable to discharge the powers and duties of his office, the Vice President shall continue to discharge the same as Acting President; otherwise, the President shall resume the powers and duties of his office.

Proposed to the states by Congress, July 6, 1965
Ratification completed, February 10, 1967
Ratification declared, February 23, 1967

Article XXVI.

SECTION 1.   The right of citizens of the United States, who are eighteen years of age or older, to vote shall not be denied or abridged by the United States or by any State on account of age.

SEC. 2.   The Congress shall have power to enforce this article by appropriate legislation.

Proposed to the states by Congress, March 23, 1971
Ratification completed, July 1, 1971
Ratification declared, July 5, 1971

Article XXVII.

No law, varying the compensation for the services of the Senators and Representatives, shall take effect, until an election of Representatives shall have intervened.

Proposed to the states by Congress, September 25, 1789
Ratification completed, May 7, 1992
Ratification declared, May 18, 1992

Chronology
1774–1804

1774   First Continental Congress meets in Philadelphia, September 5–October 26. With royal governments collapsing, eight states create provincial congresses or conventions to govern during crisis.

1775   War for Independence begins, April 19. Second Continental Congress meets, May 10. Votes to raise an army and borrow money.

1776   Congress recommends that each state draw up a new constitution, May 10. Virginia convention calls on Congress to declare independence, May 15, and adopts declaration of rights and a new constitution. Congress declares independence, July 2. New Jersey, Delaware, Pennsylvania, Maryland, and North Carolina adopt new constitutions; Rhode Island and Connecticut amend royal charters to expunge references to monarch.

1777   Georgia and New York adopt state constitutions. Congress submits draft Articles of Confederation to states for ratification, November 15.

1778   South Carolina adopts new constitution. New Hampshire elects special convention to draft state constitution. Massachusetts legislature drafts constitution that voters reject, calling for special convention to draft a new constitution.

1779   New Hampshire voters reject proposed state constitution.

1780   Massachusetts adopts new state constitution.

1781   Ratification of the Articles of Confederation completed on March 1. Congress creates executive departments of Foreign Affairs, Finance, and War. New Hampshire voters reject second proposed Constitution.

1782   Rhode Island rejects proposal allowing Congress to levy 5 percent tax on imports to pay federal debt.

1783   New York and Rhode Island scuttle second attempt to give Congress power to raise revenue. Soldiers demanding back pay surround Independence Hall on June 21, forcing Congress to leave Philadelphia. New Hampshire voters adopt new state constitution. War for Independence ends as British troops evacuate New York City, November 25.

1785   Pennsylvania assumes payment of debt United States owes to Pennsylvanians and, along with six other states, begins issuing its own paper currency.

1786   Virginia passes Statute for Religious Freedom. Convention of five states held in Annapolis, calls for a convention to meet in Philadelphia in May 1787 to revise the Articles of Confederation. Farmers in western Massachusetts protesting taxes and foreclosures shut down county courts.

1787   Massachusetts state militia prevents insurgents from seizing arsenal at Springfield. Convention meets in Philadelphia, May 14, and is attended by delegates from every state except Rhode Island. Congress adopts Northwest Ordinance for governing territory beyond Ohio River, July 13. Delegates sign Constitution, September 17. Congress submits proposed Constitution to states for conventions to ratify, September 28. Delaware convention ratifies 30–0 on December 7. Pennsylvania convention ratifies, 46–23, December 12. New Jersey convention ratifies, 38–0, December 18. Georgia convention ratifies, 26–0, December 31.

1788   Connecticut convention ratifies, 128–49, January 9. Massachusetts convention ratifies, 187–168, February 6, and recommends nine amendments to be adopted later. New Hampshire convention convenes in February, but Federalist delegates fear they will not win so adjourn until summer. Rhode Island voters reject Constitution in March 24 referendum, 2,711–239. Maryland convention ratifies, 63–11, on April 26. South Carolina convention ratifies 149–73, May 23, and recommends four subsequent amendments. New Hampshire convention reconvenes and votes to ratify, 57–47, on June 21, recommending twelve subsequent amendments. Virginia convention votes to ratify, 89–79, on June 25, and recommends forty amendments. New York convention votes to ratify, 30–27, on July 26, and recommends thirty-two amendments. North Carolina convention rejects Constitution, 183–83, on August 2, and calls for second convention. With nine states having ratified, Congress calls for elections and sets dates for new government to take effect.

1789 Presidential electors meet on February 4; all 69 vote for George Washington to be President; John Adams receives 34 votes, and is elected Vice President. Newly-elected Congress convenes in New York on March 4. George Washington inaugurated as President, April 30. Congress submits to the states twelve proposed amendments to Constitution on September 25. Second convention in North Carolina votes to ratify, 194–77, on November 21.

1790 Rhode Island convention votes to ratify, 34–32, on May 29. Pennsylvania adopts new state constitution.

1791 Vermont admitted to the Union. Ratification of ten of the proposed amendments completed on December 15. (The first proposed amendment, concerning apportionment of House of Representatives, remains unratified; the second proposed amendment will be ratified in 1992, becoming the Twenty-seventh Amendment.)

1792 Kentucky admitted to the Union. George Washington unanimously reelected with votes of all 132 electors, December 5; John Adams reelected with 77 votes.

1793 U.S. Supreme Court rules 4–1 on February 18 in *Chisholm v. Georgia* that Constitution gives federal courts jurisdiction over suits brought against a state by citizens of another state. Several state legislatures immediately call for a constitutional amendment overturning the decision. Continuing controversies over the Washington administration's policies on the national debt and foreign affairs leads to emergence of two political parties; supporters of the administration call themselves Federalists, while opponents, led by Thomas Jefferson and James Madison, call themselves Republicans.

1794 Congress proposes Eleventh Amendment, overturning *Chisholm*, to the states on March 4.

1795 Eleventh Amendment completes ratification on February 7.

1796 Tennessee admitted to the Union. John Adams, Federalist, receives votes of 73 electors, December 7, while Thomas Jefferson, Republican, receives 68; they are elected President and Vice President, respectively.

1800 Electoral votes are tied with Republican Presidential and Vice Presidential candidates, Thomas Jefferson and Aaron Burr, each receiving 73; President John Adams receives 65.

1801   House of Representatives votes between Jefferson and Burr, with Federalists supporting Burr; on thirty-sixth ballot, February 17, ten states vote for Jefferson, electing him President.

1803   Supreme Court rules unanimously in *Marbury v. Madison* that a provision of Judiciary Act of 1789 is unconstitutional, first time Court strikes down act of Congress. Ohio admitted to the Union. Congress proposes Twelfth Amendment, establishing separate balloting by electors for President and Vice President, to the states on December 9.

1804   Twelfth Amendment ratified on June 15; no further Amendments will be added until 1865. Thomas Jefferson reelected, December 5, receiving votes of 162 of 178 electors; George Clinton elected vice president.

Biographical Notes

Henry Abbot (c. 1740–1791) Baptist minister. Helped draft North Carolina constitution in 1776. Supported ratification with amendments as delegate to the North Carolina ratifying conventions held in 1788 and 1789.

Samuel Adams (1722–1803) Political organizer. Organized opposition to British colonial policies in Massachusetts after passage of Stamp Act. Served in Massachusetts General Court, 1765–74, and in Continental Congress, 1774–82. Delegate to the Massachusetts convention, 1788, where he eventually supported ratification with recommended amendments. Governor of Massachusetts, 1794–97.

Fisher Ames (1758–1808) Lawyer. Delegate to Massachusetts convention, 1788, where he supported ratification. Served in the U.S. House of Representatives, 1789–97.

David Caldwell (1725–1824) Presbyterian minister. Helped draft North Carolina constitution in 1776. Delegate to North Carolina convention, 1788, where he opposed ratification.

Patrick Dollard (1746–1800) Innkeeper and plantation owner. Opposed ratification as delegate to the South Carolina convention, 1788. Served in South Carolina assembly, 1789–90.

Oliver Ellsworth (1745–1807) Lawyer. Served in Connecticut assembly, 1775–76, and as delegate to the Continental Congress, 1777–83. Judge of Connecticut superior court, 1785–89. Delegate to the Constitutional Convention, 1787, and the Connecticut convention, 1788, where he supported ratification. U.S. senator, 1789–96. Chief Justice of the Supreme Court of the United States, 1796–1800. Negotiated convention with France, 1799–1800.

Benjamin Franklin (1706–1790) Printer, writer, and natural philosopher. Member of the Pennsylvania assembly, 1751–64. Represented Pennsylvania as colonial agent in London, 1757–62 and 1764–75. Delegate to Continental Congress, 1775–76. Served as diplomat in France, 1776–85, negotiating treaty of alliance with France and peace treaty with Great Britain. Served as president of the Pennsylvania supreme executive council, 1785–88. Delegate to the Constitutional Convention, 1787.

Elbridge Gerry (1744–1814) Merchant and investor. Massachusetts delegate to the Continental Congress, 1776–81 and 1782–85. Delegate to the Constitutional Convention, 1787. Served in U.S. House of Representatives, 1789–93. Governor of Massachusetts, 1810–12. Vice president of the United States, 1812–14.

Alexander Hamilton (1755–1804) Lawyer. Military aide to George Washington, 1777–81. New York delegate to the Continental Congress, 1782–83. Delegate to the Constitutional Convention, 1787, and the New York ratifying convention, 1788. Secretary of the treasury, 1789–95.

John Hancock (1737–1793) Merchant. Massachusetts delegate to the Continental Congress, 1775–78. Governor of Massachusetts, 1780–85 and 1787–93. Delegate to the Massachusetts ratifying convention, 1788.

Patrick Henry (1736–1799) Lawyer. Virginia delegate to the Continental Congress, 1774–75. Governor of Virginia, 1776–79 and 1784–86. Delegate to the Virginia ratifying convention, 1788.

Harry Innes (1752–1816) Lawyer. Attorney general for district of Kentucky, 1784–89. Judge of U.S. District Court for Kentucky, 1789–1816.

James Iredell (1751–1799) Lawyer. Attorney general of North Carolina, 1779–81. Supported ratification as delegate to North Carolina ratifying convention, 1788. Associate Justice of the U.S. Supreme Court, 1790–99.

John Jay (1745–1829) Lawyer. New York delegate to the Continental Congress, 1774–79. Minister to Spain, 1779–82. Treaty negotiator with Great Britain, 1782–83 and 1794–95. Secretary for foreign affairs, 1784–89. Delegate to New York convention, 1788, where he supported ratification. Chief Justice of the Supreme Court of the United States, 1789–95. Governor of New York, 1795–1801.

Thomas Jefferson (1743–1826) Lawyer and plantation owner. Virginia delegate to the Continental Congress, 1775–76 and 1783–84. Governor of Virginia, 1779–81. Minister to France, 1785–89. Secretary of state, 1790–93. Vice president of the United States, 1797–1801. President of the United States, 1801–9.

William Jones (1724–1811) Joiner and schoolteacher. Delegate from Bristol, district of Maine, to Massachusetts convention in 1788, where he opposed ratification.

John Lansing, Jr. (1754–1829) Lawyer. New York delegate to the Continental Congress, 1784–85. Delegate to the Constitutional Convention, 1787. Opposed ratification as delegate to the New York convention, 1788. Justice of New York supreme court, 1790–98; chief justice, 1798–1801; and chancellor of New York, 1801–14.

John Leland (1754–1841) Baptist preacher in Virginia, 1776–91, and Massachusetts, 1791–1841.

Robert R. Livingston (1746–1813) Lawyer. New York delegate to the Continental Congress, 1775–76, 1779–80, and 1784. Chancellor of New York, 1777–1801. Secretary of foreign affairs, 1781–83. Delegate to New York convention, 1788, where he supported ratification. Minister to France, 1801–4.

James Madison (1751–1836) Politician and plantation owner. Virginia delegate to the Continental Congress, 1780–83 and 1787–88. Delegate to the Constitutional Convention, 1787, and the Virginia ratifying convention, 1788. Served in U.S. House of Representatives, 1789–97. Secretary of state, 1801–9. President of the United States, 1809–17.

Luther Martin (1748–1826) Lawyer. Attorney general of Maryland, 1778–1805 and 1818–22. Delegate to the Constitutional Convention, 1787. Opposed ratification as delegate to the Maryland convention, 1788.

George Mason (1725–1792) Politician and plantation owner. Drafted much of the 1776 Virginia state constitution, including its Declaration of Rights. Delegate to the Constitutional Convention, 1787, and to the Virginia convention, 1788, where he opposed ratification without prior amendments.

Charles Cotesworth Pinckney (1746–1825) Lawyer and plantation owner. Officer in Continental Army, 1776–83. Delegate to Constitutional Convention, 1787, and the South Carolina ratifying convention, 1788. Unsuccessful Federalist candidate for president in 1804 and 1808.

David Ramsay (1749–1815) Physician and historian. South Carolina delegate to the Continental Congress, 1782–83 and 1785–86. Supported ratification as delegate to the South Carolina convention, 1788.

Benjamin Rush (1746–1813) Physician, educator, and social reformer. Pennsylvania delegate to the Continental Congress, 1776–77. Supported ratification as delegate to the Pennsylvania convention, 1788.

Roger Sherman (1721–1793) Merchant and jurist. Connecticut delegate to the Continental Congress, 1774–81 and 1783–84. Delegate to the Constitutional Convention, 1787, and the Connecticut ratifying convention, 1788. Served in the U.S. House of Representatives, 1789–91, and in the Senate, 1791–93.

Daniel Shute (1722–1802) Congregational minister. Delegate to Massachusetts state constitutional convention, 1780. Supported ratification at Massachusetts convention, 1788.

Amos Singletary (1721–1806) Gristmill owner. Served in Massachusetts house of representatives, 1781–84, and in the state senate, 1787–90. Opposed ratification at the Massachusetts convention, 1788.

John Smilie (1742–1812) Politician and farmer. Served in the Pennsylvania assembly, 1778–80 and 1784–86. Opposed ratification at the Pennsylvania convention, 1787. Served in the U.S. House of Representatives, 1793–95 and 1799–1812.

Jonathan Smith (1741–1802) Delegate to the Massachusetts state constitutional convention, 1780. Voted in favor of ratification at the Massachusetts convention, 1788.

Melancton Smith (1744–1798) Merchant, lawyer, and landowner. New York delegate to the Continental Congress, 1785–88. Opposed unconditional ratification at the New York convention, 1788, but eventually voted in favor of ratification with recommended amendments.

Isaac Snow (1714–1799) Mariner. Captain of privateer during Revolutionary War. Delegate from district of Maine to the Massachusetts convention, 1788, where he supported ratification.

Joseph Spencer (1745–1829) Farmer and neighbor of James Madison in Orange County. Officer in Continental Army, 1776–77. Served in Virginia assembly, 1780–81.

Samuel Spencer (1734–1793) Lawyer and plantation owner. Judge of North Carolina superior court, 1778–93. Opposed ratification at the 1788 and 1789 North Carolina conventions.

John Stevens, Jr. (1749–1838) Engineer and inventor. Served as New Jersey state treasurer, 1777–83. Wrote "Americanus" essays in support of ratification, 1787–88. Became leader in steamboat and railroad development, building the first oceangoing steamship and the first American steam locomotive.

Increase Sumner (1749–1838) Lawyer. Delegate to Massachusetts state constitutional convention, 1779–80. Served in Massachusetts senate, 1780–82. Justice of the Massachusetts supreme judicial court, 1782–97. Supported ratification at the Massachusetts convention, 1788. Governor of Massachusetts, 1797–99.

Samuel Thompson (1735–1798) Innkeeper and landowner in the district of Maine. Served in Massachusetts house of representatives, 1784–88 and 1790–94. Opposed ratification in the Massachusetts convention, 1788.

Charles Turner (1732–1818) Congregational minister. Served in the Massachusetts house of representatives, 1780, and the state senate,

1783–88. Initially opposed ratification as delegate to the Massachusetts convention, 1788, but eventually voted to ratify with recommended amendments.

George Washington (1732–1799) Military officer, politician, and plantation owner. Served as officer in Virginia militia during French and Indian War, 1754–58. Virginia delegate to Continental Congress, 1774–75. Commander-in-chief of the Continental Army, 1775–83. President of the Constitutional Convention, 1787. President of the United States, 1789–97.

Noah Webster (1758–1843) Lawyer, schoolteacher, journalist, and editor. Wrote series of essays ("Giles Hickory," "A Citizen of America") in support of ratification, 1787–88. Edited magazines and newspapers and published spelling books, grammars, and dictionaries.

Samuel West (1730–1807) Congregational minister. Delegate to the Massachusetts state constitutional convention, 1779–80. Supported ratification at the Massachusetts convention, 1788, and privately urged Governor John Hancock to intervene in support of the Constitution.

Robert Whitehill (1738–1813) Politician and farmer. Helped draft Pennsylvania state constitution in 1776. Served in Pennsylvania assembly, 1776–78, 1783–87, and 1797–1801; on the state supreme executive council, 1779–81; and on the council of censors, 1783–84. Opposed ratification at the Pennsylvania convention, 1787. Delegate to Pennsylvania constitutional convention, 1789–90. Served in the state senate, 1801–5, and in the U.S. House of representatives, 1805–13.

William Widgery (c. 1753–1822) Shipbuilder and lawyer. Served in Massachusetts house of representatives, 1787–93 and 1795–97, and in the state senate, 1794. Delegate from district of Maine to the Massachusetts convention, 1788, where he opposed ratification. Served in the U.S. House of Representatives, 1811–13.

James Wilson (1742–1798) Lawyer and land speculator. Pennsylvania delegate to the Continental Congress, 1775–77, 1783, and 1785–87. Opposed 1776 Pennsylvania state constitution. Delegate to the Constitutional Convention and the Pennsylvania ratifying convention, 1787. Helped draft new Pennsylvania constitution, 1789–90. Associate justice of the U.S. Supreme Court, 1789–98.

Robert Yates (1738–1801) Lawyer. Helped draft New York state constitution, 1777. Justice of the New York state supreme court, 1777–1790; chief justice, 1790–98. Delegate to Constitutional Convention, 1787, and to the New York convention, 1788, where he opposed ratification.

Note on the Texts

This volume collects the texts of sixty-three speeches, letters, news-paper and magazine articles, memoranda, and poems written or delivered during the debate over the ratification of the Constitution from September 17, 1787, to July 30, 1788.

The documents included in this volume are taken from a variety of sources. Thirty-one documents are printed from *The Documentary History of the Ratification of the Constitution* (29 volumes to date, 1976–2017), edited by John P. Kaminski and Gaspare J. Saladino and published by the State Historical Society of Wisconsin. Another ten documents are taken from a digital source, Founders Online, a project of the National Historical Publications and Records Commission of the National Archives launched in 2013 in collaboration with the University of Virginia Press (https://founders.archives.gov/). The remaining twenty-two documents are printed from their original appearances in newspapers, magazines, pamphlets, or early accounts of the state ratifying conventions.

This volume prints texts as they appear in the sources listed below, but with a few alterations in editorial procedure. Words crossed out with a line through them have been deleted here. Bracketed editorial conjectural readings, in cases where the original text was damaged or difficult to read, are accepted without brackets in this volume. In cases where the original text was damaged and no conjectural reading was offered, the missing words are indicated by a bracketed space, i.e., [   ]. The editors of the *Documentary History* use angle brackets to indicate parts of newspaper articles that other newspapers excerpted and printed for their own use; these brackets have been omitted in this volume. In cases where the texts of the early printings used as sources have been corrected or revised in other printings or by publication of errata, the editors of the *Documentary History* give the later correction in a footnote or insert the correction in brackets next to the original word; this volume deletes the error and prints the corrected word in the text without brackets.

The following is a list of the documents included in this volume, in the order of their appearance, giving the source of each text. In the case of documents taken from the *Commentaries on the Constitution: Public and Private* volumes of the *Documentary History*, the item assigned by that edition is also given (for example, CC:77A). The most common sources are indicated by these abbreviations:

DCM   *Debates, Resolutions and Other Proceedings of the Convention of the Commonwealth of Massachusetts, Convened at Boston, on the 9th of January, 1788, and Continuing until the 7th of February Following, for the Purpose of Assenting to and Ratifying the Constitution Recommended by the Grand Federal Convention. Together with the Yeas and Nays on the Decision of the Grand Question. To Which the Federal Constitution Is Prefixed*, edited by Benjamin Russell (Boston, 1788).

DHRC   *The Documentary History of the Ratification of the Constitution* (29 vols. to date, Madison, WI: Wisconsin Historical Society Press, 1976–2017). Volume IX (1990), Volume X (1993), Volume XIII (1982), Volume XIV (1983), Volume XV (1984), Volume XVI (1986), ed. John P. Kaminski and Gaspare J. Saladino. Copyright © 1990, 1993, 1982, 1983, 1984, 1986 by the State Historical Society of Wisconsin. Reprinted by permission.

FO/AH   The Alexander Hamilton papers at Founders Online (https://founders.archives.gov/content/volumes# Hamilton) of the Wisconsin Historical Society.

PCNC   *Proceedings and Debates of the Convention of North-Carolina, Convened at Hillsborough, on Monday the 21st Day of July 1788*, transcribed by David Robertson (Edenton, NC, 1788).

THE DEBATE OPENS

Benjamin Franklin, Speech at the Conclusion of the Constitutional Convention, September 17, 1787. *DHRC*, XIII, 213–14, CC:77A.

Alexander Hamilton, Conjectures about the New Constitution, late September 1787. *FO/AH*, accessed January 18, 2018.

James Wilson, Speech at a Public Meeting, October 6, 1787. *DHRC*, XIII, 339–44, CC:134.

Brutus I, October 18, 1787. *DHRC*, XIII, 412–21, CC:178.

A Political Dialogue, October 24, 1787. *DHRC*, XIII, 455–57, CC:189.

James Madison to Thomas Jefferson, October 24, 1787. The James Madison Papers at Founders Online (https://founders.archives.gov/content/volumes#Madison, accessed January 18, 2018).

Thomas Jefferson to James Madison, December 20, 1787. The James Madison Papers at Founders Online (https://founders.archives.gov/content/volumes#Madison, accessed January 18, 2018).

Cato III, October 25, 1787. *DHRC*, XIII, 473–77, CC:195.

Publius (Alexander Hamilton), The Federalist No. 1, October 27, 1787. *FO/AH*, accessed January 18, 2018.

OPPOSITION ORGANIZES

Elbridge Gerry to the Massachusetts General Court, November 3, 1787. *DHRC*, XIII, 548–50, CC:227A.

Letters from the Federal Farmer to the Republican, November 8, 1787. *DHRC*, XIV, 18–54, CC:242.

Thomas Jefferson to William Stephens Smith, November 13, 1787. The Thomas Jefferson Papers at Founders Online (https://founders .archives.gov/content/volumes#Jefferson, accessed February 23, 2018).

George Mason, Objections to the Constitution, November 22, 1787. *DHRC*, XIV, 152–53, CC:276B.

Robert Yates and John Lansing, Jr., to Governor George Clinton, January 14, 1788. *DHRC*, XV, 368–70, CC:447.

TOWARD A NEW UNDERSTANDING OF POLITICS

Publius (James Madison), The Federalist No. 10, November 22, 1787. *DHRC*, XIV, 175–81, CC:285.

A Countryman (Roger Sherman) II, November 22, 1787. *DHRC*, XIV, 172–74, CC:284.

Brutus IV, November 29, 1787. *DHRC*, XIV, 297–303, CC:306.

Americanus (John Stevens, Jr.) III, November 30, 1787. *New York Daily Advertiser*, November 30, 1787.

Samuel Adams to Richard Henry Lee, December 3, 1787. *DHRC*, XIV, 333–34, CC:315.

A Landholder (Oliver Ellsworth) VII, December 17, 1787. *DHRC*, XIV, 448–52, CC:351.

Publius (Alexander Hamilton), The Federalist No. 23, December 18, 1787. *FO/AH*, accessed January 23, 2018.

Brutus VII, January 3, 1788. *DHRC*, XV, 234–40, CC:411.

Publius (Alexander Hamilton), The Federalist No. 30, December 28, 1787. *FO/AH*, accessed January 23, 2018.

SLAVERY AND LIBERTY

Luther Martin, The Genuine Information VIII, January 22, 1788. *DHRC*, XV, 433–37, CC:467.

Giles Hickory (Noah Webster) I, December 1787. *American Magazine*, December 1787.

Publius (James Madison), The Federalist No. 39, January 16, 1788. *DHRC*, XV, 380–86, CC:452.

On the New Constitution, January 28, 1788. *DHRC*, XV, 486, CC:481.

Brutus XI, January 31, 1788. *DHRC*, XV, 512–17, CC:489.

Civis (David Ramsay) to the Citizens of South Carolina, February 4, 1788. *DHRC*, XVI, 21–27, CC:493.

Publius (James Madison), The Federalist No. 54, February 12, 1788. *DHRC*, XVI, 107–10, CC:524.

THE FUTURE OF THE AMERICAN REPUBLIC

Publius (James Madison), The Federalist No. 51, February 6, 1788. *DHRC*, XVI, 43–47, CC:503.

Brutus XII, February 7 and 14, 1788. *DHRC*, XVI, 72–75, CC:510.

Harry Innes to John Brown, February 20, 1788. *DHRC*, XVI, 152–53, CC:545.

Joseph Spencer to James Madison Enclosing John Leland's Objections, February 28, 1788. *DHRC*, XVI, 252–54, CC:574.

Publius (Alexander Hamilton), The Federalist No. 70, March 15, 1788. *FO/AH*, accessed February 20, 2018.

Brutus XV, March 20, 1788. *DHRC*, XVI, 431–35, CC:632.

Publius (Alexander Hamilton), The Federalist No. 78, May 28, 1788. *FO/AH*, accessed February 20, 2018.

George Washington to John Armstrong, April 25, 1788. The George Washington Papers at Founders Online (https://founders.archives .gov/content/volumes#Washington, accessed February 20, 2018).

THE STATE RATIFYING CONVENTIONS

PENNSYLVANIA

James Wilson, Opening Address, November 24, 1787. *The Substance of a Speech Delivered by James Wilson, Esq. Explanatory of the General Principles of the Proposed Federal Constitution*, compiled and edited by Alexander J. Dallas (Philadelphia, 1787), 3–10.

James Wilson and John Smilie, November 28, 1787. *Pennsylvania Herald*, December 12, 1787.

Benjamin Rush, November 30, 1787. *Pennsylvania Herald*, January 5, 1788.

James Wilson on the Slave-Trade Clause, December 3, 1787. *Debates of the Convention, of the State of Pennsylvania on the Constitution, Proposed for the Government of the United States*, compiled and edited by Thomas Lloyd (Philadelphia, 1788), 57–59.

Robert Whitehill Replies to Wilson on the Slave-Trade Clause, December 3, 1787. Philadelphia *Independent Gazetteer*, December 6, 1787.

Dissent of the Minority of the Pennsylvania Convention, December 18, 1787. *DHRC*, XV, 13–34, CC:353.

MASSACHUSETTS

Fisher Ames, January 15, 1788. DCM, 30–35.

An Exchange, January 17, 1788. DCM, 56–61.

Amos Singletary and Jonathan Smith, January 25, 1788. DCM, 136–40.

Daniel Shute and William Jones, January 31, 1788. DCM, 155–57.

John Hancock Proposes Ratification with Recommended Amendments, January 31, 1788. DCM, 161.

Samuel Adams Supports Hancock's Proposition, January 31, 1788. DCM, 162–63.

John Hancock's Final Observations, February 6, 1788. DCM, 220–22.

The Form of the Ratification of Massachusetts, February 6, 1788. *DHRC*, XVI, 67–69, CC:508.

SOUTH CAROLINA

Charles Cotesworth Pinckney, May 14, 1788. *Columbian Herald* (Charleston), June 9, 1788.

Patrick Dollard, May 22, 1788. *City Gazette* (Charleston), May 29, 1788.

VIRGINIA

Patrick Henry, June 4, 1788. *DHRC*, IX, 929–31.

Patrick Henry and James Madison, June 12, 1788. *DHRC*, X, 1209–26.

George Mason and James Madison, June 17, 1788. *DHRC*, X, 1338–39.

NEW YORK

Robert R. Livingston, Melancton Smith, and John Jay, June 23, 1788. *Debates and Proceedings of the Convention of the State of New-York*, edited and transcribed by Francis Childs (New York, 1788), 51–60.

Melancton Smith, June 27, 1788. *Debates and Proceedings of the Convention of the State of New-York*, edited and transcribed by Francis Childs (New York, 1788), 92–96.

NORTH CAROLINA

James Iredell on the Presidency and the Pardoning Power, July 28, 1788. PCNC, 129–37.

James Iredell on Impeachment, July 28, 1788. PCNC, 149–54.

Henry Abbot and James Iredell, July 30, 1788. PCNC, 217–22.

The Rev. David Caldwell and Samuel Spencer, July 30, 1788. PCNC, 226–27.

This volume presents the texts of the documents chosen for inclusion here without change, except for the correction of typographical errors or slips of the pen and the modernization of the use of quotation marks (only beginning and ending quotation marks are provided here, instead of placing a quotation mark at the beginning of every line of a quoted passage. The following is a list of typographical errors corrected, cited by page and line number: 21.21, sacrified; 36.12, Goverment; 88.4, convention; 186.1, to to; 224.20, there; 276.30, of three; 334.1, persumed; 344.27, as.

Notes

In the notes below, the reference numbers denote page and line of this volume (the line count includes headings, but not rule lines). No note is made for material included in the eleventh edition of *Merriam-Webster's Collegiate Dictionary*. Biblical references are keyed to the King James Version. Footnotes and bracketed editorial notes within the text were in the originals. For further historical and biographical background, and references to other studies, see *The Debate on the Constitution*, ed. Bernard Bailyn (2 vols., New York: The Library of America, 1993).

3.1–2 *Benjamin Franklin: Speech . . . Convention*] This speech was read for the eighty-two-year-old Franklin by James Wilson just before the final votes were taken in the convention.

3.14–18 Steele . . . Wrong.] The mock dedication to Pope Clement XI by Bishop Benjamin Hoadley (1676–1761) in Urbano Cerri, *An Account of the state of the Roman-Catholick Religion* (1715), was often attributed to Richard Steele. It includes the observation: "You are Infallible, and We always in the Right."

3.27 if well administred] Cf. Alexander Pope, *An Essay on Man* (1733–34), Epistle III, ll. 303–4: "For Forms of Government let fools contest; / Whate'er is best administered is best."

4.34–36 Then the Motion . . . accordingly.] The motion to add the form of signing to the Constitution; see p. 430 in this volume. Despite Franklin's appeal, Edmund Randolph and George Mason of Virginia and Elbridge Gerry of Massachusetts refused to sign.

5.1–2 *Alexander Hamilton . . . Constitution*] Hamilton did not publish and is not known to have circulated this private memorandum.

8.1 *James Wilson . . . Public Meeting*] Wilson spoke at a meeting in the Pennsylvania State House Yard held to nominate candidates to the state assembly. His speech was published in the *Pennsylvania Gazette* on October 29, 1787, and by the end of the year had appeared in thirty-four newspapers in twenty-seven towns across twelve states, becoming the most frequently cited document in the ratification debate.

10.34–35 cantonments . . . Ohio] The Continental Congress kept a few hundred troops in outposts along the western frontier after the Revolutionary War.

13.16 the funding law] In 1785 the Pennsylvania assembly voted to assume payment of the interest on the national debt owed to citizens of the state. The assumption measure was to be funded by selling public lands, levying taxes, and issuing paper money.

15.1 *Brutus*] The author of the sixteen "Brutus" essays (*New-York Journal*, October 18, 1787–April 10, 1788) is not known.

21.22–23 baron de Montesquieu . . . vol. 1] Baron de Montesquieu (1689–1755), *The Spirit of the Laws* (1748), volume I, book VIII, chapter XVI.

21.35–36 the marquis Beccarari] Cesare Bonesana, Marchese di Beccaria (1738–1794), *Essay on Crimes and Punishments* (1764).

27.35 beware . . . the Pharisees] See Matthew 16:6, 11–12, Mark 8:15, and Luke 12:1.

29.6 Commodore Jones] John Paul Jones (1747–1792).

29.12 Col. Carrington] Edward Carrington (1749–1810), a Virginia delegate to the Continental Congress.

29.25 W.H. B.F.] William Hay (c. 1749–c. 1826) of Virginia, and Benjamin Franklin.

29.35 Ubbo's book] Ubbo Emmius (1547–1625), *Graecorum Respublicae*, the third volume of *Vetus Graecia* (1626).

29.38 Encyclopedie] *Encyclopédie méthodique* (1782–1832), originally edited by Charles Panckoucké (1736–1793), was an expanded and rearranged version of *L'Encyclopédie, ou Dictionnaire Raisonné, des Arts et des Métiers* (1751–76), edited by Denis Diderot (1713–1784) and Jean le Rond d'Alembert (1713–1783).

31.11 Governour Randolph] Edmund Randolph (1753–1813) served as governor of Virginia, 1786–88, attorney general of the United States, 1789–94, and secretary of state, 1794–95. In the Philadelphia convention Randolph had favored a three-man executive drawn from different parts of the country.

32.37–39 As I formerly . . . on the subject.] In a letter to Jefferson dated March 19, 1787.

33.4 imperia in imperio] Governments within a government.

33.15–20 Lycian Confederacy . . . Achæan] The Lycian Confederacy was founded in southwest Asia Minor c. 169 B.C.E. and retained its sovereignty until its annexation by Rome in 43 A.D. Initially organized around the temple of Demeter at Anthele, the Amphyctionic Council later met at the temple of Apollo at Delphi. The council administered the temples and their property, organized the Pythian Games, and sought to protect the water sources of its member cities. Founded c. 280 B.C.E. by several cities in the northern and central Peloponnese, the Achæan League was dissolved following its defeat by Rome in 146 B.C.E.

38.14   Divide et impera] Divide and rule.

39.25–26   Mr. Wythe . . . MClurg] George Wythe (1726–1806), professor of law at William and Mary College and a supporter of the Constitution; James McClurg (1746–1823), a Richmond physician.

41.2   the Governour's] George Clinton (1739–1812) was governor of New York, 1777–95 and 1801–4, and vice president of the United States, 1805–12.

41.16–18   Mr. Chase . . . Mr. Paca] Samuel Chase (1741–1811), an attorney from Baltimore, and William Paca (1740–1799), governor of Maryland, 1782–85, were both signers of the Declaration of Independence. At the Maryland convention, April 21–29, 1788, Chase opposed ratification, while Paca, who proposed a number of amendments, voted to ratify. Chase later became a Federalist and served as an associate justice of the U.S. Supreme Court, 1796–1811.

41.22–23   Chancellor Pendleton] Edmund Pendleton (1721–1803) was a judge of the Virginia court of chancery, 1777–88. He served as the presiding officer of the Virginia convention in 1788, where he supported ratification.

41.24–25   Innis and Marshall] Both James Innes (1754–1798), attorney general of Virginia, 1786–1796, and John Marshall (1755–1835), then an attorney practicing in Richmond, supported ratification in the 1788 convention. Marshall later served in Congress, 1799–1800; as secretary of state, 1800–1; and as Chief Justice of the Supreme Court of the United States, 1801–35.

41.26–27   James Mercer . . . M. Page] James Mercer (1736–1793), a judge of the Virginia General Court; Richard Henry Lee (1732–1794), Virginia delegate to the Continental Congress, 1774–79, 1784–85, and in 1787, and a U.S. senator, 1789–92; his brother, Arthur Lee (1740–1792), a physician who served as a Virginia delegate to the Continental Congress, 1781–84; Mann Page, Jr. (c. 1749–c. 1810), a planter and lawyer who served in the Virginia house of delegates.

42.4   Mr. Dane] Nathan Dane (1752–1835) served as a Massachusetts delegate to the Continental Congress, 1785–88.

42.14–16   Mr. Adams . . . Your reappointment] John Adams had served as the United States minister to Great Britain since 1785. Jefferson was reappointed minister to France on October 12, 1787.

42.18–22   *made without . . . scruples*] The italicized words were written using a cipher that Jefferson had sent to Madison from Europe on May 11, 1785.

42.28   Mr. Jay] John Jay (1745–1829) was secretary of foreign affairs, 1784–89. He later served as Chief Justice of the Supreme Court of the United States, 1789–95, and as governor of New York, 1795–1801.

43.10   Broome . . . Mr. Burke] Jefferson was trying to help the family of
the late John Burke recover property they believed had "come to the hands
of" John Broome, a New York merchant.

43.14   Speech of Mr. C. P.] Charles Pinckney (1757–1824), a South Carolina
delegate to the Continental Congress, 1785–87, and to the Constitutional Convention, 1787. Pinckney later served as governor of South Carolina, 1789–92,
1796–98, 1806–8; as a U.S. senator, 1798–1; as minister to Spain, 1801–4; and
as a congressman, 1819–21.

43.19   Musæum, Magazine] *The American Museum* (1787–92) and *The
Columbian Magazine, or Monthly Miscellany* (1786–92), both Philadelphia
journals.

44.8–11   A. Stuart . . . P. Carrington] Archibald Stuart (1757–1832), a lawyer and member of the Virginia house of delegates; Patrick Henry; William
Nelson, Jr. (c. 1759–1813), a lawyer and member of the Virginia house of delegates; St. George Tucker (1752–1827), an attorney and legal scholar who later
served on the Virginia court of appeals, 1804–13, and as a U.S. district judge,
1813–25; John Taylor (1753–1824), known as John Taylor of Caroline, later became a prolific writer on politics and served in the U.S. Senate, 1792–94, 1803,
and 1822–24; Paul Carrington (1733–1818), chief judge of the Virginia General
Court and older brother of Edward Carrington (see note 29.12).

45.11–12   cyphered paragraph] See page 42.18–22 and note.

45.18   Burke's case] See page 43.9–10 and note. On September 17, 1787, Jefferson had written Madison that John Burke's cash had been given by John
Broome to William S. Browne of Providence, Rhode Island.

45.27   Mr. Bourgoin] French miniaturist François Bourgoin.

45.31–32   mr. Hopkinson] Francis Hopkinson (1737–1791), a lawyer, was a
New Jersey delegate to the Continental Congress in 1776. Hopkinson strongly
supported ratification at the New Jersey convention, 1787, and later served as
the U.S. district judge for Pennsylvania, 1789–91.

46.30–31   say, as mr. Wilson does] James Wilson, in his speech of October 6,
1787; see pp. 8–14 in this volume.

48.21   late rebellion in Massachusetts] A series of protests by farmers in western Massachusetts against tax collections and farm foreclosures led in September 1786 to the outbreak of "Shays' Rebellion," named after one of its leaders,
the Revolutionary War veteran Daniel Shays (1747?–1825). The uprising was
suppressed by Massachusetts militia in February 1787.

50.1   *Cato III*] The author of the seven "Cato" essays (*New-York Journal*,
September 27, 1787–January 3, 1788) is not known.

51.11–26   Montesquieu . . . monarchy.] *The Spirit of the Laws*, volume I,
book III, chapter 16.

52.2–3   Mr. Locke . . . *compact*.] Cf. John Locke, *Two Treatises on Government* (1690), Second Treatise.

52.4–5   *Political liberty . . . security*] *The Spirit of the Laws*, volume I, book XI, chapter 2.

52.21–22   *property . . . consist*] See note 52.2–3.

52.30–32   this state . . . Frankland] New York claims to land in Vermont, which declared itself independent in 1777, were not finally resolved until 1791, when Vermont entered the Union. North Carolina had temporarily detached its western territory as the so-called State of Franklin (1785–88), which would eventually be incorporated into the new state of Tennessee.

55.2   *The Federalist*] The *Federalist* essays were first published from October 27, 1787, to May 28, 1788; Alexander Hamilton wrote fifty-one of them, James Madison, twenty-nine, and John Jay, five.

63.1–2   *Elbridge Gerry . . . Court*] Gerry's statement was reprinted throughout Massachusetts and by at least thirty-one newspapers in eleven other states, as well as two pamphlet anthologies and *The American Museum.*

66.1–2   *Letters . . . Republican*] Published in pamphlet form, *Letters from the Federal Farmer to the Republican* circulated throughout the United States and was in its fourth printing by early January 1788. The author of the *Letters* remains unknown; "The Republican" to whom the letters are ostensibly addressed was probably George Clinton, the Antifederalist governor of New York.

67.1–2   Pope's maxim . . . is best,"] See note 3.27.

71.33   had they all attended] A total of nineteen elected delegates, including Patrick Henry and Richard Henry Lee, did not attend the Constitutional Convention; all but five of them formally resigned their appointments.

72.5   Eleven states met] Rhode Island chose not to elect delegates to the Convention. New York's vote was counted until early July, when two of its three delegates left Philadelphia, while New Hampshire's delegates did not arrive until late July.

99.39–40   the well born . . . Mr. Adams calls them] John Adams, *A Defence of the Constitutions of Government of the United States against the attack of M. Turgot*, volume I (1787), Preface.

101.34–36   perpetual jealousy . . . Mr. Dickinson] John Dickinson (1732–1808), *Letters from a Farmer in Pennsylvania to the Inhabitants of the British Colonies*, No. 11, February 8, 1768.

104.25   morrisites] The followers of Robert Morris (1734–1806), the powerful Pennsylvania banker and merchant who served as superintendent of finance under the Continental Congress, 1781–84, and of Gouverneur Morris (1752–1816), a lawyer who served as an assistant to Robert Morris when he was superintendent of finance. Both men were delegates to the Philadelphia convention and ardently supported the Constitution.

106.8–9 gentlemen in Boston . . . the press] In October 1787 some printers in Boston had refused to publish pseudonymous Antifederalist material unless they were given the writers' true identities. The refusal to print such pieces was assailed as a flagrant violation of the freedom of the press in Massachusetts, Connecticut, Rhode Island, New York, and Pennsylvania, and the practice was soon dropped.

109.1 *William Stephens Smith*] A former Continental Army officer from New York, Smith (1755–1816) served as secretary to the American legation in London, 1785–88. In 1786 he had married Abigail (Nabby) Adams, the eldest child of John and Abigail Adams.

109.13 M. de Chastellux] François-Jean, Marquis de Chastellux (1734–1788), was a French general who had served in the United States during the Revolutionary War and the author of *Travels in North America in the Years 1780, 1781, and 1782* (1787).

109.33 instance of Massachusets?] Shays' Rebellion; see note 48.21.

111.1 *George Mason . . . Constitution*] Mason wrote out the first version of his objections in Philadelphia on the back of his printed copy of the draft Constitution. On October 7, 1787, he sent a revised and expanded version to George Washington, who passed a copy on to Madison. Mason's "Objections" were first printed in the *Massachusetts Centinel* on November 21, 1787, but without the paragraph on the navigation laws (see p. 114.6–20). The full version appeared in the *Virginia Journal* the next day.

111.6–112.3 Gentlemen, At this . . . in manuscript.] The introduction and concluding statement (p. 115.8–14) were written by Tobias Lear (1762–1816), Washington's private secretary, 1785–92. Washington did not know that Mason's essay was going to be printed.

116.1–2 *Robert Yates . . . George Clinton*] Yates and Lansing withdrew from participation in the Constitutional Convention and left Philadelphia on July 10, 1787. This letter was their first public explanation of their conduct.

116.7 Mr. Hamilton] Alexander Hamilton.

116.13 the powers delegated to us] The New York legislature appointed delegates to attend the Constitutional Convention on March 6, 1787, and instructed them to limit the convention to revising the Articles of Confederation.

121.2 *The Federalist No. 10*] This essay was Madison's first contribution to the *Federalist* series.

129.1 *A Countryman*] Roger Sherman published five "Countryman" essays in the *New Haven Gazette*, November 14–December 20, 1787.

131.24–25 *George Bryan's*] The Pennsylvania Antifederalist George Bryan (1731–1791) was believed by some to be the author of the eighteen "Centinel" essays published in Philadelphia, October 5, 1787–April 9, 1788. The essays are now attributed to his son, Samuel Bryan (1759–1821).

133.8 my last number] Brutus III, published November 15, 1787.

135.1 my first number] Brutus I, published October 18, 1787; see pp. 15–26.

137.27–29 *Apostle Paul . . . cherisheth it."*] Ephesians 5:29.

139.1–9 *Elisha . . . king of Syria."*] 2 Kings 8:12–13.

140.1 *Americanus (John Stevens, Jr.)*] Stevens published seven "Americanus" essays in the *New York Daily Advertiser*, November 2, 1787–January 21, 1788.

140.3 "It is natural . . . territory."] *The Spirit of the Laws*, volume I, book VIII, chapter 16.

140.5 Civilian] An authority on the civil law.

140.16–19 "the people . . . enact laws."] *The Spirit of the Laws*, volume I, book II, chapter 2.

145.5 our General Court] The Massachusetts legislature.

145.6 my Station there] Adams served as president of the Massachusetts senate, 1787–88.

146.23 Colo Francis, Mr. A. L.] Lee's brothers Francis Lightfoot Lee (1734–1797) and Arthur Lee (1740–1792).

147.1 *A Landholder (Oliver Ellsworth)*] Ellsworth published thirteen "Landholder" essays in the Hartford *Connecticut Courant*, November 5–December 31, 1787, and March 3–24, 1788.

147.6–17 "In all our deliberations . . . indispensible."] From the letter that accompanied the Constitution when it was sent to the Continental Congress on September 17, 1787. Drafted by the Constitutional Convention's committee of style, the letter was signed by Washington.

150.3 the thirty-nine articles] The Thirty-nine Articles of Religion, adopted in their final form in 1571, defined the doctrine and practices of the Church of England.

153.29–30 "the common defence . . . welfare."] From the Articles of Confederation, Article VIII.

157.18 *nudum pactum*] Naked agreement, i.e., one that is legally unenforceable.

163.1–3 then moved . . . the United States.] In a plan proposed to the Continental Congress on March 20, 1783, by Alexander Hamilton and James Wilson that was rejected, 7–4.

171.1–2 *Luther Martin . . . Information*] The Maryland House of Delegates requested on November 23, 1787, that the state's delegates to the Constitutional Convention provide "information" regarding its proceedings. Luther Martin responded by giving a speech to the house on November 29 that was published in expanded form in the Baltimore *Maryland Gazette*, December 28, 1787–February 8, 1788. A pamphlet edition, *The Genuine Information, Delivered to the Legislature of the State of Maryland*, appeared on April 12, 1788.

177.1 *Giles Hickory (Noah Webster)*] Webster published four "Giles Hickory" essays in *American Magazine*, December 1787–March 1788.

178.3–4 habeas corpus act . . . 2d of William and Mary] The Habeas Corpus Act (1679), passed to prevent imprisonment without proper legal authority, detailed the methods of obtaining a writ of habeas corpus and imposed penalties on government officers who did not comply with writs that had been issued. In 1689 Parliament adopted a declaratory act that became commonly known as the Bill of Rights. It established a line of royal line of succession, barred Catholics from the throne, and declared that the crown could not legally suspend or dispense with laws, levy money, or keep a standing army in peacetime without the consent of parliament. The Bill of Rights also called for free elections to parliament, frequent holdings of parliament, freedom of speech in parliament; proclaimed the right of subjects to petition the crown; and declared that excessive bail and fines ought not to be imposed and that cruel and unusual punishments ought not to be inflicted.

182.38–39 the Senate of Maryland] Under the state constitution adopted in 1776, senators in Maryland were indirectly elected by electors chosen by the voters. The constitution was amended in 1838 to allow for the direct election of the state senate.

188.3–5 'squire Adams . . . St. James's] As the U.S. minister to Great Britain, 1785–88, John Adams was formally received as minister to the Court of St. James's Palace in Westminster. Adams wrote *A Defence of the Constitutions of Government of the United States of America* (3 vols., 1787–88) while he was living in England.

188.9–10 Shelburne and Pitt . . . Rush and Wilson] William Petty, second Earl of Shelburne (1737–1805), Whig statesman who served as prime minister of Great Britain, 1782–83; William Pitt the Younger (1759–1806), a Tory who served as prime minister, 1783–1801 and 1804–6; Benjamin Rush and James Wilson.

192.31–193.5 "From this method . . . positive law."] Cf. William Blackstone, *Commentaries on the Laws of England* (4 vols., 1765–69), Introduction, section 2. The Latin passage from Grotius may be translated: "The law is not exact on the subject, but leaves it open to a good man's judgment."

195.27–196.3 The court of exchequer . . . all the nation.] See Blackstone, *Commentaries*, Book III, chapter 4, section 7.

204.22   recently obtained . . . sanction of America] The Continental Congress adopted an amendment to the Articles of Confederation on April 18, 1783, changing the basis for apportioning treasury requisitions among the states from property values to population. By the time the Constitutional Convention met, all of the states except New Hampshire and Rhode Island had ratified the amendment.

220.11   A voluminous writer in favor] "Publius," in *Federalist No. 34*, January 4, 1788, written by Hamilton, and *Federalist No. 44*, January 25, 1788, written by Madison.

221.32–222.6   Originally, this court . . . to dispute."] See Blackstone, *Commentaries*, Book III, chapter 4, section 6.

223.1   *John Brown*] Born in Staunton, Virginia, Brown (1757–1837) had moved to the district of Kentucky in 1782 and established a law practice in Frankfort. He opposed ratification at the Virginia convention in 1788, then served as a congressman from Virginia, 1789–92, and as a senator from Kentucky, 1792–1805.

223.3–4   Mr. Lacasagne] Michael Lacassagne (c. 1750–1797), a lawyer, merchant, and speculator who lived in Louisville.

224.35   Mr. Al Parker] Alexander Parker, a merchant, lawyer, and surveyor.

225.5   Col. Thos. Barber] Thomas Barbour (1735–1825), a plantation owner in Orange County who had served in the house of burgesses, 1769–75. Barbour failed to win election to the Virginia ratifying convention in the voting held in Orange County on March 24, 1788.

225.26–32   Mr. Bledsoe and Sanders . . . Capt Walker] Aaron Bledsoe (c. 1730–1809) and Nathaniel Saunders (d. 1808) were Baptist preachers in Orange County, Virginia. James Walker was a Culpeper County plantation owner who served in the Virginia senate, 1777–79. He was an unsuccessful candidate for the Virginia ratifying convention.

227.6–7   Riddle . . . Sampsons Heifer] See Judges 14:12–18.

234.36–39   Junius . . . *De Lome] Hamilton quotes from the preface to the pseudonymous *Letters of Junius* (1772), which cites *The Constitution of England* (1771) by Swiss jurist Jean Louis de Lolme (1740–1806).

237.4   my last number] Brutus XVI, February 28–March 6, 1788.

240.19   a former paper] Brutus XI, January 31, 1788; see pp. 190–96.

243.5–6   *with a high . . . arm.*] Cf. Deuteronomy 26:8 and Jeremiah 21:5.

244.2–3   *Federalist No. 78* . . . May 28, 1788] The final eight *Federalist* essays (nos. 78–85), all written by Hamilton, first appeared in the second volume of the book edition published by John and Archibald McLean in New York on May 28, 1788 (the first volume appeared on March 22).

244.8–9 have been clearly pointed out] In *Federalist No. 22*, December 14, 1787, written by Hamilton.

249.38–39 Protest of the minority . . . Martin's speech] The dissent of the minority of the Pennsylvania ratifying convention was published in the *Pennsylvania Packet*, December 18, 1787, and widely reprinted; see pp. 281–306. Luther Martin's speech to the Maryland House of Delegates on November 29, 1787, was published in a pamphlet titled *The Genuine Information*; see note 171.1–2.

252.1 *John Armstrong*] A resident of Carlisle, Pennsylvania, who had served as an officer in the French and Indian War and in the Revolution, Armstrong (1717–1795) supported ratification of the Constitution.

252.7 Colo. Blain] Ephraim Blaine (1741–1808), a merchant in Carlisle, Pennsylvania, who had served as a commissary officer during the Revolution.

254.24 Dr Nisbet] Charles Nisbet (1736–1804), a Presbyterian minister, served as the first president of Dickinson College in Carlisle from 1785 until his death.

259.1–2 PENNSYLVANIA . . . CONVENTION] The convention met in the Pennsylvania State House (now known as Independence Hall) in Philadelphia. It achieved a quorum on November 21, 1787, and began debating the Constitution on November 24.

259.3 *James Wilson: Opening Address*] The text of Wilson's speech is taken from a pamphlet published on November 28, 1787, by Alexander J. Dallas (1759–1817), editor of the *Pennsylvania Herald*.

261.15 (as Montesquieu has termed it)] *The Spirit of the Laws*, volume I, book VIII, chapter 20.

261.29–31 Montesquieu . . . members;] *The Spirit of the Laws*, volume I, book IX, chapter 1.

262.7 the Germanic Body] The Holy Roman Empire.

262.13–14 Achæan and Lycian . . . Amphyctionic] See note 33.15–20.

263.20–23 at the revolution . . . the people] In 1689, Parliament offered William and Mary the throne on the condition that they acknowledge the rights and liberties later included in the Bill of Rights (see note 178.3–4). Blackstone wrote in his *Commentaries*, Book I, chapter 6, that the Revolution of 1688 made clear the existence of an unwritten "original contract" between the king and the people, under which the king pledged to govern his people according to law in return for their allegiance.

269.16–18 Sir William Blackstone . . . British Parliament] *Commentaries on the Laws of England*, Book I, chapter 2.

272.23   Virginia has no bill of rights] The Virginia convention adopted a declaration of rights, drafted by George Mason, on June 12, 1776, and a constitution, drafted largely by Mason, on June 29, 1776.

274.8   Mr. M'Kean] Thomas McKean (1734–1817) was a Delaware delegate
to the Continental Congress, 1774–76 and 1778–83; chief justice of Pennsylvania, 1777–99; and governor of Pennsylvania, 1799–1808.

276.20   council of censors] Under the 1776 Pennsylvania constitution a council of censors was to be elected every seven years to serve for a single year. The
council would review the actions of the state government to see if the constitution had been violated and, if necessary, propose amendments to be considered
by a new constitutional convention.

276.33   Civilians] Experts in civil law.

278.10   Mr. Findley] William Findley (1741–1821), a delegate from Westmore-
land County who voted against ratification. Findley later served in the U.S.
House of Representatives, 1791–99 and 1803–17.

278.20   These were the . . . in 1783] The text of Wilson's remarks is taken
from *Debates of the Convention of the State of Pennsylvania, on the Constitution*,
a pamphlet published by Thomas Lloyd on February 6, 1788. A list of errata in
the pamphlet noted that this phrase should be deleted.

280.1–2   *Robert Whitehill . . . Clause*] Whitehill's remarks are taken from
the Philadelphia *Independent Gazetteer*, December 6, 1787, where "Puff" (said
to be Benjamin Rush) reported them as the "Substance of a speech."

281.1–2   *Dissent . . . Pennsylvania Convention*] The "Address and Reasons
of Dissent" was published in the *Pennsylvania Packet* on December 18, 1787,
six days after the Pennsylvania convention voted to ratify the Constitution.
Signed by twenty-one of the twenty-three delegates who opposed ratification,
the "Address" was probably written by Samuel Bryan (1759–1821), a former
clerk of the Pennsylvania assembly who published eighteen "Centinel" essays
in the Philadelphia press, October 5, 1787–April 9, 1788.

283.10–11   in one member . . . a subsequent session] In 1776, Pennsylvania had adopted a constitution that established a unicameral legislature, a
twelve-member executive council without veto power, and a supreme court
whose judges served for seven-year terms. The constitution became the focus
of a continuing political struggle between its "Constitutionalist" supporters
and its "Republican" opponents, who favored a bicameral legislature, a single executive with a limited veto, and appointing judges for terms of good
behavior. In the October 1786 elections the Republicans gained control of
the assembly, and on December 30 the new majority appointed seven delegates to the Constitutional Convention. With the exception of Jared Ingersoll
(1749–1822), the delegates were all prominent Republicans. The eighth delegate, appointed on March 28, 1787, was Benjamin Franklin.

283.39 *The Journals . . . still concealed.] The Constitutional Convention voted on September 17, 1787, to deposit its journals in the custody of George Washington; they were first published in 1819.

284.3–4 violent threats . . . *tar and feathers*] On September 28, 1787, the *Independent Gazetteer* carried an unsigned item warning an "anonymous scribbler, in the Freeman's Journal" who had criticized the Constitution that an "incensed people" might "honor him with a coat of TAR and FEATHERS" if he continued to "sow dissension among the weak, the credulous, and the ignorant."

284.14–16 member of the house . . . federal convention] George Clymer (1739–1813), a merchant and banker from Philadelphia, served in the Pennsylvania assembly, 1785–88; in the Continental Congress, 1776–77 and 1780–82; and in the U.S. House of Representatives, 1789–91.

285.34–35 the 13th article . . . confederation] Article XIII required that changes to the Articles of Confederation be approved by the legislatures of every state.

290.24–36 "The extent of country . . . despotic power."] See p. 261.11–23 and note 261.15 in this volume.

290.37–291.6 "Is it probable . . . dominion of America."] See pp. 265.35–266.6.

294.19 The celebrated *Montesquieu* The Spirit of the Laws (1748), volume I, book II, chapter II.

298.21–23 very eminent Civilian . . . first sentence."] Possibly the English civil lawyer Thomas Lane (c. 1660–c. 1704) in his appearance before the Court of the King's Bench in *Brown and Burton v. Franklyn* (1698).

299.15–25 learned judge *Blackstone* . . . of the expence.] *Commentaries on the Laws of England*, Book III, chapter 24.

299.29–32 same learned author . . . went out together.] *Commentaries*, Book III, chapter 23.

301.11–12 late commercial treaty . . . kingdom and France.] The Anglo-French treaty of navigation and commerce, signed on September 26, 1786.

301.18–33 the celebrated Montesquieu . . . of individuals."] *The Spirit of the Laws*, volume I, book XI, chapter 6.

307.1–2 MASSACHUSETTS . . . CONVENTION] The Massachusetts ratifying convention met at the State House in Boston on January 9, 1788 and reconvened at the Long Lane Meeting House.

309.32 this article] Article I, section 2.

311.36 Mr. ADAMS] Samuel Adams.

312.4   The 4th section] The fourth section of Article I.

313.33–36 the restoration . . . the commonwealth] The restoration of Charles II to the throne in 1660 ended the Commonwealth established in England following the execution of Charles I in 1649.

316.4–6   the man that slew . . . *all wisdom*] David (see 1 Samuel 13:14 and 17:35–36) and his son Solomon, to whom God gave wisdom (see 1 Kings 4:29–34 and 2 Chronicles 9:22–23).

316.19–20   there were two . . . Caleb and Joshua] See Numbers 13, 14:1–9.

318.8   the court] The Massachusetts General Court.

319.4–5   a black cloud . . . over the west.] Shays' Rebellion; see note 48.21.

320.3   My honourable old daddy] Amos Singletary was sixty-seven, Jonathan Smith forty-eight.

322.5–6   the paragraph . . . a religious test] Article VI, paragraph 3.

323.17–20   The apostle Peter . . . *acceptable* to him] Acts 10:34–35.

323.28   (*Bristol*)] In the district of Maine.

324.5–9   the PRESIDENT . . . submitting a proposition] Governor John Hancock had been elected president of the convention, but did not attend any sessions until January 30, 1788, reportedly due to an attack of gout. On the morning of January 31, after the Federalist leader Theophilus Parsons (1750–1813) made a motion to ratify, Hancock announced that he would present a proposition in the afternoon that would "remove the objections of some gentlemen."

324.18–23   to adopt the form . . . some general amendments] For the form of ratification of Massachusetts, see pp. 329–32.

325.7–8   the motion . . . gentleman from Newbury-Port;] The motion to ratify made by Theophilus Parsons.

326.8   Our ambassadour . . . London] John Adams.

326.16   the article . . . for a revision] Article V.

332.1–2   SOUTH CAROLINA . . . CONVENTION] The convention met in the Exchange Building in Charleston on May 12, 1788.

336.12–21   a very celebrated author . . . and virtuous industry."] Benjamin Franklin, "Positions To Be Examined" (1769).

342.39   *Paley, a deacon] William Paley (1743–1805), archdeacon of Carlisle, *The Principles of Moral and Political Philosophy* (2 vols., 1785).

348.33–34   archbishop Laud . . . "*non resistance.*"] William Laud (1573–1645), Archbishop of Canterbury, 1633–45, preached that Christians should not resist the authority of the king under any circumstances.

350.1–2 VIRGINIA . . . CONVENTION] The Virginia convention met in Richmond at the temporary state capitol on June 2, 1788, then moved to the larger Richmond Theatre.

353.5 An Honorable Gentleman] Edmund Randolph (see note 31.11). Randolph had reversed his earlier opposition to the Constitution and now supported its ratification.

354.4–5 The Honorable Gentleman . . . opinion of Mr. Jefferson] On June 9 Henry had alleged that Jefferson advised rejecting the Constitution until it was amended. Edmund Pendleton responded on June 10, regretting that the "opinion of a private individual, however enlightened," had been introduced into the debate. Pendleton then quoted from a letter Jefferson had written from Paris on February 7, 1788, to his friend Alexander Donald, a Scottish merchant living in Richmond: "'I wish with all my soul that the nine first Conventions may accept the New Constitution, because it will secure to us the good it contains, which I think great and important. I wish the four latest which ever they be, may refuse to accede to it, till amendments are secured.' He then enumerates the amendments which he wishes to be secured, and adds, 'We must take care however, that neither this, nor any other objection to the form, produce a schism in our Union. That would be an incurable evil; because friends falling out never cordially re-unite.'"

356.38–39 Connecticut has preserved . . . her royal charter] Connecticut revised its royal charter in 1776 to eliminate references to royal authority. The state adopted its first post-Revolutionary constitution in 1818.

357.9 the trial by jury taken away?] Article III, section 2 of the Constitution mandated jury trials for criminal cases under federal jurisdiction, but did not require them in civil cases, an omission reversed by the Seventh Amendment.

357.13 One Honorable Gentleman] Edmund Randolph.

357.36 Our Declaration of Rights] The Virginia Declaration of Rights, adopted June 12, 1776.

358.10 The Honorable member] Edmund Randolph.

362.25 The Honorable Gentleman] Edmund Pendleton.

364.27 The Honorable Gentleman] Edmund Pendleton.

365.32 the Honorable Gentleman] Edmund Pendleton.

366.20 the Honorable Gentleman] James Madison.

368.7 the rule of the House] The convention had voted on June 3 to debate the Constitution clause by clause in a committee of the whole chaired by George Wythe (see note 39.25–27), a procedure that allowed Edmund Pendleton, the president of the convention, to join in the debate.

373.30–31 "They have done . . . to have done."] Cf. the Anglican *Book of Common Prayer* (1662), "The Order for Morning Prayer."

375.1–2   NEW YORK . . . CONVENTION] The New York ratifying convention met in the old Dutchess County Courthouse in Poughkeepsie on June 17, 1788.

375.7   gentleman from Dutchess] Melancton Smith.

380.6   honorable member from New-York] Richard Harison (1747–1829) was a lawyer from New York City who voted for ratification. He later served as U.S. Attorney for the District of New York, 1789–1801.

383.1   the committee] The convention was meeting as a committee of the whole.

394.1–2   NORTH CAROLINA . . . CONVENTION] The North Carolina ratifying convention met in St. Matthew's Episcopal Church in Hillsborough on July 21, 1788.

400.19–20   an exercise of mercy . . . Massachusetts] In November 1786, Massachusetts passed an act of indemnity pardoning all Shaysite rebels who pledged allegiance to the state government before January 1, 1787. A second act, passed in February 1787, offered pardons to rank-and-file insurgents, although those who took the oath were to be disenfranchised for three years.

405.38–39   A gentleman from New-Hanover] Timothy Bloodworth (1736–1814) was a delegate to the Continental Congress, 1786–87. Bloodworth opposed ratification at the 1788 and 1789 North Carolina conventions. He later served in the U.S. House of Representatives, 1790–91, and in the Senate, 1795–1801.

406.29–30   honourable Member from Anson] Samuel Spencer.

408.3–4   the gentleman from Halifax] William R. Davie (1756–1820), a lawyer and plantation owner, was a delegate to the Constitutional Convention in 1787 and supported ratification at the 1788 and 1789 North Carolina conventions. He served as governor of North Carolina, 1798–99.

409.12–13   worthy member from Edenton] James Iredell.

409.19   worthy member from Halifax] William R. Davie.

412.16   *the gates of hell . . . against it?*] Matthew 16:18.

Index

About the Editors

ROBERT J. ALLISON is Professor of History at Suffolk University and also teaches in the Harvard Extension School, where he received the Petra T. Shattuck Excellence in Teaching Award. Allison is the author of *The Crescent Obscured: The United States and the Muslim World, 1776–1820* (1995), *A Short History of Boston* (2004), *Stephen Decatur: American Naval Hero, 1779–1820* (2005), *The Boston Massacre* (2006), *The Boston Tea Party* (2010), *A Short History of Cape Cod* (2010), and *The American Revolution: A Concise History* (2011; reissued in 2015 as *The American Revolution: A Very Short Introduction*). His lecture courses "Before 1776: Life in the American Colonies" and "The Age of Benjamin Franklin" are available in audio and video formats as part of The Great Courses series published by The Teaching Company. Allison is president of the South Boston Historical Society, vice president of the Colonial Society of Massachusetts, a Fellow of the Massachusetts Historical Society, and an overseer of the U.S.S. *Constitution* Museum.

BERNARD BAILYN is Adams University Professor and James Duncan Phillips Professor of Early American History, emeritus, at Harvard University. Bailyn is the author of numerous books, including *The Ideological Origins of the American Revolution* (1967), winner of the Pulitzer Prize and the Bancroft Prize; *The Ordeal of Thomas Hutchinson* (1974), winner of the National Book Award; *Voyagers to the West* (1986), winner of the Pulitzer Prize; *Faces of Revolution* (1990); and *The Barbarous Years* (2012), and the editor of *The Debate on the Constitution: Federalist and Anti-Federalist Speeches, Articles, and Letters During the Struggle over Ratification, 1787–1788* (2 volumes, The Library of America, 1993). He was appointed the Jefferson Lecturer by the National Endowment for the Humanities in 1998, delivered the first Millennium Lecture at the White House in 2000, and received a National Humanities Medal in 2010.